100345545 X

I0586386

291045

- 5 DEC 1997

HERITAGE

Conservation, Interpretation
and Enterprise

SHEFFIELD HALLAM UNIVERSITY
LEARNING CENTRE
WITHDRAWN FROM STOCK

HERITAGE

Conservation, Interpretation and Enterprise

Edited by

J.M. FLADMARK

SHEFFIELD HALLAM UNIVERSITY
LEARNING CENTRE
WITHDRAWN FROM STOCK

Papers presented at
The Robert Gordon University
Heritage Convention 1993

DONHEAD

© The Robert Gordon University, Aberdeen.
Individual chapters are the copyright
of their authors.

All rights reserved.
No part of this book may be reproduced or transmitted in
any form or by any means electronic, mechanical or
otherwise without prior permission from the publisher,
Donhead Publishing.

First published in the United Kingdom
in 1993 by
Donhead Publishing Ltd
28 Southdean Gardens
Wimbledon
London SW19 6NU
Tel. 081-789 0138

ISBN 1 873394 13 6

A CIP catalogue record for this book is available
from the British Library.

Printed in Great Britain at the
Alden Press, Osney Mead, Oxford

In order to produce this book quickly for the conference
delegates, the publishers have used camera ready copy
provided by the editors and contributors

CONTENTS

Foreword   ix
Lord Balfour of Burleigh

Acknowledgements   xi

Introduction   xiii

CULTURAL LANDSCAPES
An Holistic View of the Environment

1 LANDSCAPE AS HERITAGE   3
National Scenes and Global Changes
David Lowenthal

2 THE ELUSIVE REALITY OF LANDSCAPE   17
Concepts and Approaches of Landscape
Michael Jones

3 CULTURAL LANDSCAPES   43
The Need for a Political Perspective
Harold Eidsvik

4 A STUDY IN NORDIC LANDSCAPE PLANNING   51
Magne Bruun

5 ISSUES FACING SCOTLAND   63
John Arnott

6 **THE SCOTTISHNESS OF SCOTTISH
   ARCHITECTURE**   77
   Building for People and Places
   Charles McKean

7 **FARM BUILDINGS IN NORWAY**   93
   Jan Våge

8 **TOWARDS A COMMON LANGUAGE**   101
   The Unifying Perceptions of an Integrated Approach
   Lesley Macinnes

9 **A JOURNEY THROUGH SCOTLAND**   113
   John Foster

PLANNING FOR INTERPRETATION
Working Together in Partnership

10 **DISCOVERING THE PERSONALITY OF A REGION**   125
   Strategic Interpretation in Scotland
   Magnus Fladmark

11 **THE SCOTTISH PARKS SYSTEM**   141
   A Strategy for Conservation and Enjoyment
   *Timothy Edwards, Nicholas Pennington and
   Michael Starrett*

12 **INTEGRATED STRATEGIES IN NATIONAL PARKS**   153
   Experience in England and Wales
   Peter Freeman and Tim Haley

13 **ACCESS THROUGH HOSTELLING**   161
   The Role and Policies of SYHA
   Philip Lawson and Magnus Fladmark

14 **EXPLAINING THE LOCAL HERITAGE**   175
   The Role of a Regional Archaeologist
   Ian Shepherd

15 **THE HERITAGE OF ABERDEEN**   185
   James Wyness

INTERPRETATION AND PRESENTATION
Studies in Telling the Story

16 THE NORTH EAST OF SCOTLAND AGRICULTURAL HERITAGE CENTRE 203
Interpretation at Aden
Andrew Hill

17 THE NEW LANARK STORY 215
James Arnold

18 CHATELHERAULT 235
The Restoration and Interpretation of a Folly
James Brockie

19 KELBURN COUNTRY CENTRE 241
Presenting a Family Heritage
The Earl of Glasgow

20 BAXTERS AND ITS VISITOR CENTRE 251
Gordon Baxter and Finlay Weir

21 THE BRITISH GOLF MUSEUM 259
Peter Lewis

22 AT THEIR COUNTRY'S CALL 271
The Heritage of Soldiering in Scotland
Stephen Wood

THE ARTS AND CRAFTS
Calling upon the Muses

23 OUR HERITAGE 285
Not Just an Armchair at the Fireside of History
Duncan Macmillan

24 THE TIMELESS HERITAGE OF MUSIC 301
John Purser

25 THE SCOTTISH TRADITION OF STORY TELLING   311
Donald Archie MacDonald

**26 EVERYMAN'S FURNITURE IN
LOWLAND SCOTLAND**   325
David Jones

27 BOWYERY AND FLETCHING   335
The Ancient Crafts of Archery
Hugh Soar

28 HERITAGE IS IN THE HEARTH   347
Elisabeth Luard

FOREWORD

The publication of these papers celebrates the inauguration of the Aberdeen Heritage Unit which it has been my good fortune to be associated with, as Chairman of the Advisory Board, since its first Director was appointed in April 1992.

Our aims are ambitious. We have been invited to develop the University's capability in the field of heritage studies and to foster understanding of the value of the nation's heritage and of policies for its stewardship. To this end, we will concentrate on the art of interpreting and presenting our heritage, as practised in Scotland and elsewhere; all to be achieved through programmes of education, training and research, by harnessing the multi-disciplinary strengths of The Robert Gordon University.

We have one guiding principle: that the past, the present and the processes shaping tomorrow's heritage, are all equally important.

We are all familiar with the period in the 18th Century, known as the Scottish Enlightenment, the convergence of ideas among the sciences and humanities that arose when the nation's leading thinkers and artists came together. Later scholars, like John Muir, Patrick Geddes and Frank Fraser Darling, built on this way of thinking in their exploration of man's interaction with the natural world.

We too seek to encourage studies that cross conventional disciplinary boundaries. The Heritage Unit is concerned with a great spectrum of ideas and human activity: archaeology; architecture; garden design; arts and crafts; community life; trade and technology.

Our work will emphasise the importance of observation, well-founded evidence and clear communication. The authors of these papers, prepared for the 1993 Heritage Convention at The Robert Gordon University, provide valuable insight into the art of telling stories of places and their associated heritage, to enrich people's enjoyment by stimulating their interest and awareness. The essays show how this approach can be used as a tool of conservation management to encourage sensitive behaviour, as well as a means of attracting visitors to generate income and stimulate enterprise for the benefit of local communities.

The focus of these papers, and the discussion that will spring from them, is the study of our heritage – to help us understand where we came from, what we are doing now, and where we are going.

Lord Balfour of Burleigh
Brucefield
Clackmannan

June 1993

ACKNOWLEDGEMENTS

This volume is a historic document for the university and for the City of Aberdeen. It also stands as a monument to the heroic efforts of those charged with establishing our new Heritage Unit. Within the space of nine months, a star studded cast of eminent speakers was assembled to contribute to the first major convention of its kind ever held in Aberdeen that would address some of the key issues facing European policy makers and practitioners concerned with heritage conservation, interpretation and enterprise.

I am immensely grateful to each contributor for finding time to write papers so that they could be published in time for the Convention, including the Lord Provost, Dr James Wyness, who personally penned the story of Aberdeen. My special thanks go to the Unit's Director, Magnus Fladmark who inspired the idea in the first place and who spent long hours welding the collection together into a cohesive volume. In this he was ably and tirelessly assisted by the sub-editor, Karen Sage, and I know that they would like me to thank Jill Pearce at Donhead for sparing no efforts to deliver a book of the highest possible quality within the time available. Our thanks also go to other members of staff who have contributed in one way or another, Professors Eric Spiller and Seaton Baxter, David Silbergh, Ernie Smith, Garth Strachan, Gillie Reith, Suzie Wood, Joan Hardie and Alison Macori.

The blessing of Government for the Convention was greatly valued, and I am grateful to Sir Hector Munro's presence to open the proceedings. The university is also greatly indebted to the many supporting organisations and their chief executives or chairmen who kindly made themselves available to introduce speakers and to guide ensuing discussions, i.e. Alan Alstead of the Scottish Sports Council, Aitken Clark of the Federation of Nature and National Parks of Europe, Ronald Cramond of the Scottish Museums Council, Douglas Dow of the National Trust for Scotland, Hance Fullerton of Grampian Enterprise, Tom Band of the Scottish Tourist Board, David Baird of Scottish National Heritage, Professor Donald MacKay of Scottish Enterprise National, Seona Reid of the Scottish Arts Council and Iain Robertson of Highlands and Islands Enterprise. The services of John Foster as programme adviser and chairman of the refereeing panel is reflected in the consistently high standard throughout.

Dr David A. Kennedy
Principal
The Robert Gordon University
Aberdeen

INTRODUCTION

> We don't always take enough pride in our culture, and Scotland's fine heritage is often undervalued and neglected. This Convention is the University's contribution to the debate about what we can all do to ensure that this splendid inheritance continues into the next century in good shape.

These words, attributed to the Editor in a recent press announcement, neatly summarise the rallying call that went out with invitations to the contributing authors. To engender pride in our inheritance and to ensure proper stewardship of our resources into the future, it is necessary to communicate the value and fragile nature of what has been placed in our custody by previous generations. Thus, the common thread running through these papers is the many artful ways that the story of our heritage can be told and explained.

The story can be told for many reasons, in many different contexts, and using various media. The term we use is 'interpretation', a concept that goes back to the early Scandinavian folk museums, some of which were first established in the second half of the 19th Century, but the idea was first developed as a discipline by the national parks movement in North America, under the watchful eye of their great guru, Freeman Tilden. In his book, *Interpreting Our Heritage* (1957), he refers to interpretation as, 'an educational activity which aims to reveal meanings and relationships'. According to him, 'information as such is not interpretation. Interpretation is revelation based on information'. The essence of the philosophy behind the idea can be summarised by a dictum based on Tilden that is widely used by the US National Parks Service:

through interpretation – understanding;
through understanding – appreciation;
through appreciation – protection.

As is evident by these lines, the conservation ethic was an essential ingredient of interpretation from the start, but the word 'sustainability' had not assumed its present meaning when Tilden wrote his book. The word is now pinned to the forehead of every politician, bureaucrat and ardent environmentalist you are ever likely to meet. However much you may try to avoid its use, you are likely to fail, and here is our Unit's applied definition:

> In all our activities, we endeavour to promote new attitudes to development that will enhance the quality of life and take a long term view of the environment. We do this by seeking to ensure that the needs of the present are met without compromising the ability of future generations to meet theirs. In this we regard human needs as broader than just meeting the requirements for healthy food, water and air. They also embrace the ability to enjoy aspects of our heritage that give spiritual uplift, aesthetic pleasure and cultural fulfilment.

The last sentence is important, for it accounts for the wide scope of these papers. They have been organised into four main sections. We decided to start with a discussion of cultural landscapes, a concept that is very much about interpretation, but still relatively unexplored in Britain. It has been around in some other European countries for the better part of a century, and it is hoped that the excellent contributions from our overseas guests will provide the impetus for a wider debate and action by government in this country.

The peg on which the first section hangs, is the question: are landscape designations a blessing or a curse for heritage interpretation? The authors confirm that, both in Britain and elsewhere, governments, professionals, academics and voluntary agencies have in recent years become increasingly involved with the stewardship of our environmental inheritance. This has led to a highly compartmentalised situation, each vested interest having staked out its own territory, and attitudes have become polarised and often confrontational. There is general agreement among the authors that the holistic concept of cultural landscapes can serve as a means of bringing about a wider awareness by explaining the evolution of landscapes as a product of human interaction with the natural world. This is because the concept places an emphasis on interpretation of the environment in terms of relationships across the conventional subject boundaries of nature conservation, human habitation, animal husbandry, agriculture, forestry, industrial activity etc.

The papers in the second part of the book deal with strategic policy and planning. Heritage interpretation is equally relevant as part of school and university curricula, in museums and galleries, in parks and for tourist enterprises. The question asked of authors was whether there is enough sharing of skills and information, and whether there is enough joint working to avoid duplication of services and unnecessary competition. They have examined the roles of different sectors and agencies in strategic planning for heritage interpretation, and deal with various mechanisms for integrated action, their analysis highlighting strengths and weaknesses of existing systems. Some interesting issues and challenges have been identified that need to be overcome to ensure sustainable use of resources into the next century.

The third part is a selection of case studies in the art of telling the story of a place and its associated heritage through themes and storylines that will deliver a memorable impact. Principles, methods, techniques and procedures of interpretation have common elements whatever the subject. The authors have chosen to enable exchange and sharing of experience across the full spectrum of provision for interpretation and presentation, ranging from museums to parks and estates, and dealing with both private and public sector enterprises. Leading flagship projects of long-standing are reviewed and discussed, as well as new and ambitious projects, like recent developments at New Lanark and the British Golf Museum in St Andrews which makes extensive use of modern information technology.

The last section deals with the arts and crafts. Although I have been castigated for referring to the arts as the Cinderella of interpretation, I still feel confident about saying that the mainstream of interpretation practice has focused on the natural, built and industrial heritage. In the way the authors have tackled their task, they have certainly succeeded in breaking the mould by widening the agenda to show how more conventional themes can be enriched through a study of the different arts. If confirmation was needed, they endorse that the arts should not be regarded as an elitist subject best left to experts, but as a cultural expression of human achievements and aspirations. The theme to emerge is that, rather than merely providing the illustrative frills for interpretive programmes, the arts and crafts justify interpretation in their own right. They can be the key to unlocking the intricate web linking nature, enterprise and culture in the lives of local communities.

The spirit of our age, as conveyed in this volume, is to seek rediscovery of the cultural continuum and inter-dependence of past, present and future achievements. To see things in the round, holds the key to this rediscovery. The cocooned mentality bred by a determination in certain quarters to deny any relevance of past practice and achievements, combined with 'the end of history' syndrome, make the task of heritage interpretation a great challenge. For example, reviewing a recent exhibition of modern sculpture in the *Sunday Times Scotland* (30 May 1993), Andrew Gibbson Williams expressed dismay over the fact that the art establishment still seems antagonistic towards the past and shows a cavalier contempt for public opinion. In his words, 'their art can go nowhere because it has come from nowhere'.

To any reader who may have to deal with those who have got lost in this way, I hope that the papers in this collection will be of some help. In the words of Lord Balfour, they help us to understand where we came from, what we are doing now and where we are going. To this I would add, they also help us understand how all things natural and cultural, including our private lives and personal pursuits, are closely interlinked in the subtle tapestry that is our heritage.

Magnus Fladmark
Director
The Robert Gordon University Heritage Unit

CULTURAL LANDSCAPES
An Holistic View of the Environment

The land as we see it,
is the product of human interaction
with the natural world,
and all things are interlinked

LANDSCAPE AS HERITAGE
National Scenes and Global Changes

David Lowenthal

Heritage has mounting import in countless realms of life the world over. Recent decades have seen an explosion of interest in the past embracing everything from fossils and furniture to folklore and faiths: just this year Glasgow opened a major museum devoted solely to religion.

Moreover, heritage is newly populist. No longer are only aristocrats obsessed with ancestry, only the super-rich collectors of antiques, only academics antiquarians, only a cultured minority museum-goers; millions of ordinary folk now search out their roots, mobilize to protect beloved scenes, cherish their own and other people's mementoes, and dote on media versions of history.

Because heritage so often focuses at the national level, the global spread of these trends is less apparent. Heritage normally connotes 'English', or 'Scottish', sometimes 'British', seldom 'European'. As heritage icons are often site specific, they are seldom compared from country to country even by globe-trotting professionals. Yet, heritage became an obsession in the 1970s and 1980s not just in Britain and the West but in the then communist East and shortly in the Third World as well. It is now prized and marketed everywhere.

CHANGING PERCEPTIONS OF HERITAGE

Widespread enthusiasm has changed what heritage is about. Once confined to monuments of great moment, to grand personages, to unique treasures of art and architecture, it now celebrates the vernacular and the typical. Once restricted to a respectably remote past – buildings before 1750, antiques a century old, history before Diocletian – it now embraces even last year. Temporal barriers are steadily lowered – archives open to public view not in

50 years but 30, structures listed as 'historic' built not a century but a generation ago, relics auctioned at Sotheby's not just of long-dead monarchs but extant if ageing pop-stars, school history touching on times within teachers' if not pupils' living memory ('Please sir, was the Civil War in ... the Olden days?').

Heritage now transcends the old-time realm of artefacts in two directions of moment here. One is the realm of ideas and expression. Language and folklore have long had devotees; but intangible culture is newly viewed as group legacy alongside buildings and paintings, potsherds and townscapes.

The other direction is the environment in which artefacts arise and are used. Nature conservation has ancient roots; but historic landscapes have only recently entered the mainstream of heritage. For example, the National Trust for England and Wales newly stresses its landscape legacy of heritage coasts and landed estates. Fifteen years ago, the great houses and gardens and parks alone were cherished; estate lands were ruthlessly milked to feed their fabric. Today, the concerns of a membership up five-fold make estate lands of equal heritage moment. To be sure, the Trust claims a century of continuity with founders' landscape causes, but rural decline and newly aroused public interest today involve utterly different landscape emphases.

The expanding heritage generates problems and criticisms along with insights and opportunities. Some complain heritage encompasses so much it is incapable of definition. Others spurn it as a past glamourized by dismay of the present and fears for the future. Still others resent it for trivializing and falsifying the past; heritage hucksters and a credulous public scuttle 'true' history for vapid, bowdlerized, anachronistic, Disneyfied versions. Many critics deplore heritage popularity as a threat to the past's fabric and ambience; it is being loved to death. Time is lacking here to discuss these partly justified, though I think inflated, fears.

LANDSCAPE ASPECTS OF HERITAGE

I aim to explore how heritage demands newly focus on landscape. The word landscape subsumes three vital concepts: **nature** as fundamental heritage in its own right; **environment** as the setting of human action; and **sense of place** as awareness of local difference and appreciation of ancestral roots. I note four distinct lines of public concern: for environment in general, for settings of everyday life and leisure, in awareness of natural and cultural complexity and stewardship needs, and for communities reliant on a sense of place.

Green political fortunes show that public concerns with environmental matters are volatile and often exaggerated. Much Green advocacy is hostile to habits of technology and enterprise felt vital to most livelihoods. But since Rachel Carson's *Silent Spring* a generation ago, the risks of heedless assault on our still more vital fundament have become familiar throughout the world. Few feel no concern about nuclear accident, global warming, ozone layer depletion, species loss, ecosystem diversity – risks regularly headlined in the media. Few Scots are ignorant of acid rain, oil spills, coniferization, reindeer and red deer habitat problems, Chernobylized sheep, let alone air pollution and waste disposal, soil erosion and degradation.

Unlike most of our forebears, we now see the living globe as a common legacy requiring our common care. Huge gulfs remain between risks faced and impacts understood, between ecological *nous* and economic dogma, private greed and public need, doomsters and Pollyannas. These gulfs magnify public fears of catastrophe that underlie much landscape awareness.

Linkages of present with past are felt to need not just isolated heritage icons but the cultural landscape's embedding framework. Conservation areas and national parks exemplify this urge. Schooling, the arts, and expanded leisure help us see that the ultimate aim is living rather than making a living, and to go beyond the item to the ensemble.

Scottish sages from John Muir to Patrick Geddes to Ian McHarg stress the psychic primacy of nature and a nature-respecting shaping of humane domains. Scots philosophers and poets, painters and musicians, articulate the convergence, not the opposition, of natural with human milieus.

Landscape legacies are not confined to the states in which they lie; they are the heritage of the world as a whole, exemplified in World Heritage Sites. More than cultural monuments, the world's scenic and natural treasures are protected and even enhanced by collaborative effort. Antarctica is a reserved continent, the Tasmanian wilderness escaped exploitation by means of global pressures, thousands of scientists and statesmen devote skills and resources to problems of ocean pollution, concern over space debris is international.

Urbanized, mobile, deracinated denizens of anonymous, ephemeral places mourn the loss of what seems cosy and distinctive. Some seek to regain links with ancestral locales or childhood milieus. Others cherish or reinvent the scenery and social fabric that make such places *our* place rather than just *any* place.

To be sure, the former working landscape is scarcely recoverable; if it survives as scenery it dies as a social entity, just as our own memories of the daily bygone round atrophy with age and disuse. Yet the urge to regain rural roots has begun to rehabilitate many ancestral places. Investment in rural resettlement and community services revivifies local legacies throughout Europe.

EUROPEAN LANDSCAPE ATTACHMENTS

Our new concerns are not sketched on a *tabula rasa*. Age-old landscape traditions continue to reflect the attractions (and revulsions) every culture feels toward nature as shaped and reshaped by generations of forebears. We must heed these inherited attachments in assessing newly augmented aims.

Traditional landscape links focused largely on local neighbourhoods, kinship ties with nearby places conjoining ancestry and acreage. Owning, managing, working on land were fundamental as long as farming was the main mode of livelihood. But these local ties have in recent centuries been

5

overlain by others. Landscape has notably become a compelling symbol of national identity.

National attachments reveal landscapes deployed for identity and cohesion, stimuli for group feeling and action. They form the foundations for present-day changes in how land is seen and valued, notably where environmental feelings are highly self-conscious.

Most European heritages include landscape traits felt integral to identity. Countries commonly depict themselves in landscape terms; they hallow traits they fancy uniquely theirs. Every national anthem praises special scenic splendours or nature's unique bounties.

Embedded habits and language barriers hamper comparisons. A sign in the Swiss village of Chateau d'Oex says in English: 'Please do not pick the flowers.' In German: 'It is forbidden to pick the flowers.' In French: 'Those who love the mountains, leave them their flowers.' These phrases all favour flowers, but imply divergent landscape attitudes: English good manners, German minatory prohibition, French aesthetic affection.

Patriotic feeling builds on previous talismans of space and place: 'hills and rivers and woods cease to be merely familiar; they become ideological' as sites of national shrines, battles, birthplaces. And to crush the losers' national spirit, invaders violate the vanquished locale, as the British Ordnance Survey did in the mapping and Anglicising of Erse landscapes.

NATIONAL LANDSCAPE TRAITS

Geographical virtues have long mirrored national character. Three centuries of Swiss have ascribed their sturdy independence to frugal, communitarian mountain life and the purity of Alpine altitude and air; untouched nature there still betokens ancestral simplicity. The traditional *glits* landscape of farmsteads set in fields, birch groves, and fir trees betokens enduring Latvian virtues, though most Latvians now are urban or seafaring.

National feeling finds novel charms in otherwise unsung features. The Irish peat industry's Bogland tour reflects a mystique that much 'of the most cherished material culture of Ireland was found in a bog'; the poet Seamus Heaney celebrates 'the bog as the memory of the landscape, or as a landscape that remembered everything that happened in and to it'.

Landscape traits ennoble minorities, too. Mountain fastness safeguards Basque egalitarian purity from degenerate Castile, buttressing ethnic faith against the bastardized Celts, decadent Latins, corrupted Moors of the rest of Spain. The sea sustains island autonomies from Shetland to Sardinia, Corsica to Crete.

Among Europeans transplanted overseas landscape supplants a felt lack of history or compensates too sad a saga. Tasmanians reflect on 'a history of which none of us can be proud – but the most beautiful country in the world'. Americans found their unique identity in wilderness; a natural saga older and purer than Europe's human history became the national mystique. Americans needed no 'artificial' palaces and cathedrals: 'we have giant cathedrals, whose spires are moss-clad pines, whose frescoes are painted on the sky and mountain wall, and whose music surges through the leafy aisles in the deep toned base of cataracts'. America's archetypal icon, the Wild West, stands for the freedom, exuberance, optimism derived from the unity and immensity of national space. By contrast, some Americans dismiss history-laden European scenes as too diffusely heterogeneous.

Laudatory foreign views focus on traits that epitomize the visited land by contrast with their own. Thus to Hippolyte Taine English hills seemed 'all drowned in that luminous vapour which melts colour into colour and gives the whole countryside an expression of tender happiness'. New World visitors praised Britain as 'the only country in the world that is all finished, ... the rubbish picked up, ... no odds and ends lying around', all looking 'swept and dusted that morning'. F. L. Olmsted, America's premier landscape gardener, was struck both by the 'clean and careful cultivation and general tidiness of agriculture' and the order even of English trees, 'as if the face of each leaf was more nearly parallel with all the others near it ... than in our foliage'.

Not all European landscapes are nationally distinctive, to be sure; boundaries often straddle scenic traits. Normandy and Picardy merge without a break into Flanders, Savoy into the Val d'Aosta; the Alps are indifferent to the national flags of Germany, Austria, France, Switzerland, Italy. Some nations feel the want of prideful icons; stuck with windmills and tulips, the sub-sea-level Dutch may still cherish, but nowadays can hardly celebrate, the threatened compage of water meadows, copses, dairy holdings, and meandering rivers immortalized by Rembrandt and van Ruysdael. Other states accord regional traits national status: Jutland's heaths hardly typify the Danish landscape, yet they symbolize Danish love of nature.

Territorial traumas deprive some traditional national scenery of salience. Stefan Heym rejects certain pre-war scenes: 'all those German landscapes weren't German any more. They'd been lost by Hitler.' He meant Breslau and Danzig, now Polish. But also war-erased Chemnitz and Dresden. And beyond, a larger landscape stained by Nazi memories.

CELEBRATING FRANCE

France and Britain offer multiple and contrasting landscape tastes. France celebrates its sheer multiplicity of admired features. Scholars like patriots laud the Jardin de France's natural riches for French superiority. Here was the 'genius loci that prepared our existence as a nation', writes Braudel; 'the beauty of the country, the fertility of the soil, the salubrity of the air' held by a 15th-century chancellor to 'efface all other countries'.

The French landscape is termed incomparable on several counts. First, its extraordinary range (France is the only land combining Mediterranean, Atlantic, and continental climes) lends the agricultural mosaic exceptional variety; celebrants since Michelet seize on diversity as the 'word which best characterizes France'. Second, seven millennia of unbroken occupance confer an unmatched depth of country life and lore. Third, intense peasant attachments mark lands the Revolution made definitively their own; place-names – 'cour Mathurin', 'champ de Raierie' – everywhere affirm peasant family annals. Fourth, the landscape attests total, continual fructification, scarcely an inch left untended up to the Second World War.

Fifth, peasant memory is still fresh and public sentiment rural, France having remained mainly agricultural long after Britain or Germany. Indeed, France had been Europe's most advanced and densely peopled European nation when it was an essentially peasant economy. Industrialization came slowly and late; half the French at the turn of the century, a third as late as 1954, still made their living from the soil, and peasants remain France's principal proprietors.

Farmers are indeed France's new musketeers, viewed as paragons of ecological virtue securing sacred national and family values. Artichokes and rapeseed oil are subsidized not simply against GATT machinations but for French culture. Every important political figure has close countryside ties through rural relations. Lavish subsidies protect this relic of the national patrimony. The popular hit of 1992 was 'Les mariés de Vendée', a peasant wedding folk song featuring 17th-century smocks and farm gear with electric guitars.

To sociologists like Le Play and geographers like Vidal de Blache, the heterogeneity of French landscapes and ways of life spelled strengths surpassing any other nation's. That others might claim comparable diversity made no difference; no other country felt so happy about it. Vaunted diversity underscores manifold inherited excellences: the infinite rich variety of French wines, cheeses, cuisine, customs, languages.

Yet this diversity in no way detracts from French unity. Alone in western Europe the ancient territorial state coincides with the national community (Germany and Italy were till lately fragmented, Britain and Spain remain composite in culture and language). Predestined to engross a God-given realm, France was foreshadowed in a millennium of regal conquests; medieval maps in French history texts today show embryo regions 'not yet reunited' to the nation-to-be. The Revolution further sacralized the nation: eradicating provincial bonds, republicans made France homogeneous. Though Napoleon had wider dreams, France's natural frontiers (Alps, Pyrenees, Rhine) became a fixture of national ideology. A previsioned France shaped diverse peoples into common views and allegiances – a patriotism praised for forgetting discordant Occitan, Breton, and Huguenot ways.

At the same time, the French landscape heritage is supremely artificial. Just as royal circuits were once inscribed within Euclidean geometries, so the primary school ideal of France since the 1880s is of a land 'symmetrical, proportioned, and regular'. Timeless France is a six-sided myth: the national estate as reified hexagon. Gallic geographical determinism recalls my own America's Manifest Destiny, the imperial reach 'from sea to shining sea'.

French landscape celebratory modes are also unique i.e. Tour de la France par deux enfants is the best known of travellers' panegyrics, surpassing in range and enthusiasm Arthur Young's pragmatic tours of England. Today's

'Tour de France' alone celebrates a national domain via bicycle. From the start, in 1903, the race's route limned the realm's immensity, beauty, and defenses, stressing its well protected natural frontiers. The tour underscored France's amplitude and awesomeness, Pyrenean and Alpine stretches dramatized as virtually inaccessible. Glorying in local scenes and regional customs, the Tour at the same time guards the national identity. Media displays and souvenir sales, the promotion of sports and other goods, village and town rivalries along the route exemplify rural France's transition from sites of toil to scenic tourism.

CELEBRATING ENGLAND

Britain's landscape attachments are more explicitly unique. 'An English and topographical eye' is a supposed special talent. Nowhere else is landscape so freighted as legacy. Nowhere else does the very term imply quintessential national virtues. The historian Butterfield reified that 'inescapable heritage of Englishmen', Whig history, as 'part of the landscape of English life, like our country lanes or our November mists or historic inns'. The magazine *Heritage* is subtitled 'British Life and *Countryside*'. (But they mean English, omitting the Celtic fringe, as I do here.)

Landscape is not the frame but the core of Chesterton's village scene, where 'the roofs and walls ... mingle naturally with the fields and the trees ... These were the national, the normal, the English, the unreplacable things.' Archetypal rural England, 'some very green meadow with a stream running through it and willows on its banks', inspired poets of the Great War. 'Freedom', wrote Spender, was at heart 'a feeling for the English landscape'.

The now hallowed visual cliché – the patchwork of meadow and pasture, hedgerows and copses, immaculate villages nestling among tilled fields – is not old; only the pre-Raphaelites made the 'English' landscape a medieval fantasy: fertile, secure, small-scale, seamed with symbols. But praise for *some* man-made palimpsest goes back a half millennium. Four traits link this landscape with national ethos: insularity, artifice, order, and stability. Long-crafted, well-bounded, durably ordered, the English landscape is the national heritage's staunchest support.

Insularity distinguishes Britain from all Europe, save Iceland and Ireland. Virgil mourned Britain as 'utterly marooned from all the world'. But natives find isolation an abiding joy. In Tory leader Norman Tebbit's words:

> Our Continental neighbours use 'insular' as a term of abuse, but we ... have every reason to be thankful for our insularity. Our boundaries ... are drawn by the sea – some might say by Providence. Unlike those of most other nations they have not been drawn, rubbed out and redrawn time and again ... The blessing of insularity has long protected us against rabid dogs and dictators alike.

Against their neighbours within the island they raised other barriers. The incoming Romans and Saxons saw England as 'such a precious spot of ground' as a 17th Century panegyrist put it, 'that they thought it worthy to be *fenced* in like a Garden-Plot with a mighty *Wall* [and] a monsterous *Dike*' to keep out the Scots and the Welsh.

Escaping foreign influence enabled the English to 'work out their civilization entirely by themselves', claimed the historian Buckle. Atavisms are insular: 'on these shores', 'this sceptr'd isle'. Like its medieval prototype, the English garden fences out a menacing wilderness.

The garden is not natural but crafted. Other nations extol untouched nature; English culture tames and adorns it. Emerson noted 'nothing left as it was made; rivers, hills, valleys ... feel the hand of a master'. The manmade landscape is not merely the locus of heritage but its mainstay.

Continentals cherish some primordial fundament, however reduced. The ancient forest, the savage peak, the solitude of glacier and marsh exalt national myth and spirit. But Britons celebrate only the landscape they have made and remade over the centuries: the supreme communal creation since prehistory. Even megalithic folk are lauded for adding 'a new dignity to Nature' and leaving 'English country more beautiful than they found her'. The acme of nature is a fabric woven by 50 generations of landlords and labourers.

Of this legacy the English are proudly beneficent stewards. All creatures benefit by rural guidance. The threat to 'our heritage of British country sports ... by countries [devoid of] respect for wildlife and conservation' is termed the gravest menace of European union. Rural stewardship tempers enterprise with concern for natural harmonies. But not for nature raw. 'If you could get through the bogs and jungles and the thickets [that covered] this country one million years ago, you would say, "What a dreadful place this is" ', Nicholas Ridley as Environment Minister admonished Green primitivists. 'The valleys were mosquito-ridden swamps; the mountains were covered in hideous oak thickets and there were just a few shacks, where miserable people attempted to live. Now this is a country full of wonderful landscape, ... superb cities and towns, all built by man, [and] we are constantly enhancing it.'

Order is this landscape's touchstone. It is an English creed that all land requires supervision. Nature needs vigilant guidance. Hence the impending withdrawal from cultivation of millions of acres arouses custodial alarm. 'Left to themselves, the fields would fur over with weeds, waist-high and then head-high', and eventually with scrubby forest; as drainage broke down, much would revert to waterlogged swamp:

> It would be good for birds, but also for rats, mosquitoes and accumulations of weed pollen to make the nation sneeze ... In the dimness of the tangled undergrowth there would lurk mounds of abandoned cars, refrigerators, and agricultural machines. This prospect terrifies the government, the planners, and the environmentalists. [So] they have invented the farmer as museum custodian, to preserve the look of the rural 'heritage'.

Even the encroachment of scrub seems menacing. Vacated fields are seen as not just scruffy but degenerate and lawless.

Managed landscape spells social order. To English improvers uncultivated land bespoke 'uncivilized nations'. Control is the countryside's leitmotif, obsession with order patent in chosen scenes. Mess is ill-mannered and offensive; hedges and walls mark clear-cut bounds. Neatness, 'a passion for tidiness, for trimmed edges', the National Trust aesthetic embraces castle and cottage alike.

Stability is England's fourth endearing landscape trait. Harmony is ever 'ancestral'. 'England still has quiet villages, peaceful homes and pleasing prospects, bearing the stamp of centuries of countrymen and women', says an archetypal old codger. An inveterate tree-planter, Michael Heseltine, when Environment Minister claimed to 'only copy where others pioneered. My yews were their yews, the beech their foresight, the chestnuts their commitment ... England as she was: changeless in our fast-changing world.'

'The countryside reassures us that not everything is superficial and transitory; that some things remain stable, permanent and enduring.' Rurality sanctions the status quo. Invoking rural roots, Prime Minister Baldwin termed himself not 'the man in the street even, but a man in a field-path, a much simpler person steeped in tradition and impervious to new ideas'. Elsewhere rural idiocy shames; in England it spells stability.

But rural idiots are extinct; we now have only rural entrepreneurs. For two hundred years most English people have had no intimate links with green fields. Yet, abiding affection for the landscape heritage valorizes agricultural policies as fabulous as the French. Many farm landscapes survive largely through tourism. 'In 20 years' time all Lakeland farmers will have given up farming', forecasts a local. 'They'll be called field wardens. They'll build up dry stone walls, then knock them down again to amuse the tourists. Herdwick sheep will become pets, never sold or killed. Shepherds with awfully clever dogs will move them in a perpetual circle, from field to field.'

A century ago the 'radiant beauty of ... still unsullied expanses of corn land and wind-swept moor and heather, ... and quiet down standing white and clean' struck the Liberal leader C.F.C. Masterman as a tragic irony; never had 'the land beyond the city offered so fair an inheritance to the children of its people, as to-day, under the visible shadow of its end'. But for most inheritors the countryside was 'a toy and a plaything ... for whose vanishing traditions and enthusiasms they care not at all'. Now more than ever such landscapes yield more fun than food, and city dwellers' countryside contacts are solely scenic or sportive. But they have come, more and more, to care for it.

LANDSCAPE AND EUROPEAN NATIONHOOD

English attachments to nature tamed are most intense, but not unique. Verdant, cultivated, inhabited scenes are beloved all over Europe. The wild or the ruinous may charm aesthetes and tourists, but domestic rural locales rank first in popular affection.

To be sure, early-19th century national spokesmen extolled Nature's pristine splendours, and by the century's end wild scenery featured in most national logos. Rugged mountains, dense forests, deep lakes, storm-scarred coasts and cliffs suited nascent and militant chauvinisms. But the domestic endured alongside the dramatic. And national icons today stress intimate, humanized chocolate-box scenes: a figured landscape. Not only in England do landscapes need people to elicit love. Traces of cultural heritage must be embellished. Photographers' props in Sweden enrich the classic Dalecarlian lakeland scene: a collapsible wooden fence, a model in folk costume, a replica traditional birch-bark horn, a couple of goats.

What Europe now lacks is less the landscape than its habitants. Farming technology and flight from rural life empty countrysides. Urban and suburban devotees flock to these landscapes but know little of how they were formed and are sustained. Yet their recollections, however imperfect, suffice to preserve them as icons.

The tenacity of these national icons raises questions about the new cult of regional and local devolution. National landscape tastes have largely rural roots and a populist, democratizing bent. In landscape as in language, regionalism in continental Europe still conjures up memories of privilege, injustice, and landless bondage. By contrast, national landscape icons, wild and tamed alike, bespeak liberation and freedom: liberation from subjugations both foreign and domestic, freedom for farmers empowered by sovereign status.

Nationhood for most Europeans came when they were still rural, and nationalism is linked with peasant emancipation. Save in England, rural folk saw the centralized state as a release from harsh provincial and local bondages. Despite subsequent urbanization, Europe's landscapes everywhere remain compelling icons of *national* identity.

An overview of national landscape attitudes reveals a crucial transition from rural majorities to minorities, from farm scenes to urban and industrial locales. The loss of intimate contact with rural land as the seat of livelihood and the fabric of everyday life is inexorable, with each state at some particular stage in the process. The pace and mode of change, the endurance of ties with the world left behind, new attachments to once-ancestral milieus shape diverse national responses. Let me suggest some traits common to three points on the continuum of change.

WHERE RURAL LIFE STILL PREVAILS

The traditional predominance of farming and rural life, already rare in western Europe, is increasingly challenged in eastern Europe too. The Ukraine and Byelorussia, Bulgaria and Poland still look largely rural, and the linkage of land and labor is commonplace; but the lot of many if not yet most is urban or industrial, as it is in Portugal and Greece, Denmark and Finland. Perhaps Albania and Kosovo alone remain almost wholly rural.

Yet agricultural perspectives still dominate many of these lands. Everyday rural life precludes self-conscious apprehension of landscape save as hearth and livelihood. To these farmers and herders the landscape concerns of vacationing city folk, nature cultists, ecological reformers, folklife tourists are alien and pointless. Productive landscapes may betoken national pride, but peasant loyalties are perforce mainly local and proprietorial.

WHERE RURAL LIFE IS A RECENT MEMORY

Rural labour has dropped precipitously in much of western Europe only since the Second World War. Despite a century or more of decline and departure, France, Scandinavia, Greece, the Mezzogiorno, Switzerland, Iberia have lost most of their farm workers just in the last few decades. Farming, often intensified, remains crucial; but fewer than one-fourth and often (France, Switzerland) as little as a twentieth of the labor force remain farm-based.

So recent is the exodus, though, that most keep intimate ties with rural land and pursuits. The farm is where everyone's parents or at least grandparents came from; rural landscape conjoins personal and collective heritage. Regular visits home, summer vacations, childhood memories reinforce rural images that sacralize country life, massively sustained by agricultural subsidies. As in France, remaining farmers are extolled as exemplars of social health and ecological virtue, an endangered breed the nation must treasure for its very identity.

WHERE RURAL LIFE IS LONG GONE

Rural majorities and folkways are remoter memories in a few long urbanized and industrialized lands. Britain is the prime exemplar; but in northern Italy, the United States, and much of Germany only recent incomers from elsewhere – the Mezzogiorno, the American South, the Slavic east – retain firsthand memories of rural life elsewhere.

The landscape legacy in these states is vital for national identity as for tourism; I have shown it integral to English notions of belonging. But it embodies few people's own recollections and is mostly devoid of networks of obligation and reward. Even grandparental roots hark back not to rural but to urban and industrial locales.

Personal recall is largely framed by factories and city streets. Hence, industrial archaeology, urban heritage centres, tenement and factory museums now flourish in Britain and the United States, and are coming to do so in France, Austria, Scandinavia. They attract not only visitors from abroad, but locals whose sense of purpose and order was formed in scenes of mill and mine and shipyard, not meadow and field and pasture. These remain realms of meaning, to be sure, but what they signify is less and less connected with everyday family memory.

'The mass of mankind everywhere, except in a little workshop like England, must live by agriculture', wrote a British observer just a century ago. Time has overturned this truism. Sooner rather than later, most states will increasingly slough off rural life. Every passing decade distances the Parisian further from roots in Provence and Bretagne; in time the compote and calvados cease coming from 'home', the uncles retire and the farm is sold off. We must envisage a Europe run by those severed from ancestral rural linkages and agricultural memories. No longer the font of home and family, livelihood and metier, landscapes become more and more locales of contemplation, vacation, avocation.

To invest these landscapes with the mystery and resonance of traditional heritage requires three acts of faith. The first is to bow to the inevitable withdrawal of much arable and pastoral land from present productive purposes, yet not to abandon it to indifferent neglect or anarchic greed. This requires enlarged views of what seems productive, a huge topic in itself.

The second is to bequeath the public at large, however remote from rural matters, a major share in landscape legacies. This flies in the face of landownership trends. As in early-modern Europe, formal title to land is coming to be confined to a tiny minority. Yet, all citizens and visitors have a continuing stake in it. The most superficial and ephemeral appreciator deserves some say in its stewardship, even urban weekenders who expect a tidy, quiet, odourless, pig-free countryside.

Possession is the main impediment. Urbanites talk about the view as if it belonged to them, despite their absence and negligence. 'You swallows come and go but I'm always here and don't you tell me what to do with my trees', says an irate farmer. 'I thought they were everybody's trees', muses an incomer, 'but he thought they were his.' An Oxfordshire field from the train window is a vaunted 'private view for one of the best shows on earth'; but landowners 'cannot have rural policy being dictated from the car window'. Why not? It is from cars that most people admire the landscape. All of Stonehenge that most people see may be fleeting glimpses from the highway; but it mesmerizes millions. We need alliances among those for whom landscape is a home, a locus of livelihood, and a source of even occasional inspiration.

The third act is to augment car-window views of Stonehenge, say, with perceptions of Salisbury Plain, of Wiltshire, and of the wider world beyond. Enhanced perspectives may in time make the landscape of the long-distance traveller, like that of walker and the painter, the weekender and the pensioner, more fulfilling than the grind of peasant life over millennia past would ever have led us to suppose.

The author

David Lowenthal is a Harvard graduate with further degrees from Berkeley and Wisconsin. In his varied academic career, he has worked for universities in several countries, and he became Professor of Geography at University College London in 1972. A prolific writer and lecturer of international renown, his books include *The Past Is a Foreign Country* (Cambridge University Press, 1985).

References

Barzini,L., *The Europeans*, Harmondsworth: Penguin, 1984.

Bruno, G., *Le Tour de la France par deux enfants* (1877), Paris, 1976.

Bunkse,E., 'Landscape symbolism in the Latvian drive for independence', *Geografisker Notiser*, 1990, no. 4, pp.171-72

Carson, R., *Silent Spring* (1962), Hamondsworth Penguin, 1982.

Citron, S., *Le mythe national: l'histoire de France en question*, Paris: Ed. Ouvrières, 1989.

Heiberg, M., *The Making of the Basque Nation*, Cambridge University Press, 1989.

Löfgren, O., 'Landscapes and mindscapes', *Folk*, 31, 1989, pp.183-208.

Lowenthal, D. & Penning-Rowsell, E.C.(eds.), *Landscape Meanings & Values*, London, Allen & Unwin, 1986.

Lowenthal, D., 'British national identity and the English landscape', *Rural History* **2** (1991), pp.205-30.

Lowenthal, D., 'Finding valued landscapes', *Progress in Human Geography* **2** (1978), pp.373-418.

Lowenthal, D., 'The place of the past in the American landscape,' in Lowenthal, D. & Bowden, M.J.(eds.) *Geographies of the Mind*, New York, Oxford University Press, 1975, pp. 89-117.

Lowenthal, D., & Prince, H., 'English landscape tastes', *Geographical Review* **55** (1965), pp.186-222.

Lowenthal, D., 'The American scene', *Geographical Review* **58** (1968), pp.61-88.

Newby, H., *Country Life: A Social History of Rural England*, London: Weidenfeld and Nicolson, 1987.

Nora, P.(ed.), *Les lieux de mémoire*, III *Les France*, 2. *Traditions* , Paris: Gallimard, 1992: Armand Frémont, 'La terre', pp.18-55; Thierry Gasnier, 'Le local', pp.462-525; Georges Vigarello, 'Le tour de France', pp. 884-925.

Olmsted, F.L., *Walks and Talks of an American Farmer in England* (1859); Ann Arbor: Univ. of Michigan Press, 1967.

Olwig, K., *Nature's Ideological Landscape: A Literary and Geographic Perspective on Its Development and Preservation in Denmark's Jutland Heath*, London: Allen & Unwin, 1984.

Shoard, M., *This Land Is Our Land: The Struggle for Britain's Countryside*, London: Paladin, 1987.

Walter, F., *Les Suisses et l'environnement*, Geneva: Ed. Zoé, 1990.

Weber, E., *My France*, Cambridge, Mass.: Harvard University Press, 1991.

Williamson, T.,& Bellamy, L., *Property and Landscape: A Social History of Landownership and the English Countryside*, London: George Philip, 1987.

2

THE ELUSIVE REALITY OF LANDSCAPE
Concepts and Approaches in Research

Michael Jones

The last ten years has seen a growing interest in the cultural landscape in Norway. Until the early 1980s, cultural landscape studies were a specialised research field for a limited group of cultural geographers, landscape architects and practitioners in a few other disciplines (Jones 1988a), without awakening very great interest beyond. The second half of the 1980s saw a marked increase of interest for the cultural landscape in widening academic circles as well as in central and local planning authorities. At the beginning of the 1990s, the concept of the cultural landscape has become common property, a positive word used by researchers, planners and administrators in a variety of contexts. It has become a catchword used in the media and everyday life.

A Cultural Landscape Campaign was conducted by the Ministries of Environment and Agriculture in 1988-89. The Central Office of Historic Monuments (Riksantikvaren) established a Cultural Landscape Department in 1988. In 1989, the Ministry of Agriculture introduced a Cultural Landscape Subsidy, signalling a change towards more environmentally orientated support for farming. The same year, a popular, photographically illustrated presentation of Norwegian cultural landscapes was published by Ragnar Frislid (1989 and 1990). More recently, the Directorate of Nature Management and the Agricultural Development Fund have both issued reports listing a large number of practical projects relating to the management of cultural landscapes (Bodsberg 1990, Landbrukets utbyggingsfond 1991).

Parallel with this interest, an increasing awareness of the problematical, even somewhat chaotic nature of the concept of cultural landscape can be discerned. Taking as its starting point the Norwegian discussion, this paper discusses the relationship between the concept of landscape and approaches to its study.

CONCEPTUAL CONFUSION

A series of articles in the antiquarian periodical *Fortidsvern*, helped initiate the discussion by demonstrating the variety of ways in which the cultural landscape is specified by different practitioners (Austad 1987, Brekke 1987, Christensen 1987, Magnus 1987, Norderhaug 1987, Schancke 1987). In a short reply in the following issue, Knut Fægri (1987a) held that attempts to specify the concept only caused confusion. For him, the cultural landscape was the whole landscape as it had been changed from its natural state by human activity, and not the individual elements in it as studied by separate fields of inquiry. Fægri (1988, pp.1-2) amplified his viewpoint in the preface to the published proceedings of an international symposium entitled 'The cultural landscape – past, present and future', held in Western Norway in 1986 to celebrate the 100th anniversary of the Botanical Museum in Bergen. In origin, he pointed out, the cultural landscape was the antithesis of unspoilt nature. However, modern attempts to protect untouched nature revealed that virgin landscapes were a fiction. The ensuing vegetation succession in protected areas showed that virtually all landscapes are created or modified to varying degrees by humans. Fægri preferred the idea of a gradient of human impact. In another context, he maintained that the cultural landscape was not a single landscape or landscape type, but an abstract concept. Every epoch and culture makes its own material impact on the landscape. If human influence were to be removed, a pseudo-natural landscape would develop (Fægri 1987b, pp.12,16).

The varying position of the dividing line between natural and cultural landscape was noted by Even Gaukstad (1988). He observed that the cultural landscape is a complex phenomenon, which is understood differently by different disciplines. In particular, perception of the cultural landscape in the natural sciences diverges from that in the humanities. For the former, the cultural landscape requires physical traces of human activity. For the latter, people's mental perceptions of cultural landscapes are important.

Erik Aas Jr. (1989) criticised the way in which the Ministry of Environment used the concept in its campaign. He felt that a false distinction was created between natural and cultural landscapes, when in reality all landscapes contain elements of both nature and culture. This distinction was reflected in a sectorised research and administrative apparatus, in which nature conservation and cultural conservation are separate departments instead of being united in an integrated environmental conservation.

Under the auspices of the Norwegian Research Council's research programme on the conservation of cultural heritage, two seminars were held in 1989, one on theory and method and the other on Sami (Lapp) cultural heritage. In both cases, the concept of the cultural landscape was among those discussed. Gaukstad (1990) pointed out that, while Fægri as a botanist had a logical interest in the way nature was influenced by humans, cultural historians were interested in how culture manifests itself in the landscape, as visible human products and processes, as well as how landscape is culturally interpreted. As a physical category, cultural landscape is difficult to delimit, since all landscapes are bearers of culture. Audhild Schancke (1990b) expressed scepticism concerning the cultural landscape concept. She pointed to the paradox of human landscapes being ascribed such great value at a time when nature is subject to even greater pressure from human activity. She criticised the prevailing view of the cultural landscape as put forward in Frislid's book (1989, p.7): 'the cultural landscape is all landscape which has been influenced by human activity'. Schanke stated that the Sami cultural landscape is more than the physical traces of Sami activity. It comprises also the historical and cultural values attached to the landscape, including the natural landscape, which have importance or relevance for Sami culture. Nature and culture do not need to be seen as being in opposition to one another, maintained Schancke. She queried the ideological role of the prevailing definition. For her, cultural landscape is a self-reinforcing idea lacking theoretical reflection (Schancke 1990a, p. 91).

Similar debates have appeared in agricultural research. Havard Steinsholt (1987) observed that landscape has become a rallying cry, a fashionable, positively value-laden concept. A variety of disciplines and professions have announced their interest in landscape planning, but there has been a lack of a clarifying theoretical discussion on concepts and ways of understanding reality. In Steinholt's view, landscape can be defined narrowly as the aesthetic values within a defined area, or broadly as the total interaction between humans and nature in a given area. The broader landscape idea serves as a counterweight to what Steinsholt termed the 'monocultural' thinking which prevails in conventional planning, with its legal and economic basis, and which results in the zoning of specialised land use areas. The landscape idea should not be restricted to 'monocultural' conservation areas.

Discussing the agricultural landscape, Lars Emmelin (1988, pp.247-248) emphasised that the cultural landscape concept should not be limited to especially valuable landscapes but focus on the natural and cultural values in the 'everyday' landscape of farmers. Erling Krogh (1989), noting the lack of clarity in the cultural landscape concept, argued for an understanding of landscape as a repository of the cultural values of different social groups. Anne Katrin Geelmuyden (1989b, pp.59, 61-62) criticised the incorporation of cultural landscape in planning for failing to distinguish between landscape as concrete reality, which can be manipulated by technology and science, and landscape as experience or a manner of understanding, which cannot. Landscape experience is thus reduced to decor, picture postcards, or a leisure or holiday attraction, a legitimation of economic interests in rural tourism, while concealing an accelerating environmental destruction.

DEFINITIONS AND CULTURAL APPROACHES

These debates serve to emphasise the relevance of analysing such concepts in disciplines like geography where the cultural landscape has long been on the research agenda. The present author has identified seven differing ways the concept of cultural landscape has been used in the Norwegian academic literature (Jones 1988a). These can be grouped into three main categories of usage, summarised in Table 1. The three usages have implications for the manner in which landscape is approached in landscape research and

Table 1 Different usages of the concept of cultural landscape

Categories	Landscape Modified or influenced by human activity	Valued features of the human landscape, threatened by change or disappearance	Landscape elements with meaning for a human group in a given cultural or socio-economic context
Variants	Areal category	Agricultural landscape	Subjectively interpreted surroundings dependent on ethnic group, social class, economic interest, academic discipline
	Chronological stage	Cultural heritage	
	Traces of human activity in any landscape	Scenery with aesthetical qualities	
Approach	Landscape as means or point of departure for analysing ecological and socio-economic processes	Landscape as object for planning and conservation	Landscape as manifestation of values
Methods	Ecological analysis, historical-geographical interpretation	Inventory, conservation criteria, experimental management	Cultural analysis

Source: Based on Jones 1989

Table 2 Three approaches to the study of landscape

	'Scientific'	'Applied'	'Humanistic'
Landscape regarded as:	Objective	Objective` but value-laden	Subjective
View of landscape reality	'is'	'ought to be'	'a way of seeing'
Landscape comprises:	Everything visible	Selected elements	Symbols
Research problem	Unmanageability leading to compartmentalization	Criteria for selection	Categorization of social and cultural groups

management (Jones 1989).

Landscape modified or influenced by human activity: The classical definition of the cultural landscape, as used by geographers since Friedrich Ratzel (1895-96), sees it as the landscape formed or influenced by human activity. As such, it is the opposite of the natural landscape. Emphasis is variously laid on the cultural landscape as an areal category, as a chronological stage, or as the traces of human activity in any landscape. As an areal category, the cultural landscape is opposed to areas of untouched or comparatively untouched nature. As a chronological stage, the time dimension is emphasised: as a result of human influence, the cultural landscape replaces the original natural landscape or primeval landscape. Since all landscapes are in practice influenced by humans, the cultural landscape is alternatively seen as all physical traces of human activity in any landscape. Thus the concepts natural landscape and cultural landscape are a means of distinguishing the respective roles of nature and humans in the formation of the landscape.

Within this group of usages, the cultural landscape is the physical expression of human-ecological and socio-economic change through time. The landscape is dynamic, changing continually in response to ecological processes and societal forces. Although often criticised as being one-sidedly descriptive, classificatory and morphologically oriented (English and Mayfield 1972, p. 6), landscape research can also be regarded as a point of departure, a means of gaining insights into processes of change. It provides a gateway towards understanding the forces which have formed our physical surroundings in the past and which form them today. Methods of ecological analysis and historical-geographical interpretation are central.

Valued features of the human landscape, threatened by change or facing disappearance: For conservationists the cultural landscape tends to be seen in terms of valuable characteristics or elements in the human landscape which are threatened by change. Historic or traditional landscapes have qualities which are disappearing. Emphasis is variously placed on the cultural landscape as countryside, as heritage, or as aesthetically pleasing scenery. The rural landscape is threatened by urbanisation. Traditional agricultural landscapes are threatened by modernisation or abandonment. Semi-natural grasslands are threatened by modern farming practices. Historic urban landscapes are threatened by road schemes and redevelopment. Ancient buildings and other antiquities are threatened by air pollution or the decay of time.

These usages of the concept are practical in orientation. The cultural landscape is an object for physical planning. The preservation of values represented by traditional landscapes is a problem to which planners must find practical solutions. The cultural landscape becomes an objective in itself. Central methodological challenges for research are inventory, the formulation of criteria for the selection of objects and areas for conservation, and experimentation with different methods of management. The explicit purpose of research is to serve planning and administration.

Landscape elements with meaning for a group of people in a given

cultural or socio-economic context: Here, the cultural landscape is not seen as something objective, but as a subjective interpretation of elements in one's surroundings which give meaning in a particular context. The landscape is interpreted differently by different groups of people. What is considered as significant in the landscape depends on factors such as ethnic affiliation, economic interest, social class or even academic training. A natural landscape for Norwegians may be a cultural landscape for Sami. Farmers perceive the cultural landscape differently from urban dwellers. A rural proprietor experiences the landscape of his estate differently from agrarian workers or the rural proletariat. Similarly, geographers, landscape architects, botanists, archaeologists, ethnologists and representatives of other disciplines describe and study the landscape differently from one another.

This usage accepts the precept that the cultural landscape is the manifestation of differing value judgements. The cultural landscape means different things for different groups of people. What is registered in a landscape analysis will be the result of a subjective choice. What is considered significant in a landscape reflects differing needs and aspirations among different groups of people. These may often come into conflict with one another. Values differ not only from culture to culture or sub-culture to sub-culture, but also change over time within a single cultural group. Researchers are concerned with landscape perception and the expression of different values in the landscape and in actions which lead to landscape change. The study of landscape meanings and values leads on to cultural analysis.

THE NATURE AND CULTURE OF LANDSCAPE

The concept of 'cultural landscape' is essentially a creation of the 20th Century. The concept of 'landscape' is much older and can serve to demonstrate the cultural specificity of concepts in the historical sense.

In its original Germanic form, landscape probably referred to a collection of lands (Jackson 1986, p.67). The medieval Norwegian provincial law codes are still referred to as *landskapslover* (Jones 1988a, p.153). Kenneth Olwig (1990a, pp.26-27, 1990b, pp.13,16) showed how the concept of landscape developed from its early Germanic connotation of an area belonging to and shaped by a people, to its Renaissance Dutch application, to mean such an area depicted in a painting. The technique of making a perspective drawing of a landscape was related to the techniques of architectural design and cartography. In English the term came to mean a painting of an area of natural scenery, or a painting of rural surroundings as an idealised picture of nature. The words nature and landscape became almost synonymous.

Nature became idealised as countryside, a symbol of the natural and genuine in contrast to the town. As the progressing industrialisation and urbanisation of society led to an increasing differentiation between town and country, nature became reified as landscape. Landscape gardens developed as an attempt to re-create physically the lost rural idyll. Landowners landscaped the rural surroundings of their country seats to resemble the idealised natural environment depicted in paintings. Under the influence of art, landscape became in a broader sense an area perceived as in a picture from a certain viewpoint, the human experience of scenery dependent on season, weather, emotion or fantasy.

Dennis Cosgrove demonstrated how the landscape idea reflects relations between society and land. In German and Middle English, landscape meant an identifiable tract of land, an area of known proportions and properties. Landscape painting emerged in Flanders and Upper Italy, the most economically advanced and urbanised regions of the 15th Century Europe. The development of perspective drawing, pioneered in northern Italy, was, like cartography, related to the exercise of control over land. The landscape painting represented visual control over space, and reflected the patricians' image of a controlled and well-ordered world. Artists reproduced the view of those controlling the land, not those working and belonging in it. In England, the evolution of both landscape panting and landscape gardening between the 16th and 18th Centuries was related to changing social relations to land. The pleasing prospect could be sold as a commodity, uncorrupted by the conflicts of the towns.

Geelmuyden (1989a and b) examined two contradictory aspects in the Renaissance view of landscape: on the one hand an object that can be described, and on the other the image of divine, all-inclusive nature, visible landscape served as a compensatory category for the totality of subjective human experience which was formerly the preserve of religion. With the idea that humans create their own history, historical development became an analogue to the all-inclusiveness of nature, and landscape was a means of providing historical legitimacy. English landscape gardens suppressed the realities of production in the industrial and urban areas, although their prerequisite was the wealth generated by technological and capitalistic growth. Landscape gardens came to exert a powerful influence on later landscape ideals. They embodied the aesthetic idea of nature. Two central aesthetic concepts were the picturesque and the sublime. Geelmuyden pointed to the contradiction between the visual, comprehensible properties of the picture, something which can be scientifically analysed and manipulated, and the ethereal, incomprehensible qualities of the sublime, representing total, fleeting and subjective experience.

Orvar Lofgen, compared the landscape perception of traditional agrarian society with that of modern industrial society. In traditional agrarian society, the landscape was a means of production and nature the source for the satisfaction of a multiplicity of needs. Nature was magically laden. Superstitions, folk tales and poetry provided rules of behaviour, reflecting the values of farming society regarding the use and misuse of nature. In modern industrial society, the landscape is subordinate to technology, economic rationality and the profit motive. Modern values such as effectivity and specialisation result in the transformation of nature to a source of satisfaction for leisure activities. Nature is described in aesthetic and romantic terms. It is experienced as beautiful scenery from viewpoints along the road or from the summer cabin.

In academic research, with its ideal of objectivity promoted by positivism, the landscape as an object of study came to be seen as an area of special character, with its associated forms and inter-related features. The most common usage of landscape is as the sum of our visible surroundings, the total complex of visually perceptible forms within a given area, both natural and human (Jones 1988a, p.153). Nonetheless, concern with both the visible landscape, consisting of natural forms and the forms of human occupance, and the aesthetic landscape, as a symbolic creation giving insight into value systems, has a long tradition in geography (English and Mayfield, 1972). Tarja Keisteri (1990, pp.32-42) has shown how the double meaning of landscape as a defined area of land and as a picture of such an area is paralleled in various European languages. In geography, usage has variously connoted an area, the physical forms of an area, functional processes within an area, and aesthetic and subjective impressions of an area. The geographical concept of landscape today, according to Keisteri, can be said to retain both the visible and subjectively experienced aspects.

Several conclusions can be drawn from this brief review of the concept landscape:

1. The landscape concept retains several layers of meaning. As it developed from an area associated with scenery, the idea of possession and control did not entirely disappear. Hence the power of the national-romantic aesthetic documentation of nature and scenery during the 19th Century Norwegian national revival can be understood.
2. The landscape concept embodies several unresolved conflicts: between collective belonging and individual control, between the subjective and the objective, and between the mental and the material.
3. The concepts of landscape and nature are interlinked. As human society becomes more technical and its surroundings more artificial, the apparently simpler and more nature-near life of the countryside becomes idealised as natural. However, as rural areas become more subject to technology and more integrated into an urban lifeform, comparatively untouched nature is something which becomes available only in isolated reserves. Traditional human landscapes become defined as cultural landscapes, which arouse a desire for documentation and possession through preservation, in the same way as untouched nature.
4. Concepts such as nature, landscape and cultural landscape can only be understood and interpreted in their historically specific social and cultural context.

CULTURAL AND SOCIAL CONSTRUCTIONS

Under the impact of impulses from semiotics and social theory, landscape can be understood not simply as a physical reality but as the mediator of values and ideas produced in society. Semiotic theory, developed from the linguistic studies of Ferdinand de Saussure (1955), leads to the interpretation of landscape as a system of symbols. Structuration theory (Giddens 1979, 1984) suggests that perceptions of reality, for example landscape, nature or environment, are produced through an interaction between individual agency and social context. The meaning of landscape needs to be interpreted in a socio-historical or cultural context.

In geography, culture is often understood in the broad sense as the totality of human endeavour, including beliefs and values, actions resulting from these conceptions, and the physical products of human activity. In another sense, culture is understood as the sum of perceptions, values and motives of a social group, formed through a process of learning and socialisation; human actions and artefacts are then regarded as manifestations of culture. In the process of socialisation, the ideas and interests of certain dominating groups become accepted as valid for the social group or society as a whole. These ideas tend to be adopted and internalised by the dominated sub-groups (class, gender or minority groups). However, minority and popular sub-cultures also explicitly or implicitly challenge dominant values. In the words of Peter Jackson (1989, p.1), 'culture emerges as the domain in which economic and political contradictions are resolved.' The meanings attached to the landscape will hence tend to be produced by dominant groups and maintained by institutions representing their interests. Such ideas are reproduced, as well as contested, in the relations between these institutions and users of the landscape. Different sub-cultures also produce their own varieties of landscape. Thus landscape reflects both physically and conceptually social relationships and constellations of power in society.

CHANGE AND CONSERVATION

Change and conservation of the landscape are generally presented as opposites. Proponents of change argue that 'we cannot conserve everything', or 'the old is a hindrance to new thinking; it must give way to the new; every age must be allowed to set its stamp on the landscape.' But is this an argument that 'nothing' can be conserved? Conservation interests argue, on the other hand, that 'things are changing too quickly' and 'historical values/cultural values/ecological values are threatened with destruction by processes of change'. The desire for conservation can be regarded as a critique of the forces of change. Conservationists query processes of change and attempt to moderate them. However, even the most ardent conservationist does not argue that nothing can be changed.

There is a hidden paradox in the dichotomy of change versus conservation. All change implies that something is preserved. In urban renewal projects, cemeteries, churches and pubs are often retained. Monuments, and especially the symbols of power, tend to show longevity in the landscape regardless of how much change occurs around. Ownership structures also tend to be long-lived, and will often reassert themselves in the landscape despite urban development, redevelopment or rebuilding after a catastrophic fire.

Nor can conservation be absolute. In all conservation there is some degree of change. Protected buildings will decay unless they are maintained; maintenance implies that old materials are replace by new. Choices are made as to whether a protected building is restored back to its original appearance, perhaps involving the removal of later additions and alterations, or whether the interior is modernised to meet modern standards of comfort and sanitation. Since most ecosystems are influenced to some degree by human activity, their protection requires measures to prevent the succession of vegetation. Different types of management, depending on the state of knowledge and available finance, affect the landscape in different ways. Many types of traditional agrarian landscape can ultimately only be preserved if the traditional forms of farming that led to their occurrence are maintained; inevitably compromises will have to be made regarding the degree of concession to be made to market forces, or the extent to which museum management is practicable. In national parks and other types of reserve, choices must be made regarding how much management is necessary to prevent damage from visitor pressure or to provide information to visitors and in what form. Conservation creates its own landscape, in which preservation and change are regulated in accordance with prevailing ideas and the significance attached to particular landscape features.

The paradox of attempts to conserve the cultural landscape, which is commonly defined as the result of change, has been pointed out by Schancke (1990a, pp.92-95). Historical change is presented as a value, thus in a sense legitimising change elsewhere. Just as the 'framing' of landscape in art was steered by a particular viewpoint, the 'framing' of areas of landscape through conservation also reflects a particular viewpoint, while divorcing the protected areas from socio-economic processes creating landscape (Olwig 1990a, pp.27-29). Although conservation involves a critique of change , the delimination of protected landscapes helps deflect attention from the forces leading to change elsewhere.

Neither are conservation and change neutral. Conservation presents itself as a critique of tendencies of globalisation and the ensuing disappearance of regional cultures. However, there exists a tension between the ideology of conserved landscapes and the creativity of the landscapes of popular and other minority sub-cultures, which also contain elements of opposition to globalisation (cf. Jackson 1989, p.5). The interesting question is: what changes when something is conserved? What is conserved when things are changed? Interpretation along these lines can give insights into hidden values, deeper thought structures, ideologies, taboos, and the relationships of power in society.

In 1965, David Lowenthal and Hugh C. Prince made a presentation of English landscape tastes on the basis of a selection of literature from the 17th to 20th Centuries. The idealised images and visual prejudices which recurred revolved round a set of themes which Lowenthal and Prince identified as: the bucolic, the picturesque, the deciduous, the tidy, facadism, antiquarianism, rejection of the present, rejection of the sensuous, rejection of the functional, historical associations and *genius loci* (the sense of place). They were quick to stress that the attitudes identified were not necessarily those of the common man, but representative of that minority who have been most active in creating landscape taste.

Some of the social mechanisms whereby landscape values are produced and reproduced can be illustrated by analysis of people's expectations towards the recreational environment of Oslomarka, the forested area to the north of the Norwegian capital (Oraug et al. 1974). At the beginning of the 1970s, a growing conflict between recreational and forestry interests became acute in Oslomarka. The authors examined the kinds of experience that had given rise to the expectations of recreationists towards Oslomarka. They focused on the role of literature and art in producing and reproducing conceptions. Artistic endeavour documents experiences (positive or negative) and at the same time through documentation contributes to maintaining those experiences. The conceptions of later generations concerning Oslomarka were strongly influenced by the descriptions of writers such as Bernhard Herre, Peter Christen Asbjornsen and Johan Dahl, as well as the pictures of artists such as Theodor Kittelsen and Eric Werenskiold. The national romantic school in literature and art created a conception of how Oslomarka should look. The later conflicts between recreationists and forestry interests arose because a landscape with clear cuttings and roads for forestry vehicles did not accord with the landscape that recreationists expected to see.

Shelagh Squire (1986) illustrated how the creative literature of romanticism coloured popular perceptions of landscape. The poet William Wordsworth played a special role in creating an appreciation of the English Lake District as an aesthetic and attractive landscape. Romantic literature emphasised the emotional rather that the rational, the natural and rural as opposed to the urban. The portrait of landscape in romantic literature was coloured by intense emotion and imagination. However, the romantic portrait was selective. Rural poverty was neglected: factories, mines and quarries were ignored. The elusive and subliminal dimensions of landscape were to the forefront. Public fascination with this mythologised and emotional portrait led to the emergence of a tourist landscape. Wordsworth's poetry inspired and educated elite to visit the Lake District. With the help of a popular travel guide, written by Wordsworth, and the extension of the railway network, the conditions for mass tourism were laid. The popularity of romantic literature fostered tourism, and poetical accounts played an important role in creating tourist assessments. This illustrates how the face of reality alters under different perceptual gazes. The transformation of an actual landscape into a literary landscape helped change attitudes towards wilderness and natural beauty. The literary landscape became in turn a tourist landscape.

THE TOURIST GAZE

In his book with this title, John Urry (1990) analysed the systematic ways of 'seeing' adopted by tourists. Part of the tourist experience is to view scenes and landscapes which are different from their everyday life. Tourists look at the environment with enhanced interest and curiosity. Urry examined how this gaze is socially organised and systematised. The tourist gaze is constructed with the help of professionals in the tourist industry. Urry illustrated how the gaze varies in different societies, social groups and historical periods. There is no universal experience which is true for all tourists at all times. The tourist gaze is directed in the anticipation of pleasure, and constructed and sustained with the help of mass media. The gaze is directed at features of the landscape which are separated from everyday experience. There is a greater sensibility to visual elements. People linger over a view which is frequently captured through photographs, film or picture postcards, enabling the gaze to be endlessly reproduced. The tourist gaze is directed at signs of unique, the typical (often confirming preconceived notions derived from the discourse of travel and tourism) or the traditional (in unfamiliar environments).

The tradition of visiting the seaside or the countryside dates back in Britain to the 19th Century. This has led to the appreciation of special types of landscape, for example, village landscapes and country houses in parks. The last 20 years has seen the development of a new tourist interest in townscapes and industrial landscapes. The rapid decline of manufacturing in Britain in the 1970s and 1980s resulted in a sense of loss as the landscapes, technologies and social life of industrial areas were transformed. At the same time, industrial premises became available for alternative uses. The result has been the reshaping of urban and rural landscapes as heritage (Urry 1990, pp. 107-108).

In the global division of the tourist industry, Britain has specialised in the historical and 'quaint'. Robert Hewison (1987) critically examined what he termed the heritage industry. He claimed that Britain is manufacturing heritage instead of goods. Heritage gives a refuge in a time of change and dissolution of old values connected with the industrial past. Hewison argued that nostalgia is a social construct. He saw heritage as anti-democratic, concealing social and spatial inequalities, masking commercialism and consumerism, and ultimately altering or destroying the buildings and landscapes that were supposedly being preserved. He distinguished between authentic history (continuing and therefore dangerous) and heritage (dead and therefore safe), and argued that history had to be saved from the conservationists.

Urry (1990, pp.110-112) criticised Hewison for ignoring the broad popular basis of the conservation movement and taking too little account of the link between the conservation of cultural heritage and the development of broader environmental policies in the 1980s. In Urry's view, Hewison failed to see that the same heritage can be viewed in differing ways. Urry's critique is that the heritage industry distorts because of its predominant emphasis on visualisation, while other types of social experience are neglected.

New modes of visual perception, primarily photography, are significant part of the tourist gaze. Urry's argument is that photography is also a socially constructed part of seeing and recording. It involves in a sense appropriation of the scene of object being photographed, in a kind of knowledge and power relationship. Photography provides apparent evidence of reality. Yet, the photographer selects, structures and shapes what is photographed and often idealises images. Photographs do not directly reveal their constructed nature nor ideological content. As everyone becomes a photographer, so everyone becomes an amateur semiotician. Photography involves the democratisation of all forms of human experience, by turning everything into photographic images and by enabling anyone to photograph them. It gives shape to travel, giving a reason for stops and imposing an obligation not to miss certain scenes. A hermeneutical circle develops, in which a set of photographic images is sought after (as seen on television or in brochures), captured, and demonstrated as evidence (Urry 1990, pp.136-140). The implications for landscape are that anybody's view is valid in the post-modernistic sense, at the same time as the structural forces controlling the mass media, the photographic industry and the tourist industry exert an underlying influence on the way landscape is perceived.

AGRICULTURE AND ENVIRONMENTALISM

The touristic attractions of the Norwegian landscape, both its impressive nature and human artefacts, are extolled in a recent committee report on rural tourism for the Ministry of Agriculture (NOU 1990:14, pp.33-34, 36). The cultural landscape is mentioned as a resource for tourism in the sections dealing with both Norway's natural resources and its cultural resources. In particular, 'the cultural landscape which is created by an active agriculture' is emphasised as an important asset. Farming is seen as having a central role in the maintenance of Norway's distinctive cultural landscape.

In Norway, as in several other West European countries, the agricultural landscape has attracted a great deal of attention in recent years. Cultural landscape values are increasingly mentioned, by the farmers' organisations in negotiations with the government, by the agricultural authorities when they defend farming subsidies, and by government ministers when environmental considerations are brought forward in arguments justifying agricultural subsidies in the international negotiations within the General Agreement on Tariffs and Trade (GATT).

Because of the problems of agricultural surpluses and growing international demands for a reduction of subsidies on agricultural production, an attempt is being made to find alternative sources of income for Norwegian agriculture; the cultural landscape is seen as offering an opportunity (Krogh 1989, p.65). The new cultural landscape subsidy is at the same time an important symbol for the presentation of a new environmentally oriented profile in agricultural policy. The subsidy operates at present on two tiers. Provided their farming practices are not seen as directly detrimental to the landscape, all farmers are eligible for the lower tier, which is in reality a subsidy on the acreage kept in agricultural production. The second tier can be applied for by farmers for active landscape management, beyond conventional farming operations. It is conditional on a management agreement. Criteria for acceptable management of the cultural landscape (meaning agricultural landscape) include paths for public access, the upkeep of areas around ancient monuments and the maintenance of biological diversity. As this support is oriented towards the environment rather than production, the subsidy is acceptable internationally.

It is timely to ask what the historically specific situation is that can help give an understanding of the attention bestowed on the cultural landscape of agriculture beyond its value for plant and livestock production. Two points can be made. The first is that high costs, large subsidies and problems of overproduction have led to a crisis of legitimacy for agriculture. The prime right of farming interests to possess the countryside is being challenged in a more fundamental way than earlier. It is significant that farmers have become a small minority in the urbanised West European countries. The second point is that there is an increasing awareness of environmental problems in a society at large. The agricultural landscape lies in people's awareness somewhere between the city and the unsullied nature. The city is the technical, urban-industrial landscape where most people live, while nature is understood as comprising wild animals and plants and those parts of the environment subject to spontaneous and self regulatory processes, but which are increasingly subject to interference and destruction by urban-industrial society. Furthermore, this society's demands for economic effectivity and specialisation are transforming the familiar agricultural landscape so that it is becoming unrecognisable, while producing at the same time environmental problems such as soil erosion and pollution from animal manure, artificial fertilisers and pesticides. Not only that, it seems as though even farmers and farming society are becoming dispensable. If farmers are no longer needed to produce food, then they must produce something else if they are to survive. Environmental quality, including a positively value-laden cultural landscape, are seen as a possible response. Experience of a varied countryside and the opportunities it provides for relaxation and recreation are more acceptable to the predominantly urban population than the production of agricultural surpluses at an unacceptable price both financially and environmentally.

The movement towards a 'greener' agricultural policy in Denmark has been described by Olwig (1986, pp.113-132, 1988). He has critically examined legislation aiming to promote habitat reconstruction in marginal agricultural areas. Objectives included nature protection, nature rehabilitation, afforestation and the planting of vegetation belts along water-courses in order to reduce pollution. Up to 20% of Denmark's agricultural area is to be taken out of production during the next 20 years, especially in marginal areas where farming is unprofitable under the prevailing technological and economic conditions. The environmental authorities are presented with a remarkable opportunity to introduce measures for the re-creation of nature. The Danish Health Society, which for 120 years has reclaimed the heaths and drained the bogs, can now find new tasks in heathland conservation and the restoration of water-courses. The justification for such measures lies in the agricultural surpluses resulting from the European Community's agricultural policies, and the consequent attempts to reduce these by taking farmland out of production. The solution adopted is to concentrate agriculture on the best soils, where heavily capitalised, specialised, intensive production is already well-established, and to reduce agriculture in economically marginal areas. A polarisation of land use occurs between areas with protected 'natural' landscapes where continued modernisation is permitted. Alternative solutions, such as a general reduction of production by introducing less intensive but more environmentally friendly methods everywhere, are less politically acceptable than measures to re-create nature in marginal areas. The 'nature' of these areas consists in reality of traditional cultural landscapes, but their protection as 'nature' masks the social origin of these values (Olwig 1986 p.132).

In West Germany, a radical change in direction was made by the land consolidation agency in the early 1980s. The traditional aim of land consolidation (*Flurbereinigung*) was the reallocation of land and structural rationalisation in order to promote mechanised farming. Hedges were removed, streams placed in culverts and wetlands drained. Instead, the authorities now strive to reallocate land in such a way that production costs are lowered without contributing to increased food production and without despoiling the natural and cultural values of the landscape. Nature and landscape protection, recreational use and village renewal have developed as important tasks. Land consolidation is used as a means of multiple land-use planning in rural areas, with both ecological and economic aims. The creation of biotope networks and the 're-naturalisation' of water courses are important measures. Corridors for flora and fauna are created, wetlands recreated, streams reopened and new meanders formed, and nature reserves established (Ronningen 1989, 1991a, pp.36-73, 1991b, pp.61-65).

Again, these measures can be seen in relation to the problems of the European Community's agricultural policies. The aim is to reduce agricultural surpluses by taking land out of production. However, intensive farming practices continue on the areas remaining in production. The new 'ecological' land reallocation gives new, socially acceptable tasks to the planning apparatus, which has faced increasing criticism from a more and more environmentally aware public. The state can demonstrate that it is responsive to the growing green movement. The new measures gain support from the urban population, which uses the countryside for recreation, is interested in wild animals and plants, and dominates the green movement.

31

Paradoxically, several of the land consolidation operations are initiated by motorway construction. A West German objective was that nowhere should lie further than 50km from a motorway. The construction industry has a strong interest in motorway building. The car society is backed by powerful economic interests. It would appear to be easier to focus on ecological measures in the countryside than to solve the problems of traffic. By focusing on the landscape ecology, attention can to some degree be diverted from problems which are harder to solve, such as pollution from traffic, thermal power generation and so on (Jones 1991).

Jürgen Ossenbrügge (1988) linked investment in environmental measures with the new capitalistic model of flexible accumulation and the accompanying restructuring of space. Environmental problems and associated social problems from the middle of the 1970s have led to greater environmental awareness among the general public. While state regulation of the economy has otherwise been reduced, environmental enhancement has become a new field for government regulation and investment. This provides support for the construction industry as well as new environmentally oriented enterprises which have grown up in the private sector. It helps to reduce unemployment and social conflicts while giving new possibilities for capital accumulation. The radical critique is that there is no basic change in the production processes which cause the environmental problems.

AN ACADEMIC BATTLEFIELD

The idea of landscape as simultaneously physical reality and a social or cultural construct can help explain why different academic disciplines use the concept of cultural landscape in different ways. Different disciplines and schools within disciplines structure the concept according to academic traditions, paradigms, concepts and methods into which the particular discipline's practitioners have been schooled or socialised. Perceptions vary according to the scale of observation, differing emphasis on the natural or cultural components of the landscape, differing weight on form, function or process, and differing stress on static or dynamic aspects (continuity or change).

The cultural landscape has become a new market for researchers. Different disciplines attempt to market their identity and comparative advantage (Krogh 1989, p.65). The cultural landscape has become something of an academic battlefield as different disciplines compete for research funds and thereby influence. A similar struggle for influence and power takes place in administration and planning.

Human geographers frequently describe the cultural landscape in terms of land use. Mapping and regional description are traditional approaches. The generally unasked question is: what are the value judgements made when selecting which elements are to be mapped or not (cf. Axelsen and Jones 1987), or deciding what is to be stressed and what is to be omitted in a regional description?

Landscape architects use aesthetic concepts such as variety, harmony, totality, vividness, linearity, repetition and structure to describe the cultural landscape. To what extent can these be said to be universal concepts, and to what extent do they reflect a set of values learnt through processes of socialisation among landscape architects? What is the correspondence between such concepts and those used by ordinary users of the landscape such as tourists and recreationists, who describe it as pretty, ugly, nice or beautiful?

The interest of architects in the cultural landscape is focused especially on buildings and their relationship to their surroundings. Architects have a well-developed aesthetic sense derived from art history. Birgit Cold (1989) distinguished between three levels of aesthetic experience: the first is the experience of the individual, which is dependent on particular situations; the second is the intersubjective experience shared by a society within a particular epoch: the third is the 'eternal' aesthetic experience, based on an agreement that certain aesthetic experiences appear to be valid for all epochs and all (or most) cultures. However, it can be queried whether architects and art historians themselves play a central role in influencing individual and intersubjective experience, and in contributing to the transfer of apparently universal experiences from one epoch to another.

Archaeologists tend to place archaeological finds and ancient monuments in the context of a prehistoric or medieval landscape when they use the term cultural landscape. An ironical view is that the cultural landscape of archaeologists is that around ancient monuments (Schancke 1990a, p.92). Ethnologists are generally concerned with buildings and other cultural relics from more recent times when they speak of the cultural landscape, and in common with social anthropologists are concerned with the maps of meaning which different cultures and sub-cultures construct to interpret their physical surroundings. Cultural historians, in general, justify their selection of information in terms of theories of historical association or cultural identity: elements in the landscape have a historical meaning for a cultural group and they represent collective memories. The landscape's symbolic value is part of a group's feeling of identity or sense of place. However, one of the most difficult problems faced is to select the criteria upon which different ethnic and social groups, cultures and sub-cultures can be identified and delimited from one another.

Agricultural economists approach cultural landscape by regarding it as an externality of agricultural production and propose economic incentives (for example, management agreements) to reduce negative externalities or enhance positive externalities. But how are decisions made as to whom or to which areas such financial incentives are to be applied?

Botanists are primarily interested in culturally influenced ecosystems when they examine the cultural landscape. Ecological diversity in plant species and vegetation complexes on semi-natural grasslands, which are dependent on grazing or haymaking for their maintenance, is an example. Zoologists are interested in the cultural landscape as environment for insects or animals. In landscape ecology, the cultural landscape, especially the agricultural landscape, is associated with the function of human-made features as habitat for flora and fauna. The landscape ecologist describes the cultural landscape in terms of patterns, mosaics, edges, corridors, networks and gradients. The effect of fragmentation of the landscape as environment for plant and animal species is important. Functioning ecological systems, biotope networks and natural processes in the cultural landscape are in focus. Nature is regarded as having an intrinsic value in itself, and the maintenance of ecological diversity is a primary motive for such studies. The cultural in the landscape tends to be relegated to a backdrop. Yet, how is the border between nature and culture decided? Through their choice of conversation criteria, human beings determine what is worthy of conservation. Some species are more equal than others. Human societies delimit nature reserves and national parks and regulate their use. 'Natural' processes in the cultural landscape are dependent on continued human management for their existence. When planning authorities re-naturalise water courses and re-create natural biotope systems, it is a cultural landscape both physically and ideologically that is created. The paradox is that, in landscape ecology, the cultural is presented frequently as natural but the reverse is not taken into account.

The underlying question is: where do the individual disciplines obtain their academic authority from? What is the underlying set of value judgements that determines what is relevant knowledge for a particular discipline? Academic disciplines are not neutral. They have their subjective values which are the result of the particular way in which each discipline has been institutionalised and used by society. This influences the way in which the landscape is perceived and what is considered important to register when it is investigated. This also applies when scientists are called in as experts to give planners and administrators advice on what is worthy of conservation and what can be permitted of change. For each discipline concerned, the landscape is both an objective reality and a set of symbols which depends on a particular form of socialisation.

To document is also to interpret. The enormous wealth of detail in the landscape is reduced to what is regarded as important and meaningful. Like landscape paintings and photographs, scientific documentation produces expectations. Documentation implies possession through knowledge. Conflicts arise between the interests of different disciplines. When the landscape becomes the object of planning and administration, the choice of documentation becomes a means of control over the landscape and thereby influence through the career possibilities offered to the practitioners of different disciplines concerned with landscape.

OBJECTIVITY, SUBJECTIVITY AND INTER- SUBJECTIVITY

In conclusion, three basic approaches to the study of landscape can be identified (Table 2).

In the first approach, the landscape is regarded as something objective, a set of physical forms which can be objectively registered. The underlying idea is that the landscape has an objective existence, the landscape 'is'. The reality of landscape can be investigated scientifically by observation. A natural scientific paradigm with strong positivistic undertones tends to dominate this approach consciously or unconsciously. The landscape is defined as 'everything visible'. However, the practical problem arises: how can 'everything' be studied without becoming unmanageable? The solution is to divide it up into different spheres according to specialist disciplines. Similarly, in landscape planning and administration, totality is divided up into different sectors and departments, employing people with differing qualifications. Each discipline or sector applies its particular concepts and methods, its particular perspectives and training to the object of study. Thus, despite the scientific ideal of objectivity and neutrality, the totality of landscape is seen from differing viewpoints, reflecting often unconscious value judgements inherent in disciplinary socialisation and the acceptance of particular paradigms (cf. Jones 1985 on value judgements in research).

In the second approach, the landscape is regarded as a value-laden reality, a reality consisting of physical forms that can be objectively registered, but where attention is focused on special natural or cultural elements which are considered as especially valuable, particularly if they are threatened with destruction or change. The underlying idea is that within the objective reality of landscape there are certain things that have a special right to existence. This is the landscape as it 'ought to be'. This approach has strong normative undertones in which knowledge is applied to planning. The landscape is perceived as a 'selection' of especially valuable elements, such as ancient monuments, historic buildings, traditional forms of land use, rare natural phenomena and so on. The problem then arises for both academics and administrators. On the basis of which criteria is the selection of especially valuable items to be made? There is room for much disagreement between different academic disciplines and administrative sectors. Although value judgements are more to the fore here, the danger is particular values will be given a special legitimacy by being referred to as scientific evidence or as 'intrinsic' values. The relative strengths and degrees of acceptance of different disciplines will determine which values prevail over others. At the present time, ecological values tend to win greater acceptance than aesthetic values. A further point of discussion concerns the role of expert views in relation to the views of the public at large. The debate between 'expert' and 'user-oriented' studies is well-known in landscape evaluation (Penning-Rowsell 1981, p.31 Jones 1986, p.232). A further problem is whether the results of user preference studies, using aggregation to gain the majority view, should be treated as consensus values, or whether the divergent values of minority groups should be considered.

In the third approach, the landscape is regarded as something subjective, a mental perception of reality. The underlying idea is that landscape is 'a way of seeing'. The manner in which landscape is perceived is dependent on individual experience and socially conditioned expectations. The landscape consists of 'symbols' which express individual and social values, depending on culture. This is the mental landscape, the subjective, human picture of reality. This approach has a humanistic point of departure, concerned with the interpretation of meaning. For the researcher, the objective of study is people's conceptions of the landscape. The research problem is then: how can people be categorised into meaningful social and cultural groups with regard to the way they see the landscape? For the planner or the administrator, the problem becomes a political one: how to arbitrate between different groups with diverging perceptions, values and interests related to the landscape?

Can these three standpoints be united? A key concept is inter-subjectivity. The point of departure is that reality is neither wholly objective nor wholly subjective. We can assume that there is a reality existing independently of human perception of it. The manner in which humans perceive this reality and their ability to perceive it is mediated by society. An interaction takes place between the physical reality of landscape and the subjective conceptions which humans form of this reality in varying social contexts. Varying degrees of agreement or consensus will develop regarding how this reality is experienced. These are inter-subjective conceptions. The fruitful fusion of impulses from social theory and cultural theory suggest methods for investigating how inter-subjective consciousness of different types of landscape arises.

THE NEED FOR REFLEXIVITY

In 1972, Paul Ward English and Robert C. Mayfield summarised the criticisms against classical studies of the cultural landscape in geography as being concerned with empirical facts more than theory, content more than context and form more than process. They identified three special weaknesses: the difficulty of studying the transition from natural to cultural landscapes when all landscapes have in reality been influenced by humans, often in unknown ways; the difficulty of description and classification because of the huge number of variables involved; and preoccupation with the visible landscape, leading to neglect of the less obvious, invisible forces influencing spatial patterns of human behaviour.

Theories of landscape change are central. Attempts to understand landscape change require the combination of intentional, functional and structural explanation (Jones 1988b). Acceptance of the idea that all landscapes are cultural landscapes, in the physical sense, implies that ecological processes cannot be viewed a-historically but must be seen in historically specific contexts. Further, cultural landscapes need to be understood not only as the physical traces of human resource use over time, but also as sets of human beliefs and conceptions concerning the landscape. As the manifestation of cultural processes, cultural landscapes express the relationships between material practice and cultural production. Ideas and strategies for landscape conservation also need to be seen as a social process. A central research perspective is the question of who owns and controls the landscape, directing both its physical and ideological formation and change.

Inter-subjectivity implies that inventory and documentation of the landscape require critical awareness of the reasons for the selection of what is registered, and analysis of the meanings and values communicated. The academic study of landscape requires reflexivity concerning its purpose, both in geography and other disciplines. All choices of subject are socially and culturally mediated. The same applies in landscape planning. Both object and subject should be kept in view when documentation is a tool for the conservation of landscape or elements in it.

In landscape planning, the cultural landscape is a moral landscape. It cannot be divorced from dominating ideologies in planning and political circles. Reflexivity means also a critique of the exercise of power through the presentation of hidden values as universal. Insights into social and cultural differences in the perception of landscape provide a challenge to the belief of experts in their own objectivity (Krogh 1989, p.69). Applied work by academics requires self-reflection over the value judgements concealed in the theoretical bases and methodologies of particular disciplines.

Olwig (1990a, p.17) has noted the increasing power of ecological disciplines as nature is 'placed under administration'. Aesthetic evaluations are on the defensive in the face of criticism for being subjective, ephemeral, varying from individual to individual, varying according to period or fashion, or dependent on social status (Nordisk ministerroad. Miljåørapport 1987:3, p.64). However, less insistence on the universality of landscape experience and aesthetic appreciation and the appreciation of nature are social and cultural processes.

An important prerequisite for inter-disciplinary communication is conceptual analysis. Inter-disciplinary communication requires that individual disciplines do not define landscape narrowly nor exclusively from their own perspective (Krogh 1989, p.69). A will to reach mutual understanding is a precondition for dialogue. This is necessary in democratic, participatory planning, where solutions must be negotiated among a variety of competing interests. Landscape can be seen as one arena for communication (Emmelin 1988, p.58, Geelmuyden 1989b, p.62).

Practical landscape conservation should mean more than the protection of areas and physical elements in the landscape. It implies also an attempt to influence public consciousness and interpretation of the forces producing change. It implies awareness of and active participation in the process by which the inter-subjective acceptance of values takes place. The challenge for planners and administrators concerned with landscape is to justify the choices and actions they make. Criticism of the forces which make conservation necessary is as important as the conservation of demarcated landscapes.

When landscape is approached as a 'way of seeing', the researcher is attempting to argue from a world of exterior appearances to a world of inner meaning. Inter-subjectivity implies that meaning is formed in a social and cultural context. Individual creativity, subjective perception and ideas cannot be interpreted without reference to the constraints provided by social stratification and cultural structures (Jackson 1989, p.22). Cosgrove (1984, p.11) stressed that 'landscape is an ideologically charged and complex cultural product'. The changing values and ideas attached to the landscape concept provide an illustration of the production and reproduction of culture as social practice in historically and geographically specific contexts.

The author

Michael Jones is Professor of Geography at the University of Trondheim. As a student at University college London, he wrote his doctorial thesis on Human Responses to Land Uplift in Finland, a subject on which he has written two books. He went to Trondheim in 1975 to help establish a new department of geography and he is an authority on the subject of cultural landscapes.

The Editor is grateful to Scandinavian University Press for permission to reproduce the above text which appeared in *Norske Geografisk Tidsskrft* (Norwegian Journal of Geography), Vol 45, No 4, 1991, pp.229-244.

References

Aas, E., Jr., *Landskapsvern i Norge*, in Samtiden, No.*4, 1989*. pp.47-53.

Austad, I., *Våre gamle kulturmarker*, in Fortidsvern, No.3, 1987, pp20-23.

Axelsen, B., & Jones, M., *Are all maps mental maps?*, in GeoJournal, *No.14(4)*, 1987, pp447-464.

Bodsberg, K., *Kulturlandskapsprosjekter: En oversikt over tiltak som er satt i gang for å verne og utvikle norske kulturlandskap*, Directorate for Nature Management, Trondheim, 1990.

Brandt, J., *Afgrunden mellem landskabsøkologi og landskabsplanlægning*, in Sådan ligger landet: en antologi om det åbne land, Dansk Byplanlaboratorium, 1987, pp.129-140.

Brekke, N.G., *Byggeskikk og kulturlandskap*, in Fortidsvern, No.3, 1987, pp7-11.

Christensen, A.L., *Kulturlandskapet - på godt og vondt, Fortidsvern 3, 1987*, pp.4-6.

Cold, B., *Om arkitektur og kvalitet*, in Arkitektur of kvalitet: Arkitekturavdelingens skriftserie 1, Norges Tekniske Høgskile, Trondheim (Mimeo), 1989, pp.3-16.

Cosgrove, D., *Social Formation and Symbolic Landscape*. Croom Helm, London, 1984.

English, P. & Mayfield, R.C., *The cultural landscape*, in English, P.W. & Mayfield R.C. (eds), Man, Space, and Environment: Concepts in Contemporary Human Geography, Oxford U.P., 1972, pp.3-9.

Emmelin, L., *Kulturlandskapet: en utfordring til samarbeid mellom landbruk og naturvern*, in Landbrukets Arbok, Tano, Oslo, 1988, pp.246-271.

Fitzsimmons, M., *The matter of nature*, in Anitpode *21(2)*, 1989, pp.106-120.

Frislid, R., *Norske kulturlandskap*, Landbruksforlaget, Oslo, 1989.

Frislid, R., *Man in Nature: Cultural Landscapes of Norway*, Landbruksforlaget, Oslo, 1990.

Fægri, K., *Kulturlandskapsbegrepet*, in Fortidsvern, No 4, 1987.

Fægri, K., *Kulturlandskapet i historiens lys*, in Konferanserapport, Kulturlandskap: Bruk og vern, Samarbeidsgruppa i Sogn og Fjordane (Mimeo), September 1987b, pp12-18.

Fægri, K., *Preface*, in Birks, H.H., Birks, H.J.B., Kaland, P.E. & Moe, D. (eds) The Cultural Landscape: Past, Present and Future, Cambridge UP, 1988, pp1-4.

Gaukstad, E., *Kulturelandskapet og skinnenighetens harmoni*, in Dugnad, No 14, 1988, pp11-30.

Gaukstad, E., *Kulturlandskaps-begrepet*, in Kulturminnevernets teori og metode, Seminarrapport fra Utstien kloster, May 1989, Norges allmennvitenskapelige forskningsråd, Oslo, 1990, pp128-144.

Geelmuyden, A.K., *Landskapsopplevelse og landskap: Ideologi eller ideologikritikk? Et essay om de teoretiske vilkårene for vurdering av landskap i arealplanleggingen*, Norges Landbrukshøgskole, Institutt for landskapsarkitektur, Doctor scientiarum thesis, 1989a.

Geelmuyden, A.K., *Vurdering av opplevelseverdier i landskapet: et kritisk blikk på metodespørsmålet*, in Landbrukøkonomisk Forum 6(4), 1989b, pp54-63.

Giddens, A., *Central Problems in Social Theory: Action, Structure and Contradiction*, in Social Analysis, Macmillan, 1979.

Giddens, A., *The Construction of Society: Outline of the Theory of Structuratuion*, Polity Press, 1984.

Hewison, R., *The Heritage Industry: Britain in a Climate of Decline*, Methuen, 1987.

Jackson, J.B., *The vernacular landscape*, in Lowenthal, D. & Penning-Rowsell, E.C. (eds) Landscape Meanings and Values, Allen & Unwin, London, 1986, pp65-77.

Jackson, P., *Maps of Meaning: An Introduction to Cultural Geography*, Unwin Hyman, London, 1989.

Jones, M., *Datakilder, datainnsamling og verdisyn*, in Dale, B., Jones, M., & Martinussen, W. (eds) Metode på tvers: Sumfunnsvitenskapelige forskningsstrategier som kombinerer metoder og analysenivåer, Tapir, Trondheim, 1985, pp57-84.

Jones, M., *Landscape and welfare: a conceptual convergence?* in Jones, M., (ed) Welfare and Environment, Tapir, Trondheim, 1986.

Jones, M., *Progress in Norwegian cultural landscape studies*, in Norsk Geogr Tidsskr, No.42, 1988a, pp153-169.

Jones, M., *Land-tenure and landscape change in fishing communities on the outer coast of Central Norway, c.1880 to the present: Methodological approaches and modes of explanation*, in Geog. Ann 70b(1), 1988b, pp197-204.

Jones, M., *Kulturlandskapet: et ord med mange meninger*, in Spor 8 (2), 1989, pp4-5 and 49.

Jones, M., *Økonomi og økologi: Utfordringer for landbruket*, in Bærekraftig utvikling: en utfordring for geografer i forskning, forvaltning og utdanning, rapport fra Norske Geografers Forening, Seminar 10-12 Jan, 1991, Trondheim, Skrifter fra Norske Geografers Forening, ny serie 2, 1991 pp43-52.

Keisteri, T., *The study of changes in cultural landscapes*, in Fennia 168(1), 1990, pp31-115

Krogh, E., *Kulturlandskap som forskningsobjekt*, in Landbruksøkonomisk Forum 6(4), 1989, pp64-70.

Landbrukets utbyggingsfond, *Prosjekt-og tiltakskatalog 1990: Kulturlandskap*, Lanbrukets utbyggingsfond & Statens fagtjeneste for landbruket (Mimeo), 1991.

Löfgren, O., *Människan i landskapet: landskapet i människan*, in Honko, L., & Löfgren, O., (eds) Tradition och miljö: Ett kulturekologiskt perspektiv, Liber Läromedel, Lund, 1981, pp235-260.

Lowenthal, D., & Prince, H.C., *English landscape tastes*, in Geog. Rev. 55, 1965, pp186-222.

Magnus, B., *Arkeologenes kulturlandskap*, in Fortidsvern 3, pp14-16, Nordisk ministerråd, *Miljørapport: Natur og kulturlandskapet i arealplanlegging, Forvaltning av ressurser og verdier*, 1987.

Norderhaug, A., *De urterike slåtteengene*, in Fortidsvern 3-1987. pp12-13.

NOU., *Norsk bygdeturisme: En næring med framtid*, Landbruksdepartementet, Norges offentlige utredninger 14, Oslo, 1990.

Olwig, K., *Hedens natur: Om natursyn og naturanvendelse gennem tiderna*, Teknisk Forlag, København, 1986.

Olwig, K., *Landbrugspolitik i grøn inpakning*, in Byplan 40(3), 1988.

Olwig, K., *Naturens synliggørelse*, in Kulturminnevernets teori og metode, Seminarrapport fra Utstein kloster 8-11 May 1989, Norges allmennvitenskapelige forskningråd, Oslo, 1990a.

Olwig, K., *Why does geography have difficulty dealing with nature/culture issues?* paper for the 11 Nordiska Symposiet för Kritisk Samhallsgeografi (Mimeo), 1990b

Oraug, J., Østensen, F., Lind, T., & Rosenfeld, I.S., *Forventninger til rekreasjonsmiljøet i Oslomarka: Analyse av fotografier, tegninger og litteratur med motiver fra skog generelt og Oslomarka spesielt*, NIBR arbeidsnotat 10/74, Oslo, 1974.

Ossenbrugge, J., *Regional restructuring and the ecological welfare state: spatial impacts of environmental protection in West Germany*, in Geographische Zeitschrift 76(2), 1988, pp78-96.

Penning Rowsell, E., *Fluctuating fortunes in guaging landscape value*,in Progress in Human Geography 5(1), 1981, pp25-41.

Ratzel, F.,*Die deutsche Landschaft*, in Halbmonatshefte der Deutchen Rundschau 4, 1985-6, pp407-428.

Rønningen, K., *Jordskifte som planinstrument i natur-og landskapsvernarbeidet i Bayern*, Hovedoppgave ved Institutt for jordskifte og arealplanlegging, Norges Landbrukshøgskole, 1989.

Rønningen, K., *Jordskifte og kulturlandskap: Hva kan vi lære av bayersk jordskifte?* Institutt for planfag og rettslære, Norges landbrukshøgskole melding nr. 48,1991a.

Rønningen, K., *Planlegging i kulturlandskapet trenger jordskifte*, in Landsbruksokonomisk Forum 8(2), 1991b, pp57-70.

Saussure, F. de. *Cours de linguistique générale*, in Balley, C. & Sechehaye, A. (eds) collab. with Reidlinger, A., Pyot, Paris, 1955.

Schancke, A., *Det samiske landskap*, in Fortidsvern 3-1987. pp17-19

Schancke, A., *Samfunnsteori og forvaltningsideologi i kulturminnevernet*, in Kulturminnevernets teori og metode, Seminarrapport fra Utstein kloster, pp8-11, May 1989. Norges allmenvitenskapelige forskningsråd. Oslo, 1990a, pp79-97.

Schancke, A., *Samisk kulturlandskap*,in Samisk kulturminnevernforskning, Rapport fra seminar i Guovdageaidnu Kautokeino, 22-24, Nov. 1989, Norges allmenvitenskapelige forskningsråd, Oslo,1990b.

Squire, S., *Wordsworth and Lake District tourism: romantic reshaping of landscape*,in Canadian Geographer 32,.1988, pp237-247.

Steinholt, H., *All kultur er dyrken, først og fremst av landskap: Noen tanker et stykke ut i en planleggingsdebatt*, in Kart og Plan 47(6), 1987, pp609-616.

Urry, J., *The Tourist Gaze:Leisure and Travel in Contemporary Societies*,Sage, London, 1990.

3

CULTURAL LANDSCAPES
The Need for a Political Perspective

Harold Eidsvik

Heritage is still a little understood concept, but it is becoming increasingly important to help us to see the environment from a new perspective. Conventionally we think about heritage primarily as buildings, and sometimes as land that has been passed down through generations. As an inheritance, heritage usually involves the breaking up of an estate and distribution of silver, furniture, buildings and land to numerous heirs. Thus what was once a unity becomes scattered and isolated, leading to a loss of knowledge and value of heritage as a larger entity.

Jeremy Carew-Reid of the International Conservation Union (IUCN) noted that, 'What we are discovering is that the things viewed as heritage are woven within systems which, as a whole, are always much greater in importance than their constituent parts. This means that unless we recognise and understand all parts of the system, and their relationships, one to the other, we cannot expect to manage and conserve the heritage items which are of specific immediate significance.'

Nature cannot survive if it is managed in isolated pockets. It must be managed in full consideration of all land uses. Similarly, a nation's heritage will not survive if it is not protected through some organised process. This may involve for example inheritance laws, or laws relating to land transfers and zoning changes. Cultural landscapes are a part of our inheritance which will not survive if opportunism and neglect become a driving force in land use change.

In 1962, UNESCO passed a recommendation for safeguarding the beauty and character of landscapes, that was concerned not only with truly natural landscapes but also with those on which man had left his imprint in both a rural and urban context. It was concerned not only with their natural beauty but also with the witness they bore to the interaction between nature and culture. Today concepts of 'protected or cultural landscapes' as found in

World Heritage publications bear witness to and elaborate upon the evolution of this early UNESCO recommendation.

Long-term protection to benefit future generations does not occur by accident. It occurs because there are committed politicians. Incidentally, committed politicians occur only when there are committed people to spur them into action. A colleague put it this way, 'No community, no state and no nation in the world can accomplish its preservation goals without recognising and controlling the various political elements at play.' From local involvement preserving a building, to the designation of World Heritage Sites, continued political stimulus is essential.

Early in the 17th Century La Rochefoucauld said, 'A word to the wise is unnecessary.' Although more than 84% of the Scottish people urge the establishment of national parks, politicians in government have not acted. Perhaps a word to the wise is necessary and perhaps these discussions on cultural landscapes may help towards this end.

DEFINITIONS

In order that we have some common understanding of terms, I would like to put forward some definitions taken from Bing Lucas (1992):

Conservation: The management of human use of the biosphere so that it may yield the greatest sustainable benefit to present generations, while maintaining its potential to meet the needs and aspirations of future generations. Thus conservation is positive, embracing preservation, maintenance, sustainable utilisation, restoration, and enhancement of the natural environment.

Protected Area: Any area of land that has legal measures limiting human use of the plants and animals within that area; includes national parks, game reserves, protected landscapes (cultural landscapes), multiple use areas, biosphere reserves, etc.

Landscape: Many things are encompassed in our understanding of the word landscape, the geological structure of the land, its soil, animals and its vegetation, the pattern of human activity, fields, forests, settlements and local industries, both past and present. It is a matter not only of beauty, of aesthetic appreciation of nature and architecture, but of the whole ecology of an area and the history of its occupation and use by people.

Protected Landscape or Seascape: these are designated to maintain nationally significant natural landscapes which are characteristic of the harmonious interaction of people and land, while providing opportunities for public enjoyment through recreation and tourism within the normal life-style and economic activity of these areas.

It is interesting to note that for whatever reason IUCN has in the last category above chosen to use 'protected landscapes', whereas many others use the term 'cultural landscapes'. In practice they are synonymous, although, as we all know, not all cultural landscapes are protected.

CHANGING CONCEPTS

The World Conservation Union had its origins, first in preservation, and then in the protection of flora and fauna. It was not until the 1980 World Conservation Strategy that it made a major shift toward the concepts of sustainable development, and a broader perception of nature conservation. In 1978 its Commission on National Parks and Protected Areas (CNPPA) began to shift its perspective from nature reserves and national parks to a full range of protected areas including 'protected landscapes'.

When the World Conservation Union published the 1980 United Nations List of National Parks and Equivalent Reserves it did not include categories. It added a footnote with respect to the National Parks of England and Wales saying that 'the national parks of the United Kingdom do not meet the criteria of government ownership as most lands are private.' It could be said that the Union was, by stressing government ownership and nature conservation, a very conservative organisation trying to hold back the pressures of tourism and other forms of development that ensued following World War II. Subsequently, it has taken on a much broader perspective.

The expanded role of the World Conservation Union was foreshadowed in the 1978 CNPPA paper on categories which introduced the concept of protected areas to encapsulate the national parks of the United Kingdom. Protected landscapes were to encompass two types of areas, 'semi-natural' and 'cultural landscapes'. These were seen as areas managed primarily by 'man' and not by 'nature'. Today of course this thinking has shifted to recognise that there is hardly a place on earth, including all parks and nature reserves, which are not under the pervasive influence of man.

The concept of 'protected landscapes' took a major step forward with the International Symposium on Protected Landscapes, held in the Lake District in 1987. This symposium was to a considerable extent spurred on by the deferment of the Lake District nomination to the World Heritage List. Neither the World Conservation Union nor the International Council on Monuments and Sites (ICOMOS), could reach agreement on what constituted a 'cultural site' under the World Heritage Criteria.

THE WORLD HERITAGE CONVENTION

The World Heritage Convention, as it is commonly known, was launched in 1972, through the combined efforts of UNESCO and the World Conservation Union. Today it has 132 states participating from the 172 governments that participate in UNESCO. The World Heritage List includes 378 sites, of which 276 are cultural, 87 are natural and 15 are mixed sites.

The World Conservation Union and ICOMOS are the principle technical advisors to the World Heritage Committee which designates sites for the World Heritage List. They are guided by the terms of the Convention and by operational guidelines which have been adopted by the Committee. The original provisions for the listing of cultural landscapes in the Convention and in the guidelines were not very clear, and thus the Committee devoted considerable time to their clarification at its 1992 meeting in Sante Fe, New Mexico.

Essentially, the Committee endorsed the Convention which provided for the recognition of cultural landscapes in Article 1 as, 'combined works of nature and of man'. They went on to say that cultural landscapes are illustrative of the evolution of human society and settlement over time, under the influence of the physical constraints and/or opportunities presented by their natural environment and of successive social, economic and cultural forces, both external and internal. They should be selected on the basis both of their outstanding universal value and whether they are representative in terms of a clearly defined geo-cultural region and also for their capacity to illustrate the essential and distinct cultural elements of such regions.

NEW CONCEPTS

The Committee defined cultural landscapes as embracing a diversity of manifestations of human interaction with its natural environment. These are:

First, clearly defined landscapes designed and created by man. This embraces garden and park land landscapes constructed for aesthetic reasons. Versailles, or some of the works of Capability Brown are illustrative.

Second, organically evolved landscapes resulting from an initial social, economic, administrative and/or religious imperative that have developed into their present form by association with and in response to their natural environment. There are three sub-categories:

1. a relict or fossil landscape where evolutionary processes came to an end at some time in the past, its distinguishing characteristics still being visible in material form (agricultural terraces in Peru exhibit these characteristics);
2. a continuing landscape is one which retains an active social role in contemporary society closely associated with the traditional way of life, and in which the evolutionary process is still in progress;
3. an 'associative cultural landscape' is one in which powerful religious, artistic, or cultural associations relate to the natural elements rather than to material cultural evidence which may not exist (Mount Fuji might meet these criteria).

The World Heritage Committee assigned the responsibility for evaluating cultural landscapes to ICOMOS in co-operation with the World Conservation Union. To achieve this, the former will need to expand its technical capabilities to include professionals in the fields of landscape architecture and landscape ecology as well as planning. Alternatively, they could collaborate with existing professional organisations.

DISCUSSION

In a holistic sense, during the last decade, cultural landscapes have begun to emerge as a critical part of the global conservation programme. There remains a challenge for the World Conservation Union to emerge from its focus on pure nature and for ICOMOS to shift from its focus on buildings, monuments and archaeological sites. Clearly both organisations are charged by the World Heritage Committee to expand their horizons. Concepts such as environmentally sustainable development challenge traditional conservation practices, where undisturbed or fully protected natural areas form the core of the conservation programme. There are those who believe that sustainable development will bring about a balance between conservation and development, and that central planning will create a harmony in which protected areas are no longer essential. Unfortunately, I know of no place in the contemporary world where this has been successful. Even with protected areas the loss of biodiversity continues at an accelerated pace.

There is little doubt that everyone recognises that protected areas, which encompass only about 5% of the world, will not survive in a sea of development, sustainable or otherwise. There is an essential need, however, to recognise that effective planning must take place in all surrounding areas, for, without the core of protected areas, most national or internationally famous sites will be destroyed. To comprehend the situation one needs only to look at the sterile conifer forests, planted row on row, or at the continuing controversy over peat cutting, or the continuing dialogue about the future of the Cairngorms. All is not well in the native land of John Muir. Hopefully, the potential for integrated management policies offered through Scottish Natural Heritage will lead to a brighter future.

Landscape destruction will come about as a result of deliberate development action driven by narrow economic forces or it will come about from benign neglect. Regrettably in Scotland it is perhaps a combination of both. The Cairngorms would in the eyes of many illustrate both problems.

On the other side of the coin, a concern for the individual as well as the collective welfare must be central to any programme. In this respect there has been little recognition of the landmark decision taken at the 1975 General Assembly of the International Conservation Union in Zaire. This decision stressed that local communities should not have their lifestyle disrupted by the establishment of protected areas. It went on to say that local people must be involved in all land use decisions which affect their lifestyle. These concepts have been put into practice and are now reflected in strategies such as the 1980 World Conservation Strategy, The Brundtland Commission and the 1992 Earth Summit in Rio.

It is advantageous for specialised groups and interests to speak of protected areas as being 'set aside' from society and its economic interest. The concept of protected areas as single use areas in contrast to multiple use areas is often used in a pejorative sense by those who do not support them. Frankly, this is misleading and far from the truth. Protected areas are specifically designated to attain more effective management than surrounding lands. Management is aimed at attaining special conservation objectives for which specific areas were designated. Rather than a single use, most protected areas produce a range of benefits from the protection of species, sustaining local culture, the provision of recreational opportunities, the provision of watershed protection, and the prevention of soil erosion, as well as stimulating regional economic development.

Protected areas, individually taken, are rarely economically self-sufficient. Collectively, they make significant contributions at the local, regional and national level. In Croatia prior to present hostilities the Plitvice National Park was the economic engine of the region, generating a gross income of $50,000,000 per year and a net income of seven to eight million dollars. In Canada the National Parks of the Atlantic Region are central to both the employment and the incomes of the region. It is misleading to stress that protected areas disrupt traditional economic activities. However, without formally established protected areas, society will lose many of its monuments, historic buildings, and archaeological sites as well as its biological diversity.

CONCLUSION

The people of Scotland have good reason to be proud of their heritage, 'the magnificent scenery of mountains and lochs, wild heath covered moors and woodlands of pine and birch,' encompass much of the nation's scenic heritage. Today only a small part has in depth legal protection through the designation of National Scenic Areas and Sites of Special Scientific Interest. One must ask if this is sufficient to conserve the rich natural and cultural heritage with which Scotland has been endowed. As Roger Carr said in writing to the Secretary of State for Scotland: 'Continued delay incurred through repetitive examinations of the problems can only further exacerbate them.'

New concepts such as the protection of cultural landscapes under the World Heritage Convention provide new opportunities for conservation. As stated above, sometimes a word to the wise is unnecessary. The rest of the world knows that you have a country of exceptional scenic values and deep cultural traditions. Perhaps the time has come to send a word to the wise by joining the Friends of the National Parks in Scotland and supporting the work of the Scottish Council for National Parks. As an adviser to the Council,

I ask you to recognise that my statement may carry some bias.

The author

Harold Eidsvik is Senior Programme Officer, World Heritage Centre in Paris, and the views expressed in this paper are those of the author and do not necessarily coincide with those of UNESCO or the World Heritage Centre.

References

Carr, R., Letter to the Secretary of State for Scotland.

Carew-Reid, J., *The Conservation of Heritage of National Significance*, Workshop Proceedings, 18-23 August 1991,Khatmandu, Nepal.IUCN,1992.

Eidsvik,H.K.(ed), *United Nations List of National Parks and Equivalent Reserves*, IUCN,1980.

Eidsvik,H.K. *A Framework for the Classification of Terrestrial and Marine Protected Areas*, CNPPA/IUCN, 1990.

Lucas, P.H.C.(Bing) *Protected Landscapes: A Guide for Policy-makers and Planners*, Chapman and Hall,1992.

UNESCO, *Recommendation Safeguarding the Beauty and Culture of Landscapes* (1.12.62), in The World Heritage Newsletter,UNESCO, February 1992.

4

A STUDY IN NORDIC LANDSCAPE PLANNING

Magne Bruun

The origin of the term 'cultural landscape' may be traced back to the early part of this century, when it was introduced first and foremost by German ecologists, with the following meaning: 'A landscape which to a substantial degree has been altered from its natural state, by human activities and use' (Krebs,1923).

The term was used according to this meaning by professional groups such as landscape architects and geographers, largely as a tool to describe landscapes influenced and altered by man where skilful management prescriptions would be necessary agents if an equilibrium were to be maintained. Its counterpart is the 'natural landscape' which is not or only slightly modified by man, and where an ecological equilibrium is maintained and secured by nature's own forces and laws.

During the last decade, there has been a rapidly growing, multi-disciplinary interest in studies related to cultural landscapes, and a subsequent proliferation of diverging interpretations and definitions of the concept itself has occurred. A recent report on Agricultural Landscapes issued by the Nordic Council of Ministers (1991), reveals no less than seven different definitions of the term. Interpretations vary from the original ecological definition to notions implying landscapes that have a special meaning to each individual. One might feel justified in suspecting that each discipline which has taken an interest in the subject, feels obliged to design its own definition. Jones (1991) stresses this elusiveness of the concept. The confusion has sometimes appeared so overwhelming that several authors have suggested that it might be best to forget about it all and stick to the general term 'landscape'.

A DEFINITIONAL CONTEXT

Cultural landscapes exist in interaction between man and nature, and there is no distinct zone of transition between what may be termed natural and cultural landscape. Forman and Godron (1986) have described a landscape modification gradient in five stages:

1. Natural landscape – without significant human impact;
2. Managed landscape – harvested land, e.g. pastures;
3. Cultivated landscape – agricultural land with patches of natural or managed landscape scattered within;
4. Suburban landscape – a mixture of commercial and residential areas, cultivated land, and natural areas;
5. Urban landscape – densely built-up areas.

In Norway, areas in the managed landscape category have been predominant parts of our farming systems until quite recently. Even as late as 1939, natural meadows made up more than 30% of the total area under grass production. At that time, one tenth of Norwegian farms had summer pastures for dairy herds in upland areas (seters), utilising the fertile alpine grasslands. Along the western coast, the age-old system of barren heath lands and moors were still managed the traditional way as winter pastures for sheep. Today, such extensively used farmland areas have long been abandoned and taken over by natural regeneration of woodland vegetation, if not totally converted into commercial forest through reforestation schemes. This exemplifies the dynamics of cultural landscapes, their vulnerability to changing economic and social circumstances.

The wildlands of the Nordic mountain regions are examples of natural landscapes which only to a slight extent have been modified by impacts of human use. National Parks have been established in such areas, in order to preserve natural ecosystems without any management to interfere with nature's processes, with the exception of measures needed to keep recreational use under control. On the other hand, these wildlands have not altogether been untouched by man. The largest wilderness tracts of Northern Europe are found in the National Parks of Swedish Lapland, but even these areas have been used by Lappish people since the end of the Ice Age. Facts like these add interesting dimensions to the debate of what a cultural landscape really is.

A DESCRIPTIVE MODEL

If we leave the urban and suburban landscape out of the discussion, the rural areas provide the arena where the future of cultural landscapes really are to be modelled. Competing land use interests, expanding suburban areas, and industrial and transport development are factors that have made a strong impact on the traditional rural landscape wherever economic development has taken place. Agricultural regions of high potential for intensive production have been subject to radical processes of reorganisation and mechanisation, while areas that have turned out as marginal under the new economic order, have been left to abandonment and dereliction. This development is typical all over the industrialised world.

Throughout the first three decades after the end of World War II, this process was looked upon as something inevitable, and the landscape and heritage amenities that were thus sacrificed, were considered to be of no significant value and a necessary price to pay for progress at any rate. An increasing environmental awareness during the 1980s placed the issue on the political agenda for the first time. Cultural landscape no longer was the concern only of a limited group of planners and conservationists.

In response to this, the Nordic Council of Ministers, which is a co-ordinating body facilitating collaboration among the five Nordic countries at governmental level, launched a three year project to develop methods and guidelines for the integration of natural and cultural landscape values into the process of physical planning. As a foundation for this study, a general model for the identification and description of cultural landscape was called for. This model focused on three basic landscape characteristics, i.e. natural components, cultural components related to land use and man-made features, and visual appearance and scale (Bruun 1987a).

The **natural components** are, of course, always present. They form the very backbone of any landscape. Land form, climate and soils will always be prevailing factors as determinants of land use and settlements. Advanced technology and organisational skills of man may modify the restraints set by nature, but it remains most unlikely that we ever shall be able to grow maize successfully near Archangelsk or Hammerfest.

Other natural components are of a more subordinate character, and may easily become disrupted or overthrown by the impact of technology. Natural vegetation belts and woodlands, brooks and wetlands, ponds and meadows, etc. are all elements that modern rationalisation tends to erase from the cultural landscape. The results are well-known: impoverished ecology, dramatically increased susceptibility to erosion and other environmental hazards, and sadly reduced visual qualities.

Man-made landscape components may be divided into two groups:

Land use, historic and contemporary is a powerful characteristic of most cultural landscapes. Agriculture with intensively cultivated crops, animal husbandry with extensive pastures, and prevailing forestry are land uses that put most distinctive marks on the landscape. In some cases, land use may seem a very stable factor, but strong political and economic changes may cause disruptive impacts. It is important to keep in mind the effects of historic land use patterns, and to develop efficient tools to identify and study the imprints of history in the landscape that we see today.

Man-made elements like buildings, archaeological monuments, vernacular architecture and other man-made features may be important factors defining the character and heritage of a given landscape that underline its historic continuity.

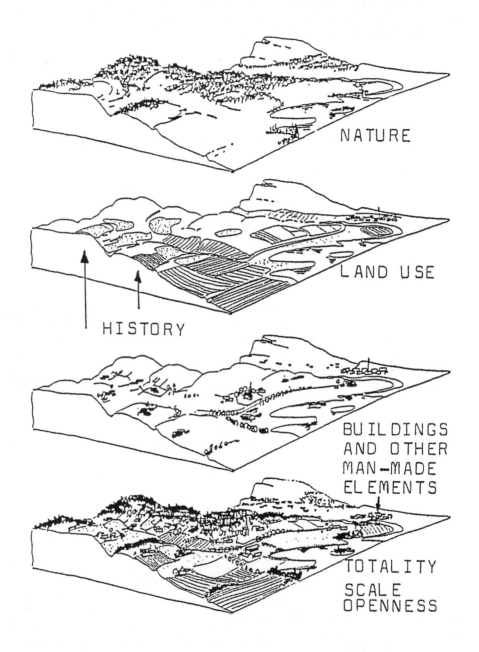

NATURE

LAND USE

HISTORY

BUILDINGS
AND OTHER
MAN-MADE
ELEMENTS

TOTALITY
SCALE
OPENNESS

Figure 1 A simplified illustration of key factors in the regional description of cultural landscapes.

Other aspects are **visual characteristics and scale**, which govern the overall impression or the totality of the landscape, including spatial relationships and scenic qualities. These are factors of particular importance in a process where the aim is to integrate strategies for conservation of landscape amenities into physical planning at an equal level with economic and development interests.

In the Nordic project this descriptive model with the above categories of major landscape characteristics provided the basic criteria for regional classification of cultural landscapes. The need for such classification is dictated by several factors:

1. Administrative boundaries of regional and district authorities are usually poorly related to landscape characteristics and often cut across consistent landscape entities.
2. Conservation philosophy puts emphasis on representativity, the typical natural or cultural environment, and calls for a framework of reference: typical in relation to what?
3. Regional identity has received increasing attention also in relation to the landscape around us and regionalisation may become an important tool to aid the interpretation of these values.

The project report presented preliminary sketches for such regionalisation, and in Norway this work has been taken up by the Norwegian Institute of Land Inventory in a nationwide project which started in 1991 (NIJOS 1991). An interesting parallel to this is found in the province of Emilia-Romagna in Italy, where a classification into landscape regions was carried out in connection with the Regional Landscape Plan in 1986, based on similar criteria to those in the Nordic project (Bottino 1987).

LANDSCAPE PLANNING

The next step in the Nordic project was to make decisions about major criteria for the identification of conservation values as a basis for the planning process. Conservation values were considered in terms of natural, cultural, and scenic or aesthetic values in the landscape. Natural and cultural values have traditionally been looked upon as separate sectors, perhaps mainly because they have been studied by different disciplines without any common platform of training or methodology. In the real landscape, however, these values occur within the same areas and systems.

Aesthetic or scenic values have, strangely enough, had a very low level of prestige in conservation work and physical planning, at least in Norway. The rational attitudes induced by functionalism in the earlier part of the century may serve as a partial explanation for this situation. Since scenic values are often closely connected to nature or cultural monuments and sites, there has also been a tendency to see them as integral parts of nature conservation, with no need for any special attention. The results of such attitudes are easily observed in the Norwegian countryside as well as in urbanised areas. Recent action by the Ministry of Culture in Norway may signal a new political awareness in this field.

Coherent landscape planning calls for co-ordination of conservation interests, and many agencies have made efforts to define criteria for this purpose. Based on this material, the Nordic project identified and developed key criteria that could serve as common denominators for different categories of conservation values in the landscape. The application of these criteria was tested in model areas, especially in the district of Rygge in the South East of Norway.

Representativeness is a key word in this context. Safeguarding of areas or locations which are typical of the natural and cultural heritage of a given region has been one major conservation goal in recent years. Areas typical of the natural heritage are identifiable, e.g. as fringes or large tracts of original forest cover, such as relics of deciduous hardwood forests in the Rygge area. Areas typical of the cultural history are found for instance where archaeological monuments abound or where farmsteads have occupied the same sites since prehistoric times. Typical scenic qualities need not necessarily be outstanding panoramic views, but are frequently found in rather ordinary areas where the unity of the landscape has been preserved and spared from unsightly and badly conceived development. Representativeness is not confined to continuous areas only, but may also relate to linear structures in the landscape, such as the mosaic of stone fences which is typical of many regions along the Atlantic coast.

Diversity is another major criterion. Ecological diversity is endangered from many directions, and stresses the need for protection of a widest possible range of natural habitats. Marginal zones or fringes in the rural landscape are important: woodland edges, stone fences, shorelines and brooks that still remain in the cultivated landscape, all add to the biological diversity. So do woodland lots, forest segments or wetlands. Cultural diversity is often found in areas of a long historic continuity, where traces of previous epochs still exist. Scenic diversity is considered a sign of high aesthetic or recreational value, but is a highly relative quality. What may be seen as rich and varied in one particular landscape region, may appear rather commonplace in another where nature has more to offer.

Rarity and vulnerability are criteria complicated by relativities. Unique geological formations or endemic plant life, for instance, may be defined as rare in a global sense. The elm groves north of the Arctic Circle in Norway are no doubt rare for the latitude where they are found. On the other hand, the diverse natural meadows that once were common sights in the rural lowlands, are rapidly disappearing and becoming rare in the agricultural landscape of today. The same process is taking place in regard to hedgerows and stone fences in many regions.

Virgin areas are not solely restricted to wilderness tracts and primeval forests far from the madding crowd, but may also occur on more or less isolated sites fairly close to farmlands and roads. Woodlands in close proximity to farms and villages are sometimes virtually undisturbed, contrary to remote forests that often are subject to modern management for timber production.This became quite evident during the Rygge study. In a cultural sense, virgin areas may be associated with 'historic landscape', tracts which have escaped from changing land use and development since a certain period in history.

Other criteria that should be mentioned are so called **intrinsic values**. In earlier conservation policies such criteria were considered particularly important in relation to features like magnificent trees, majestic waterfalls, or other objects that caught special attention. Intrinsic values of cultural monuments, implying for instance architectural significance, are often rated equal to rarity. **Symbol and identity** values which are so often brought into the limelight in professional debate nowadays, are closely related aspects. In scenic terms, intrinsic values are often related to such qualities as splendour, striking contrasts and intensity. In unspectacular rural landscapes such conditions are hardly to be expected, but in cases where contrasting landscape elements converge, combined with sweeping views, even the ordinary agricultural scene can assume a touch of intensity.

As a result of a landscape analysis where these criteria have been applied, consistent areas may be identified, where there is a concentration of values within one or more of the categories described. But the result may also be the identification of linear features of equal interest. Such features are often of crucial importance in a conservation strategy, not least because they frequently occur in zones of transition without strong conflicts with competing land use.

Land use interests that were considered in connection with conservation values in the project, included agriculture and forestry, water related interests, suburban development, transportation, and outdoor recreation. Several of these interests are dependent on the same resources that are in focus for conservation. Agriculture and forestry depend on conservation of the natural productivity of the land. Outdoor recreation calls for a landscape where nature, cultural and aesthetic values are maintained. Residential and urban planning goals emphasise scenic qualities and the natural environment, at least in principle.

An important goal of the Nordic project was to develop a land classification system based on a balanced evaluation between economic and conservation interests. Such an evaluation will indicate 'yes areas' and 'no areas', and help in defining possible directions of future development (Bruun 1987b). Important conclusions of the Rygge study were later adopted by the local planning authority and included in the master plan for the district.

AGRICULTURE IN A CHANGING SOCIETY

Recent history and the present day crisis in Norwegian intensive farming are paralleled in almost any western country. Although the total area of farmland in Norway covers only 3% of the surface of the country, the productivity of Norwegian farming ranks among the highest in the world, thanks to advanced technology and artificial fertilizers. The intensification of North American farming in the 1970s, where the slogan 'plant fencerow to fencerow' was taken literally and the last remnants of shelter belts from the 'dust bowl' period were removed (Ulrich 1989), had its counterpart in Norway. Gullies were levelled out, wetlands drained and forests cut down in order to expand the area of arable land.

To combat the adverse effects of these processes, more ecologically sustainable farming practices are called for. Since 1990, the Norwegian government has initiated programmes to reduce the amount of fertilisers, returning arable land liable to erosion to permanent vegetation cover, to restore protective hedgerows along ditches and watercourses, etc. Subventions to farmers are granted on the conditions that woodland edges and lots are not disturbed, that brooks and open ditches are not filled, and that the biological diversity is retained. Remaining forests and woodlands are especially in an endangered position in many cultivated landscapes, but represent important climatic, hydrological and biological functions.

Contrary to the problems of surplus production and over-exploitation of ecological resources in primary farming regions is the rapidly increasing deterioration of the cultural landscape in abandoned or economically declining areas. All over Europe the cultural landscapes are being recognised as important parts of our heritage and a cornerstone for our identity as Europeans. This understanding is particularly connected with the historical heritage of marginal upland and coastal communities (Council of Europe 1988).

Reforestation programmes for marginal farmland have been introduced by the Norwegian government, much to the concern of conservationists who fear dense plantations of Norway or Sitka spruce on formerly sunny meadows and fields. However, the goals set by the Forestry Act of 1976 firmly state that consideration should be given to animal and plant life, ecology, recreation, and scenic quality. Reforestation plans have to be approved against this legislative background.

The crisis of declining rural landscapes is not solved through nature conservation measures alone. Reserves of high priority cultural landscapes, amnaged by the support of public funds may protect isolated ecological communities or sites of historic importance, but do nothing to support a living, working landscape in a viable community. A different course was staked out by the Council of Europe in a report that advocated a re-definition of the role of the farmer. Instead of being looked upon only as a producer of food and fibre, the farmer should be recognised as a keeper of the countryside in the interest of the entire society, and receive economic compensation accordingly (Council of Europe 1988b).

Norwegian systems to support farmers who keep areas of special historic value or biological diversity are founded on this kind of philosophy, but there are strong reasons for believing that this is insufficient to provide a meaningful life in otherwise doomed communities. Another more positive approach is about to catch attention among agricultural departments and

Plate 1 The heritage of the Norwegian seacoast is threatened by radical changes of economic conditions.

Plate 2 The old farms of the western regions of Norway, with their stone fences, gardens and pastures, are facing an uncertain future, unless efficient rural strategies are put into effect.

farmers, where the cultural landscape by itself is considered a resource for economic activity. This is very much in line with European declarations that marginal areas should become 'innovation areas', instead of being characterised by abandonment and dereliction (Council of Europe,1988 b).

Rural tourism is an important part of new strategies for the countryside and plays an increasing role in Norwegian development. Opening up of the countryside for public outdoor recreation is another important deal, with promising potentials to foster a new sense of solidarity between city dwellers and those living and working in the countryside. This requires planning for multiple use of the cultural landscape, an approach which in recent years has been favourably received by the farmers' organisations in Norway.

Sustainable development of the cultural landscapes in rural areas is a challenge of great complexity, to which no adequate answer has been found yet. Landscape planning, having due regard to the natural and cultural heritage and the scenic qualities of the cultural landscape, is a necessary tool in this process. It is a prerequisite if we are to make comprehensive strategies for rural communities a reality in the future. Without it, the challenging task of integrating heritage conservation and development may be a difficult road to follow.

The author

Magne Bruun is Professor of Landscape Architecture at the Norwegian University of Land Use. In addition to the work for the Nordic Council described in this paper, he is known for his many publications on the history of Norwegian gardens, cultural landscapes and studies on landscape classification. He has also been involved in several projects to restore historic gardens.

References

Bottino, F.,(ed) *Obiettivi, oggetti, elementi costitutivi del Piano*, in Urbanistica, May 1987, pp.54-73.

Bruun, M., *Regioninndeling av landskap*, in Natur-og kulturlandskapet i arealplanleggingen 1.,Nordic Council of Ministers, Oslo, 1987, pp.11-40.

Bruun, M., *Natur-og kulturhistoriske verdier i landskapet*, in Natur-og kulturlandsk 2. Nord. Counc. of Ministers, Oslo, 1987 b, pp. 9-76.

Council of Europe, *A new management of the environment in rural areas*, Environmental Encounters No.4., Strasbourg, 1988, pp.38.

Council of Europe, *Proceedings of 2nd European Colloquy on the Future of the Countryside*, Lisbon June 1987, Strasbourg, 1988 (b.), pp.131.

Forman, R. & Godron, M., *Landscape Ecology*, New York, 1986.

Frislid, R., *Norske Kulturlandskap*, Landbruksforlaget, 1989.

Jones, M., *The elusive reality of landscape*, in Norsk Geografisk Tidsskrift 45, 1991, pp.229-244.

Krebs, N. *Natur- und Kulturlandschaft,* in Zeitschrift der Gesellschaft für Erdkun, Berlin, 1923.

Marsh, W. L. *Landscape Vocabulary*, Los Angeles, 1964, pp.316.

NIJOS, *Reiseliv og areal*, Norwegian Institute of Land Inventory, 1991.

Nordic Council of Ministers, *Kulturlandskap og jordbruk*(English summary), Oslo, 1992,pp.205.

Ulrich, H. *Losing Ground*: *Agricultural Policy and the Decline of the American Farm*, Chicago, 1989, pp.278.

Plate 3 Undisturbed, historical landscape around the ruins of Selje Monastery, abandoned early in the 16th Century.

5

ISSUES FACING SCOTLAND

John Arnott

The first point to be made is that almost the whole of Scotland is a cultural landscape, reflecting the interaction between man and the environment in a process going back for thousands of years. There may be some mountain tops ungrazed by sheep and unmarked by walkers' paths, but in general right down from the brochs of Shetland and the cleits of St Kilda through the ancient cultivation ridges of the highland glens to the heavily modified lowlands the hand of man is to be seen.

Before looking at the issues facing that cultural landscape today it might be helpful to look back briefly at how it came into existence and the forces that shaped it over the centuries, some of which are still at work today. I shall be talking solely about rural Scotland; the urban landscape is another story.

Scotland has been heavily glaciated in the past, giving us the familiar rounded forms of the mountains and the steep-sided trenches of the glacial valleys. Most of it emerged from the last blanket of ice only about ten thousand years ago. Much of its rock is acidic, and its climate is cool, windy and moist. Particularly in the uplands which cover about 70% of the country this all adds up to a land of rather low productivity except in a few areas.

But the surrounding seas are, or have been, highly productive and this has affected the landscape through the pattern of fishing villages and crofter fisher townships. Though it is a comparatively small country, Scotland has a coastline of 11,000 kilometres, long enough to stretch from here to Singapore, and home to some of the country's most spectacular wildlife in its great sea-bird colonies and its hosts of wildfowl and waders.

REMOVAL OF TREES

In spite of not being very productive the land could certainly grow trees; perhaps 50 or 60% of it was covered in Scots pine and in oak and birch and other broad-leaves in prehistoric times. Destruction of these began as soon as man appeared on the scene. It is known for example that Scots pine was cleared at Loch Garten in 2090 BC and that there was extensive clearing 2000 years ago, but little is known about the rate of clearance over a long period since then. By 1600 perhaps only 4% of the land remained wooded, and it has been argued that by then man had already had a major impact on the land through podsolisation of the earth in the change from forest to heathland.

It is a process which continued for various reasons: agricultural clearance, fuel, or allegedly removing cover for bandits and wolves, until the commercial value of the forests was appreciated in the 18th Century. Even in 1775 Dr Samuel Johnson was able to remark: 'A tree might be a show in Scotland as a horse in Venice'.

Dr Johnson was on a tour visiting some of the great lairds and magnates of the highlands. These were among quite a small number of large landowners who exercised an enormous amount of power and influence throughout the whole of rural Scotland and who have had a profound effect upon the cultural landscape of the country. This was not only through direct ownership of the land and therefore control over building and land use, but also politically. Two hundred years ago, in 1788, no county electorate exceeded 200 votes. In the whole of rural Scotland there were 2,655 votes of which 1,318 (half of them) are believed to have been fictitious, having been created by magnates to ensure their hold over elections.

Farming up to that Century had been on a runrig system of small unenclosed fields growing barley and oats with common grazing for sheep, goats, and particularly black cattle. These cattle were Scotland's principal export for 150 years up to the middle of the 18th Century, and the drove roads along which over the years millions of them were driven are still a notable feature of the countryside.

18TH CENTURY IMPROVEMENTS AND THE CLEARANCES

Black cattle meant cash. More black cattle meant more cash, and this started a process of overgrazing and environmental impoverishment which we see continuing to this day, only now with sheep and deer. But the 18th Century was also the time of agricultural improvements: new crops like potatoes and turnips, better stock, new machinery, enclosure by hedge and dyke, bigger and better buildings, longer leases, and after the 1745 rising greater security.

All this was driven originally by quite a small number of landowners, changing the face of lowland Scotland and some of the uplands, and setting a pattern of mixed and varied farmland which survived until the recent emphasis on the highest possible productivity.

This was the time, too, of another initiative of the big landowners: the planned villages, some 150 of them, still among the treasures of the Scottish countryside. Their well proportioned stone houses share a common attitude and spirit of the times with their grander cousins in Edinburgh's New Town and the country palaces of the nobility, all being built at the same time, the Age of Enlightenment.

It was a time of expansion and also a time of expense for landowners with access to London and appearances to keep up. Rents on the lower ground could be doubled or trebled with the greater yields brought by agricultural improvements. On the higher, more infertile land this was not possible. The answer there lay in sheep which would provide a higher return, and so followed the miserable period of the clearances, when thousands of people were forcibly removed from the land in the north and west to make way for sheep, and were encouraged to emigrate or were resettled in crofting townships along the coast in a pattern which is familiar today. Many of these crofts were not large enough to support a family, with the intended result that labour was available for gathering kelp. This, too, has consequences for today, though it is worth remembering that voluntary emigration from the land to the growing cities was on a comparable scale in the south of Scotland, without quite the same legacy of bitterness.

THE ROMANTIC MOVEMENT

Then came the Romantic Movement which was to have a profound effect on Scotland, continuing to the present day. Macpherson's invention of the Gaelic poems of Ossian with their epic tales of heroism had an enormous influence throughout Europe; (it was Napoleon's favourite book), and so did the novels of Sir Walter Scott which inspired innumerable operas, ballets and other works. A mountain landscape which had previously been regarded with awe and horror quite suddenly became the sublime and majestic setting of heroic fantasy.

Dr Johnson on his 1775 tour had said: 'Seeing Scotland is only seeing a worse England. It is seeing the flower gradually fade away to the naked stalk. An age accustomed to flowery pastures and waving harvests is astonished and repelled by this wide extent of hopeless sterility.'

The agricultural improvements did something for that. By 1845 the New Statistical Account could say of the parish of Airlie in Angus: 'Almost all the fields are enclosed, either with hedges or dry stone dykes. The former, with the interspersed woodlands, give to a great part of the parish a warm, clothed appearance.'

It was otherwise in the hills and mountains, that is to say most of the country, now perceived elsewhere in Britain and Europe as a romantic, mist-girt home of a warrior race. Sir Walter Scott's poem The Lady of the Lake might almost be said to have founded the Scottish tourist industry, with visitors flocking to Loch Katrine. Indeed if Scotland can lay any claim to include an IUCN 'associative cultural landscape' the Trossachs must be a contender.

The paintings of McCulloch and Landseer and many others moved away from the ordered elegance of the 18th Century to misty, dramatic mountains, affecting peoples' perceptions of what is beautiful scenery to this day. The stark beauty of the tundra-like Flow country of Caithness had few friends when it came to be smothered under trees. The haunting, spacious beauty of estuaries with their teeming wildlife has been similarly under-valued.

THE SPORTING ESTATE

All this Gothic magic put many people under its spell, including the young Queen Victoria who loved the highlands, and in the 1840s bought the Balmoral estate for summer visits. This set in train a fashion among wealthy people in England for acquiring large tracts of highland country as sporting estates to be enjoyed in August and September as private Arcadias. This was, and is, an expensive hobby, and the castellated shooting lodges which were built on the estates were, and are costly to maintain. So the red deer acquired economic as well as trophy importance. This is what lies behind two of the major impacts on the landscapes of today: the lack of regeneration of native trees as a result of heavy grazing by red deer and by sheep, and paradoxically the proliferation of densely packed plantations of exotic and profitable conifers.

19TH CENTURY CONSTRUCTS

It is also something of the story that lies behind a series of constructs that have been wished on to the Scottish cultural landscape from outside Scotland: the clearance of people for sheep, the exclusive sporting estate, the import of game laws, the fiscal encouragement of blanket forestry, the over-grazing of hill country, all resulting in the under-resourcing of a fragile landscape of which too much has been asked.

Nor, speaking of culture, is it confined to land use, but also the whole tartan touristic perception of Scotland, which is pervasive and insidious, as well as essential to the country's economy, bringing in billions of pounds. How many Scotsmen who today wear the philabeag, the short kilt, know that it is the invention of an 18th Century English steelmaster in Inverness whose workers were overheating in the great kilt? Or know that many of the tartans they wear are inventions of the Sobieska-Stuart brothers in their bogus volume 'Vestiarum Scoticum', catering to the tartan mania induced by the visit of George IV to Edinburgh in 1822, stage-managed by Sir Walter Scott? It is all a debasement of a folk culture which found its apotheosis in the maudlin, sham sentimentality of Sir Harry Lauder.

Some of this history is widely resented, and by no-one more so than the people of north and west Scotland, who have been at the receiving end of some of these constructs, some well meaning (like Lord Leverhulme's patronage of Lewis) and some not so well meaning. That accounts today for the widespread suspicion and antipathy among people in the north and west towards any bright ideas about land designation for their areas coming from the south. Anyone who has spoken to public meetings there, as I have, can feel the hostility to suggestions from outside. In devising better measures for securing the most harmonious cultural landscape we have to remember this.

CONFIDENCE IN OURSELVES

The roots of this resentment go back a long way, and underlie a lack of social confidence at variance with other countries comparable in many ways, such as in Scandinavia. The removal of the royal court from Edinburgh to London in 1603 contributed to this, as did the Union of Parliaments in 1707, whatever its benefits otherwise. So did the suppression of Gaelic and of Scots. Some of my former colleagues encountered the English language only when they first went to school where they were for ever forbidden to speak in Gaelic, their mother tongue. Scots was similarly confined to the play ground. It is not too fanciful to say that the lack of a Scots translation of the Bible in the 17th Century played a significant role in this. English became the language of sacred and secular authority. The recent Lorimer translation came, perhaps, 350 years too late.

FORESTRY

And so we come to the 20th Century. The foundation of the Forestry Commission in 1919 was well meaning too. Vast amounts of timber had been felled in World War I and a strategic reserve was considered imperative. Between the wars land was cheap. In Scotland, North American conifers grew fastest, particularly Sitka spruce and lodgepole pine. Trees grow straighter if they are densely planted. Fences to keep out deer are cheaper if they run in straight lines. The result of all this is the hard rectangle of dark, uniform, even aged conifers blanketed across the countryside, perhaps the most obvious impact ever to have been visited on the landscape of Scotland.

Tree cover has increased to about 13% of the land surface (compared to about 27% in France and 30% in Germany), divided roughly equally between the Forestry Commission, now the Forestry Enterprise, and private owners. Many of the latter were encouraged to invest in forestry by tax advantages until 1988, and it is likely that many forest owners, working through forestry companies, never see their trees or the effect they have had on the landscape. The government target for new afforestation has been 33,000 hectares a year, mostly in Scotland and in the private sector, although the actual recent planting has been a good deal less than this.

RED DEER

I mentioned fences to keep out deer, but away from these exclosures the red deer has been one of the main reasons for the continued denuded appearance of much of the uplands with little or no regeneration of their natural woodlands. This is particularly noticeable in the remnants of the old Caledonian pine forests, amounting now to perhaps 1% of their former extent. They are one of the glories of Scotland, a natural sculpture gallery of dramatic forms in the pines and junipers, with their ground cover of blaeberries, home to crossbills and crested tits and red squirrels. They are full of magnificent mature and ancient trees but very often there is no sign at all of a younger generation coming up to replace them.

The Red Deer Commission estimates that there are over 300,000 red deer in Scotland, a massive increase over the figure a generation ago, and considers that this is far too high both in the interests of the deer and of the environment. Some owners (although of course the deer is a wild animal and belongs to no-one until it is shot) still apparently believe that more hinds mean more trophy stags, although this is not the case with surplus stags being pushed to the periphery and the lower ground where they are shot by others. Hind shooting in winter is expensive in manpower.

MODERN AGRICULTURE

The lower ground, in which the surplus stags come foraging, has of course seen the biggest changes in the last 50 years with the drive for maximum food production. The better agricultural ground in the east and south has seen the same pressures for intensive monoculture as the rest of western Europe, with the wholesale grubbing out of hedges and felling of field margin trees, the filling of ponds and the loss of much diversity both through direct action and indirectly through the use of herbicides and insecticides.

Farming is obviously heavily conditioned by the Common Agricultural Policy, not only in the richer lowlands but also the less fertile uplands. Almost all the hill country of Scotland (70% of it) is designated as a Less Favoured Area by the CAP, entitling its sheep farmers to a number of benefits including Hill Livestock Compensatory Allowance, compensatory that is for their more difficult conditions. In recent years the average subsidy paid through HLCA in the whole highland area has been greater than the average net farm income. In other words the primary agricultural land use throughout most of Scotland has been operating at an overall net deficit.

Lamb, or sheep-meat as the bureaucrats call it, is one of the few agricultural products in the EC which is not in surplus, but clearly there is an element of social subsidy in this, in that it is more productive to rear sheep on lower, more fertile ground. Farming is the sheet anchor of rural communities. If the farmers leave much else goes with them. It is a strange paradox that it was the sheep which drove so many people from the land nearly 200 years ago, and yet it is the sheep that are now keeping people there. The difference is that the urban tax payer is now footing the bill. Britain is a net payer to the EC and so all EC expenditure in Britain is provided by the British tax payer.

PUBLIC ATTITUDES TO THE ENVIRONMENT

This introduces a new player in the cultural landscape: the city dweller, who has a reasonable interest in how his taxes are spent. And a new player in another sense, in an awakening realisation of the beneficial effects of a natural environment for recreation, getting away from the stresses and artificiality of town and city life. Even with the high standard of living of much of our society there is still a yearning for simpler, more natural surroundings.

So, what is the view of urban man and woman about the landscape? Two surveys of attitudes to the environment were carried out in 1991 and there was an earlier one in 1987. Two were conducted by System Three for the Countryside Commission for Scotland and the other was carried out by The Scottish Office. They were large representative samples which meant that almost all were town or city dwellers. They are too detailed to go into at any length but I would like to pick out a few of the points relevant to this paper.

Respondents in a System Three survey were given a list of six aspects of the country's heritage and asked to rate each one as: 'very important', 'important', or 'not important'. The list was: historic buildings, Scots language and music, scenery, wildlife, archaeology and Gaelic culture. The percentages given as 'very important' were: scenery 73%, wildlife 66%, historic buildings 49%, Scots language and music 42%, archaeology 28% and Gaelic culture 20%. In answer to another question 93% considered that scenery and wildlife needed more protection. In the Scottish Office survey two thirds of respondents felt that the government should pay more incentives to farmers to protect the countryside.

When given a list of different types of scenery, first preference was given to 'lochs surrounded by hills', and the second most popular was 'views at the coast with islands in sight'. It is interesting to note that the Chinese word for scenery translates literally as 'rocks and water'; it seems to be a widespread view. Bottom of the list with only 4% came 'lowland farmland with small woods'; a marked difference here from Dr Johnson in 1775 with his preference for 'flowery pastures and waving harvests', but illustrating the still dominant Victorian romantic view of the mountains.

In the System Three survey of April 1991 when asked if they thought that there should be National Parks in Scotland 84% of respondents said 'yes'. In the Scottish Office survey of December 1991 when asked if they thought that some parts of Scotland should be set aside as National Parks so that they are protected from development, 90% said 'yes'. Also in that survey 60% supported open access to areas of hill and moorland, and this brings us back to recreation in natural surroundings.

ACCESS AND THE LAW OF TRESPASS

Contrary to popular opinion there is a civil law of trespass in Scotland which applies in open and unenclosed land just as it does in domestic gardens and other lowland property. Anyone present on privately owned land without permission can be told to leave and if necessary be removed by force, even if no damage is being done. It is also a criminal offence under an Act of 1865 to camp or light fires on private land without permission.

There has, however been a long tradition of toleration of access to the hills and moors, with a few notable exceptions. Generally speaking people can walk in open country without being turned away, but the possibility always exists, which leads to uncertainty. It inhibits some people from going where they would in fact be tolerated and it may greatly affect the quality of enjoyment and the spiritual benefit to be gained by many people. 'Being where one has no right to be' (a definition of trespass) inserts a negative and disquieting element between the walker and the natural environment of which, for a short time, he is a part.

The Scottish Landowners Federation which includes about 30% of landowners in its membership is in favour of toleration of responsible access which respects the needs of other land uses. One of these, as I have mentioned, is the sporting estate which in a great many cases still requires an input of money. Letting deer stalking can be a profitable source of revenue, and stalking can be disrupted by walkers even some considerable distance away. Mountain bikes, and their eroding effect, have also increased antagonism towards access, and so has the erosion caused by walkers' boots on many of the most popular hills. The landowner sees his property being damaged but receives no revenue to restore that damage.

This is where the Countryside Commission for Scotland (CCS) used to come in with its twin interest of conserving the natural beauty of the landscape and facilitating enjoyment of it. Among many other things it grant-aided footpath repair which can be an expensive business in remote areas, up to over £1,000 per 100m in the most difficult cases.

The CCS, now subsumed into Scottish Natural Heritage, was one of a whole range of government agencies and departments with an influence on the landscape, sometimes at odds with each other. Each had its own sectoral interest, whether promoting increased agricultural or timber production, building bigger roads or quarries, or sports facilities, or more housing, or protection of wildlife and scenic beauty.

The situation is changing now, though slowly. Government departments now have a general duty to have regard to the environmental consequences of what they do. There is a much greater awareness now of the natural environment arising from a whole sea-change in attitudes which has occurred at an accelerating rate ever since European Conservation Year in 1970 and the work which led up to it.

THE HOLISTIC VIEW AND SUSTAINABILITY

It is possible that the NASA space photographs taken in the 1960s played a part in this: those powerful images of the blue planet hanging in the blackness of space. They concentrated the mind as no image had ever done before on how finite and fragile were the earth's resources. And they gave sharp focus to the concept of a holistic view of the world with its whole web of interconnecting life. As John Muir, the Scot who played such an important role in nature conservation in America, put it: 'Try to take out anything by itself and you find it hitched to everything else in the universe.'

Along with that wider view has come the concept of sustainability, a word enshrined in Scots law for the first time in the Natural Heritage (Scotland) Act of 1991. There is of course a lot of discussion about what exactly it means, and putting the word into Statute will mean calls for exactness, but even in general terms it is forcing people to think in a practical way about what it means to hand on the world in at least as good a condition as that in which we found it.

These notions lie behind a lot of encouraging developments which are now in train in the cultural landscape, so what are the prospects for a more harmonious relationship between man and the environment in Scotland? A lot is being done, but a great deal remains to be done.

BUILDINGS IN THE COUNTRYSIDE

Take buildings in the countryside for example. We have a sophisticated system of local authority planning and development control, accountable to elected representatives, and we have a rich vernacular tradition of building going back to those 18th Century planned villages and beyond. All this does not prevent the construction of buildings which are out of sympathy with their surroundings in location, and design, and materials. You can see them all over the countryside, singly or amassed in villages like Aviemore and Tyndrum.

This does not mean to say that there should be dull uniformity or a slavish copying of the past; there is plenty of room for fresh ideas and new materials. What it does mean is that we are in danger of losing what is distinctively ours and thus diminishing our cultural landscape. The issue for the future here is a very broad one of education and enlightenment and the will to care about the landscape by everyone concerned: planners, councillors, architects, builders and buyers. I am afraid that that is a tall order.

FARMING TODAY

Turning to farming, there are major changes going on driven by the Common Agricultural Policy. At present £240m a year in CAP money goes into Scottish farming out of the total EC expenditure here of some £280m: over 80% of it. It is expected that the present CAP reforms will add a further £120m a year to this. Some of this is, in effect, social support as I mentioned earlier. Part of it is going into an increasing number of environmentally friendly programmes. We have had five Environmentally Sensitive Areas (ESAs) and five more are now being put in place.

These provide payments for farmers to maintain traditional practices, such as in the crofting machair lands of the Western Isles using seaweed for fertiliser and later cutting of grass for hay which protects nesting birds, or in Breadalbane for avoidance of overgrazing and for repairs to dykes and hedges. It is a popular scheme in that it is voluntary, though the take-up has been variable throughout Scotland. One of the new areas in the southern uplands will have as one of its objectives the restoration of heather moorland, of which so much has been lost through improved grazing and forestry.

We have never had a tradition of farm woodland with trees grown as a crop, as in much of Europe, largely because of our system of land tenure with so many tenancies, in which trees planted by the tenant become the property of the landlord. This difficulty is being got round and the Farm Woodland Premium Scheme provides compensation for loss of income as a result of farmland being converted to woodland.

More ground is going out of production with short and long term set-aside of arable land and this might have a significant effect on the landscape. So, too, could the new EC Agri-Environment Regulation (EC 2078/92) which will provide further support for organic farming, habitat creation, heather regeneration and other beneficial effects.

There are two issues here for the future. One is whether a way can be found to maintain a farming industry in a way which is sustainable and enhances the landscape through diversity, and at the same time respects the ethos of the farmer which is one of being productive and growing things. There are only so many dry stane dykes to be repaired, or trees to be planted or ponds to be dug. Farmers do not want to be park-keepers.

The other issue is whether the resourcing of environmental measures in the long term will be pitched at a sufficiently attractive level to farmers to make them want to enter voluntary agreements, and thus produce a significant overall result. The Scottish Office Agriculture and Fisheries Department has said that it proposes to increase its spending on environmental schemes to about £11m on 1994/95 and £14m in 1995/96: this out of a production support budget of perhaps £360m or more. It remains to be seen whether the effects of this are any more than window dressing.

FORESTRY TODAY

Forestry, too, has been subject to major changes in recent years, though of course the effects take much longer to show. The Forestry Commission, having been driven for most of its life to produce maximum yields of timber both in its own forests and in grant-aiding private planting, is now setting much higher environmental standards of design and species mix, with more open spaces and with varied age classes as second and third rotations come in. Grant-aid is now available for restoration of native pine woods and semi-natural woodland.

There is an ambitious project to improve the run-down countryside between Edinburgh and Glasgow with large community and commercial woodlands. Regional Council Indicative Forestry Strategies are beginning to take some of the heat, and uncertainty, out of the location of new forests. Much new planting will still be of North American conifers but their appearance over time may be less of a blight that it has been in the past.

There are two major issues in this area for the cultural landscape. One is the mooted wholesale privatisation of the Forestry Enterprise's estate. The main buyers of this are likely to be big international pulp and paper companies. If this happens, will the remaining part of the Forestry Commission, the Forestry Authority, have the powers and the political clout to enforce the higher environmental standards they are now practising in their own forests?

The other issue relates to access. The Forestry Commission has long encouraged and facilitated informal recreation on its land, calling some of it Forest Parks. Will that same enlightened attitude continue under new ownership? Securing binding access agreements by local authorities prior to the sale is a costly and time consuming process.

THE RED DEER QUESTION

There are question marks, too, over the red deer issue. The government has recently held a consultation exercise as a result of which the powers of the Red Deer Commission may be strengthened, but unless there is a large cull of deer in some upland areas there is little chance of restoring them to the more natural vegetation cover they once enjoyed. The issues here are of rights of ownership and long term sustainability.

CONSERVATION ORGANISATIONS

The effects of the deer are of great interest to Scottish Natural Heritage, brought about last year by the amalgamation of the Nature Conservancy Council for Scotland and the Countryside Commission for Scotland, and bringing together at long last two essentially interdependent organisations. SNH has introduced a heavy cull on its own land and the result in regeneration of trees can already be seen.

The NCC made its biggest contribution to the cultural landscape through the designation of a kind of landbank of species and habitats and geology in the network of Sites of Special Scientific Interest, though the NCC did not tend to see the landscape in cultural terms. 'Scientific' was a word it used often and science became almost a kind of icon to it, almost an end in itself rather than a means to an end, although the whole idea of protecting wildlife is in itself a cultural concept and to an extent an aesthetic one.

The Council was given the enormous task by Statute of identifying and designating the SSSIs; there are some 1,300 of them in Scotland and it did create a degree of aggravation among the people managing the land, some of whom felt that nature was being protected from people, rather than for people. We may hope that most of that trouble is now in the past. But the division between the scientific and the aesthetic is one which is deeply rooted in our society, clearly causing the separate foundation of the countryside and wildlife agencies in the 1940s and perhaps only now being slowly bridged by a more holistic view. This wider view of ecology, in which mankind is seen as one of a great many players rather than standing apart from the rest of the natural world, is also becoming apparent in the voluntary bodies, some of which are now major landowners such as the National Trust for Scotland, the Scottish Wildlife Trust and the Royal Society for the Protection of Birds.

As well as the SSSIs there are more than 40 other designations applied to the countryside in Scotland. Another one is the National Scenic Area of which 40 were selected by the CCS, amounting to about 13% of the land surface. They are designed to protect the finest landscapes by bringing additional scrutiny to bear on larger developments and have had some success in doing this.

Other designations apply to countryside around towns and to the Green Belts around cities, restoring an often seriously degraded landscape. Others relate to recreation, including 36 Country Parks, averaging about 180 hectares, and four much larger Regional Parks where recreation co-exists, not always easily, with other land uses.

THE MOST VALUED LANDSCAPES

The problems of co-existence become particularly acute in some of the most beautiful and highly regarded landscapes. Everyone wants to use them, not only for the traditional uses of farming and deer stalking, but also for forestry, for nature conservation, for hydro-electric schemes, for walking and climbing, skiing, sailing and mountain biking, and for hotels, time-shares and conference centres.

The two areas under greatest pressure from all this are the Cairngorms and Loch Lomond, and they represent a kind of touchstone for how society values its cultural landscape. They have been the subject of seemingly endless inquiries for more than 60 years, while the pressures have mounted and the landscape has suffered. What lies at the heart of the question is the need to bring a coherent planning regime to the area, a strategy for conserving and enhancing it, a staff dedicated to these purposes, and sufficient resources to implement the strategy through incentives to the people on the ground who actually manage it.

As far back as 1931 the Addison Report recommended a National Park for the Cairngorms. This was repeated in the 1940s by the Ramsay Reports which recommended that the Cairngorms and Loch Lomond (as well as three other areas) should be National Parks, and this was the conclusion in a CCS report in 1974, although it called them Special Parks. At the end of an exhaustive inquiry in 1990, requested by government, the CCS again recommended National Parks for the Cairngorms and Loch Lomond.

Two working parties were then set up by government to examine these areas in detail. At the time of writing the Loch Lomond group had not completed its work but the one for the Cairngorms produced its report earlier this year. It sets out a comprehensive management strategy for the area, and for its implementation recommends a partnership board bringing together all interested bodies in order to co-ordinate their policies in compliance with the strategy. It would be a new designation, a Natural Heritage Area, enabled by the 1991 Act. The board would have no powers or significant funding of its own, but would work through other organisations such as local authorities and government agencies. Concern has been expressed that, given the number of local authorities involved (whether or not they are reorganised) and all the continuing difficulties of the past, this will not be a robust enough structure to answer the needs of the Cairngorms, or provide sufficient safeguards to achieve World Heritage Site status which the government is seeking.

The response of the government to the Report is not yet known, but up to now there has been a marked contrast between its attitudes north and south of the border towards National Parks, which would provide the necessary structure for the Cairngorms. There have been National Parks in England and Wales for 40 years, strongly supported by all governments which have regarded them as the jewels in the crown of the countryside. In Scotland there has been caution and reluctance by government to countenance them, founded in part by an antipathy towards them by landowners and by some elected representatives, which has its roots in the social history about which I was speaking earlier. The issue here, and it is crucial for the cultural landscape of Scotland, is one of political will.

ACCESS AND ENJOYMENT

The last issue for the future I want to talk about is access and enjoyment of the countryside, the subject of a major review carried out by Scottish Natural Heritage during this year. There are two aspects of access I would like to highlight. One is the public rights of way system to enable people to walk in the countryside, particularly near towns and cities where most of them live. We have an archaic and inadequate system based on outmoded travelling needs and it badly needs revision.

The other aspect is access to open and unenclosed land on mountain and moorland. With the development of the sporting estate last century which I spoke about earlier came the application of the concept of exclusive use carried over from the widely accepted notion of domestic privacy for lowland houses and estates to very much larger areas of open hill country where it is out of place and has never been widely accepted. The time has come to examine the practicability of a general right of responsible access to open country, subject to some exclusions for land management purposes and for privacy, and similar perhaps to the systems in Scandinavian countries.

Walking in the countryside, whether lowland or upland, is the most popular form of outdoor recreation. The issue here is whether the silent majority will make its voice heard in new arrangements for access which, while safeguarding the interests of land managers, will provide for the needs and aspirations of a largely urban population as we enter the 21st Century.

To sum up, we have a unique cultural landscape in Scotland with a great richness and variety of countryside and coast of great beauty, patterned by social forces over hundreds of years. In the last generation there has been a revolution in awareness of how its component parts interact. It is a landscape which deserves better treatment than it has had. A great deal is now known about how to restore and enhance it. What is needed, and what remains the principal issue, is the will to do it.

The author

John Arnott is a regional board member of Scottish Natural Heritage. A broadcaster and recipient of the 1985 Sony Award for Radio Features, he was Edinburgh Manager of BBC Scotland and served as Vice-Chairman of the Countryside Commission for Scotland, 1986-92. A keen ornithologist and environmentalist, he chaired a panel on Scotland's Mountain Areas, 1989-90 and served on the National Parks of England and Wales Review Panel, 1990.

References

Blunden, J. and Curry, N.(eds) *A People's Charter?* HMSO, 1989.

Countryside Commission for Scotland, *The Mountain Areas of Scotland: Conservation and Management*, CCS, 1990.

System Three Scotland, *Report of a Survey of Scotland's Scenery and Wildlife*, Countryside Commission for Scotland, 1991.

Countryside Commission for Scotland, *Report of a Survey towards Conservation of the Countryside*, CCS, 1987.

Fladmark, J.M., Mulvagh, G.Y. and Evans, B.M., *Tomorrow's Architectural Heritage*, Mainstream, 1991.

MacEwen, A. and M., *Greenprints for the Countryside?* Allen and Unwin, 1987.

McVean D.M. and Lockie, J.D., *Ecology and Land Use in Upland Scotland*, Edinburgh University Press, 1969.

Magnusson, M. and White, G.(eds), *The Nature of Scotland*, Canongate, 1991.

Muir, R., *Reading the Celtic Landscapes*, Michael Joseph, 1985.

Naismith, R.J., *Buildings of the Scottish Countryside*, Victor Gollanz, 1985.

Nicholson, M., *The New Environmental Age*, C.U.P., 1987.

Parry, M.L. and Slater, T.R. (eds), *The Making of the Scottish Countryside*, Croom Helm, 1980.

Scottish Office, *Commonsense and Sustainability: a Partnership for the Cairngorms*, HMSO, 1993.

Scottish Office, *Public Attitudes to the Environment in Scotland*, HMSO, 1991.

Smout, T.C., *A History of the Scottish People 1560-1830*, Collins, 1969.

Smout, T.C., *A Century of the Scottish People 1830-1950*, Collins, 1986.

Smout, T.C., *The Highlands and the Roots of the Green Consciousness 1750-1990*, in Proceedings of the British Academy, Vol.76, pp.237-263.

6

THE SCOTTISHNESS
OF SCOTTISH ARCHITECTURE
Building for People and Places

Charles McKean

The notion of cultural landscape, in a physical sense, is intriguing since it accepts that the landscape which we see, and the things within it, are the products of a culture: that is to say, of man-made aspiration, to a greater or lesser extent deliberate. That is certainly the case so far as architecture is concerned. Building is one of the most expensive and labour-intensive activities which man ever undertakes; and an examination of who built, what they built, and why they built represents indisputable evidence of social history in stone.

Scotland is a curious case: a country suffering from an advanced case of amnesia. There are few books on the history of Scottish architecture that can be safely recommended as a general introduction to what was built. That is because, for the past 300 years, Scottish architecture has been interpreted as a difficult provincial manifestation of English or British architecture. Until the last ten years, there had been pitifully little examination of building typologies and very little detailed analysis. There have been some deeply profound misunderstandings. These misunderstandings have infected the whole way we regard the Scottish character, and Scottish history, and indeed, what makes us Scottish.

I will illustrate the point through comparing conventional mythologies with historical evidence, followed by general examination of the essentials of Scottish architecture as it reflects evolving Scottish life. Finally, this paper ends with an examination of the periodic revivals of nationalism in architecture, and how they have reflected broader cultural landscapes.

Although the focus is upon Scotland, for we are in Scotland, some of the principles are universal. Underlying this entire collection of papers is the distinction between heritage and history. Architecture represents essential history: and, if properly understood, provides a corrective to heritage interpretation and myth. Yet people are often more inspired by myth than by reality; what people believed happened has proved more important in the sum of human affairs than what actually happened. Conversely, people inspired by myth are often less able to adapt to contemporary life than people inspired by history if that myth has become seriously dislocated from the truth. Our current rediscovery of the essentials of Scottish architecture will necessarily lead to a revaluation not only of certain important aspects of Scottish history, but of our entire persona.

MYTH ONE: PROVINCIAL

This myth is the legacy of principally 19th and 20th Century architectural history books which have sought to find a place for Scottish architecture within the canon of British architecture and usually failed to do so. In the *National Trust Book of English Architecture*, Sir James Richards embraced both Charles Rennie Mackintosh and Robert Adam; without any understanding that the buildings Adam designed for Scotland were fundamentally different to those he designed in England; or that one of Mackintosh's most vehement lectures was a lament that growing Englishness in the late 17th Century killed off the Scottish native architectural genius. Mackintosh was wrong, but less wrong than Richards in trying to shoehorn him into a niche which he would have found profoundly distasteful. MacGibbon and Ross developed the thesis of the time lag, to the effect that what happened in England would follow in Scotland some decades or centuries later: and was it not quaint that at the time when other countries were enjoying the Renaissance, Scotland was still building Romanesque details?

Now what was the reality? Scottish architecture may be a footnote to architectural history, but has nothing to do with British architectural history. Scotland was a part of mainstream Europe from the 15th to 17th Centuries. The border to England had been closed since about 1296 with very little traffic going north and south save armies in pursuit of conquest. The internationalism of Scotland still remains in much of our language and place names – Champfleur, Champeney, Little France, Belleville etc.; and an Englishman was so rare in Scotland in the late 16th Century that when they imported one to teach French in the Grammar School of Edinburgh, he was universally described as Nicolas L'Anglois. What does the architecture tell us? As I will explain in more detail, the plan of the major lairds' houses of this period was very similar to those of the chateaux of the Loire – usually three rooms in sequence, a bedroom tower at one end of the *corps de logis*, a stairtower in the opposite corner. Scottish city centres, just as in Salzburg and

Chiavari, consisted of arcades with tenements above. Those Romanesque details may be attributed to Spain; and a plan close to that of Sir Robert Smythson's great house at Wollaton, of 1592, appears 60 years earlier from the hand of Sir James Hamilton of Finnart at Craignethan, Lanarkshire.

MYTH TWO: POVERTY

The absence of glorious medieval and Renaissance buildings comparable to those in Europe or England has been taken to be a sign of poverty; a myth that has been compounded by the compilation of principally 19th Century evidence about the working conditions of country people an farm servants. The reality is significantly different. Timothy Pont's map of, for example, the Clyde Valley as it was in 1596 reveals a density of substantial chateaux as great as that of the Loire. Ambassadors viewing the dead at Flodden commented on the outstandingly rich apparel of the Scottish nobility, and the comments by visitors on the lavishness of the interior of the Palace of Huntly (Strathbogie) are similarly awestruck. We may have been wrong to treat as laughable Pitscottie's report of Mary of Guise's wonder at the cathedral, priories, abbeys and fine houses of St Andrews. He quoted a similar reaction from the Ambassador of the Pope to King James V's timber hunting castle erected near Blair Atholl in 1531: wondering how such lavishness could exist in a country known as 'the arse of Europe'.

The quality of architecture reveals that there was substantial money to build, and substantial money to gild and decorate. What we have, for example, in the Provand's Lordship in Glasgow, with its bare rubble walls and occasional arras or chest, is heritage or myth. Provand's Lordship used to be harled (rubble was never, never visible), and it is certain that inside would have been plastered with vivid murals, and the ceiling timbers would have been brightly painted. The best local artist was normally employed for that job. The evidence is all there in the buildings and in their accounts, but we have chosen not to see it. The envoy flitting between Mary of Guise and her brother the Duke in the 1550s wrote 'nothing is short here but money'. The county was rich in kind, with some of the best wine to be had in Europe. What Scotland was short of, was cash. Sadly, the dismal ruins we have inherited in place of past splendours are not the consequence of poverty so much as the consequence of invasion from England, two Jacobite forfeitures, and, above all, the vast influx of money in the 19th Century.

MYTH THREE: VERNACULAR

Perhaps the worst myth of all. It has recently been endorsed by the Scottish Arts Council, which, in its Charter for the Arts, stated 'Scotland has a strong tradition of vernacular architecture'. Ignorance at that level illuminates the extent of our problem. Vernacular, by definition, means an absence of deliberate intellectual or artistic input, and the product, instead, of the materials and skills to hand. Both Robert Billings, in 1854, and Mackintosh in 1892, recorded their belief that the buildings of the 16th and 17th Century Scotland were the work of architects, and the product of deliberate design decisions. It can be assumed from some of Robert Adam's buildings that he had the same view.

Our re-examination of that period reveals Billings & Mackintosh to have been correct. One by one the names of these people are emerging. There were those who worked their way up from building as masons to act as architects. We can trace their details, their plan forms and their massing from one building to another. On the other hand, there were nobles or gentry involved in building by way of making *platts* and controlling expenditure. Pre-eminent were Sir James Hamilton of Finnart, William Schaw of Sauchie and Sir James Murray of Kilbaberton, a grand succession eventually to end in Sir William Bruce. Of course there was vernacular building, in its proper place, but the aggregation of these myths all tend towards the same end: namely Scotland as a poverty stricken province without cultural significance.

MYTH FOUR: CALVINISM

We have been so preoccupied with the Reformation, Calvinism, and some of the more overt manifestations of such developments, that we have believed its own propaganda. We assumed that the instruction in, 1567, that ministers should avoid luxurious apparel and dress in sad brown applied to everybody. We have even assumed that abbeys and priories were instantly demolished and the titles abandoned in 1560. History reveals otherwise: although they were principally landowning titles, abbots and priors existed into the 17th Century as did Bishops. Catholicism persisted in parts of Scotland without a break (mainly in Moray where the evidence is clearly to be seen in churches in Glenlivet), Episcopalianism persisted without a break (principally in Buchan, where the evidence is once again apparent in the plan form of churches), and Calvinism itself, the Church of Scotland, was very much less rigorous and radical than the histories of John Knox, James Melville, Johnston of Warriston and other would have us believe.

We now know that 16th and 17th Century buildings were designed with a super-structural flamboyance and colour that we would now regard as vulgar: with a vividness of gilding, external painting, internal decoration fittings and hangings that makes a nonsense of our perception of Scotland as a version of Little Holland. There has been an equal under-appreciation of great composers such as Robert Carver (easily the equal of Thomas Tallis), of poets like David Lindsay, Dunbar, Douglas and Montgomery, of the other arts of the Scottish Renaissance Courts, and indeed of painting. We are only very tentatively at the beginning of discovering who the painters might have been, because the records are so scant, and the evidence has been largely destroyed. One day Andrew Bairhum and George Jameson's uncle might be restored to us.

MYTH FIVE: CASTLE COUNTRY

Gordon District boasts of itself as castle country. Touraine boasts itself as the *'pays des chateaux'*. Preponderantly, the buildings in Gordon and the buildings in Touraine were erected in the same period. Preponderantly, they share a similar plan form, although those in Scotland are, necessarily, adapted for Scottish conditions, Scottish materials and Scottish climate. Preponderantly, Touraine sees itself as the heart of the French Renaissance; whereas Gordon markets itself as some form of Caledonian killing field. Those buildings in Gordon are chateaux, erected at a time when, under the influence of the Gordon Earls of Huntly, north east Scotland enjoyed a period of unexampled wealth and splendour, largely exempt from the dynastic troubles and English invasions that afflicted the districts further south. The inhabitants of Gordon and north-east Scotland traded directly with the Baltic, inter-married with the Baltic, and established trading posts, colleges, and churches throughout the Baltic. If you wish to see what Gordon District really was like, you need to go to Stockholm, Danzig, Riga, and countless other places from whence the influence derived. Gordon is the heartland of Scotland's reaction to the northern European Renaissance.

MYTH SIX: THE INDUSTRIAL BABYLON

Reawakened by the controversy over the 1990 Glasgow Year of Culture, class warfare in Glasgow needed to portray the 18th Century city as a provincial, if not jokey small community, in order to emphasise how the rise in cotton, heavy engineering and shipbuilding in the mid 19th Century, created an Industrial Babylon. Historic Glasgow had to be diminished in achievement if this post-Victorian representation of the city, as a place in which workers themselves had managed to pull themselves up by their bootstraps, was to be given adequate value. That picture, which dominates 20th Century literature (and there is no lack of evidence to support such a perception), is fundamentally partial.

The architecture reveals that Glasgow, after its freedom from the archbishops in the mid 17th Century, was the boom town of late 17th Century Scotland, rebuilding itself on the most advanced European model in 1652 and 1677. Glasgow developed the Virginia trade, and Glasgow had Britain's first Palladian mansion, indeed the first building by Colen Campbell. In Glasgow did Sir William Bruce build his finest arcaded and colonnaded town house, in the Saltmarket. Glasgow developed the street of suburban Tobacco Lord villas, unique in western Europe, and Glasgow developed the American pattern of placing public buildings in the centre of urban squares like Ivy League court houses. In Glasgow you can find buildings whose nearest parallels are in Annapolis.

It was to Glasgow that nine-tenths of all tobacco imports into Europe was dispatched; and a Glaswegian Tobacco Lord, John Glassford of Douglaston, in 1774, earned £1.5m, about £300m today. It was in Glasgow that merchant John Stirling had the stunning conception of building a wholly private town square to the design of Robert and James Adam, part of which was completed. To Glasgow did Sir John Soane bring his only town house design outside London (in Buchanan Street). Glasgow attempted the only private sector New Town to be funded in Scotland (the Merchant City). Throughout its history, appears the Glasgow entrepreneur: rich, pushy, adventurous, who created Glasgow then, as he does now. It is all there in the architecture, but Glaswegians have chosen to avert their eyes. A different non-conforming mythology prevailed.

MYTH SEVEN: THE LOSS OF KING AND COURT

Political mythology has it that once James VI left Scotland for England in 1603, the country's fortunes went into near-terminal decline. It was certainly the case that the greater aristocrats who stayed behind in Scotland felt themselves increasingly peripheralised by a London-based court. To everybody else, facts were otherwise. Recent research by Michael Lynch, confirmed by the architecture, has revealed the precise opposite. Once the King and his squabbling coterie were safely out of the way in London, the country, and in particular the capital, enjoyed a period of unequalled mercantile prosperity. During this period much of Edinburgh's High Street was refaced in ashlar arcades like Gladstone's Land; the capital was able to afford dressed stone civic buildings like the Tron Kirk, Parliament House, and the splendid George Heriot Hospital. It was at this time that new universities were completed in Glasgow, Aberdeen and Edinburgh. It was the era of Sir William Dick of Braid, with his banks in Edinburgh and London, and his agent in Paris.

The gentle countryside surrounding the capital was spotted with villas of rich merchants and nobles, the houses of Ravelston, Dean, Colinton, Pilrig, Kilbaberton, Woodhouse, Malleny, Liberton and Craigcrook. It was the period when the splendid Wryghts House was constructed by Bruntsfield Park. At the bottom ends of the wynds in the Old Town lay new noblemen's houses, like those for the Earls of Selkirk and Traquair; or those of rich merchants like Robert Gourlay. Out there in the Home Counties arose the unequalled splendour of Linlithgow, Winton House, and Prestongrange; to say nothing of the splendours arising further afield, particularly in the north east with Pitsligo, Pitullie, Fyvie and Boyne. The architecture itself bears testimony to what has been a mislaid generation: a generation, however, which represented indigenous Scottish culture at the peak of its achievement, and back to which all subsequent revivals appeared to hark.

BROADER ANALYSIS

So much for myths. Scotland's architecture reveals a different Scottish history to that which we have all been taught: a history considerably different to that embodied in most heritage presentations. What, therefore, is its underlying structure? Sir Banister Fletcher adumbrated that the architecture of all countries throughout the world is governed by the same factors: geology, geography, climate, economics, politics, religion and skills. Here is how those characteristics applied to Scotland.

So far as **geology** is concerned, Scotland is a country of stone, many different stones, but stone nonetheless, and after the early Middle Ages, a country almost entirely bereft of trees save in the great Caledonian Forest at Rothiemurchus. Scottish architecture therefore developed upon the structure of a stone vault. Long-span timber was extremely rare, and therefore used only in buildings adjacent to great forests, or where the wealth of the client could afford imports, and thus restricted only to the King or the very greatest of Lords.

When it comes to **geography**, Scotland is a small, pendicular country falling off the north-west corner of Europe where, Tacitus claimed, that 'the world and all things come to an end'. When communication was entirely by sea, it was far less remote than it appears today. In the early Middle Ages, influences from Europe entered Scotland through England, over land; but after the wars began c.1296, that stopped, save where attached to English expansion. Thereafter, cultural influences and high quality craftsmanship were imported expensively from across the sea. A different tradition persisted in the west of Scotland, (probably emanating from Ireland) revealed in the non-hierarchical curtain-walled buildings of the Highland areas in total contrast to the hierarchical Norman buildings of Comyns, Moravias, de Vaux, which, even then, had been suitably adapted for Scottish materials and climate. Carving and elaboration signals wealth; and Scottish buildings are tighter in plan, more squeezed vertically, with less elaboration.

Once the barrier severed links between Scotland and England, Scots first internalised and developed the tower house, an architecture of strong geometry and sparse elaboration. 16th and 17th Century inspiration from France, Spain, Italy, Sweden and Holland transformed that native product into a truly indigenous architecture of startling style and vividness.

In terms of **economics**, Scottish wealth derived from crops; and to judge by Pont's record of buildings, the cultivated areas predominantly followed the coastline or river valleys. Large tracts of the country remained uncultivated. There was a great deal of building, most of it almost certainly by local masons, embellished by free masons, who were directed toward dressed stone superstructures or details, which they sometimes signed.

Mid-Victorian wealth, however, proved to be more damaging than scarcity of cash. Most Scots regarded the period c.1840 as a golden age: wealth was increasing, new classical suburbs were complete, and most towns were graced with impressive neo-classical schools, art galleries, churches and hospitals. The old still survived, albeit decaying and overcrowded, to act in pleasurable contrast to the new. Barely years later, Scotland's economy had swollen and the country waxed large. Town centres became gravely overcrowded, insanitary and dangerous, and the country's heavy industry provided the money with which to rebuild. The Victorian boom period proved close to being the most culturally destructive passage in Scottish history, as the memory of what had been achieved before 1707 was obliterated.

Religion offers a key to understanding Scottish buildings. The peculiar nature of Scottish Presbyterianism, in which the audience engages in discussion with the Minister, explains the God box churches of the 18th and 19th Centuries of such a different plan to contemporary buildings in England. The influx of poor people, particularly from Ireland, most of whom were Catholic, into the cities of Scotland in the mid 19th Century explains the proliferation of Catholic churches in Dundee, Glasgow and the industrial areas of Aberdeen and Edinburgh: for the Catholic church was the church of the underdog. Once Episcopalianism became legitimised in the early 19th century, covertly Jacobite families emerged from the obscurity with which they had protected themselves during the previous 70 years, married money and commissioned some of the most extraordinary extravagance in Scottish building history.

Politics influenced Scottish architecture in that its own identity developed as the consequence of the war with England and alliances with Scandinavia and Europe. European attitudes far beyond architecture duly entered the bloodstream. For example, English visitors to Edinburgh in the 18th century usually found the city distinctly continental in ambience. However, once Scotland's trading links with Europe were compulsorily severed after 1707, there was a diminution of northern European influence, replaced, in due course, by a British one. Thenceforth, Scotland was expected to perform the role of North Britain. By then, however, Scottish culture had matured, and its inherited continental attitudes proved surprisingly persistent. The revival of Scottish architecture, in the 1840s, the 1890s, the 1930s were closely associated with broader cultural and political nationalist movements, as indeed was the case in Europe. The erection of the Wallace Monument in 1859 attracted laudatory telegrams from the Italian patriot Garibaldi and the Hungarian patriot Kossuth.

Scotland's indigenous **skills and technology** were masonic. There is no significant tradition of timber framing or technology, as a consequence of the absence of long-span timber. It was thus a country of heavy mass. Framing, that is to say iron framing, entered the country tentatively in late 18th Century mill architecture; but it blossomed from the 1850s. It was a new technology to Scots, but, blessed by association with the world-wide reputation earned by Scotland in heavy engineering and shipbuilding, it came to be profoundly influential. Thereafter, the issue was one of whether structure was the servant of architecture (Mackintosh), or architecture was decorated structure (James Miller); or whether the two could synthesise (Alexander Thomson). That debate persists even now. The notion of architecture as decorated, (and increasingly undecorated), structure began to predominate as the dictates of economy prevailed. Inter-war houses were designed so that they could be erected by unemployed shipyard and steel workers, or even coal mines. Undecorated structure, in which the programme of production mattered more than any other consideration, peculiarly suited the Stalinist Calvinists of the post-1945 period. Great output was achieved; Glasgow, after all, had more system-built towers of flats and more motorway miles per head of population, than anywhere else.

REVALUATION

Scotland is fortunate in its concentration of architectural and other historians; and in the substantial national archive based in Edinburgh. Part of the rediscovery has been fuelled by the essentially visual nature of the RIAS/Landmark Trust Illustrated Architectural Guides to Scotland, which at 16 volumes, is about half way through its sequence. From the thousands of their illustrations (a particular concentration upon historic illustration of buildings either altered or demolished) patterns have begun to emerge, which shed light upon an architecture of which we have been largely unaware.

Typologies have appeared which, insofar as post 1500 buildings are concerned, relegate the traditional concepts of castle, tower house and barmkin to the cupboard. These discoveries have been confirmed by European comparisons, technical studies dating buildings by wall thickness, by colour and harling, and by massing and detail has revealed much about Scottish Renaissance buildings. They have an inherent proportion. Far-fetched as though this may sound when considering Scotland against the myth, the plan of buildings like Craignethan (1532), the fortifications of Leith (1548), and the oriel windows of Balvenie (c.1560) testify to mainstream European Renaissance influence in early 16th Century Scotland.

The 1992 bicentenary of Robert Adam promoted a similar revaluation of his work in Scotland, in particular of his villas and castles. British architectural historians tend to classify Adam's castles as mock-Gothic. There is not a single Gothic window in those castles: they are designed with a strong geometry distinctly resembling early 17th Century Scottish architecture. To Robert Adam we owe the grouping of otherwise ordinary terraced houses, behind a palace-frontage, the re-use of Scottish Renaissance detail, and the grandeur of his vision of what the principal entries into Edinburgh should look like. Adam deployed vigorous skyline of pitched roof and tall chimney stacks long after the time when English roofs had disappeared behind balustrades.

The examination of Scottish architecture between the Wars undertaken for *The Scottish Thirties*(1987), revealed comparable aspiration. Previously judged as a provincial echo of the International Style, Scottish buildings during that period formed part of a continuum with the Scottish literary renaissance and were the product of a different programme: namely to develop a 20th Century Scottish architecture, its roots much more in 17th Century Aberdeenshire than in 1927 Stuttgart.

The evidence for such revaluations has been available for a long time, but was either ignored or misinterpreted because it did not fit. Scottish architecture, less lavish than in Europe, with its emphasis upon weather protection, has produced sufficient buildings of a quality to merit the most miserable interpretation. But the cultural history of other countries has never been formed solely from the second rate. The Scottish problem has been to accept second rate as the best and revalue the remainder downwards accordingly.

SYNTHESIS

The bones of our Scottish architectural culture, which arises from its landscape, its people and its economy, must now be apparent. Massive stone buildings of the Middle Ages displayed little ornament (because expensive), the best by French masons like John Morvo. The native inspiration was one of sturdy geometry. A nobleman or laird's house developed into the indigenous building form of a tower, in which principal rooms were vertically disposed above each other.

With the arrival of the Renaissance, that vertical plan was replaced by horizontal one, offering a more luxurious lifestyle within an apartment of three chambers each one opening into the next in sequence. The last chamber, a bedroom, was usually in a tower expressed with its own private staircase, which the laird could use to visit his lady in the apartment above. The contrast with, for example, the horizontally proportioned English manor house, picturesquely obscure in its moated and bosky fastness, its principal rooms arrayed around the courtyard on a ground floor, is striking. Scots Renaissance chateaux are vertically proportioned, principal rooms invariably upon the first floor until the mid 17th Century, sitting upon kitchens and cellars. Their increasingly flamboyant superstructures in a largely treeless country were designed to be read from a distance like the heraldry of an army. Skylines mattered; and Scotland was peculiarly fond of towers. The towered Scots Tolbooth is unique to the country; and Glasgow and Edinburgh's Universities, George Heriot's Hospital, Dundee's almshouses and Stirling's Guildhall, amongst many others, are focused upon prominent towers. Where dressed stone could not be afforded the rubble would be harled or smooth plastered, using whatever brilliant pigment could be imported. The dressed stone was limewashed in a different colour, and from the interaction between the two, as well as from the massing, form and detail, emerged the Scottish Renaissance.

That combination of geometry, plan, and skyline persisted into the early 18th Century and informs much of the work of William Adam, Scotland's finest architect of the period. The plan, for example, of Duff House, is clearly derivative from the earlier period. The dressed stone of William Adam's great mansions was rare, expensive, and thereby restricted to the very wealthy, or new money like Lord Braco. The generality of early to mid 18th Century houses evinced plain harled geometry, with sparingly applied detail, and perhaps only a pediment for show. The contrast between dressed stone and harling remained the principal aesthetic. Many mid 18th Century houses retained the European pattern of subordinate ground floor, with a gigantic piano nobile above, the entire composition embellished, in true continental style, with that vividly swept roof and prominent chimney stacks.

The motive force in north Britain (as in the rest of Britain) was to emphasise through building the landowner's control over his estate, and his determination to invest in the most advanced forms of husbandry and agricultural improvement. But the songs north and south of the Border remained distinctive. Robert and John Adam were either the inheritors of a surviving Scots tradition through their father, or the perpetrators of the first Scottish revival. Robert's work was informed by the mastery of composition and internal space which he had imbibed in Rome. But the means he deployed for that effect were essentially Scots and geometric. He evinced a certain fondness for picturesque effect. For, by the late 18th Century, Scotland was becoming the romantic location *par excellence*, to which people came to be terrified by untamed nature and wild beasts, to say little of the savages who had come so close to overturning the Hanoverians in 1746.

Adam's successors were less certainly Scots and more flamboyantly picturesque: and their country mansions aped Tudor and Elizabethan houses promiscuously. The Scottish inferiority complex ensured that lairds preferred to purchase the most fashionable English architects for the new houses which were being rebuilt at a rapidity partly on the proceeds from the Montgomery Act (a tax efficient vehicle for investment in agricultural improvement and enclosure), and partly because an English education had convinced Scots lairds of the uncouth and inappropriate nature of the building which they had inherited.

That same agricultural improvement and Scotland's growing trade provided the wealth for the golden age of Scots urbanism. Between 1770 and 1840, splendid new towns were added to Edinburgh, Aberdeen, Perth, Glasgow and Ayr, and was only prevented in Dundee by an obsessive non-interventionist approach of the Lord Provost Alexander Riddoch, who prided himself that his was the only city in Scotland that had not gone bankrupt. Nowadays, few remember the bankruptcies, but everybody notices Dundee's lack of integrated streets and squares in the gracious Classical manner that so grace its rivals.

The predominant New Town buildings were rows of classical terraced houses, (although Edinburgh's New Town cross streets were tenement flats suitably decorated to look like terraced houses) highlighted by stately classical churches, hospitals, Athenaea, Town Houses, Art Galleries, Schools and Museums. One of Robert Adam's legacies was the belief that a public building should evince a nobility and grandeur far beyond that needed solely for functional purposes. There was sufficient money for ashlar. A study of those buildings and their massing reveal a sturdiness, a geometry and lack of elaboration, when compared with comparable buildings in Bristol or London, which identify them as being part of the Scottish tradition. Great walls of buildings, inheritors of the six-storey tenements facing Edinburgh's High Street, were duly succeeded by walls of tenements of the later Victorian period. Unfortunately, those classical suburbs sucked the professional and the middle classes from the old cities, just as their later successors sucked the skilled artisans. Those left behind in the city centres were those who could not afford to move: thus, laying the foundations of mid 19th Century urban squalor, and the health-impelled improvement programmes that necessarily followed.

With the opening of new quarries, and the eventual availability of rail-delivered machine-cut stone, Scotland's architectural characters became predominantly one of ashlar stone. Plastering and harling became associated with the building of the poor and, as a consequence, many an older building had the harling picked off in a fit of 'rubblemania'. People came to desire their money's worth of stone.

By the mid 19th Century, Scots architecture had split between the attractions of the past, and those of the future. The impetus of the first proper Scottish revival, perhaps impelled by the novels of Walter Scott and the erection of the Scott Monument, derived architecturally from the publication of four volumes: *The Baronial and Ecclesiastical Architecture of Scotland* by Robert Billings. Those books gave the Scottish laird the confidence to instruct his mason or his architect to use Scottish forms and details rather than necessarily aping English ones. Many very large Victorian Scottish country houses with a standard Victorian country house plan were embellished with 17th Century Scottish details.

Such romanticism would not suit town centres. The Scots, fundamentally pragmatic, believed that architecture should reflect function. Picturesque baronialism might be all very well for the countryside and lairds, but conveyed entirely the wrong signals for city centre offices, warehouses, mercantile emporia, mills and banks. Banks had to be secure. No matter how romantically baronial a bank manager might be in private at night, banks took the form of Italian palazzos or classical palaces – opulent, reliable and sturdy. Great warehouses and mercantile emporia were, by contrast, designed from the inside out, adapting Italian, French or any other flamboyant European or Far Eastern style that was thought to fit. Thus was architecture as decorated structure brought to life.

The next revival, at the turn of the century, coincided with Sir Patrick Geddes' proposed reinhabitation of the Old Town of Edinburgh, an interest in arts and crafts, and the establishment of the Chair of Celtic Studies at Edinburgh University. This second revival was more learned than the earlier, being base upon the study and measurement of buildings of the 16th and 17th Century period, under the guidance of Sir Robert Rowand Anderson, Sir Robert Lorimer, James Mclaren and others. But a division appeared between those who went back to the 17th Century, like Sir Robert Lorimer, to stay there and those like Mackintosh, who returned to that period for inspiration, but synthesised to produce a contemporary architecture. It was, if you like, the battle between the sentimentalist (Lorimer) and the romantic (Mackintosh).

That battle was little evident in the city centres. The development of American iron-framed techniques, and the introduction of the mechanical lift led to buildings soaring from the ground to Glasgow's grid-iron pattern and standard floor-plates: thus producing a continuation and development of the notion of architecture as decorated structure in counterpoint to the revivalists. The rather thin nature of speculative office development, which thus made its first appearance in Glasgow, was concealed behind the profusion of cheaply available carved stone, and the flowering of Glasgow's figurative sculpture with which these buildings were adorned.

It did not take much, in the rather more straitened period between the Wars, for the stone and figurative sculpture to be stripped off such buildings, leaving but the bare structure behind. The inter-war period in Scotland reflected an economy which was the worst in the western world, without the revival during the 1920s enjoyed by the others. Vast acreages were overwhelmed by suburban housing and bungalows, with amorphous urbanity and remorseless sprawl. The economy was so poor that, in 1934, the tenement (banned under arts and crafts influence in 1918 as being the cause of ill-health and poor achievement) was reintroduced, although Continental models were studied to make the native product more appealing. It was an architecture of survival. It reflected the need to attract new industry to new industrial estates, new housing in the form of both private sector and working-class suburbs, and buildings for a new form of transport – the motor car. There was, however, a new ingredient, consumerism from which arose the architecture of self-indulgence, leisure and entertainment. The 1930s have become associated particularly with the architecture of cinemas, dance halls, ice rinks, seaside pavilions, cafes, roadhouses and restaurants: because the smooth imagery of those buildings reflected something of the clean white optimism through which people sought to emerge from the past.

That was the context of the third Scottish architectural revival which paralleled the Scottish literary renaissance. Predominantly associated with bourgeois houses, the aim of its leaders was to seek inspiration from the period of 1600, Scotland's most national period, with its strong geometric forms and sparingly applied decoration, and adapt it to contemporary techniques for a contemporary architecture.

The Empire Exhibition in Glasgow in 1938 very nearly achieved the goal of the previous 100 years: the synthesis of two opposing strands of Scots architecture: decorated structure on the one hand, and Scottishness on the other. Its combination of the most advanced prefabrication techniques, and the aesthetic of white architecture of the Scottish Revival was remarkable. Before it could breed children, war intervened.

Post-war Scotland's focus was on rebuilding its housing and industry as quickly as possible. The country's eye was on production, and architecture as structure, not even decorated any more, if that structure provided the *units* that the social programmes required. Buildings resulting from such programmes remain the most prominent manifestations of post-war Scotland. A submerged passacaglia of smaller churches, houses, the occasional school, the very occasional office block, factory or distillery, seemed to exemplify the inheritance of the past: brilliant walls, strong form, picturesque skyline, and geometric modelling. In short, these were works of architecture rather than of programme.

THE PRESENT DAY

Where we are now depends upon whether we are considering Scottish cities, Scots suburbia, or the Scottish countryside. All are threatened by the consequences of mythology. As we rebuild our cities after the 1960s depredations, it is not to the 17th Century European pattern of arcaded streets, but to the 19th and 20th Century pattern of road-widened walled streets. The 1968 Glasgow gale brought the programme of eliminating tenements from the face of Scotland to a merciful end; and we have been knitting the ravaged pieces together, but only rarely in an architectural culture worthy of our 17th Century forebears.

Suburbs, which first flowed north after World War I, threaten to become the country's dominant aspect as we link one city to the next in an urban form neither urban nor Scots. There is perhaps no greater problem at the moment than the development of a pleasing Scottish suburb of which we could be proud.

Worst of all is the countryside. Despite valiant attempts, notably by the Countryside Commission in *Tomorrow's Architectural Heritage*, the Scottish countryside is being suburbanised, diminished and devalued, by a combination of ignorance, amnesia and myopia. It begins with the road engineers, is followed by the town planner, and society concurs. What has happened to the Highland village of Strontian, to Fort William, to Aviemore, to Gardenstown and to Mintlaw is a matter of shame: needlessly wide roads, intrusive pavements, a scurvy of signs, a tweeness of cottages, and the blankness of flat, dog-infested grass. These are the spoor of suburbia, and instead of enobling nature and benefiting from it, we are close to reducing our natural heritage to valuelessness. Perhaps the initiative for a Central Scotland Forest, and the associated architectural competition for New Ideas in Rural Housing are glimmers of light. But are they? Central Scotland has the vision of trying to retrieve what its forefathers threw away, at a time when rural Scotland is still busy destroying what it has.

If architecture is a representation of a living culture, then it tends to follow rather than lead society. Yet in a battle of myths and images, good architecture could offer the country a lead in its search for itself. To do that requires a clear understanding. People will develop an appropriate contemporary architecture when they understand with greater clarity from whence they came. Only by an acceptance of this can we hope to forge a contemporary Scottishness of Scottish architecture.

The author

Charles McKean is Secretary and Treasurer of The Royal Incorporation of Architects in Scotland. A journalist, author and campaigner for a greater pride in Scottish culture, his many achievements include masterminding a series of local architectural guides, many of which he has written himself. His major works are *The Scottish Thirties*(1987), *Architectural Contributions to Scottish Society since 1840* (1990), *Edinburgh – Portrait of a City* (1991).

References

Billings, R., *The Baronical and Ecclesiastical Architecture of Scotland.*
Fenton, A & Walker, B., *The Rural Architecture of Scotland*, John Donald, 1981.
Fladmark, J.M. et al, *Tomorrow's Architectural Heritage: Landscape and Buildings in the Countryside*, Mainstream, 1991.
Howarth, T., *Charles Rennie Mackintosh and the Modern Movement*, Routledge, 1990.
McWilliam, C., *Scottish Townscape*, Collins, 1975.
Naismith, R.J., *Buildings of the Scottish Countryside*, Gollancz, 1985.
Reiach, A. & Hurd, R., *Building Scotland: Past and Future*, Saltire Society, 1944.
Robertson, P. (ed), *Charles Rennie Mackintosh: The Architectural Papers*, White Cochade, 1990.
Royal Incorporation of Architects in Scotland, *The Architecture of the Renaissance*, 1990.
Savage, P., *Lorimer and the Edinburgh Craft Designers*, Paul Harris, 1980.
Tait, A.A., *The Landscape Garden in Scotland 1735-1835*, Edinburgh University Press, 1980.
Willies,P., *New Architecture in Scotland*, Lund Humphries, 1977.

RIAS/Landmark Trust Architectural Guides:
Beaton, E., *Ross and Cromarty*, 1992.

Brogden, W.A., *Aberdeen*, 1986.
Burgher, L., *Orkney*, 1991.
Close, R., *Ayrshire and Arran*, 1992.
Finnie, M., *Shetland*, 1990.
McKean, C., *Banff and Buchan*, 1990.
McKean, C. et al, *Central Glasgow*, 1989.
McKean C., *The District of Moray*, 1987.
McKean, C., *Edinburgh*, 1992.
McKean, C., *Stirling and Trossachs*, 1985.
McKean, C. & Walker, D., *Dundee*, 1984.
Pride, G.L., *The Kingdom of Fife*, 1990.
Swan, A., *Clackmannan*, 1987.
Walker, F.A., *The South Clyde Estuary*, 1986.
Walker, F.A. and Sinclair, F., *The North Clyde Estuary*, 1992.

7

FARM BUILDINGS IN NORWAY

Jan Våge

The farmstead is an essential part of our cultural landscape and should be viewed as such. This paper deals with farm buildings used directly for production, as well as the farmhouse and the setting, covering development during the last 150 years. I conclude with the current process of seeking new activities in green tourism with the aim of supporting a viable living in the countryside and giving new life to old buildings.

Up until the middle of the 19th Century, the basis for Norwegian farming was self-sufficiency. The towns were small and so were the market possibilities. The farmer traditionally took advantage of a broad spectrum of resources, such as hunting, fishing in the sea and in rivers, forestry for timber and fuel, as well as arable crop and dairy farming. Most of the farmers, especially those in the upland areas, were dependent on the mountain out farm (seter) during the summer months. This was often located miles away and normally had a byre, a small barn and a cottage with one room for habitation and one used as a dairy.

Altogether there were many buildings on each farm, up to 25 to 30 on the bigger ones, including a number of small buildings located away from the steading, for use as field barns, and for fishing, hunting and forestry. Each had a particular functional purpose. Heated buildings and animal-houses were normally constructed of logs throughout the country, but in the more simple outhouses, like barns, different construction systems were used in different parts of Norway. In the west of the country, barns were of stave construction with rafters supporting the roofing material and horizontal exterior cladding, while in the east, barns were made of logs with purlins in the roof construction and vertical exterior cladding.

During the last three hundred years many farms have been repeatedly sub-divided. Before the land reallocation process, which started in the middle of the last century, buildings for up to 15 farms were grouped together in nucleated settlements and the different districts of Norway had developed one or two dominant steading types on the lines of a Scottish 'fermetoun' prior to the agricultural improvements in the 18th Century. These are still called a 'tun' in Norwegian (the Norse from which the English word 'town' is

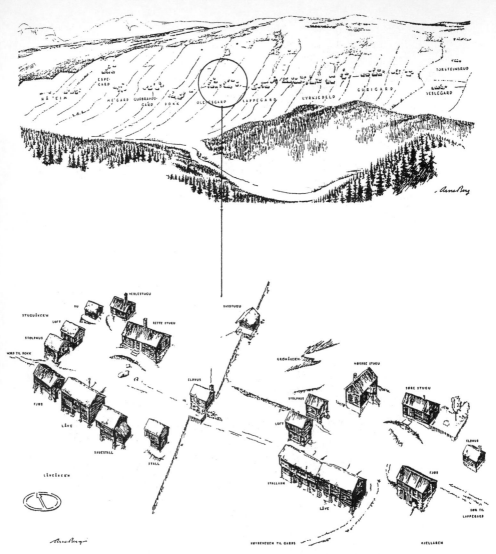

OLEIVSGARD i LEVELD
gnr. 66
i ÅL i Hallingdal kring 1900

Leveld is the original name of the farm. Many farms in the sketch on
the previous page have been parcelled out from this. Sometimes after
division had been carried out the name of Leveld went over to the whole
cluster of farms, and the original farm was called Oleivsgard from
the 18th century. This was divided into two equal parts in 1815.
The two holdings, Nordre and Søre, each have their own farm tun,
and the square pattern is clear even though they have been built
on a hill.

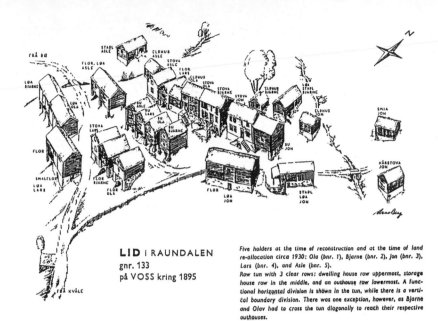

LID I RAUNDALEN
gnr. 133
på VOSS kring 1895

Five holders at the time of reconstruction and at the time of land re-allocation circa 1930: Ola (bnr. 1), Bjarne (bnr. 2), Jon (bnr. 3), Lars (bnr. 4), and Asle (bnr. 5).
Row tun with 3 clear rows: dwelling house row uppermost, storage house row in the middle, and an outhouse row lowermost. A functional horizontal division is shown in the tun, while there is a vertical boundary division. There was one exception, however, as Bjarne and Olav had to cross the tun diagonally to reach their respective outhouses.

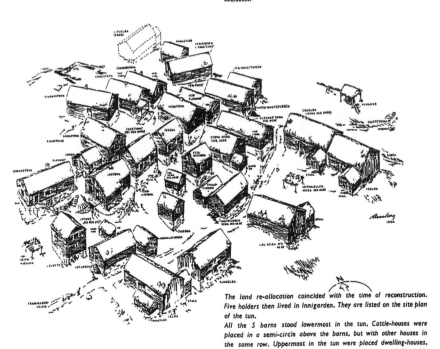

The land re-allocation coincided with the time of reconstruction. Five holders then lived in Innigarden. They are listed on the site plan of the tun.
All the 5 barns stood lowermost in the tun. Cattle-houses were placed in a semi-circle above the barns, but with other houses in the same row. Uppermost in the tun were placed dwelling-houses, eldhus, and small storage houses. Each holder generally had his houses grouped together.
'Dei der nede' (the farm below), bnr. 1, and Sjur, bnr. 2, moved out at the time of land re-allocation. Shortly afterwards Per, bnr. 3, and 'Dei der oppe' (the farm above), bnr. 9, also moved out.

INNIGARDEN PÅ KLAKEGG
gnr. 14
i JØLSTER kring 1880

derived) and there are six main types, some of which are divided into sub-categories. There was, of course, a lot of tuns with forms of less definite shape. I have used a selection of Arne Berg's drawing, originally published in *Norske Gardstun* to illustrate the typical arrangement of buildings.

In about 1850 various events took place which caused change and accelerated development in farm buildings. A growing population, increasing industrialisation and urbanisation brought new markets, and improved communications made it easier to serve the towns. Animal products became more important for farmers, but we became dependent on the import of wheat from America. The prospects of alternative job opportunities and the possibility of emigration made labour more expensive and the importance of uncultivated land decreased as farmers could not afford the cost of manual labour. Instead, new land was brought under cultivation and people were replaced by horse-drawn equipment. The old self-sufficiency system was gradually replaced by a more market orientated system. In Norway this process took place very late compared to Britain and the pace of change was very rapid. The haphazard sub-division of land in the past made it necessary to rationalise holdings by reallocation and the traditional dense settlements were dispersed into the countryside as new single farmsteads. This process went on up to World War II and culminated in 214,000 units in total, each comprising 0.5 ha or more of cultivated land.

New farm buildings from the period 1850 - 1950 were of a rather unique design. They were based on the use of horse and gravity, and were designed as a compact multi-purpose building round animal husbandry. A ramp led to the hayloft on the first floor, animals were kept on the ground floor, and the manure was accumulated in a basement cellar below. In addition there was space for unthreshed grain, the new threshing machine, and for the grain after threshing. The topography often made it easy to build the access ramp which connected with an inside bridge on the level of the eaves. The horse brought the wagon in and the hay was thrown into the loft. It was then fed to the animals below and they in turn filled the basement so that much of the indoor transport was based on the force of gravity.

Over time the building materials used to make farm buildings also changed. Timber was still the dominant construction and cladding material, but log walls were replaced by brick walls for animal accommodation and concrete replaced stone for foundations and new basement cellars.

The new farmhouse had to accommodate the farmer's family, as well as grandparents and sometimes seasonal labour. The rather square ground floor was divided into four or five rooms served by one chimney. The bedrooms were upstairs, and underneath a cellar was introduced for storing potatoes, to provide a washroom, workshop etc. The exterior became more directly influenced by international styles introduced to farmers by new hotels and railway stations. Compared to the many local designs of the older farmhouses, the new ones had a more standardised design.

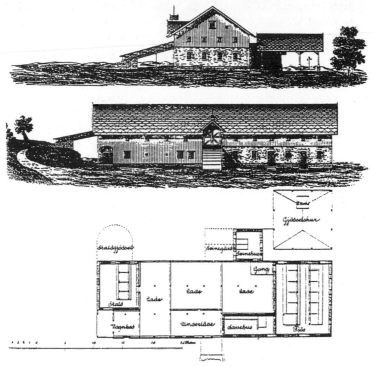

Figure 3 A multipurpose farm building from Eastern Norway about 1900. Rooms for dairy cows, horses, sheep and pigs.

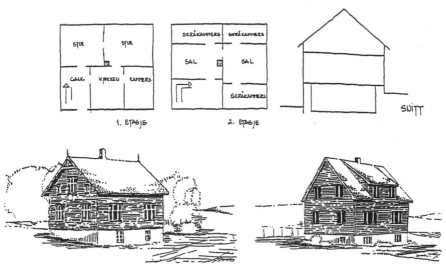

Figure 4 Farm houses from Western Norway, 1920 and 1950. Hall, kitchen and three rooms on ground floor. Two bedrooms upstairs.

The last 40 years have brought changes on both the farms and in the countryside of Norway at an increasing pace. Since 1950 the number of active farming units has decreased by two-thirds to a total of 80,000 and this has led to partial or temporary usage and abandonment of thousands of steadings.

The explosion in the use of modern machinery of the 1950s and the clearing of ground for new and more intensive cultivation led to the need for bigger units. Stimulated by an active pricing policy, we have seen a high level of specialisation. The use of combine- harvesters and new conservation systems for grass have become active forces in modelling new farm buildings.

On the grain growing farms in the South-East, the new needs were accommodated by rearranging the multi-purpose buildings or constructing new garages and sheds for the machinery and grain drying equipment. A large number of new livestock buildings were built. Today, more than two-thirds of all farm animals are housed in buildings that are no more than 30 years old. The change in style from the first half of the century is remarkable.

The part of the new farm complex used for livestock is normally a well-insulated, single-storey building with a slatted floor for cattle and sheep with a manure cellar underneath. Vertical or horizontal silos are hidden inside a more elevated, uninsulated structure which also contains limited space for some hay and for other storage purposes. Sometimes silos are still built as free-standing towers. Wood is still used as the main material for the construction of walls and roofs.

The post-war farmhouse is just like any other Norwegian detached house from this period: it is made of wood, is often prefabricated, and it is a single-storey building with a cellar. The pitch of the roof is at an angle of about 22-25°. Unfortunately, these buildings are often not designed and located to fit in well with the existing built form and layout. The challenge for the future is to find a way of designing both farm buildings and houses that are in better harmony with the cultural traditions of local communities.

The situation in Norway today is characterised by a stable national population with a strong tendency towards centralisation. We are experiencing unemployment problems and there is overproduction, not least in agriculture. The Norwegian economy depends very much on primary industries like agriculture, forestry, fishing and North Sea oil and gas, and there is a broad political agreement that the economy of remote rural areas needs to be subsidised to encourage people to stay.

As farming is becoming less important as a provider of employment, the farmers' organisations and the government now collaborate to promote new activities and jobs in the countryside, opportunities for women being seen to be of special importance. Like everywhere else in the world, tourism is seen as a growth industry that can benefit the farming community. Tourism is not an entirely new business for Norwegian farmers. Along the mountain footpaths and trails there is a long tradition of farmers providing walkers with food and overnight accommodation at the 'seter'. Anglers and mountaineers from many countries, including Britain, have generally favoured farm accommodation.

Many farmers have sold or leased ground to meet the ever-increasing demand for second homes. During the last 20-30 years some farmers have also entered the business of providing self-catering accommodation for overnight stays or on a weekly basis. Some of these new units are associated with camping sites, while others are dispersed in the landscape, normally not too far from the steading.

It is considered that this sector has growth potential. Efforts are now being made to provide a better organised and more effective advisory service and financial support through a central fund. This is being established through negotiations and price agreements between the farmers' organisations and the government. Investment for tourism on farms receives that same economic support as farm buildings and there is a special grant for women starting their own enterprise. In special cases, it is also possible to obtain a grant for the rehabilitation of farm buildings worthy of conservation.

How significant is the heritage of farm buildings and houses as a resource for tourism? In Norway, open air folk museums have been well established for at least one hundred years. As well as the well known museums in Oslo and Lillehammer, almost every self-respecting local community has its own museum with old steadings. About 1,800 farm buildings and houses are located in such museums, and they are a local resource of some significance for the interpretation of our rural heritage. Indeed, it is not too boastful to say that many of our finest timber buildings surviving from the Middle Ages, are quite important in European terms. Although some of them have been moved to open-air museums, many remain near working farms in places like Telemark and Numedal, where they could provide an important resource for developing farm tourism.More than half a million buildings have been recorded in an ambitious project to register all physical elements of our cultural heritage made before 1900. The project started in 1972 and is programmed for completion in 1995. As many as 70% - 80% of the buildings are on farms, and about 50 - 60% are classified as worthy of conservation in one form or another. This is a large number compared with the 2,000 buildings listed today. The situation in Norway is the same as that in Britain, described by Dr R.W.Brunskill in *Traditional farm buildings in Britain*. He concludes that it is quite clear that since few traditional farm buildings are suitable for continued use in their original function, those which survive have either to be put to new uses on the farm or allowed to remain under-used, empty or to fall into ruin.'

The re-use of old buildings does not represent new thinking for Norwegian farmers, but it is a tradition that has not been encouraged in the last 50 years. It seems sensible to use our stock of old buildings for green tourism rather than to see them fall into neglect, and for this we should draw on the experience of farmers already established in the tourist business. A holistic approach will be required to ensure that both interior and external features are properly conserved, as well as the traditional setting of buildings. In an attempt to help ensure that not too many mistakes are made in future, my university is involved in a project to review different business options and to formulate advice on good design practice for rehabilitation and conversion of old buildings.

The author

Dr Jan Våge is Reader in the Department of Agricultural Technology & Building at the Norwegian University of Land Use. He is author of *Historisk utvikling av bygnnigan på gardsbruk* (Landbruksbokhandlem, 1990). During a study attachment with the Countryside Commission for Scotland, he became associated with early work on *Tomorrow's Architectural Heritage* (1991).

References

Berg, A. ,*Norske Gardstun*, Univesitetsforlaget, 1968.

Brunskill, R.W., *Traditional Farm Buildings in Britain*, Victor Gollancz, 1983.

Bugge, S. & Norberg-Schulz, C., *Early Wooden Architecture in Norway*, Buggekunst NAL 1969.

Buggeland, T & Ågotnes, J., *Maihaugen: De Sandvigske Samlinger 100 år* (English Summary), J.W.Cappelens Forlag, 1987.

Donnelly, M.C., *Architecture in the Scandinavian Countries*, MIT Press, 1992.

Forseth, T. & Giljane, T., (eds), *Byggskikk i Norge*, Bonytt, 1986.

Hauglid, R. et al, *Native Art of Norway*, Dregers, 1977.

Holan, J., *Norwegian Wood: A Tradition of Building*, Rizzoli International, 1990.

Hjulstad, O., *Uthushistorie*, Landbruksforlaget, 1991.

Kyllingstad, R., *Tun og Gardshage*, Landbruksforlaget, 1984.

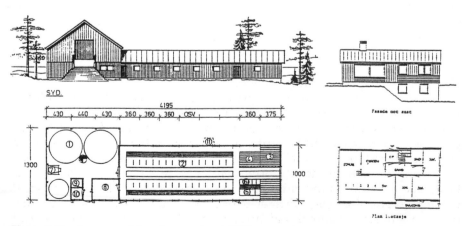

Figure 5 Cowhouse and farmhouse about 1975.

8

TOWARDS A COMMON LANGUAGE
The Unifying Perceptions of an Integrated Approach

Lesley Macinnes

Different people looking at any landscape will notice different things. At the extremes, some might see a natural wilderness bearing the numerous scars of artificial interference by humans; others a wholly human landscape set against a natural backdrop. The several shades of grey in between demonstrate the immense variety in any landscape and the wide range of interests of any on-looker, from quaternary geology to recent industrial archaeology, from beetles to ecosystems, from holiday maker to agricultural worker. Depending on your perspective, a green patch of grass breaking up the purple-brown of a heather moorland may be a productive oasis, a degraded piece of land or the platform for a prehistoric house. Objectively we may all realise that no view is the whole truth, that there can be no single definition of what constitutes landscape, that each perception is valid and depends on a variety of factors and influences, such as topography, climate, past experience and present purpose (Coones 1985). Yet such different perspectives can lead not only to healthy diversity, but also to a host of competing aims and objectives that can make consideration of any issue affecting landscape very complex indeed.

The same problems are encountered when we consider the cultural landscape (Roberts 1987, 77-86; Jones 1988, 154-8). This term is used in a number of different ways. It may, for instance, refer to distant archaeological patterns of settlement and land-use, to deliberately designed landscapes, to areas developed for industrial purposes, or to a geographical region defined by a common cultural identity. Any perception of what forms the cultural landscape depends on individual preconceptions and interests. However, it is the presence of people, whether past or present, explicit or implicit, that makes a landscape cultural and distinguishes it from the natural. Yet one might question whether such a distinction has any real significance, for it is increasingly widely acknowledged that much of the landscape, in Britain and Europe at least, has been heavily modified by thousands of years of human activity (e.g. Hoskins 1977; Simmons 1989).

COMPARTMENTALISATION

Different perceptions are to be welcomed in themselves as they reflect the variety and diversity that is to be found in the landscape. Complementary perceptions can, however, harden into oppositions, such as between human or natural, urban or rural, scenic or productive, or into a choice between preservation or development. Tension between opposites can be creative, but it can also form firm boundaries whereby any one perspective can be held to be more significant, more acceptable, more worthy of support than another. A healthy diversity of views can then become fossilised into compartmentalised approaches to landscape and can effectively obscure the recognition that each opposite is in reality a different component of the same thing (cf Coones 1992, 34-5).

There is, of course, a need to have administrative structures which deal with individual aspects of the landscape, as each has different needs. But problems can arise when administrative responsibility for landscape issues is split between a large number of organisations (Miles 1992, 98; Evans 1992, 247). This has resulted in, for example, a division both within production, principally between farming and forestry, and between production and conservation. Further divisions occur between the natural and the built heritage, land management and planning, and urban and rural concerns. Sub-divisions within each of these concerns exacerbate the problem. Within nature conservation, for instance, the focus of an individual organisation may be on a single species, to the exclusion of different species as well as other interests.

Such divisions can be a particular problem for the landscape. Concern for this has tended to lie predominantly with conservation organisations, dealing particularly with the natural and scenic aspects of the land. The role of planning in mitigating the more adverse effects of development is recognised, but the ability of the major production activities of forestry and agriculture to shape the landscape has generally been neglected or underestimated until relatively recently. The cultural landscape has also suffered. Indeed, cultural matters, however defined, have often not been considered relevant to landscape issues at all, leading to divisions between managing the cultural and the natural aspects of the landscape and, more acutely, between the needs of nature conservation and those of the rural population.

Concessions are now increasingly being made between these divisions, for example in the form of balancing duties enshrined in legislation. However, these are usually set within the context of one organisation considering its effect on other interest groups rather than attempting to achieve a fully integrated approach. It can, in fact, be immensely difficult for different organisations to achieve any overview or unity of approach within such a divided administrative structure. Although organisations increasingly work together, there is usually a lead body in any partnership, and therefore a paramount interest. This can be the case with both production-led management, such as Environmentally Sensitive Areas, and that led by conservation concerns, such as Sites of Special Scientific Interest. As a result it is difficult to achieve a truly integrated policy which embraces the individual parts within a wider whole. This is true for both the landscape in general, and the cultural landscape in particular.

UNIFYING PERCEPTIONS

The links between the different aspects of landscape are rich and complex, and an appreciation of these links can not only benefit each aspect individually, but can also make the whole greater than the sum of its parts. With appropriate mechanisms these links could be used to enhance both strategic planning and tactical action.

One major unifying factor in our perception of landscape is its time-depth, in particular how people have interacted with it over time (Macinnes and Wickham-Jones 1992a). This can help demonstrate the links between different compartments within our modern approaches to the landscape and highlight the dynamic relationship between human activity and the natural world. Looking at a piece of moorland in Scotland, for instance, many people will be aware that the land is the product of particular forms of management over the last two or three hundred years, for sheep, deer and grouse. Some will also be aware that the land was afforested in its original post-glacial state. Modern management may therefore concentrate on one or other of these forms of land-use as the principal option. However, the full story is much more complex and belies such a simple choice. Most areas of moorland will bear evidence of lengthy human occupation, from at least 5000 years ago, altering in scale and character to adapt to changing external or social circumstances. The recent survey of north-east Perthshire by the Royal Commission on the Ancient and Historical Monuments of Scotland (RCAHMS) has demonstrated this very clearly. At Pitcarmick, for example, an extensive area of open moorland is covered with the physical remains of several phases of settlement and associated field systems which show how the density and character of human use of the land has changed since the late Bronze Age (RCAHMS 1990, 70-8). Similarly, in a lowland area now under intensive agriculture it is difficult to appreciate that things have not always been as they now appear. In some cases direct evidence of past occupation survives beneath the soil to be reflected in growing cereals as cropmarks (e.g. Fulford and Nichols 1992). Other readily visible aspects of the landscape, such as hedgerows and stone dykes, can also demonstrate how patterns of land-use have changed (Hodges 1991, 26-34).

We learn from this evidence of time-depth that the use and appearance of the landscape have continually changed and altered, and that human management has been a consistent factor in this. Over the landscape as a whole, settlement has ebbed and flowed, leaving its remains almost in the form of tidal marks. Reasons for success or abandonment have been complex. For instance, land exhaustion might have contributed to the onset of peat growth which engulfed many areas of past settlement, such as at Achnacree in Argyll (Barrett et al 1976). Climatic deterioration has been an important factor in the success or failure of settlement, particularly in upland areas (Burgess 1980, 239-40). Even the effects of climatic pollution have been documented, such as the eruption of Hekla, an Icelandic volcano, around 1160 BC which scattered deposits of volcanic dust across the Bronze Age landscape in northern Scotland and may have contributed to its abandonment (Dugmore 1991; cf Burgess 1989, 325-8). Human mismanagement has also played its part leading to episodes of soil erosion, such as at Suisgill in Sutherland (Barclay 1985, 195-6). The success or failure of past settlements and societies is usually likely to have resulted from a combination of such factors (Whittle 1982).

We can better appreciate from this evidence the extent to which human actions have affected the landscape in the past. The causes and effects of previous management actions can be explored through a combination of disciplines, such as geology, palaeobotany, soil science, ecology and archaeology, to give some insight into the problems of today. This may help distinguish between management practices which are suitable for a particular area and those which are not. It may remind us how to use the land on a scale consistent with both its nature and the availability of local resources. It may even help rediscover traditional skills which have been lost, as the Libyan Valleys project sponsored by UNESCO demonstrated when it sought to establish how simple irrigation systems had facilitated cultivation of dry valleys in the Roman period (Barker and Jones 1982; cf Pitts 1992, 204-5).

Similarly, we can better appreciate the degree to which we can choose management options for the future (cf Pye-Smith and Hall 1987, 115-34). The landscape can be managed for a variety of purposes: for its nature conservation, geological, archaeological or historical interest; for its scenic and recreational value; as well as for its productive capacity. However, while we have tended to consider that a piece of land should be managed primarily for a single purpose, the evidence of the past in the landscape reminds us that different activities are closely inter-connected, inter-related and inter-dependent. We need to bear such lessons in mind as we think about future management, and in particular the question of sustainability.

Such an exploration of time-depth also suggests that most of the landscape is in a sense cultural. Although, as noted above, the cultural landscape is generally considered distinct from the natural landscape, the broader perspective of time suggests a dynamic relationship between the human settlement and management of the landscape on the one hand, and the natural processes of erosion, decay and recovery on the other. This makes it more difficult to distinguish meaningfully between cultural and natural (cf Jones 1991, 229-31). An area of moorland might be seen as natural with a wealth of wildlife, but might also be cultural, bearing evidence of past human occupation and use, as discussed above; a designed landscape is cultural, but has natural elements deliberately included within its overall design (e.g. Tait 1980 passim); even industrialised landscapes, the most obvious of cultural landscapes, were often specifically located to make use of natural resources and, in all but the most toxic cases, quickly revert to nature when abandoned (Clark 1992, 149-50).

These examples demonstrate a fluid state in the relationship between the cultural and the natural which cannot readily be accommodated within our compartmentalised approach to the landscape. To recognise fully these inter-relationships we need to break down the barriers by which we consider one aspect cultural, another natural, one productive, another less useful. In doing this we can begin to develop a more integrated approach to the description of landscape and to the management of all its aspects. Such an approach should not simply acknowledge the relationships between each aspect, but should seek to address the whole as well as the parts (Macinnes 1991, 205-9 and 215; 1993, 255). Interpretation may prove to be a particularly useful tool in establishing the common ground and developing the common language that are needed to achieve this aim.

A MORE INTEGRATED APPROACH

Some models for an integrated approach to landscapes do exist (Smith 1992; cf Blunden and Curry 1988, 199-204). These are found principally in multi-functional bodies like the National Parks or the National Trust, though even these bodies do not have comprehensive responsibilities. For instance, the recent review of National Parks recommended that their responsibilities be extended to include archaeological and historical interests (Edwards 1991, 11). The relationship between production and conservation has developed in a particularly fruitful way in recent years. Both farming and conservation schemes, like Environmentally Sensitive Areas, the Countryside Stewardship Scheme and Tir Cymen, are beginning to encourage a more holistic approach to the landscape and are reintroducing the concept of stewardship. Similarly, forestry is being encouraged to become multi-purpose. Closer integration is also facilitated by the balancing duties which are increasingly placed on organisations to encourage them to take into account other interests, particularly environmental. As noted above, however, the weakness of these schemes is that the onus tends to fall on one interest group to decide how to accommodate competing interests in seeking to achieve its own prime objectives. The challenge facing us now is to strengthen these initiatives by acknowledging the essential unity behind our individual perceptions of landscape, recognising the links between individual interests and translating these insights into our administrative structures at both strategic and tactical levels.

The relationship between cultural and natural is similarly under increasing scrutiny both nationally and internationally. Of particular note is the recent definition of cultural landscape by UNESCO in relation to World Heritage designations. This aims to transcend the boundaries between the existing categories of cultural and natural sites in recognition of the fact that the landscape is often important as a combination of the two (Prott 1992, 73-4; ICOMOS 1993, 5-6). Usually, however, such considerations are led from either the natural or the cultural side and fall short of being truly integrated. As a result they fail to gain the maximum value of a truly inter-disciplinary approach, where different disciplines contribute to each other and all inform and enrich the whole. There is far greater potential to the inter-relationship between disciplines than merely recognising physical overlap in their management, as the following example of the relationship between archaeology and nature conservation might demonstrate.

There is considerable widespread recognition of the importance of natural biodiversity, and strategies are being devised to manage this resource sustainably for the future (e.g. IUCN, UNEP and WWF 1991). However, both our understanding of the diversity of the natural world and the management of it can be enhanced in a number of ways by considering the historical context that helped create it and which continues to affect it. At the level of physical landscape, the presence of archaeological and historical features contributes to the variety which supports diverse wildlife. Such remains can be as significant in inspiring a sense of place as the natural components of the landscape. Moreover, in many cases it was the original use of historical features that encouraged or introduced many species that now contribute to the natural diversity. This is particularly evident in designed landscapes, but occurs in other contexts as well; for instance wild celery still survives at Craigmillar Castle in Midlothian, where it was imported for use in the kitchen in the medieval period. In other cases it is the colonisation and influence of earlier structures that supports diverse populations; for example, barn owls and bats inhabit ancient monuments, particularly with the increasing loss of their traditional nesting sites in farm buildings; and the lime mortar used in medieval buildings can lead to localised lime-rich grassland supporting a wide variety of species, as at Tantallon Castle in East Lothian. In these situations, the management of the historical and natural aspects of landscape needs to be closely aligned to maintain overall diversity.

When enhancement of the natural environment is proposed through the reintroduction of native species, archaeological investigation, historical research and palaeobotanical analysis can help to ensure that our choices are historically accurate and suitable for the particular location (Barber and Welsh 1992, 42-6). Such work can also contribute to our understanding of important modern environmental problems, such as soil erosion, not only by demonstrating specific examples of where this has occurred previously, but also by improving our general understanding of the complex interaction between human actions and the state of the environment over time, as considered above. Investigations, such as in the Bowmont Valley in Roxburghshire, have demonstrated how erosion and depositional processes have been affected by human management practices on the one hand, and have themselves affected evidence of that management on the other (Mercer and Tipping 1988; Mercer pers. comm.; cf Bell 1982, 132). In helping to

106

establish the results of past management practices and their effects on the present landscape and biodiversity, such research could help to ensure that management decisions made now are set within a longer perspective and are as appropriate as possible. For instance, comparing the modern farming pattern with the post-medieval landscape might suggest that modern crofting should be the norm rather than the exception in order to sustain the environment successfully and support a dispersed human population (cf Willis 1991, 28-33; SCU and RSPB 1992, 18-20).

Similarly, investigations carried out for the understanding of the natural aspects of the landscape can benefit our understanding of the archaeological and historical heritage. For example, such research can provide valuable information about the environment on which past societies depended, the resources that were available and the types of land-use that were introduced. Moreover, the management of an area for its natural interest, such as a Site of Special Scientific Interest or National Scenic Area, can enhance the setting of specific archaeological and historical features which would otherwise be managed as individual sites, thereby giving a better impression of their original context in the landscape.

Such connections between archaeology and nature conservation can be used to enhance the management of each interest, both strategically and tactically. This sort of inter-relationship could, moreover, be explored in a similar way between many different disciplines, such as conservation and farming. Recognising the potential value of such links could enrich our understanding of the landscape as a whole and lead to a more integrated approach to its management. In many cases, this approach would lead to a richer and more varied landscape than management for a single purpose might achieve. There might be more cooperation, less need for competition, a fuller understanding of the nature of the modern landscape and the human impact on it, and a greater respect for the huge diversity of elements that constitute it. The potential for conflict between different interests could be reduced by maximising the mutual benefits of managing different aspects of the landscape, and by undertaking research to develop appropriate methodologies and techniques to achieve these ends. Furthermore, the educational potential of recognising the value of the whole landscape and of demonstrating the underlying unity between apparently diverse interests is immense. This is a particularly important challenge for the field of environmental education.

THE VALUE OF INTERPRETATION

An important key to developing a more integrated approach to landscape is interpretation. Like other landscape interests, interpretative schemes have also tended to be compartmentalised more often than integrated. Yet interpretation can allow all aspects of a landscape to be explored and brought together for purposes of enjoyment, education and demonstration. It can lead by providing models to follow. One example might serve to illustrate its potential benefits.

The Kilmartin Glen in Argyll is very rich archaeologically. The area is particularly well-known for its funerary and ritual landscape of Neolithic and Bronze Age date, comprising burial cairns, a stone circle, a henge and standing stones (Ritchie 1988, 48-52). There are also significant monuments of later date, including the hillfort of Dunadd, an early capital of the Scots. It is in addition an important scenic area, with considerable natural heritage interest, including a Site of Special Scientific Interest and a National Nature Reserve. Other features of natural and historic interest abound, including several forest trails and the Crinan Canal, a major monument to the industrialisation of Scotland.

This area has far greater potential for interpreting the landscape as a whole than is being achieved at present. Many individual elements in this landscape are open to the public, and current interpretation focuses on these separate features, particularly the numerous archaeological sites in state care. Within our present compartmentalised approach, individual organisations concentrate on their own areas of interest, with no easy mechanism to link these into an interpretation of the landscape as a whole.

However, a new initiative is seeking to integrate the disparate efforts that have been applied to this landscape. The numerous organisations, both national and local, with concerns and responsibility for various aspects of the landscape gathered recently to discuss how to work together to achieve a greater whole. A report is presently being prepared which will identify the range of interests, as well as the aims and aspirations of the individual groups, and suggest how these might be linked together more effectively. There may be several unifying themes, but it is already clear that a major one will be the relationship between people and the landscape over time. This theme could lead, for example, to the interpretation of archaeological features in the context of their natural environment, helping an appreciation of how they originally functioned, as well as why some survive and others do not. Similarly, the impact of the Crinan Canal on the landscape could be charted from its original industrial use to its current value for wildlife and recreation; or the effect of the extensive peat extraction at the end of the last century on the landscape as a whole could be documented more fully.

In demonstrating the links between individual elements of the landscape, both natural and cultural, and showing the complex way they have interacted with each other, this approach to interpretation could enrich people's understanding and enjoyment of the landscape around them. It also has potential benefits for both education and tourism. Furthermore, interpretation on this basis could give a broader perspective to the continuing management of the land by setting the modern forest environment within its natural and historical context, for instance, or showing how farming has shaped the landscape over time. This might lead, moreover, to a greater recognition of the diversity of features within the modern landscape and better accommodation of their individual management needs. Appreciation of such factors is an important basis for sustaining diversity within the landscape, improving cooperation between different organisations and achieving a management strategy that accommodates a wide range of interests.

TOWARDS A COMMON LANGUAGE

This paper has explored how a consideration of time-depth can affect our perceptions of landscape, and in particular challenge our view of it as either cultural or natural. The example of archaeology and nature conservation has sought to demonstrate how the links between different disciplines can work together for their mutual benefit and, as a result, lead to a more integrated approach to the understanding and management of landscape. The approach illustrated here could be applied in many other contexts and could make a valuable contribution in the move towards maintaining diversity within the landscape and achieving a sustainable approach to the environment.

Taking further steps towards such an integrated approach to the landscape requires that we continue to transcend the barriers between different interests and organisations. It also requires that we develop more partnerships on specific projects so that we can begin to gain a broader understanding of how individual aspects of the landscape fit together and complement each other. Furthermore, by establishing the dialogues necessary to achieve aims of mutual benefit, we may begin to develop a common language that reflects this more integrated approach. As a result we might achieve a greater awareness of, and respect for, the landscape itself, recognising the essential unity behind its diversity.

The author

Dr Lesley Macinnes is a Principal Inspector of Ancient Monuments with Historic Scotland. She wishes to thank G.J. Barclay, D.J. Breeze and W.S. Hanson for their helpful comments on earlier drafts of this paper.

References

Barber, J. and Welsh, G.M., *The potential and the reality: the contribution of archaeology to the green debate*, in Macinnes and Wickham-Jones 1992b, pp.41-51.

Barclay, G.J., *Excavations at Upper Suisgill, Sutherland*, Proc. Soc. Antiq. Scot 115, 1985, pp.159-98.

Barker, G.W.W. and Jones, G.D.B., *The UNESCO Libyan Valleys survey: palaeo- economy and environmental archaeology in the pre-desert*, Libyan Studies 13, 1982, pp.1-34.

Barrett, J, Hill, P. and Stevenson, J.B., *Second millennium BC banks in the Black moss of Achnacree: some problems of prehistoric land-use*, in Burgess, C. and Miket, R. (eds)

Settlement and economy in the third and second millennia BC, Oxford, 1976, pp.283-7.

Bell, M., *The effects of land-use and climate on valley sedimentation*, in Harding, 1982, pp.127-142.

Blunden, J. and Curry, N., *A future for our countryside*, Oxford, 1988.

Burgess, C., *The age of Stonehenge*, London, 1980.

Burgess, C., *Volcanoes, catastrophe and the global crises of the late second millennium BC*, Current Archaeology 117, 1989, pp.325-329.

Clark, C., *The brown debate: archaeology; ecology; and derelict land*, in Macinnes and Wickham-Jones 1992b, pp.146-51.

Coones, P., *One landscape or many? A geographical perspective*, Landscape Hist. 7, 1985, pp.5-12.

Coones, P., *The unity of landscape*, in Macinnes and Wickham-Jones 1992b, pp.22-40.

Dugmore, A.J., *Tephrochronology and UK archaeology*, in Budd, P, Chapman, D, Jackson, C, Jannaway, R. and Ottaway, B. (eds) Archaeological sciences, Oxford,1989,pp.242-50.

Edwards, R., *Fit for the future; report of the national parks review panel*, Cheltenham, 1991.

Evans, D., *A history of nature conservation in Britain*, London, 1992.

Fulford, M. and Nichols, E. (eds), *Developing landscapes of lowland Britain. The archaeology of the British gravels: a review*, London, 1992.

Harding, A.F. (ed), *Climate change in later prehistory*, Edinburgh, 1992.

Hodges, R.,*Wall-to wall history: the story of Roystone Grange*, London,1991.

Hoskins, W.G.,The *making of the English landscape*, (third edition), London, 1977.

ICOMOS, *World Heritage Cultural Criteria and Guidelines*, ICOMOS Landscapes Working Group newsletter (January 1993), (International Council on Monuments and Sites), 1993,pp.1-7.

IUCN, UNEP and WWF, *Caring for the earth. A strategy for sustainable living*, (The World Conservation Union, United Nations Environment Programme and the World Wide Fund for Nature), Gland, Switzerland,1991.

Jones, M.,*Progress in Norwegian cultural landscape studies*, Norsk Geografisk Tidsskrift 42,1988, pp.153-69.

Jones, M.,*The elusive reality of landscape. Concepts and approaches in landscape research*, Norsk Geografisk Tidsskrift 45,1991, pp.229-44.

Macinnes, L., *Preserving the past for the future*, in Hanson, W.S. and Slater, E.A. (eds), Scottish archaeology: new perceptions, Aberdeen,1991,pp.196-217.

Macinnes, L., *Archaeology as land-use*, in Hunter, J. and Ralston, I. (eds), Archaeological resource management in the UK: an introduction, Stroud,1993,pp.243-55.

Macinnes, L. and Wickham-Jones, C.R., *Time-depth in the countryside: archaeology and the environment*, in Macinnes and Wickham-Jones 1992b, pp.1-13.

Macinnes, L. and Wickham-Jones, C.R. (eds), *All natural things: archaeology and the green debate*, Oxford, 1992b.

Mercer, R. and Tipping, R., *Bowmont Valley*, in University of Edinburgh Department of Archaeology 34th Annual Report, Edinburgh, 1988, p.23.

Miles, J., *Environmental conservation and archaeology: is there a need for integrated designations?* in Macinnes and Wickham-Jones 1992b, pp.97-104.

Pitts, M., *Manifesto for a green archaeology*, in Macinnes and Wickham-Jones, 1992b, pp.203-213.

Prott, L.V., *A common heritage: the World Heritage Convention*, in Macinnes and Wickham-Jones, 1992b, pp.65-86.

Pye-Smith, C. and Hall, C., *The countryside we want*, Bideford,1987.

RCAHMS, *North-East Perth: an archaeological landscape*, (Royal Commission on the Ancient and Historical Monuments of Scotland), Edinburgh, 1990.

Ritchie, A., *Scotland BC*, Edinburgh,1988.

Roberts, B.K., *Landscape archaeology*, in Wagstaff, J.M. (ed), Landscape and Culture, Oxford,1987, pp.77-95.

SCU and RSPB, *Crofting and the environment: a new approach*, (Scottish Crofters Union and the Royal Society for the Protection of Birds), Inverness, 1992.

Simmons, I.G.,*Changing the face of the earth: culture, environment, history*, Oxford,1989.

Smith, K., *Protected landscapes: integrated approaches to conservation management*, in Macinnes and Wickham-Jones,1992b, pp.127-33.

Tait, A.A., *The landscape garden in Scotland 1735-1835*, Edinburgh, 1980.

Whittle, A., *Climate, grazing, man*, in Harding 1982, pp.192-203.

Willis, D., *The story of crofting in Scotland*, Edinburgh,1991.

Plate 1 The fishing village of Crail nestling in the coastal landscape of Fife

Plate 2 The powerful presence of Slioch towering above Loch Maree in the Wester Ross National Scenic Area

A JOURNEY THROUGH SCOTLAND

John Foster

As will be evident in this brief journey through space and time, my view of Scotland is essentially of a country with many facets, a country in which it is impossible to be bored if one has an eye to see and a mind to comprehend. It is also a country of great contrasts, from the crowded cities of the central belt, through a variety of handsome country towns and a multitude of villages and tiny hamlets to the sparsely populated countryside and coast of the Highlands and Islands.

Much of Scotland is a working countryside and the buildings in it are therefore an integral part of it. Farming goes on wherever possible, from the fertile lowlands of Central Scotland to the high mountain country of the far North West, and because it is such a long-settled country, our view of its physical character, its scenery, is very much coloured by our knowledge of its many past events and people.

This interaction between place and people over many centuries has produced its own distinctive pattern of history and culture, from the prehistoric standing stones of Stenness on Orkney, through the many ancient castles round our coast, to the very different, and so functional, buildings of our own day and age.

There are also the vagaries of our oceanic climate with frequent gales, Arctic conditions on our mountain tops and periodic coastal haar. An ever changing pattern of weather through the seasons is the outstanding characteristic of the Scottish climate which governs our lives, with sun and cloud alternating in a wholly unpredictable medley of light and shade.

Let us start our exploration of Scotland in my birthplace, **Glasgow** so recently European City of Culture, although an ancient place with a university founded in 1451. Here the 18th Century Tobacco Lords traded to their great advantage with the fast developing Americas and from here too in more recent times countless ships were launched which made 'Clyde built' known worldwide.

Part of the wonder of Glasgow for me, however, is not so much within the city itself, but what lies close by. **Only a few miles away is Loch Lomond**, with the islands of the Highland Fault at its southern end and Ben Lomond dominating its northern reaches. From the slopes of the Ben, looking west can be seen the spread of **the Arrochar Alps** - Beinn Ime, Beinn Vane and The Cobbler - all so beloved of the tough Glasgow school of mountaineers in the lean years of the 1930s.

Looking west too, many Glaswegians can recall the great days of the Clyde pleasure steamers, of which only the Waverley now hangs precariously to life. These steamers sailed to many places, favourite among them **Rothesay and the Kyles of Bute**, whose vicinity was changed for a time during the 1970s by the huge onshore oil development at Ardyne. This, like the steamers, is history also and the site is now a modest fish farm.

From **the high road to Tighnabruaich**, west of the Kyles of Bute, the mountains of North Arran make a distinctive skyline and on Arran itself, at the north west tip, the ruin of Lochranza Castle reminds us that here in 1306 Robert Bruce landed on his return from Rathlin Island to fight another day for Scotland. Crossing **over the Roof of Arran by Goatfell** and dropping down to Brodick is another castle, the traditional seat of the Dukes of Hamilton, with its 18th century formal garden.

Across the Clyde estuary from Brodick lies **the rich coastal farmland of Ayrshire.** One of its most prominent headlands is National Trust for Scotland property. On it stands **Culzean Castle**, a fine Adam building and the seat of the Kennedy family. Since 1969, the Culzean policies have also been a Country Park, the first to be established in Scotland, and now enjoyed by well over a quarter of a million visitors every year.

In this fertile part of Ayrshire, one time **home of the young Robert Burns**, we can appreciate some of the changes which have occurred in Scottish agriculture since the last war. Manual labour, horse-drawn machinery and steam engines have been replaced by diesel power and electricity. The once familiar round hay ricks have largely disappeared; instead outsize helpings of 'shredded wheat' now rest uncomfortably in the harvested fields. Pigs and poultry have almost completely disappeared into large, intensive-rearing sheds, leaving only a few hens running about here and there to remind us of times past.

Further south in **the Stewartry of Kirkcudbright,** dry-stane dykes have long been a feature, as they are in many other parts of Scotland. The tradition is very much kept alive here in the biennial competition of the Stewartry Dry-stane Dyking Association which draws dykers from far north in Scotland and from all the way down the Pennines. This is also the home of the well-known breed of cattle called the Belted Galloway and of its less familiar all white cousin with black ears.

The towns hereabouts, sturdy places of stone and slate, have long had a tradition of painted buildings, fitting homes for the many artists who have settled here over the years. The Stewarty is also home to **Dundrennan Abbey**, where looking down the long nave to the skeleton of its once magnificent west window, visitors are led to wonder on the thoughts of Mary Queen of Scots as she passed this way on her last journey to England and an untimely execution.

On our way eastwards, let us briefly go north, to the bare moorland country where **Leadhills** and **Wanlockhead** share the honour of being the highest villages in Scotland. In Leadhills there is an old Miners' Library founded in 1741 and in the churchyard a memorial to the late John Taylor, a tenacious soul who clung to life in this bleak place for all of 137 years.

Moving on, **the Borders**, renowned for its great abbeys and many fine mansions, has witnessed a number of changes in recent years. Forests now climb over many of the once bare Border hills. **The Megget Valley** has greatly changed in character, with the construction of the massive reservoir there to help keep Edinburgh supplied with clean water.

Fortunately, much of the long-standing border scene remains. **The Tweed still flows**, as it did in Sir Walter Scott's time, through a manicured landscape of field and woodland. And **St Mary's Loch** has changed little since James Hogg, the Ettrick Shepherd, a poet and contemporary of Scott, looked down on it in his own lifetime from the hills he knew so well.

At its eastern limit the border country drops dramatically into the North Sea in a long line of cliffs and bays. At **St Abbs Head** there is a spectacular clifftop nature reserve. Here the National Trust for Scotland and the Scottish Wildlife Trust collaborate in protecting this popular headland and its wildlife habitat for all of us to enjoy.

Down the coast from St Abbs, the little fishing port and holiday resort of **Eyemouth** has a splendidly protected harbour. Out beyond the harbour, in the bay, one day in 1881, when the fishing fleet was still under sail, a disastrous storm blew up and 189 local fishermen lost their lives. A magnificent tapestry, comprising a million stitches, was made by the people of Eyemouth for the centenary of that terrible event and now takes pride of place in the local museum.

Moving northwards across the fertile farmland of West Lothian, **the City of Edinburgh** soon appears, dominated by its ancient castle. Scotland's capital since the 12th Century, few cities offer so many contrasts within their boundaries. It has **its venerable Royal Mile and its magnificent Georgian New Town**; there is the wildness of Arthur's Seat standing guard over Holyrood Palace, and Cramond within the city's boundary seems a hundred miles from the bustle of Princes Street. It is hardly surprising that Benjamin Disraeli called Edinburgh 'the most beautiful city in the world'.

The Central Belt of Scotland has long been a place of industry. Grangemouth with all its trappings of the oil age big time exemplifies this perhaps better than anywhere, while the old mills and tall stone houses of **New Lanark**, now happily restored and a candidate for the World Heritage List, testify to the pioneering age of the first industrial revolution when David Dale and Richard Arkwright established a planned village there in 1784.

Much has happened since the heyday of New Lanark and mining and heavy industry have taken their toll on the once green countryside of this part of Scotland. But great strides in restoration have been made in recent years and not all of the countryside of the Central Belt was destroyed by industry. **Almondell Country Park** in West Lothian, where children can learn about things natural and see them at first hand in a still unspoilt river valley, is just one of many places now protected for the benefit of present and future generations.

Out at the eastern limit of the Central Belt is the **Kingdom of Fife** the south coast of which, along the Forth estuary, King James VI called its 'fringe of gold'. Today that fringe has the jewels of its fishing settlements still firmly sewn into it - **Crail**, the most far flung, **Elie, St Monance, Pittenweem and Anstruther**, still a fishing port of consequence. Here a fisheries' museum not only tells the story of far distant fishing grounds, but also gives a fascinating glimpse of domestic life in **the East Neuk of Fife** in times past.

Nearby is **Largo**, where the figure of Alexander Selkirk, better known as Robinson Crusoe, looks down on the place that has not forgotten him even after 300 years. Inland, **under the shadow of the Lomond Hills, is Falkland Palace** with a history stretching back five centuries or more and a royal tennis court that is almost as old.

North from Fife we reach **the Royal Burgh of Perth**, formerly St. Johnstoun, one time capital of Scotland. Here in 1559 in St John's Church John Knox preached his sermon urging the 'purging of the churches from idolatry', which raised a destructive storm far beyond his intentions. Today Perth is a mature and confident town, sitting comfortably along the banks of the broad River Tay in the knowledge that it is rivalling Inverness as the fastest growing town in Scotland. But Perthshire is also synonymous with the Highland Fault and with holiday towns such as **Pitlochry, Dunkeld and Crieff**, which looks south to the rounded lowland hills of the Ochils and west to the southern outliers of the more rugged mountains of the Highlands.

Further into this mountain edge is the long, narrow glen containing Loch Voil. This is the country of **Rob Roy Macgregor** who gave the word 'blackmail' its earliest meaning in our language. After his turbulent young years and, surprisingly, a relatively tranquil later life, he lies buried in the **old churchyard at Balquidder with his wife and his son Coll.**

Moving west, the annual rainfall increasing every mile along the road, the aspect changes and the softer country of Central and Southern Scotland gives way to **Caledonia**, stern and wild, so much portrayed, written and sung about over the centuries. **Rannoch Moor**, were it not for the trunk road which slices through it, would surely be the nearest thing in Scotland to wilderness. This is the kind of scene the 18th century historian, Edward Gibbon, described so tellingly as 'Foul weather, desolate landscape, backward and unfriendly natives'!

Beyond Rannoch is **Glencoe**, often dark and forbidding, reminding those who traverse it of the dark deeds of the infamous massacre of 1692, which even today neither the Campbells nor Macdonalds are allowed to forget.

Glencoe today is under the protection of the National Trust for Scotland, as are two other places in the Highlands which have similar melancholic connotations. One of these is **Glenfinnan where Prince Charles Edward Stuart raised his standard** at the east end of Loch Shiel in 1745 prior to his army's long triumphant march to Derby. At that time Glenfinnan was anything but a place of melancholy, but in one short year of history it was to become so. The second place is **Culloden Moor** where the aspirations of the

116

Jacobites to the throne died at the hand of Cumberland's soldiery along with more than a thousand clansmen on 16 April 1746.

South from Culloden is the Grampian Massif, with **Cairngorm and the Lairig Ghru** at its heart. **Aviemore,** with its multi-million pound centre serves the tourist and provides its own dry ski-ing facilities when there is no snow on the mountain tops. But important though Aviemore is to the local economy, the true heritage of Scotland lies elsewhere, high above the Strath where the mountains stretch to the horizon and the chairlift stops only 400 vertical feet below the summit of Cairngorm, at the Ptarmigan Restaurant, designed by Jan Magnus Fladmark as a young architect. This much used mountain has many problems, not least those derived from a sheer lack of understanding of its Arctic climate by many of those who ski and climb on it.

Out beyond the Grampians to the north-east is that hard knob of land called **Aberdeenshire** - tough farming country, but also the country of the great castles of Mar, which surely must be as much a part of Scotland's heritage as the soil on which they stand, as is indeed the greatest collection of standing stones in the whole of Scotland. The soil itself is worked to good effect, not least **in the magnificent parterre garden at Pitmedden.**

Like Edinburgh and Perth, **Aberdeen** is an ancient place. Its earliest charter as a royal burgh goes back to 1179 and the foundation of St Machar's Cathedral to the 14th Century. Today the city is a busy, thriving place - academically, with its second university, The Robert Gordon University, proclaimed just last year and, commercially, with a North Sea oil and gas servicing and supply base which has brought great prosperity in the past couple of decades. But its most distinctive feature is undoubtedly the granite from which so much of it is built - a stone which has made it known the world over as the Granite City.

The coast in these parts has its quota of fishing villages. Well placed though they are in sheltered bays, the houses above the beach nevertheless hunch their gables against the fierce North Sea gales. Back **along the Moray Firth, by Lossiemouth and Findhorn,** the coast takes on a different aspect - one of flat shingle beaches stretching as far as the eye can see.

Moving to the west, at Loch Duich, the imposing peaks of **the Five Sisters of Kintail** make a dramatic skyline. One of the outstanding features of this part of the west coast is the contrast of sea loch and mountain. The deep fjords in from the Sound of Sleat, Loch Nevis and Loch Hourn, hold between them **the high country of Knoydart,** with its fine deer forest and its special qualities of remoteness where the hand of man has had little impact.

North of Kyle of Lochalsh is **Lochcarron,** where, in sharp contrast to the wilds of Knoydart **there are palm trees in the little village of Plockton** thanks to the beneficial Gulf Stream. Across from Plockton, on the Atlantic shore of the Applecross Peninsula is **Applecross Village** which, until a few years ago, was an isolated place indeed, accessible only by boat or **over the high pass of the Bealach Nan Bo.** Today visitors can drive right round Applecross Peninsula in an afternoon on the new road opened in 1976.

Travelling northwards and inland we come to that classic of north-west highland lochs, **Loch Maree,** dominated on its north side by the powerful presence of Slioch. Nearby is **Gairloch**, much changed by tourism, and expanded greatly since the war. A few miles away, at **Inverewe**, it is hard to believe that 120 years ago, when Osgood McKenzie took over the land, there was little except a stunted tree or two. Now, under the management of the National Trust for Scotland, its rich range of vegetation draws visitors from many lands.

Driving north from Inverewe, before reaching Ullapool, there is **the spectacular gorge of Corrieshalloch** - a walk across its flimsy suspension bridge is an experience to be remembered!

Ullapool was a planned town established by the British Fisheries Association two centuries ago and today it is still a trim and orderly place, busy with visitors in summer. Founded on fishing, Ullapool remains a fishing port, although today catches are more often transferred to eastern European factory ships out in Loch Broom rather than being brought ashore for the home market.

This north-west corner of Scotland has a special character of wildness and remoteness which is accentuated by the way the individual mountains rise so abruptly from the relatively flat rock, heather and bog. Out beyond Kinlochbervie, the hard road ends at the tiny crofting settlement of Sheigra, ten miles south of **Cape Wrath, the last inhabited land on this coast.**

So much for the mainland of Scotland - what about the 800 or more islands scattered around the coast? Moving north first, across the Pentland Firth from John O' Groats we come to **Orkney**, which, in comparison to the rugged mountains and moorlands of the northern mainland we find a relatively green country, busy with farming wherever soil and shelter will allow.

But Orkney has its high drama of scene also, no more so than on the west coast of Hoy. The 450 feet High Stac of the **Old Man of Hoy**, first climbed only about 30 years ago, is backed by spectacular sandstone cliffs. Other vertical features, seen locally, very different in scale, are whalebones used as fence posts, reminding us of Orkney's past links with the sea.

Orkney has long been a place of human activity, from the **ancient houses at Scara Brae**, more than 4,000 years old, through long-standing settlements such as Kirkwall, the capital, dominated by the massive form of **the Norman cathedral of St Magnus**, to a more recent example of man's ingenuity, **the Churchill Barriers which protected Scapa Flow** from enemy submarines during the last war. Close to one of these barriers is another war-time reminder, the so-called Italian Chapel, now a carefully protected monument to the Italian prisoners of war who patiently changed an old Nissen hut into a place of worship, using whatever odd bits of wood and timber they could find.

The most recent evidence of man's ingenuity is quite different - **on Flotta there is now an oil terminal**, a vast operation carefully designed to fit into the local environment, in both social and visual terms. This is one of Scotland's oil development success stories and it moves us logically on to **Shetland**, to another huge development, this time on Sullom Voe. In its day, this was the largest civil engineering construction site in Western Europe. While Orkney absorbed its oil enterprise successfully, the same cannot be said of Shetland, where oil brought great changes to the social and economic make-up of the island group, quite apart from changing its physical appearance.

Shetland, like Orkney, has its human roots deep in the past. **The Broch at Mousa** probably goes back to pre-Christian times, the Castle at Scalloway, at one time capital of the islands, is almost 400 years old, and **in Lerwick, Britain's most northerly town**, the festival of 'Up Helly Aa' is an annual reminder of the ancient Scandinavian origins of the people of these parts.

Shetland also has a very distinctive physical appearance. The islands are bare, virtually treeless, offering little natural shelter to man or beast. Their rocky coastline is thick with offshore skerries and on the high cliffs of **the Gate of the Giants at Esha Ness** the sea pinks underfoot have the shortest stems in Scotland to protect them from the fierce Atlantic gales.

West of the Scottish mainland are the Hebrides, a pride of islands known far beyond Scotland for their great scenic qualities. The islands of **the Inner Hebrides** lie close to the mainland coast and there is great interplay between the two elements of island and mainland.

Skye is perhaps the most widely known of all the islands, through story and song as well as scenery. **Sailing into Loch Scavaig** in the light of the early morning, few could fail to be moved by the sight of the Cuillins' rocky outline, knowing that behind the coast ahead lies Loch Coruisk, held deep within a tight ring of gabbro ridges.

Within sight of the Cuillins, to the south, are the so-called **Small Isles** of Canna, Rhum, Muck and Eigg. Looking out from the shore at Glen Brittle, on Skye, **Canna** fills the horizon. It is a green island with a long human history, although today it is the home of a mere handful of people compared with the four hundred who lived on the island in the last century.

Across the Sound of Canna is **Rhum**, which, by comparison, is a large, brooding island, the summits of Halival and Askival rising to more than 2,500 feet. A National Nature Reserve, owned by the Nature Conservancy Council in 1957, Rhum, like Canna, was once a busy place. It bears evidence of the sad human story common to much of the Highlands and Islands, of poverty and emigration, voluntary and otherwise. Here, **from the township of Kilmory**, 400 islanders emigrated to Canada in 1827, leaving behind only the graveyard and the ruins of their croft and the wild ponies that still graze the machair hereabouts.

On Loch Scrisort, by contrast, **is Kinloch Castle**, the showplace built by Sir George Bullough at the beginning of the century, in its day a world away from the traditional lifestyle of the local people. Stranger even than the castle is the imposing Bullough mausoleum, standing among the lazy old beds in a remote bay on the west side of the island.

To the south of Rhum is **Muck**, the smallest of the island group, and **Eigg** with its distinctive barrel-shaped sgurr which identifies it so unmistakably from the mainland.

Moving down the mainland coast, across the long peninsula of Ardnamurchan, **the Island of Mull** dominates the view out from Oban.

Duart Castle, seat of the Macleans for more than seven centuries, guards the promontory where the Firth of Lorn meets the Sound of Mull.

On Mull things are very different in scale from the Small Isles. Its main town of **Tobermory** is home to 600 folk, where a century ago there were 2,000. Mull has many aspects to its character from the bare rocky summit of Ben More to the remote shores of Loch Scridain with its 1,200 feet high cliffs and **50 million years old fossil trees at Burg**.

West of Mull is **the Island of Iona**, reached from Fionnphort by ferry boat. In contrast to the more forbidding mountain country of Mull across the Sound, Iona is a sunny place, a place of green crofting land. The glory of Iona is its abbey and all that it stands for in the Christian history of Scotland. Beside it is **St Oran's cemetery**, Scotland's oldest Christian burial place where 48 Scottish, eight Norwegian, four Irish and two French kings are said to rest. Here, surely, is a prime example of where the built heritage, the abbey, and the scenic heritage, the island itself, come together, the one enhancing the other.

Within close range of the west coast of Mull there are other notable islands too, some, like **the Treshnish Isles** are small, in a sense little more than lumps of grass-covered rock rising above the sea, but each distinctive in its own way. One of them, **Staffa**, is unique in the geological story of Scotland. Along with Iona, it is in the care of the National Trust for Scotland.

Of all the islands south of Mull, the group which is my special favourite is the Garvellochs, **the Isles of the Sea**. There are four of them, lined astern in the Firth of Lorn, presenting steep cliffs to the open Atlantic and more gently sloping land on the sheltered eastern side. To one of those, we are told, St Columba used to withdraw from Iona at intervals for prayer and contemplation, and today the remains of an ancient monastery bear testimony to that legend. But the monks and the local inhabitants of these islands are all long gone. Only sheep, ferried over from the mainland, now graze on the old lazy beds and wild flowers are left to thrive in profusion.

Riding the Atlantic for 130 miles from Barra Head to the Butt of Lewis, is the long line of islands known as **the Outer Hebrides**. **Their capital is Stornaway**, a substantial town of 6,000 people, and an ancient settlement in its own right, but nowhere near as old as **the Callanish Stones**, 15 miles to the west, which date back three and a half thousand years.

Travelling south from Stornaway, the traditional form of cultivation of these parts, lazy beds, are still worked. Further south in Harris, the landscape becomes literally a rock desert, the worst land for crofting in the Hebrides, through which passes what is reputedly the most corkscrew road in Scotland.

In the western part of Harris, the juxtaposition of land and sea is at its most dramatic on the **machair coast at Luskentyre** and out past the 19th Century sporting lodge, where James Barrie gained the inspiration for his play *Marie Rose*, **to the road end at Husinish** where somehow a tiny crofting township still manages to survive in distant isolation.

Further south, on **Uists and Benbecula**, the predominant scene is one of a great confusion of land and freshwater lochans, with more water than land in many parts and the crofts crowding behind the coastal machair. On **Barra**,

Compton Mackenzie's last home, the scene is different again, with a dark backcloth of hills rising behind the village of Castlebay and the forbidding shape of the now restored Macneil stronghold of Kisimul Castle.

In the far south there is **Mingulay, an island immortalised in song**. It is a lonely place. The last of the local people -there were once forty families living on the island - left in Edwardian times. Their houses are now all but buried in the encroaching sand and the land they tended has long since been given over to sheep.

West from Mingulay, there is just one more place which is still Scotland, apart from Rockall. That, of course, is **St Kilda**, where the Nature Conservancy Council and the National Trust for Scotland came together to protect this far-flung island group, and where, at Village Bay on Hirta, the Trust has done so much to rebuild, painstakingly as a labour of love, so many of the old ruined houses of the islanders.

The last of the traditional community of St Kilda left in 1930, but they left their mark, not simply in **Village Bay**, but wherever sheep, now wild, still graze, as on the steep slopes of the island of Boreray, and wherever on the high cliffs they reaped the fulmar and gannet harvest, so vital to their existence.

Hard by Boreray, is Stac Lee, the largest gannetry in the northern hemisphere, only one of many reasons why St Kilda is not only an important part of the heritage of Scotland, but is now recorded on the World Heritage List.

In this remote place we end our brief journey through Scotland. It has been no more than a series of brief snapshots and very much more would need to be written to do anything like justice to this long-settled country of such remarkable contrasts and quality of scene. The challenge ahead for everyone with a concern for Scotland's future is how to sustain these contrasts and qualities in the face of the economic and other pressures which face the country today.

The author

John Foster, CBE, is Vice-Chairman of the Advisory Board for The Robert Gordon University Heritage Unit. Formerly Director and Chief Executive of the Countryside Commission for Scotland, he received a CBE in 1985 for his pioneering contribution to Scottish countryside policies. His slide-tape programme for visitors at the Commission's Battleby headquarters is remembered as a model to have inspired many, and the above text is based on notes for a presentation made in honour of Sir Jamie Stormont-Darling on his retirement as Director of the National Trust for Scotland in 1983.

References

Cooper, D., *The Road to Mingulay - A View of the Western Isles*, Routledge & Kegan Paul, 1985.

Countryside Commission for Scotland, *Scotland's Landscape Heritage*, CCS, 1978.

Countryside Commission for Scotland, *The Mountain Areas of Scotland - Conservation and Management*, CCS, 1990.

Fenton, A., *The Shape of the Past - Essays on Scottish Ethnology*, John Donald, 1985.

Fladmark, J.M. , Mulvagh, G.Y., & Evans, B.M., *Tomorrow's Architectural Heritage - Landscape and Buildings in the Countryside*, Mainstream, 1991.

Grimble, I., *Scottish Isles*, BBC, 1985.

Haldane, A.R.B., *The Drove Roads of Scotland*, David & Charles, 1952 (new edition 1973).

Hetherington, A. (ed.), *Highlands and Islands - A Generation of Progress*, Aberdeen Univ. Press, 1990.

Johnston, J.B., *Place-Names of Scotland*, S.R. Publishers Ltd., 1934. Reprinted 1976.

MacDonald, M., *The Clans of Scotland*, Brian Trood Publishing House, 1991.

Millman, R.N., *The Making of the Scottish Landscape*, Batsford, 1973.

Mitchison, R., *A History of Scotland*, Methuen, 1970.

Murray, S., *A companion and Useful Guide to the Beauties of Scotland (1799)*, Byway Books, 1982.

Murray, W.H., *Highland Landscape*, A Survey commissioned by the National Trust for Scotland, 1962.

Murray, W.H., *The Companion Guide to the West Highlands of Scotland*, Collins, 1968.

Naismith, J., *Buildings of the Scottish Countryside*, Gollancz, 1985.

Roy, K., *Travels in a Small Country - A Scottish Journey*, Carrick Publishing, 1987.

Smith, R., *Walking in Scotland*, Spurbooks, 1981.

Steven, C., *The Story of Scotland's Hills*, Robert Hale, 1975.

PLANNING FOR INTERPRETATION

Working Together in Partnership

Planning together,
is the key to securing
shared ownership
of policy and action

10

DISCOVERING
THE PERSONALITY OF A REGION
Strategic Interpretation in Scotland

Magnus Fladmark

This paper is about strategic planning of interpretation, sometimes referred to as regional interpretive planning, which should not be confused with the distinctly different activity of planning interpretation at a single site. As a methodology of working, the idea has been around in Britain for the last 25 years. The author traces how it was brought to Scotland, examines the main strategic initiatives mounted north of the Border under the leadership of the Countryside Commission for Scotland, and concludes by drawing some lessons that seem pertinent for future development of practice in this area of heritage work.

Two names have been closely associated with the introduction of interpretation to Britain, first to the national parks in England and Wales, and later to Scotland. They are John Foster and Don Aldridge, and the story started in the Peak District National Park where the former was appointed Director in 1954. There he pioneered the introduction of heritage interpretation into the operational procedures of the park, and he went to North America in 1964 for the specific purpose of studying how the concept of interpretation was practised in the US National Park Service. Don Aldridge was appointed the Peak's first Information Officer, also in 1964, and he obtained a Churchill Fellowship which enabled him to follow in Foster's footsteps to North America in search of knowledge.

THE PEAK BLUEPRINT 1966

These were early days. The book entitled *Interpreting Our Heritage* by Freeman Tilden, had been published less than ten years earlier, in 1957. Aldridge met Tilden on his travels and returned to the Peak imbued with great enthusiasm for the subject and set about converting ideas into reality. At a conference at Keele University in March 1965, Foster called for a national policy requiring interpretation to be a mandatory element of park planning in all national parks, and the earliest written evidence of success in this crusade is to be found in the First Review of the Peak Park Development Plan (1966). Chapter 12 of this document was headed *Information and Interpretation Service* and set out a strategic framework for the future.

The chapter bears witness to the persuasive powers of Foster and Aldridge. Board members had clearly accepted that the information service should be broadened to include 'interpretation' as reflected in the title, and the philosophical basis for their new policy was expressed as follows:

> . . . there has been a change of emphasis in the approach to visitor services, in that the Board have become increasingly concerned with the need to provide interpretation and not merely information. Interpretation involves giving more than purely factual information to visitors, by attempting to provide them with explanatory material which will enhance their enjoyment of the park. Interpretation too reveals relationships in the environment which can help visitors to understand park values, that is those scenic and recreational values which are considered to be of the greatest importance in the Peak.

The Peak authority had accepted that implementation of this philosophy required a new information base and the plan stated: 'Effective interpretation must begin with an inventory of the natural, archaeological and historical resources of the National Park, followed by the preparation of a master plan of interpretation.' It was proposed that an inventory be drawn up under the following headings: Geology; Geomorphology; Pedology; Ecology; Climatology and Meteorology; Archaeology and Pre-history; Social History, Saxon – Mediaeval; Social History, 17th to early 19th Century; Economic History of Agriculture, Forestry and Mining; Economic History of Transport and Mills.

The next step in the methodology was the choice of themes as a precursor to formulation of an integrated strategy for interpretation, and the plan went on to say that a selection would be made from the inventory:

> . . . of those major themes and concepts which can be presented to the public effectively in accordance with the principles of interpretation already stated. For example, there are important themes or stories in the natural and semi-natural landscape of the Peak which lend themselves to this treatment in that they underline the unique character of the region's physical landscape. Archaeology and prehistory and more recent social history have similar themes, like the story of Bronze Age and Romano-British settlement, the Royal Forest of the Peak and the romance of the castles and halls, and the growth of the early tourist industry. The history of enclosure, early lead mining, and the development of road, canal and rail transport

and the invention of the factory system are also features which lend themselves to thematic treatment.

The presentation to the public of the material of each theme could best be done through new visitor centres which would have a museum function, in that they would exhibit authentic specimens or reproductions and would make use of models and other modern museum techniques of presentation. Initially three new visitor centres would separate the themes into groups, and display one group of themes in each location. It is suggested that there should be (a) a museum of the physical environment, (b) a museum of archaeology and history, (c) a museum of industrial archaeology.

Another significant part of the methodology was based on the assumptions that strategic planning for interpretation could only be effectively implemented by working together in partnership, and that there has to be active collaboration with other agencies operating existing visitor facilities. The authors of the plan were quite specific on these two points by asserting that :

> . . . there must be closer co-operation between the Board's information and interpretation service and the Universities, Institutes of Education, adult and school education services, museums and land user interests in the Park (such as the National Farmers' Union and Forestry Commission), and also with those private individuals and companies who already successfully operate facilities which are broadly speaking interpretive in their nature.

To appreciate the true significance of these proposals, it is necessary to remember that the national parks were still in their infancy. Most park authorities were just starting to grapple with the basics of providing for visitors by printing guidebooks and information leaflets, and in the absence of evidence to the contrary it is safe to say that the 1966 Peak plan was the first real attempt to formulate a coherent methodology for strategic interpretation in Britain. It is referred to in this paper as the *Peak Blueprint* against which subsequent development of the concept will be measured. The five main elements of the methodology are clearly identified in the above passages: compiling a resource inventory, theme selection, avoiding duplication, strategy of delivery, and partnership in both preparation and implementation.

MOVING TO SCOTLAND

A study of how the Peak Blueprint evolved in practice over the next 20 years is best pursued north of the Border for the good reason that John Foster returned to Scotland in 1968 to become the first Director of the Countryside Commission for Scotland. His continued commitment to advancing the cause of heritage interpretation was signalled by Don Aldridge's early appointment as Assistant Director in charge of education and interpretation. Action was quick to follow and the first course on interpretation methods organised in

Scotland, possibly also a UK first, was held at Kindrogan in October 1969. The subject featured as a regular theme in the Commission's early annual reports, and a paper by Aldridge on *Regional and National Interpretive Plans*, which appeared in the Museums Journal (December,1973), gives an interesting state of the arts review.

In the absence of a strategic policy framework of any kind, the issue of duplication was a constant problem, and the Commission was clearly being called upon to arbitrate in cases where several developers were promoting similar and geographically overlapping proposals. The normal response was to set up working groups of affected parties to hammer out mutually acceptable plans to avoid unnecessary duplication and competition. Cited examples were visitor centre proposals for the Caledonian Pine Forest in Speyside and for the story of red deer in Torridon. Many other cases are referred to in annual reports, and Aldridge stressed the need for flexibility in these plans to allow for constantly changing circumstances.

From the perspective of a national agency, plans for specific areas stopped short of strategic consideration of whole regions. Citing the example of American national parks, Aldridge drew attention to the tendency for ignoring important sites outside the park system. He referred to the often neglected point that a region must be identified before it can be defined, and suggested a strategic national framework by saying that 'we could divide Scotland into ten or possibly twenty regions, each with a personality reflecting not only in its land form, but in its land use, vegetation and regional ethnology.'

The personality of a region is the most significant concept to emerge from Aldridge's article (see also under *Other Initiatives*). To discover this personality, he argued that the resource analysis needs to transcend and cut across subject boundaries. The study of time chronologies and spatial distribution must be combined to enable elucidation of criteria like significance and rarity, and he suggested that the strategist should start by posing the sort of questions that visitors may ask: *what happened here? did it always look like this? who lived here? how did they live?* The ideas discussed in the 1973 paper appeared as a chapter in a subsequent book by Aldridge, entitled *Principles of Countryside Interpretation and Interpretive Planning* (1975).

APPLICATION IN ORKNEY

Reorganisation of local government was in the wind, the new development pressures expected from the discovery of North Sea oil and gas gave urgency to action in certain parts of the country, and the first opportunity to apply the Peak Blueprint in Scotland came in the early 1970s. Foster gave the following account of this experience in his address to the First World Congress on Heritage Presentation and Interpretation in Banff fifteen years later:

> We cut our teeth on this concept in the Orkneys, using the local authority and voluntary organisations to draw together an inventory of the heritage

features which would demonstrate the 'personality' of the island group. A study of this inventory prompted two major themes for interpretation. The first was *the role of stone* in Orkney life. The second was *the changing land use* and its effect on landscape and wildlife.

. . . there was obvious scope for developing a number of sub-themes. For example, the stone story could relate the geological formation of easily worked flagstone to its widespread use by man, including stone 'furniture' in dwellings and farm buildings, from Skara Brae into the last century. Grinding stones too offered a continuous story from Iron Age querns to the many watermills, some still in use today.

The story of changing land use could incorporate sub-themes on the pattern of farming over the years and the effects of continuing land reclamation on Orkney's wildlife, especially moorland and marshland species. Another possibility was wartime in Orkney, identifying the construction of the Churchill Barriers to protect the fleet within Scapa Flow and demonstrating the effect of these on the adjoining shores.

We also identified other possible topics, perhaps not directly related to the principal themes, but nevertheless capable of being linked into them: the cliffs and their seabird colonies, the beaches with their special plant communities and the close relationship of Orkney with the sea through the herring industry, whaling and sea transport.

Having identified the themes, we were able to pick out from the inventory those elements which were already presented to the public and to assess how adequately this was done. We also identified the most important elements which were not yet presented and explored the feasibility of presenting these in a recognisably linked way, taking into account their particular sensitivities and the risk of damage by visitors.

From this emerged an overall regional interpretive plan which related the elements on the ground to opportunities for making a comprehensive range of interpretive provisions, avoiding duplication and using to best effect the variety of public and voluntary bodies available for the task. The plan also recommended the most suitable types of provision in each case and suggested priorities which were realistic in terms of available resources.

Finally, we looked at ways whereby the various locations and topics might be brought together in orientation terms in the two main towns of the islands at which visitors arrive by air or sea: places where strangers could readily get some initial understanding of the range of heritage features in the islands so that they could plan field visits to best effect.

Although the word 'sustainability' had yet to enter the vocabulary of environmentalists, the Orkney plan of 1974 was firmly based on the principle that visitor impact must not jeopardise the integrity of the natural and cultural heritage that is the subject of interpretation. Sites in the resource inventory were classed into the following categories:

1. Sites of great interpretive interest, capable of intensive development designed to take pressure from more vulnerable sites.
2. Sites of interpretive potential, capable of absorbing visitor pressure with car parks and footpaths but which might require some control of access due to environmental sensitivity.
3. Vulnerable sites to which attention should not be drawn.
4. Recreation sites where interpretive facilities might take advantage of the fact that people are gathering there already and a conservation message would thereby reach a large audience.

GRAMPIAN REGION

As might be expected, with the accelerating pace of oil related development, the next initiative came three years later in the North East at the behest of the then Director of Planning in Grampian Regional Council, Trevor Sprott. The Commission was invited to give advice and to support a project for producing a regional interpretation strategy, and it would appear that the approach to this task might have been influenced by a simulated game playing exercise sponsored by the Carnegie (UK) Trust that is described in Aldridge's 1973 article in the Museums Journal. Partnership through joint working was given top priority and the mainspring of the operation was an event, since referred to as 'the Aboyne Workshop', that took place there over three days in November 1976. The organisations invited by the sponsors to participate were the district councils, Scottish Office Ancient Monuments Division, Scottish Tourist Board, Forestry Commission, National Museum of Antiquities, Scottish Country Life Museums Trust, National Trust for Scotland, Royal Society for the Protection of Birds, the Scottish Wildlife Trust, the National Farmers' Union of Scotland and the Scottish Landowners' Federation.

The 36 participants were organised into five syndicate groups according to professional expertise and organisational interest, i.e. geology, natural history, cultural history, farming and forestry and fishing. No attempt was made to collate a comprehensive resource inventory in line with the Peak Blueprint. The brief for each group was simply to prepare a report that would: (i) identify heritage characteristics of the region suitable for interpretation; (ii) assess whether interpretation of selected themes was already adequate; and (iii) suggest specific sites where gaps in the market could be filled.

The outcome of the exercise was published as a report in 1977. It contained the findings of each group, which had been the subject of wide consultation, and these were drawn together into a strategic framework that was regarded as the start of an ongoing process. The enthusiastic mood of the time is reflected in the following passage:

> Much of the long-term benefit of a regional interpretive planning exercise of the kind described in this Report must, in fact, depend upon on-going liaison between all the organisations concerned. The benefits to be derived from frank consultation are well-known, and the tangible evidence of this lies in the production of this Report. Without the whole-hearted willingness of those involved, to exchange ideas freely and to inform others of their intentions for development, the production of an Outline Framework for Countryside Interpretation in Grampian would not have had the authority and standing which it now has.

It would appear that the intention of 'on-going liaison' was not pursued as vigorously as planned. However, the document became a valuable framework for strategic reference by decision-makers at national, regional and district levels during the following decade. So much so that the regional council decided to undertake a review and update in 1987, headed by their newly appointed regional archaeologist, Ian Shepherd. Thirty-six other bodies were consulted and a half-day forum was held to seek endorsement of revised policies. A quality assessment of existing facilities was attempted, comprising a total of 273 sites subdivided into 17 categories.

Environmental education was identified as a priority area for better market penetration of heritage interpretation. The means chosen to achieve this was, a *Directory of Environmental Study Sites* (1993) which has been compiled and published with support from Grampian Enterprise and Moray, Badenoch and Strathspey Enterprise. Categories of sites in the directory are agriculture, ancient monuments, country parks, ecclesiastical sites, outdoor centres, forest walks and forestry, great houses, industry, landed estates, long distance walks, museums and wildlife sites.

Another significant development in Grampian of some interest is the emergence of a hierarchical system of interpretation planning through a recent decision by Gordon District Council to prepare a *Countryside Interpretive Strategy* (1992), possibly the first time that this has been done by a district in the context of an existing regional framework. The two main aims of the Gordon strategy are to assign priorities to existing and proposed heritage initiatives, the most important being a visitor centre on Bennachie and an archaeological trail, and to provide a framework for more integrated delivery of interpretation and more effective use of the local ranger service. Although not specifically intended as a framework for community action, a recent initiative by Donside Community Council to promote *The Alford Nature Plan* (1992), with support from the Nature Conservancy Council, can be seen as an example of the emerging hierarchical system reaching down to grass roots level. The settlement is located in the Vale of Alford and is strategically important because of its proximity to Haughton Country Park and Bennachie, and the main thrust of the plan is heritage interpretation to benefit both local residents and visitors to the area.

CENTRAL REGION

Central Regional Council was the third local authority in Scotland to adhere to the spirit and methodology of the Peak Blueprint, following close on the heels of the original Grampian initiative. In its 1980 annual report, the Countryside Commission for Scotland refers to discussions with several regional authorities about promoting strategic plans. A two-day workshop in Stirling is mentioned the following year, and in 1984 the Council published its strategy with support from the Commission. The style of operation was the same as in Grampian with a strong emphasis on joint working and partnership. A series of workshops were held and subject groups were charged with providing specialist input to the report, and the range of organisations invited to participate was similar to that in Grampian.

The museum and education sectors would appear to have been equal partners to the planners who had provided the main impetus and leadership in Grampian. Environmental education was given pre-eminence from the start and the document was issued for use in schools. Whereas Grampian concentrated on the countryside, Central Region sought better integration of provision between rural and urban areas, and the latter adopted a descriptive rather than a prescriptive style in the final document. The Central Region authors 'stressed that inter-relationships between subjects are the key elements of interpretation' and the report provides a well integrated text of exemplary quality on the cultural heritage of the region. It may indeed have been the first public document of its kind in Scotland to have used the term 'cultural landscapes'. Although the term was not defined as such, the whole report can be regarded as one of the best Scottish texts produced on the subject of cultural landscapes.

LOCH LOMOND

While work on the Central Region strategy was in progress, the Loch Lomond Planning Group decided to form a special group of officials from the constituent authorities of what was later to become the Loch Lomond Park Authority to produce a plan of interpretation. Their first task was to review work done by a previous Technical Group in 1974, and after a year of deliberation the new group produced, *Loch Lomond Interpretive Plan : Draft for Discussion* (1984). As the fourth major Scottish initiative to adhere to both the spirit and methodology of the Peak Blueprint, it was perhaps the most inspired, partly thanks to Carol Swanson of Strathclyde Regional Council who carried out much of the work.

The general theme adopted by the plan was summarised in the word 'Crossroads' which represented an aggregation of the following sub-themes identified in 1974:

1. The physical junction of highland and lowland landscapes which produces scenic and biological crossroads (Highland Fault Line).

2. The known/unknown crossroads twixt the early explorers in pre-history and early historical times (Pictland, Dalriada and Strathclyde).
3. The routeways for exchange of ideas, trade and conflicts among people of different cultural backgrounds (clan raids, cattle bond boats, drove roads and military roads).
4. The spread of different ideologies and religious ideas, including the early church and modern tourism.
5. The present-day dynamism of multi-purpose land use.

Although some elements of the proposed strategy have been taken forward into subsequent park policies, it is a matter of some regret that an area considered by many to be worthy of national park status still has no formally adopted strategy for interpretation. Lack of resources and pressures by other priorities has left the Loch Lomond Park Authority unable to proceed with implementation as intended by the authors of the draft plan.

THE HIGHLANDS AND ISLANDS

The 1977 achievement of producing a strategy for interpretation in Grampian Region attracted much attention in heritage circles. It caused a rush of blood to the brains of politicians and officials alike, both in national agencies and local government, but the only other region to reach the goalposts to date was Central as described above. However, there have been several other initiatives which deserve a place in the early history of strategic interpretation in Scotland, although none of these were fully comprehensive in the sense of the Peak Blueprint and some have dealt with sub-regional areas only.

The first organisation in the North to make a move was the Highlands and Islands Development Board. They appointed David Hayes of Landmark to research and write a report that was published in 1979. The prime motivation for the study was a concern about the standard of provision for tourists, perceived to be low, and the task given to him was a qualitative review of heritage resources and interpretation at key sites within the Board's area.

For the purpose of study, the area was sub-divided into 17 parts, from the Isle of Bute in the South to Shetland in the North. He proposed that a strategy should be drawn up for the whole region, and the report specified the scope and format for local plans. To address the issue of quality assurance, the report had a section setting out detailed advice and guiding principles on how to go about developing a new visitor centre, valuable advice drawn from his own experience at Landmark and earlier studies in USA. The principal recommendation of the 'Hayes Report' were that:

1. There should be an overall strategy for the Highlands and Islands. This . . . should identify the gaps, both in terms of geographical distribution of major facilities and in terms of content, or principal themes.
2. There should be a series of local interpretive plans for each district, especially for those that are heavily dependent on the tourist trade.

3. Subsequent to the agreement of a strategy for the Highlands and Islands, the existing system of museums and visitor centres should gradually be expanded to form an integrated network covering all major aspects of our heritage.
4. It is suggested that there should be regular local meetings of all organisations and individuals involved in the interpretation of our heritage.
5. A local interpretive plan for a district in the Highlands should be drawn up and be implemented under Section 5 of the Countryside Scotland Act with the Countryside Commission for Scotland's and the Highlands and Islands Development Board's support.

Although the Countryside Commission's annual reports in the late 1970s refer to meetings taking place among interested parties, it seems that the above recommendations were not acted upon in the way intended by Hayes. However, the Commission accepted the challenge by obtaining support from Highland Regional Council to undertake two studies, 'to identify roadside locations, along the coast, from which it was possible to obtain views of the characteristic scenic types and principal settlement and land use patterns represented within the study area.'

The work was led by Valerie Thom and two reports appeared from her hand: *Countryside Interpretation in Wester Ross: Kyle of Lochalsh to Ullapool* (1981) and *Countryside Interpretation in North-West Scotland: Ullapool to Durness* (1981). Taken together they set out a strategy for a motoring trail for the entire coastal zone from Kyle of Lochalsh to Durness. A total of 38 sites with high quality views were selected, and it was proposed that trail leaflets be produced to provide interpretation of these views. A small leaflet for the *Wester Ross Coastal Route* was produced by the local tourist board, and the Nature Conservancy Council published a well illustrated broad sheet entitled, *Caithness and Sutherland: Places to Visit for Wildlife and Landscape* (1992). A recent report by Angela Mackay, *Interpretation of the Natural Environment in North West Sutherland* (1992), is an interesting attempt to identify ideas for interpretation by local people.

Thanks to its extensive geographical remit, the Hayes Report was by necessity a succinct document, and it devoted exactly half of one page to the Western Isles. The author observed that, ' . . . for any local resident or visitor interested in finding out more about the wider heritage of the Outer Hebrides there is at present nowhere to go.' Fifteen years later a consortium was formed of The Western Isles Island Council (Planning, Education and Museums), Western Isles Enterprise and Tourism Programme, Nature Conservancy Council and the Royal Society for the Protection of Birds. This partnership engaged the Centre for Environmental Interpretation to produce, *Western Isles Interpretation Strategy* (1992).

From the documentation available, it would appear that the study involved only part of the Peak methodology. A resource inventory as such was not compiled. From a combination of local knowledge, drawn from consortium members, and reconnaissance by the study team, the following themes were identified : the natural environment (The Machair Islands), the history of settlement (6000 Years Living Next to the Sea), Celtic/Gaelic culture (The Hebrides – Heartland of Gaelic Culture) and economy and employment (A Permanent Struggle for Human Survival).

The main elements of the strategy were a principal orientation centre in Stornoway; sub-centres in Castlebay, Lochboisdale, Lochmaddy and Tarbert; a network of small sites with shelters and leaflets; theme booklets and other publications; and priority was to be given to involving local people and support would be given to local historical societies. The report set out an exhaustive list of ideas for site-based capital works, together with revenue projects like a machair ranger service in South Harris and a management and training programme. Several of these proposals were being actively pursued by consortium members under the Western Isles Tourism Programme at the time of writing.

OTHER INITIATIVES

To the names of Foster and Aldridge, must be added those of Professor Alexander Fenton and Ross Noble. Both have made significant contributions to furthering the cause of strategic interpretation in Scotland. As the then Director of the National Museum of Antiquities, Fenton worked closely with Aldridge on several projects. One such project, pertinent to the subject of this paper, was a national strategy for folklife parks and museums. As early as 1971, Aldridge wrote a report for the Countryside Commission on *Folklife Parks as Interpretive Media*. In this appeared for the first time a map showing how Scotland might be divided into 12 ethnological regions. Although drawn for the purpose of museums planning, the proposed geographical sub-divisions would make a good basis for future regional strategies after suitable adjustment of boundaries to take account of landscape, hydrology, ecology and demography.

Two sub-regional initiatives are of interest in the Borders. One was centred on Biggar where the Gladstone Court Museum was opened in 1968. Within a few years the Trustees had commissioned Ross Noble, then Travelling Curator of the Scottish Country Life Museums Trust, to prepare proposals for an open-air museum and centre for the interpretation of local culture. His report, *Country Heritage: An Interpretive Plan for Biggar and District* (1976), was clearly inspired by the Peak methodology. Although only partial in scope, the Biggar proposals were formulated under the assumption that they would 'contribute to a regional interpretive plan (still awaited) which will include provisions and services operated by a variety of organisations and individuals.' Noble set out a table of possible locations for interpretive centres and identified appropriate media which were listed against proposed themes and story lines with a strong emphasis on ethnological chronologies.

The other sub-regional initiative in the Borders came 16 years later when Scottish Borders Enterprise engaged the Centre for Environmental Interpretation to undertake, *The River Tweed Interpretation Strategy* (1992).

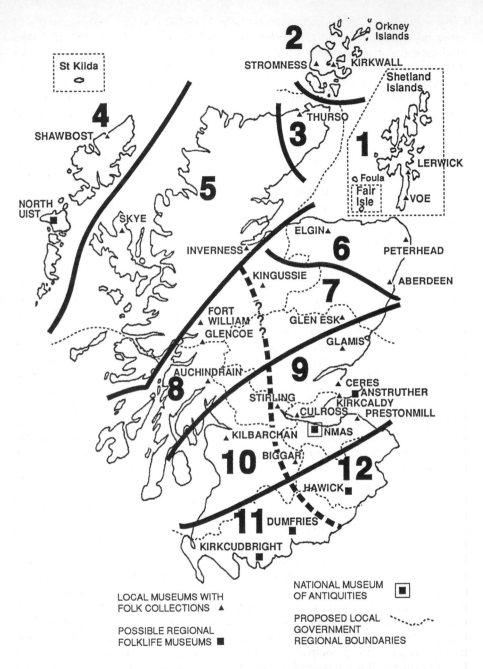

St Kilda

2

Orkney Islands

STROMNESS ▲ ▲ KIRKWALL

Shetland Islands

4

SHAWBOST ▲

3

▲ THURSO

1

LERWICK ▲

NORTH UIST ■

SKYE ▲

5

○ Foula
Fair Isle
▲ VOE

INVERNESS ▲

ELGIN ▲

6

PETERHEAD ▲

KINGUSSIE ▲

?

▲ ABERDEEN

7

FORT WILLIAM ▲
GLENCOE ▲
GLEN ESK ▲

? ?

GLAMIS ▲

AUCHINDRAIN ▲

8

9

CERES ▲
STIRLING ▲ ▲ ANSTRUTHER
KIRKCALDY
CULROSS ▲ PRESTONMILL ▲

KILBARCHAN ▲

■ NMAS

10

BIGGAR

12

HAWICK ■

11 DUMFRIES ■

KIRKCUDBRIGHT ■

LOCAL MUSEUMS WITH FOLK COLLECTIONS ▲

NATIONAL MUSEUM OF ANTIQUITIES ■

POSSIBLE REGIONAL FOLKLIFE MUSEUMS ■

PROPOSED LOCAL GOVERNMENT REGIONAL BOUNDARIES

THE ETHNOLOGICAL REGIONS OF SCOTLAND
Based on Don Aldridge 1971 (Graphics by Michael Spence)

Only a summary of the report was available at the time of writing, and this revealed little about the methodology which enabled the authors to assert 'that considerable long-term economic advantages to the area could be gained if the River Tweed was better known and appreciated. Its profile is too low in tourism promotion or as a natural resource of national significance. The River Tweed should be as internationally recognised as the Rhine, the Loire or the Danube in mainland Europe'. The themes identified through which this might achieved, were: (i) the ecology of the river; (ii) river management; (iii) life story of the salmon; and (iv) fishing. It was proposed that the strategy be comprised of the following initiatives: an access project; publications; a grant-aided programme; public art in parks and riverside locations; town twinning; and a modern visitor and interpretive centre.

Three projects were mounted in Tayside Region during the 1980s, and taken together these represent important building blocks on which a future regional strategy could be developed by a suitably structured partnership. The first was *Tayside Environmental Resources Guide* (1980), produced by the Advisory Group for Environmental Education in Tayside. This contains a detailed directory of sites for each of 18 sub-regional areas. The sites were selected for their suitability in environmental education, and each entry gives details of geography and land use, cultural and natural history, art and architecture, industry and technology, and infrastructure and access.

The second study, *Dundee's Heritage: A Strategy for Interpretation* (1984), was undertaken by Don Aldridge for the Dundee Project of the Scottish Development Agency. The report was faithful to the methodology first propounded by the author in the 1966 Peak Blueprint, and more than half the document was dedicated to a resource analysis and possible themes for Dundee's hinterland. In two subsequent reports, he developed thematic stories relating to whaling, RRS Discovery and DC Thomson. Among these, the idea of bringing Captain Scott's ship back to Dundee, was probably the most inspired proposal ever made in the history of Scottish interpretation.

The third initiative in Tayside, *Highland Perthshire: A Strategy for Interpretation* (1986), was undertaken by Aldridge and Christopher Dingwall for a consortium comprised of the Countryside Commission for Scotland, the national agencies for development and tourism, together with Highland Perthshire Development Company, Perthshire Tourist Board and Tayside Regional Council. Each step in the methodology of the study is clearly set out in the report which is recommended as an excellent general introduction to discovering the personality of a region. It describes the area's resources with interpretation potential; possible themes and story lines are explored in relation to likely providers and various market segments; and the idea of an interpretation gazetteer is explored. There is a nice concluding section on the methodology and principles of interpretation, and the report laid the foundation for the successful Locus project in Aberfeldy. Indeed, there are few places in Scotland where interpretation has been considered that do not carry the traces of Don Aldridge's influence. His latest contribution is to have updated his own 1975 publication by writing *Site Interpretation: a Practical Guide* (1993), for the Scottish Tourist Board.

This paper should be regarded as a descriptive analysis, if such a thing is possible, rather than a critical appraisal of Scottish achievements in the last 20 years. The events are too recent and many of the practitioners are still working actively in the service of interpretation. To undertake a fair and even handed assessment would be a major undertaking best left for another occasion. However, some concluding recommendations are made below. They are the author's suggested agenda for action to consolidate existing achievements so that Scotland can continue to provide leadership on the international stage into the next century. It is proposed that the theme for this agenda should be: *From national to local strategies and vice versa.*

It is reasonable to say that the regional strategies referred to above have had, for good historical reasons, a bias towards the rural hinterland. Future strategies should include the capital cities and towns of a region (like in Orkney and Dundee) to provide truly comprehensive strategies to enable proper consideration of 'gateway' provision where most visitors enter a region.

Future strategies should also be more comprehensive in terms of subject matter. In the past there has been an emphasis on natural resources and artefacts. The scope of resource inventories should be extended to include information on Doric language, story telling, literature, crafts and textiles, the performing and visual arts, food and the culinary arts, politics, religion, sports and soldiering etc.

There should be a national framework for defining regional areas on the Aldridge model that would be suitable for producing interpretation strategies. The initiative for this should come from the Scottish Office, the obvious mechanism being in the form of National Planning Guidelines. A Government Circular would also be required to lay down criteria for the production of interpretation strategies for each region, much in the same way as for Indicative Forestry Strategies and Green Charters.

The proposed Scottish Office Circular should seek the establishment of a Standing Conference or Heritage Forum for each region to sponsor, direct and oversee the production of regional strategies. National agencies should include Historic Scotland, Scottish Arts Council, Scottish Museums Council, Scottish Natural Heritage, Scottish Sports Council and Scottish Tourist Board. In addition to local area tourist boards and the tourist industry, local authorities should field representatives from education, museums and galleries, parks and planning. Voluntary bodies like the National Trust for Scotland, Scottish Youth Hostels Association, Scottish Wildlife Trust and the Royal Society of Birds should be invited to participate, as well as the Scottish Landowners' Foundation and the National Farmers' Union of Scotland.

A top-down system like this will only work meaningfully if provision is made for a complimentary bottom-up approach to facilitate grass-root community participation. Although by accident rather than by design, this is in effect what happened in the case of the Gordon District Strategy and the Alford Nature Plan within the context of the Grampian Strategy. The circular should address itself to how this two-way flow of information and decision-making might be handled to best effect. Indeed, all business associated with the work of a Forum should be conducted in the public domain. Some of the strategies to date have had only limited effect as their policy content has been a matter strictly between the client organisation and its author consultant.

It is unfortunate that the initial enthusiasm for joint working in the 1970s was not carried forward into sustained action. For any strategy to be effective, there needs to be a mechanism for regular review so that policies can be adjusted to meet changing circumstances. Only Grampian Region did this, with a time gap of 10 years, which is rather too long. In addition to establishing a standing Heritage Forum in each region, it is recommended that modern information technology should be used in the production of future strategies. This would make regular updating and sharing of information easier tasks, as well as extending the range of potential data users to schools, local area tourist boards, visitor centres and tourist enterprises.

The urgency to take action along these lines is dictated by two main considerations. The first is tourism, our main national industry, which needs a system of strategic interpretation to develop and deliver an enhanced product in both domestic and overseas markets. The second reason is that a concerted campaign of interpretation is required to encourage sustainable stewardship of our natural and built heritage, as well as to engender a greater pride in our cultural traditions among Scots of all ages, particularly among the young.

The author

Magnus Fladmark is Director of the Robert Gordon University Heritage Unit, and he was Assistant Director of the Countryside Commission for Scotland 1976–92. An Honorary Fellow of Edinburgh University, he has contributed to several major policy initiatives and publications, including being co-author of *Tomorrow's Architectural Heritage* (1991). He is chairman of the Geddes Awards for environmental excellence.

References

Advisory Group for Environmental Education in Tayside (AGEET), *Tayside Environmental Resource Guide*, Tayside Regional Council, 1980.

Aldridge ,D., *Folklife Parks as Interpretive Media*, Countryside Commission for Scotland, 1971.

Aldridge, D., *Museums and Historic Interpretation with Reference to an Ideal National Pattern and the Scandinavian and American Analogies*, in Proceedings of a Conference on Country Life Museums, Countryside Commission for Scotland, 1972.

Aldridge, D., *Environmental Awareness: Regional and National Interpretive Plans*, in The Museums Journal, Vol. 73, No. 3, Dec. 1973.

Aldridge, D., *Principles of Countryside Interpretation and Interpretive Planning*, HMSO, 1975.

Aldridge, D., *Dundee's Heritage: A Strategy for Interpretation (including its hinterland)*, Scottish Development Agency, 1984.

Aldridge, D. & Dingwall, L ., *Highland Perthshire: A Strategy for Interpretation*, Highland Perthshire Development Company *et al*, 1986.

Aldridge, D., *Site Interpretation: A Practical Guide*, Scottish Tourist Board, 1993.

Central Regional Council, *Strategy for Interpretation in Central Region*, Central Regional Council & Countryside Commission for Scotland, 1984.

Centre for Environmental Interpretation, *Western Isles Interpretation Strategy*, Western Isles Enterprise *et a.l*, 1992.

Centre for Environmental Interpretation, *River Tweed Interpretation Strategy*, Scottish Borders Enterprise, 1992.

Countryside Commission for Scotland, *Programme for Kindrogan Interpretive Methods Course*, (8 Oct. 1969), Countryside Commission for Scotland, 1969.

Countryside Commission for Scotland, *Proposals for Interpretive Planning in Orkney*, Orkney County Council & Countryside Commission for Scotland, 1974.

Donside Community Council, *The Alford Nature Plan*, Nature Conservancy Council *et al.* , 1992

Foster, J., *Heritage Presentation and Interpretation: Some Scottish Initiatives*, in proceedings of The First World Congress on Heritage Presentation and Interpretation in Banff, Canada, 30 Sept. – 5 Oct. 1985, Heritage International, 1986.

Gordon District Council, *Countryside Interpretive Strategy*, Gordon District Council,1992

Grampian Regional Council, *Regional Interpretive Planning in Grampian*, Grampian Regional Council & Countryside Commission for Scotland, 1977 (reviewed, 1987).

Grampian Regional Council, *Directory of Environmental Study Sites*, Grampian Regional Council *et al.*, 1993

Hayes, D., *Visitor Centres and Interpretive Facilities*, Highlands and Islands Development Board, 1979.

Loch Lomond Interpretive Group, *Loch Lomond Interpretive Plan: Draft for Discussion*, Loch Lomond Planning Group, 1984.

Mackay, A., *Interpretation of the Natural Environment in North West Sutherland*, Highland Regional Council and Scottish Natural Heritage, 1992.

Nature Conservancy Council, *Caithness & Sutherland: Places to Visit for Wildlife & Landscape*, Nature Conservancy Council, 1991.

Noble, R.R., Country Heritage: *An Interpretive Plan for Biggar and District*, Biggar Museum Trust, 1976.

Peak District National Park, *Development Plan First Review: Report & analysis of Survey*, 1966.

Thom, V., *Countryside Interpretation in North West Scotland: Ullapool to Durness*, Highland Regional Council & Countryside Commission for Scotland, 1981.

Thom, V., *Countryside Interpretation in Wester Ross: Kyle of Lochalsh to Ullapool*, Highland Regional Council & Countryside Commission for Scotland, 1981.

Tilden, F., *Interpreting our Heritage: Principles and Practices for Visitor Services in Parks, Museums, and Historic Places*, University of North Carolina Press, 1957.

11

THE SCOTTISH PARKS SYSTEM
A Strategy for Conservation and Enjoyment

Timothy Edwards, Nicholas Pennington
and Michael Starrett

Scottish Parks is both a *System* and an *Association*. The System was proposed by the Countryside Commission for Scotland in 1974. The Association was born in 1991 as a result of the coming together of a group of professional land use planners and managers who had, for the most part, worked within the System. Many still work within that System, although the work of Scottish Parks as an Association reaches into the wider Scottish countryside, where the experience and background of its membership has many applications, as reflected in our full name, The Association of Scottish Parks and Countryside Officers.

This paper looks at the historical context of the Scottish Parks System within a framework of strategic planning for heritage conservation and enjoyment through interpretation. It examines the manner in which attitudes, philosophies and approaches to the subject were formulated by the original vision of the Parks System. It identifies opportunities for the role of both the System and the Association in the future interpretation and management of Scotland's countryside. It is concluded with an appeal for a sound national overview to back up locally taken decisions. The views are based on 20 years of working experience during which strengths and weaknesses have been identified and highlighted.

THE DIAMOND NECKLACE

Today's country parks, all 35 of them, together with four regional parks, have been described as 'the Golden Chain'. And quite rightly: your parks *are* the Golden Chain, the String of Pearls, the Diamond Necklace, which now adorns and embellishes the most populated parts of Scotland's Countryside, meeting the needs of their millions of visitors, while at the same time promoting the aims of conservation through good management and of information and education through your Ranger Services.

This statement was made by Magnus Magnusson on 15 November 1991 on the occasion which marked the launch of The Association of Scottish Park and Countryside Officers. His words succinctly summed up one of the major achievements of an organisation which had been in existence almost 24 years to the day, and which in his role as Chairman of Scottish Natural Heritage, he was about to 'inherit'. That earlier organisation was the Countryside Commission for Scotland, and The Countryside (Scotland) Act 1967 stated that:

> There shall be established a Countryside Commission for Scotland who shall exercise the functions conferred on them by this Act for the provision, development and improvement of facilities for the enjoyment of the Scottish Countryside, and for the conservation of the natural beauty and amenity thereof. In the exercise of their functions the Commission shall have due regard to the need for the development of recreational and tourist facilities and for the balanced economic and social development of the countryside.

Whilst some might find the grammatical construction of the above passage clumsy, few, if any would argue with the intentions and sentiment of the new legislation. From out of the above grew Magnusson's diamond necklace. The constituent parts of the necklace, the country and regional parks, were linked by one of the Commission's major policy statements, a Park System for Scotland, in 1974. The regional parks required further legislative provision and this was provided by the Countryside (Scotland) Act 1981 which saw a Regional Park as: 'an extensive area of land, part of which is devoted to the recreational needs of the public'. To continue the Magnusson jewellery analogy, Regional Parks were the 24 carat version being seen 'as larger and more diverse in character than a country park'.

THE INTERPRETIVE LINK

The Scottish parks and countryside system provides opportunities for interpretation within a national context, as well as for the development of innovative approaches to countryside management and integrated land use. In this regard, the most recent legislative provision which removed the Countryside Commission for Scotland and the Nature Conservancy Council (Scotland) and substituted Scottish Natural Heritage, will be the touchstone for policy, action and a guiding hand in years to come. The mission statement of The Natural Heritage (Scotland) Act 1991 is worded as follows:

> There shall be established a body to be known as Scottish Natural Heritage whose general aims and purposes shall be:
> a) to secure the conservation and enhancement of, and
> b) to foster understanding and enhancement of the natural heritage of Scotland; and SNH shall have regard to the desirability of securing that

anything done, whether by SNH or any other person, in relation to the natural heritage of Scotland is undertaken in a manner that is sustainable.

In comparing the statutory remit of the new organisation with that of the former Commission, one finds many of the same words: conservation, enjoyment, enhancement, recreation etc. However, two words appear now in the legislation which were not included in the 1967 Act. The words are: *understanding* and *sustainability*. For understanding read 'interpretation' and for sustainability read 'common sense'.

It is in some ways regrettable that words such as these should have to become enshrined in legislation (so much for the voluntary principle) before they are taken seriously. Their inclusion is in no way an indictment of the former Commission, which in all senses embraced the principles of sustainability. Its approach to interpretation was through the dynamism and vision of its staff, and the philosophical vision which it instilled through training and association with its principal partners. In this respect the historical development of a national Countryside Ranger Service, motivated and driven by its desire to extend to the wider public and land managers, an understanding of the link between resource (land) management and interpretation, must also rank as a major achievement by the Commission.

However, the establishment of the 'diamond necklace' and the Countryside Ranger Services are one and the same thing. Those involved in rangering, and the majority of those responsible for their management, have been influenced by the Commission's vision and philosophy of interpretation. It is for this reason that the opportunity exists to extend the application of those principles to the enjoyment, enhancement and conservation of Scotland's natural heritage.

THE COUNTRY PARKS

Under the Countryside (Scotland) Act 1967, 'A country park is a park or pleasure ground which by reason of its position in relation to major concentrations of population affords convenient opportunities to the public for enjoyment of the countryside or open air recreation'. So said the Act. Interestingly enough, the mention of 'nature study', 'information' and 'display centres' (the nearest things to interpretation) come under the section dealing with 'powers of the Forestry Commissioners'. It is obvious that we have the Countryside Commission for Scotland to thank for the philosophy towards country parks with regard to a balanced approach between conservation and recreation. It could so easily have been otherwise.

Although the majority of country parks are in local authority control (there are now 36), some are based on traditional family estates, that are now owned and run by voluntary organisations such as the National Trust for Scotland. The location and emphasis of each park varies considerably, resulting in a less than symmetrical necklace, with the jewels of varying size

VISITORS TO COUNTRY PARKS

	1990	1991	1992
ADEN	186,906	205,955	207,907
ALMONDELL/CALDERWOOD	110,000	160,000	135,000
BALLOCH	270,000	295,000	250,000
BALMEDIE	100,000	110,000	150,000
BEECRAIGS	400,000	394,000	401,000
BONALY	52,000	50,000	55,328
BRODICK CASTLE	66,915	69,492	63,513
CALDERGLEN	260,000	400,000	225,000
CAMPERDOWN/TEMPLETON	600,000	500,000	550,000
CASTLE SEMPLE	250,000	232,500	230,311
CHATELHERAULT	300,000	278,346	254,553
CLATTO	90,000	90,787	90,525
CRAIGTOUN	95,000	115,744	105,355
CROMBIE	44,742	45,750	49,477
CULZEAN	365,000	385,781	353,204
DEAN CASTLE	100,000	100,000	200,000
DRUMPELLIER	363,000	462,925	463,000
EGLINTON	35,871	37,550	88,602
FORFAR LOCH	263,231	230,623	129,371
GARTMORN DAM	16,000	84,144	127,080
GLENIFFER BRAES	400,000	400,000	400,000
HADDO	150,000	190,000	155,000
HAUGHTON HOUSE	17,000	26,000	104,000
HILLEND	160,000	160,000	347,412
JOHN MUIR	200,000	262,833	279,904
LOCHORE MEADOWS	400,000	420,000	357,000
MONIKIE	180,000	180,733	147,209
MUGDOCK	220,000	280,000	255,000
MUIRAVONSIDE	100,000	107,622	115,000
MUIRSHIEL	45,000	42,000	39,708
PALACERIGG	120,000	125,000	125,000
POLLOK	900,000	900,000	750,000
PLOKEMMET	347,846	328,322	286,000
STRATHCLYDE	6,452,808	6,493,749	6,500,000
TOWNHILL		25,000	47,000
VOGRIE	45,000	130,000	209,052
TOTAL	13,706,319	14,319,856	14,246,511

Source: Countryside Commission for Scotland

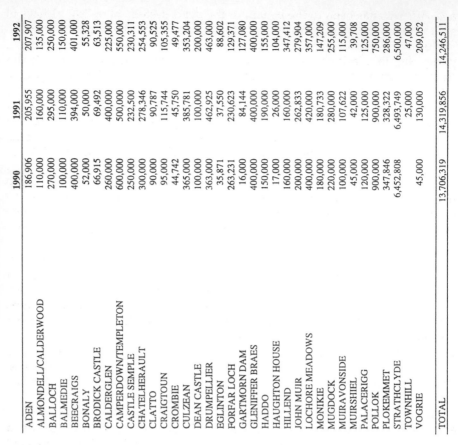

SCOTTISH PARKS
(Graphics by Michael Spence)

WESTER ROSS
INVERNESS
PROPOSED GREAT GLEN WAY
SPEYSIDE WAY
ADEN
CAIRNGORM
GLENMORE FOREST PARK
ABERDEEN
DUNDEE
FIFE REGIONAL PARK
QUEEN ELIZABETH FORREST PARK
WEST HIGHLAND WAY
FORT WILLIAM
GLENCOE & GLEN NEVIS
ARGYLL FOREST PARK
LOCH LOMOND REGIONAL PARK
CLYDE MUIRSHIEL REGIONAL PARK
GLASGOW
BRODICK
CULZEAN
GALLOWAY FOREST PARK
EDINBURGH
PENTLAND HILLS REGIONAL PARK
JOHN MUIR
SOUTHERN UPLAND WAY
PENNINE WAY
BORDERS FOREST PARK

PROPOSED NATIONAL PARKS
REGIONAL PARKS
COUNTRY PARKS
FOREST PARK
NATIONAL FOOTPATHS

and cut. This has been to the benefit of the parks system, allowing visitors to gain a diverse range of experiences, all with a countryside 'theme'.

However, the 'countryside theme' has become rather inward looking, partly due to a lack of national guidance or policy regarding interpretation from government agencies. The present pre-occupation with site specific interpretation is perhaps contrary to the original philosophy as promoted by the former Commission, but there is little doubt that country parks can, and should, act as a springboard to the wider countryside for urban dwellers: in a continuum from a more familiar, relatively managed and planned landscape, to the countryside beyond. In fact, country parks have the potential to be deliberately used as a management tool, playing a specific role in an interpretative strategy for the wider countryside by introducing topics in the field of conservation and heritage discovery that are, in most cases, new to the visitor. This is not, of course, to negate the importance of site specific interpretation. The countryside beyond should be an additional feature worked into the parks' interpretative plan.

The potential for interpretation in fields of archaeology, history, ecology and the environment within country parks are immense, but it has been a rather 'ad hoc' affair. Everyone knows that country parks provide a map, some leaflets, countryside events, some photographs and recycled posters. Have we actually taken the time to sit back and think through what information the visitor is taking away? There has been little guidance as to the best way to interpret your site. It has been up to the 'on site' managers to decide how this can be achieved within the constraints of their resources and staff, sometimes with the input of consultants, whose knowledge of the site and nature of the visitor might be very limited.

There is also a trend towards the use of modern information technology, to allow the technology to do the communicating for us. This can be a retrograde step, as it often fails to deliver the message intended. Successful interpretation demands participation by your audience and, if possible, communication with the interpreter to permit a two way dialogue. The technology trend, of course, is finance driven. It is much easier to purchase the required technology from capital allocations than it is to find the revenue finance to pay for a user friendly human. Too often, the interpretation side of a park has been ranked low in order of priority and has been instigated without a plan or mechanism for review and evaluation. All interpretative initiatives must arise out of an interpretative plan, based on market research with a constant process of self-evaluation and development. This structured approach, which also involves the collection and analysis of visitor data, could be improved upon at many sites.

Setting aside the question of guestimates, it can be seen that the country parks in Scotland receive a large number of visits each year, over 14 million from local residents, day trippers and 'overnighters'. The opportunity exists, by networking the 36 country parks, to put across a particular message or theme and influence a large section of the population. Any special initiatives or campaigns in relation to, say the principle of sustainability, could be conveyed via a structured interpretative plan at these locations, creating a much greater impact than from a single site. Networking the parks also creates the opportunity to pool resources, combine skills and influence lifestyles.

Through recent initiatives such as the establishment of an Environmental Task Force by the Scottish Office and the Scottish Tourist Board, it has at long last been recognised that the Scottish environment plays a major role in attracting tourists to the country. The parks and countryside system that exists in Scotland offers the opportunity of accessible countryside, specifically managed to receive large numbers of visitors. However, very few country parks play a role in interpreting the Scottish environment or provide a place where information is readily available. In these difficult financial times, using an existing structure, such as the country parks, as sites for tourist information, seems a sensible approach. Most country parks produce a programme of interpretative events, but very few have tried to link this to tourism visitors. Interpretation forms a pivotal position in the relationship between the tourist industry and the environment, and the potential exists for the parks system to play a significant role in promoting green tourism in partnership with the farming community and organisations like the Scottish Youth Hostels Association.

The role that the country parks play in the field of environmental education, through the work of rangers with schools and teachers, is well known and respected. Striking a partnership with the education departments of local authorities has occurred in some locations but by no means all. A recognition that country parks can interpret many areas of the curriculum, outside the classroom, could be the start of joint and more structured programmes for educational interpretation. Despite many shortcomings and missed opportunities, the parks can play a major role in natural heritage interpretation. With just a little polishing of the jewels by more thought, strategic planning, generous funding, and training, the system could be made to shine even more brightly.

THE REGIONAL PARKS

The four areas designated as regional parks range in size from 40 to 270 square kilometres. The most obvious contrast with the Country Parks must, therefore, lie in their relative scales. Located at four corners of Scotland's Central Belt, they also represent a wide spread of landscape types, although all feature high ground and embrace extensive water bodies. If scale is an obvious difference, other attributes mark and reinforce the contrasts too. Within them, each of the parks displays landscapes of great variety, widely contrasting wildlife habitats and land uses. They reflect many cultures and traditions, and their local communities, in villages or scattered farmsteads, add to their diversity. The mix is of a complex living and working landscape that is not found in the same scale and diversity in the country parks.

The Park Authorities created to operate over the designated areas have a duty to conserve those qualities which make the parks special, to enable the visitor to enjoy fine countryside and to do these things in a way which pays proper regard to the concerns of the local communities. What interests us in this context, is the potential role of interpretation and how it should be developed. All of the suggestions made in relation to country parks are pertinent to the System as a whole, e.g. green tourism, the scope for networking and need for still better training. However, the regional parks offer further challenges and opportunities with associated priorities which may be special to them. Unlike the country parks, most of the land in the regional parks is not owned or managed directly by the Park Authorities and the scope to influence events directly is usually severely limited. A primary concern is to conserve outstanding heritage assets in situations where pressures for change are very real. If conservation objectives are to be achieved, this must in the circumstances be done almost entirely through others. In other words, through persuasion. It follows that those of us working for the Park Authorities must understand what is special and be able to communicate that appreciation to others. The ability to interpret and communicate to decision makers and users, whether they are politicians or school groups, farmers or rambling clubs, is therefore crucial.

The promotion of enjoyment for its own sake is, of course, another key concern of any Park Authority. Most of us are 'blind', most of the time, to what is 'special' around us, and, a little illumination, through skilled interpretation will usually fascinate and entertain. A problem in the regional parks is, usually, which of the myriad themes to concentrate on, and, it is at this point that we begin to feel the requirement for a 'strategic' approach to interpretation. There is a clear need for an order and logic to any story and it will help if each relates to others. However, if we are to open eyes and ears, hearts and minds to what is special in the countryside, the quality of the story telling is most important. Further more, a function of interpretation that we cannot afford to ignore is its potential role as a visitor management tool. As advertising can influence buying habits, so can promotion backed up by interpretation, influence the pattern and intensity of use of our countryside.

In any area rich in sources of irritation and conflict between visitor and local interest, a critically important further aspect of visitor management lies in encouraging responsible behaviour. Again, there are opportunities through skilled interpretation to convey an understanding of a problem and a sympathetic response. Instruction or special pleading are poor substitutes. As an aside, few will convey a message about sheep worrying by dogs, or the implications of leaving field gates open, more effectively than a farmer regularly frustrated by these problems and there may be lessons to be learned about speaking from first hand experience. Another aspect we must not forget is safety. A sign saying 'Don't Swim' conveys nothing of the numbing effect of cold water and strong currents which may drag a child to an early death.

If interpretation is so critical a factor in these key areas of resource and visitor management, its central role in the overall management of the park can hardly be overstated. Yet, interpretation remains a means of achieving objectives, not an end in itself. This brings us back to the question of how to handle the subject in strategic terms. The traditional interpretative plan has tended to focus on selecting themes and developing storylines, and then determining how best to convey them within a conservation and visitor management framework. Given its potential role in strategic resource management, is this an adequate approach ?

FUTURE ACTION ON INTERPRETATION

Although much has been achieved, a great deal remains to be done to develop the system of parks and countryside services to its full potential for conservation and enjoyment. In particular, there are opportunities for improving our capability in the field of heritage interpretation. A partnership between Scottish Natural Heritage, which has the statutory obligation and the budget, and Scottish Parks, which has the experience and skills, is the key to making the diamond necklace shine more brightly. Opportunities which should be given high priority in the years ahead are:

1. Scottish Natural Heritage to fund a review of the role and function of existing systems and to formulate a national policy of interpretation for implementation by Scottish Parks within a co-ordinated programme of themes and initiatives ;
2. to develop the function of an interpretative plan in each park, from merely 'telling a story', to a management tool for influencing visitor movement, attitudes and behaviour (including a rigorous system of visitor monitoring in all parks);
3. Scottish Parks to link together with organisations like the Scottish Tourist Board, tour operators, the Scottish Youth Hostels Association, Local Enterprise Companies, etc. to produce a co-ordinated approach to interpretative opportunities for visitors, including activity based holidays and weekend breaks;
4. production of an interpretative publication highlighting the Scottish parks and countryside system as a positive opportunity for visitors to Scotland;
5. establishment and development in Scotland of the necessary research and development capability within the academic community to deliver the required training and skilled support for heritage interpretation.

FUTURE LINKS INTO THE WIDER COUNTRYSIDE

Many local authorities operate a 'countryside service' that in many ways is similar to a regional park, but without the statutory designation. These services can cover vast areas but most concentrate on the more popular and heavily used locations due to limited staff resources Here again, the opportunity exists for providing environmental interpretation, and for linking into existing tourist facilities and attractions, as well as promoting green tourism as suggested above in relation to the parks. Indeed, such services, as with the parks, can provide interpretation that helps to mediate between landowner and visitor, where conflict arises. This highlights the role parks can play in educating visitors about the wider countryside. Environmental management projects, such as the Countryside Around Towns initiatives (green belt projects), can also be viewed as a potential force towards interpreting the countryside for urban dwellers by promoting the heritage value of land adjacent to our major towns. The role of all these parks, services and projects is an important one, as most visitors to Scotland's countryside go there because of the beauty and richness of our cultural landscapes. This environmental resource is Scotland's finest and most sustainable. It is only through interpretation that visitors will increase their enjoyment of the countryside and consequently their respect for the heritage resources which attracted them there in the first place.

There are major strategic issues facing policy-makers in the years ahead. The first is the need to look at the 1974 proposals by the Countryside Commission for a closer integration between country parks and urban parks. Some progress has been made in this direction through the Countryside Around Towns projects, e.g. the Strathclyde River Valley Strategy extends into the heart of Glasgow, but more needs to be done to formalise the networking between the two types of parks. This issue, like many others, is an urgent matter for resolution in advance of the proposed re-organisation of local government. Related to this issue is also the question of whether major private sites, developed in recent years with help from the public purse, should be allowed to enter the Register of Country Parks. Examples of such sites that would be strong candidates to qualify are Kelburn, Finlaystone and Formakin.

The second strategic issue that requires urgent attention is closer integration of parks with the system of access to the countryside for walking, cycling and horse riding, that has been developed during the last 20 years. We now have three major long distance routes (national trails) in the West Highland Way, the Southern Upland Way and the Speyside Way. Plans for a fourth route, the Great Glen Way, was well advanced when the Countryside Commission closed for business in 1992. Many local authorities have been very active in developing regional and local routes, and funds have been allocated for implementing a cycle way between Edinburgh and Glasgow. There is a need for this emerging network of routes to be seen as a means of linking the regional and country parks into a national system of recreational access to the countryside which would greatly enhance the quality of life for Scots and be a tremendous boost to our tourism infrastructure.

The third and greatest issue, of the wider countryside concerns whether Scotland should have national parks or not, a part of the 1974 Park System proposals that has been the subject of most study, debate, and campaigning, including a degree of angst on the part of both national and local government, but which has not been implemented. The former Commission chose to call them 'special parks' in 1974, but after a long inquiry during the late 1980s, it took the plunge and produced a report, *The Mountain Areas of Scotland* (1991), advancing strong arguments for the introduction of national parks under new legislation in the areas of Loch Lomond/Trossachs, Glencoe/Glen Nevis, the Cairngorm and Wester Ross. This document in many ways built on the model of integrated land management so far practised only by the regional parks in Scotland, but they operate without the powers required to cope with the problems now existing in the nationally important areas.

Rather than accepting these proposals for park authorities with strong planning powers, visitor and land management functions, and new funding from the public purse at a level in keeping with that received by existing national parks in England and Wales, the Government has issued counter proposals for Natural Heritage Areas operated on the voluntary principle. The feasibility of such a scheme has been investigated by working parties for two areas. The report for Loch Lomond is awaited, and the proposals by the Cairngorm working party, produced under the chairmanship of Magnus Magnusson, is currently the subject of public consultation. The areas in question represent more than mere jewellery for show in speech-making, they are the finest pieces of Scotland's natural heritage which deserve the best stewardship and protection the nation can provide. If decisive action for their proper stewardship and protection is not taken soon, their sustainability must remain in doubt, and the Scottish Parks system might forever remain incomplete. Who would be willing to interpret that for future generations?

The authors

Dr Timothy Edwards is Manager of Mugdock Country Park and Secretary of Scottish Parks. An ecologist with a doctorate in ecological entomology he has worked in Africa and Northern Ireland where he established a volunteer conservation organisation.

Nicholas Pennington, a geographer and town planner, is Park Officer for the Loch Lomond Park Authority and Vice-Chairman of Scottish Parks. He has worked in Jamaica, for Ross and Cromarty Council and for the National Park Authorities in the Peak District, the Yorkshire Dales and in the North York Moors where he was Deputy National Park Officer.

Michael Starrett holds qualifications in ecology and education. A member of The Landscape Institute of Leisure and Amenity Management, he is Manager of Pentland Hills Regional Park and chairman of Scottish Parks. Before coming to Scotland in 1986, he worked as a warden in the Mourne Mountains in Northern Ireland.

References

Aldridge, D., *Principles of Countryside Interpretation and Interpretive Planning*, HMSO, 1975.

Cairngorm Working Party, *Common Sense and Sustainability: A Partnership for the Cairngorm*, Scottish Office, 1992.

Countryside (Scotland) Act 1967 and 1981, HMSO.

Countryside Commission for Scotland, *A Policy for Country Parks in Scotland*, 1970.

Countryside Commission for Scotland, *A Park System for Scotland*, 1974.

Countryside Commission for Scotland, *A Policy for Regional Parks in Scotland*, 1982.

Countryside Commission for Scotland, *The Mountain Areas of Scotland*, CCS, 1991.

Dawer, M. *et al*, *The Countryside Around Towns in Scotland*, Countryside Commission for Scotland, 1976.

Fladmark, J.M., *The Countryside Around Towns: A Programme for Partnership and Action*, Countryside Commission for Scotland, 1988.

Magnusson, M., *Scottish Parks*, speech made at the launching of the Association of Scottish Parks and Countryside Officers on 15 November 1991.

Natural Heritage (Scotland) Act 1991, HMSO.

Scottish Natural Heritage, *Natural Heritage Areas: Criteria for Designation*, discussion paper issued by SNH, 30 April, 1993.

Scottish Tourist Board, *Tourism and the Scottish Environment: A Sustainable Partnership*, STB, 1992.

Strathclyde Regional Council, *The River Valleys Strategy*, SRC, 1990.

Tourism and Recreation Research Unit, *Recreation Site Survey Manual: Methods and Techniques for Conducting Visitor Surveys*, SPON, 1983.

INTEGRATED STRATEGIES IN NATIONAL PARKS
Experience in England and Wales

Peter Freeman and Tim Haley

This has not been an easy paper to write. The truth of the matter is that there is no integrated strategy for interpretation in any national park in England and Wales, in spite of the fact that interpretation came to the British parks in the 1960s. Regional strategies for site interpretation have their origins in the 1966 Peak District National Park Development Plan First Review. A strategy was produced for Exmoor National Park in 1979 with help from the Countryside Commission (England and Wales), and Dartmoor produced a detailed interpretive plan in 1991. What happened to all this work you may well ask, because surely interpretation is a good thing, and interpretive planning would seem to be an effective way to avoid unnecessary duplication.

To answer the question requires a step back to the 1950s and the publication of Freeman Tilden's, *Interpreting Our Heritage,* in which the concept and philosophy of heritage interpretation, developed by the United States National Park Service in the preceding decades, was encapsulated in the dictum: 'Through interpretation, understanding; Through understanding, appreciation; Through appreciation, protection.' The definition of interpretation used by the US National Park Service could simply be expressed as 'Interpretation is the art of explaining the significance of a place to the public who visit it, in order to point out a conservation message.' Visitor centres, guided walks, camp fire talks, slide shows and on-site panels were all techniques used on site to explain a heritage theme of a particular park to a visiting audience. Although Tilden gave the subject of interpretation a philosophical base, it should be remembered that these techniques have been evolving since the 1920s in one of the most advanced park services in the world.

THE LAKES IN CONTEXT

In the 1960s these techniques were transplanted into a very different park system in England and Wales. We both work for the second oldest national park in Britain, in the Lake District, and our ranked counterpart in the United States is Yosemite. Both parks are similar in size, the Lake District encompassing 885 square miles, and Yosemite 1,000 square miles. There the similarities end. Yosemite is owned by the nation, there are very few roads, only park and contracted personnel live inside the park (about 500 persons), four million day visits are made annually, the progress of visitors beyond the honeypots is strictly controlled, and within the park the service has federal jurisdiction, including all law enforcement duties and its own jail. Only 4% of the Lake District is owned by the park authority, there are over 40 roads leading into the park, 38,000 people live within the park, and 16 million day visits are made annually, and the park authority shares its planning responsibilities with the districts and the county. It is no surprise, therefore, that even today, recognition by both visitors and locals of the location, purpose and value of the Lake District National Park is low when compared with Yosemite. In the 1960s this was even more the case, when only the Peak District and the Lakes were distinguished as planning authorities, with 30 and 15 staff respectively, whilst the other parks were little more than a name on the map with one or two county personnel responsible for park work.

There was no park ownership, no central administration, no national corporate identity, no park uniform, little or no funding and no 60 years of cultural development. Into this near communication vacuum, came a developed and sophisticated technique called interpretation: Freeman Tilden's 'Educational activity which aims to reveal meanings and relationships.' The United States had developed a clear identity for its parks system which was recognised and respected by nearly all America. Thoreau, Muir, and Leopold had all contributed towards a landscape ethic, which found its first expression in the United States parks, and its citizens were proud of this fact. The conservation ethic for national parks was simple – *in parks man is subservient to nature* – and the identity, purpose and values of parks were clear to the vast majority of American citizens. Within this communication framework, interpretation could flourish and the explanation of place could unfold within a well developed supportive framework.

INTERPRETATION IN THE 1970s

In Britain the circumstances were very different. By the early 1970s, when the American concept of interpretation had filtered via the Countryside

Commission (England and Wales) and the Peak District to all national parks, the only professional post filled in each park was that of Information Officer, and only one park had a designated National Park Officer and none had an ecologist. Direct grant from the Commission ensured that money was available annually for information services. Not surprisingly, interpretation imperfectly understood, but the best funded and most coherent concept on the national park table at the time, achieved a status well suited to its undoubted benefits.

In 1974, the Sandford Committee on national parks concluded that, 'There is no more fruitful way of promoting at a single stroke the conservation of the countryside and enjoyment of visitors' than by interpretation. The fundamental problem was that in Britain, albeit by proxy, interpretation was being asked to do two jobs. On the one hand, that of establishing a corporate identity and communicating park values, whilst, on the other, the explanation of a place to increase visitor understanding. The problem was exacerbated because the newly established park authorities focused quite reasonably on their under-developed planning and park management responsibilities, and largely left their information officers to continue on their relatively well developed path. Consequently, fundamental communication issues which, if solved, would have provided a helpful framework for interpretation, were not addressed until the 1980s. Each park successfully employed its own individual brand of interpretation practices and techniques, but interpretive planning was going nowhere fast.

THE EXMOOR EXPERIMENT

In 1979 the Countryside Commission (England and Wales) decided to give interpretive planning an impetus by mounting an experimental project in Exmoor National Park to define a strategic interpretation framework which could be a reference point for those contemplating new developments elsewhere. The key to the successful employment of this technique was that new developers could be made aware of current developments and thus of the need to avoid duplication. Bodies making grants available for such schemes, and those seeking grants from these same agencies, would be able to order their priorities on a more comprehensive and forward looking assessment than was usually the case. It was also envisaged that the strategic planning of interpretive facilities could play a significant part in helping to accommodate the impact of tourist and recreational developments, and sites vulnerable to public pressure could be identified and alternative and less sensitive locations developed. This applied to natural and archaeological sites in particular, and such a regional framework would be able to help planning and tourist authorities provide robust areas, to meet public demand, where the pattern of visitor use, site facility and on-site management combined to afford maximum enjoyment and understanding with minimum affect on the resource.

Despite an enthusiastic project officer and a well run experiment, the result for Exmoor was that very little happened. Notwithstanding the theoretical advantages outlined above, it proved hard to produce a report around which potential investors and operators could rally. Most individuals who develop an interpretive enterprise do so out of a personal enthusiasm which is often hard to harness within a regionally planned framework. Many organisations who develop facilities do so to achieve corporate goals whose influence usually overrides a voluntarily agreed plan. Again, and affecting all groups, is the increasing shortage of money from grant giving agencies, trusts, sponsorship etc. In cases where the money is actually available, there is also the problem associated with increased targeting of that money.

Finally, as success and survival increasingly depend upon numbers, spend per head, and cost effectiveness, there is the question of competition. Sir Thomas Lipton, of Lipton Grocery fame, is on record as saying, 'Show me a high street where there are three greengrocers and that is where I'll put a Lipton's.' The same increasingly applies to interpretation facilities. Nent Head, in Cumbria, provides one of the best potential sites for on-site interpretation of the techniques and social habit of 19th Century lead mining in Britain. Development has foundered because there is not a sufficient market. Thirty miles away to the west in the Lake District, two investments have been made in the last two years on the theme of Beatrix Potter at quarter of a million pounds each.

So the Exmoor experiment failed as did a similar initiative run as part of the same Countryside Commission (England and Wales) programme in Nottinghamshire. By the mid 1980s the concept of interpretation as a regional arbiter in the location of visitor provision had failed to take hold both within park authorities and in the surrounding regions. The failure stems from the length of time taken to recognise that the principles and techniques espoused so eloquently by Freeman Tilden worked because they were developed over time on land owned by one authority whose ethic and corporate identity was clearly recognised and appreciated by a huge majority of its audience.

THE EDWARDS' REPORT

In the mid 1980s the Commission ran a national park awareness campaign. At the outset it asked a series of questions aimed at establishing the level of understanding of national parks and their purpose. The results alarmed the Commission and park authorities who concluded that, what seemed to be missing, was an overall clarity of purpose and subsequent co-ordination of needs that would ensure effective use of resources in communicating park purpose. In 1989, the Commission set up the National Parks Review Panel, under the chairmanship of Professor Edwards, to identify the main factors and developments in the future which were likely to affect the ability of National Parks to achieve their purposes. In the Panel's 1991 report, *Fit for the Future*, the opening paragraph on information, interpretation and education read as follows:

Our initial reaction was one, paradoxically, of mixed admiration and confusion. We recognise the value of the National Park Information Services and acknowledge their high quality, but we found it difficult to detect any coherent policy direction. Information services have taken on more and more mantles over the years, in an apparently indiscriminate way, so that they are now a mixture of park interpretation, tourist information points and shopkeepers; they reach out to many thousands in the information centres but to only a few hundred through guided walks; and they seem to target variously the public at large, decision makers, teachers, pupils, the well versed, the little versed and the unversed. Such a catholic approach may be admirable, but we detected that it was often too broad to be effective. A clearer direction is needed.

A further quotation from the same chapter of the Edwards' report develops the argument a stage further, and two crucial points in this extract are highlighted:

Many definitions of the functions of national park information, interpretation and education services have been attempted. Some have confused national park awareness with national park promotion. **The form of words we select for use in our report is 'the successful communication of national park values to all sections of the community'.** This definition has three components:
- **information** has long been provided on such basic items as places to visit, accommodation, routes and timetable.
- **interpretation** of the landscape and culture is fundamental to the understanding – and thus, enjoyment – of the national parks. The landscape has been interpreted in a variety of ways through, for example, signed trails, guided walks and national park information centres.
- **education:** the wide dissemination of the aims and qualities of national parks to the whole population, young and old, and through formal and informal channels. To this end, national park authorities have provided youth and schools services, specialist staff and study centres.

At the heart of all these activities lies a need to explain, to both the national and local audience, the role and purpose of national parks and their place in the wider environmental context. **The park information services are central to an increased awareness of, and support for, landscape and nature conservation.**

In the summary of evidence received by the Edwards' report, the Panel states that it received little evidence on information, interpretation and education in national parks. It states, 'in many ways it seems to be a forgotten issue, or perhaps the service is taken too much for granted.' There is some truth in the latter statement but the fundamental reason that these services are a forgotten issue is because they have not demonstrated by achievement the role that their communication powers can play to support a park authority's objectives.

A STRATEGY FOR COMMUNICATION

Park authority objectives will most readily, and in some case only, be achieved by persuasion. That persuasion is achieved by communicating to as wide a public as possible an understanding of park values. It is suggested that there is currently a greater understanding, in the minds of the British public, of the problems of the tropical rainforests than of their own national parks. These points were debated at length by the Lake District National Park Authority following the publication of *Fit for the Future*. A comprehensive local survey revealed recognition of the area as a national park by 63% of locals and by 52% of visitors. Tests of awareness and knowledge of who runs or controls the area showed that at best, 36% of locals recognised that the park authority had some part to play under one or other of its titles. Visitors fared worse at 19%.

A working party of members and officers was then established, and its conclusion was that there was an overriding need to establish a communication strategy for the national park authority. In this interpretation would be but one technique to achieve communication objectives. The essential purpose of the strategy is to provide a framework which will enable the authority to explain more effectively its role and purpose, enhance public awareness and understanding of its policies and actions, and thereby achieve the ultimate goal of influencing public attitudes, opinion and behaviour. It is not a new challenge and there is a sound information base on which to build.

What is required is a more co-ordinated approach based on corporate objectives, and a focus of limited resources on these objectives. This is not the place to examine in detail the elements of the communication strategy. It is sufficient to say that the approach owes much to company corporate image development, or as the Edwards report states, 'is based on a professional marketing approach and marketing plan. This approach which is designed to get the right message to the right people, needs targets, data collection and monitoring.' In short, its essential purpose is to elevate our audiences up the communication ladder shown in the diagram. On the face of it, this is a model not far removed from Tilden, probably because Tilden was in fact describing the basic communication process as applied to the US park system through the technique of interpretation. We are taking a wider view of communication based on market research, corporate objectives and the particular circumstances of our own land management system.

It may seem from the foregoing that the park authority has little interest in an integrated approach to interpretation, or even in interpretation itself. This would be to misread the position. For example, we are working with others on the development of an information database for the Lake District, and aim by the year 2000 to be recognised nationally as the comprehensive and authoritative source of environmental information about the Lakes area. The potential for interpreting this source of information for the benefit of the landscape and for visitor enjoyment will be enormous. The authority provides an extensive network of site interpretation based on traditional techniques of exhibitions, displays and outdoor panels, and operates what is possibly the largest regional programme of guided walks and interpretive events in the country.

This year the park authority won the Hunter Davies Book of the Year Award with an innovative hill walking publication for families, which drew rave reviews from the judges who commented on the concept's national application. With the assistance of arts funding, the authority has also developed, with the Over The Top Puppet Company, a travelling show for schools which is well received despite a cost covering presentation charge. This year also sees the redevelopment of the Blencathra Centre, from hostel accommodation to study centre, in partnership with the Field Studies Council, thus bringing to the Lake District the foremost field study practitioners in the country.

CONCLUSION

The authors of this paper, who between them have worked in five different national parks for a total of 35 years, believe in the value of interpretation and, in an ideal world, in the logic of integrated national park interpretive strategies. The reasons as to why such plans have not been effective south of the Border are practical and operational. If an integrated strategy for interpretation is to bloom in the future, then it will have to take account of the practical difficulties experienced in the past as well as the comments of today's field practitioners.

The authors

Peter Freeman began his career as an Information Assistant with the Peak District in 1969. He became Deputy Information Officer in 1974, before moving to Dartmoor National Park Authority as its first Interpretation Officer, and then became Northumberland's first Head of Visitor Services in 1979. This was followed by a similar first appointment in the Lake District in 1986, and he is the only person to have worked in four National Parks.

Tim Haley came from a career in the private sector, and was appointed Assistant Information Officer in the Yorkshire Dales in 1983. He joined the Lake District National Park in 1989, as Manager of the Brockhole Visitor Centre on the shores of Windermere, with additional responsibility for management of the Park's field events programme.

References

Countryside Commission, *Exmoor National Park Interpretive Plan Study*, Countryside Commission, 1979.

Countryside Commission for Scotland and Countryside Commission, *Guide to Countryside Interpretation Part One, Principles of Countryside Interpretation and Interpretive Planning*, HMSO Edinburgh, 1975.

Countryside Commission for Scotland and Countryside Commission, *Guide to Countryside Interpretation Part Two, Interpretive Facilities and Media*, HMSO Edinburgh, 1975.

Dartmoor National Park Authority, *Interpretation Strategy*, Dartmoor NPA, 1991.

Department of the Environment, *Report of the National Parks Policies Review Committee, Chairman Lord John Sandford*, HMSO, 1974.

National Parks Review Panel, *Fit for the future, Report of the National Parks Review Panel, Chairman Prof R Edwards*, Countryside Commission, 1991.

Peak Park Joint Planning Board, *Peak District National Park Development Plan First Review*, PPJPB, 1966.

Tilden, F., *Interpreting Our Heritage*, The University of North Carolina Press, 1957.

BEHAVIOUR

ATTITUDE (apathy)

CONVICTION (indifference)

PERCEPTION (misperception)

UNDERSTANDING (misunderstanding)

KNOWLEDGE (ignorance)

AWARENESS (disinterest)

THE COMMUNICATION LADDER
negative responses may occur at any step as shown in brackets

13

ACCESS THROUGH HOSTELLING
The Role and Policies of SYHA

Philip Lawson and Magnus Fladmark

The hostelling movement has been a vital force in opening up opportunities for young people to travel and see places that might otherwise not have been accessible to them. The less privileged and less well-off in society have been our target, and this paper examines how the early hostels enabled large numbers of young townspeople to discover the delights of the countryside and mountains of Scotland. This awakening of a desire to explore places previously beyond reach, laid the foundations for what later came to be known as the leisure boom, made possible by a shorter working week, greater affluence and increased mobility. To this, government has responded in the last 20-30 years, by developing a recreational infrastructure of parks, walkways, cycling routes and visitor attractions. Without places for people to stay, the new provision for outdoor recreation would have been of little consequence, and our role has been to meet the demand for accommodation where it was most evident.

The main thrust of the paper, against the background of our past contribution, is a look at public policies for providing access to the nation's heritage, and to examine how the hostelling movement can continue to play a full part in making these policies more effective in the interest of heritage conservation and recreational enjoyment. An important aspect of our role stems from the international nature of hostelling. More than half of our visitors come from outside of Scotland, and our contribution to the tourist economy of local communities is considerable. We also look at how the stewardship and presentation of the heritage vested in our own hostels can be better presented and appreciated, and we touch on the skills and capability of our wardens in working with other agencies to provide the information needed by visitors to find, enjoy and appreciate the local heritage on the doorstep of our hostels.

WHENCE WE CAME

The Youth Hostel movement was founded in 1909 by a German schoolteacher, Richard Schirmann, who saw the need for providing overnight accommodation so that school groups could get out to experience the countryside and for city children to have a country holiday. At first, schools were used during the vacation periods, but later permanent hostels were established and the German Youth Hostels Association came into being. The hostelling idea spread rapidly throughout Europe in the 1920s and 1930s and the Scottish Youth Hostels Association was formed in 1931. In many countries, including Scotland, the emphasis was on young adults travelling as individuals and in groups, rather than on school parties of younger children, and there was a strong international aspect to the movement which encouraged the formation of the International Youth Hostel Federation. The system of reciprocity established by the Federation makes it possible for a person who is a member of any one association to use the youth hostels of all the other associations throughout the world.

A brief history of the Association was written in 1959 by Alex Beith, a founder member and former Hon Vice President. The following passages by Beith give a vivid picture of the social conditions, the ideas and aspirations which led to our establishment and which still colour the character of our organisation and its ethos:

> In the early 1930's the dream of a chain of Youth Hostels throughout Scotland inspired hundreds of young men and women to devote themselves with furious enthusiasm to the many arduous tasks which had to be performed before their vision could become a reality. Of the many 'Movements' in Scotland in this century probably no other so inspired the dynamic, creative force of the young people as the Youth Hostels Association, and the existing chain of hostels, covering pretty well the whole of the country, is an enduring tribute to their enthusiasm and industry.

> It would be an over simplification of the problem to suggest that the economic depression of the 'Hungry Twenties' was the main dynamic of the increase in popularity of the outdoor movement in Scotland, but beyond doubt it exercised an important influence. Also beyond doubt was that, between 1920 and 1930, the need to escape from the cramped and unhealthy living conditions in industrial areas became almost a blind urge for many thousands of young people. The evidence was patent in the remarkable growth of hiking, climbing, camping and cycling as popular pastimes.

Annual holidays presented even greater difficulties. In north-west Scotland - one of the most magnificent walking and climbing areas in Europe - hotel accommodation was inadequate to cater for more than a limited number of fishers and such like who formed the mainstay of the hotel business. And in nearly all, moreover, the tariff, however reasonable, was beyond the means of the young people who were in increasing numbers invading this wonderland for walkers.

The cycling movement was already organised and had built up a system of recommended accommodation throughout the country inspected by regional consuls. The rambling clubs increased in number and strength and, although they soon formed themselves into the Scottish Ramblers' Federation, this was a young organisation, active in the interest of their members but without the organisation and financial resources of the national cycling clubs. Less mobile than cyclists, their need for some kind of organised cheap accommodation on their travels was more urgent.

In the West of Scotland, where the ferment bubbled most furiously, came the first attempt to deal with the problem. In 1929 the Rucksack Club was formed with a limited capital subscribed by rambling clubs and individuals interested in encouraging walking and climbing. Although the Rucksack Club's appeal for subscribing members met with only moderate success, it managed to establish two wooden huts at Kinlochard and Arrochar (near each site there is now a youth hostel). Only in retrospect is it easy to understand why the Rucksack Club was not a successful movement. But tribute must be paid to those who had the courage and initiative to play John the Baptist to the SYHA. In 1932, the SYHA took over the assets of the Rucksack Club.

The impact which the new organisation made in its early years was considerable. Writing in 1939, in his classic book on climbing and hiking, *Always a Little further*, Alastair Borthwick declared '. . . I cannot rid myself of the conviction that the youth hostel movement is one of the more important social innovations of this century.'

WHERE WE ARE NOW

From small beginnings in 1932 when we provided for 22,366 bednights in 19 hostels, the Association has grown into the premier provider of low cost accommodation in Scotland. We now have 86 hostels, and in 1991-92 we catered for a grand total of 633,817 bednights which represents a substantial contribution to the Scottish tourist economy. The hostels vary in size, from the very large in places like Edinburgh, Glasgow, Aberdeen and Inverness, to the smaller in places like Falkland, Loch Ossian and Achmelvich. Ten hostels are housed in buildings listed as being of architectural and historic significance, and several others are located in conservation areas.

Each hostel is run by a warden, who would be more appropriately described as a 'hostel manager', whose manyfold tasks require the qualities of a Renaissance polymath. Foremost is the duty to manage the property and support staff, the latter being a big job itself in the larger urban hostels. We are introducing a computerised booking system which requires new and special skills, and in some hostels food is served so there is a catering function to look after. Then there is the customer care function, and, since so many of our visitors come from overseas, some of our hostels serve as key tourist information centres. We have always given high priority to providing guidance on local heritage attractions. Our staff work closely with local organisations, and the hostels hold literature produced by others on museums, galleries, historic houses and on local walking and cycling opportunities etc. Indeed, over the years, the Association has produced at its own hand a wide range of heritage interpretation literature in the form of maps, leaflets and guidebooks.

In response to market demand we also offer a range of activity holidays, some entirely provided by ourselves at places like Loch Morlich and Rowardennan, others offered in association with private operators. These holiday packages are at present based on the activities of cycling, walking, golf, pony trekking, sailing, skiing and wildlife and nature study. At our own two centres we offer multi-sport holidays which extend the range of activities even wider to include canoeing, archery, windsurfing, and orienteering. In partnership with the relevant transport operators and Historic Scotland, we offer two touring holiday packages, described as follows in our promotional literature:

> **Scottish Wayfarer:** Go-as-you-please and tour all of Scotland at your own pace. Our Scottish Wayfarer offers you great value and freedom to explore the beauty of Scotland. Travel the magnificent 'Road to the Isles' through lonely Rannoch Moor and Glencoe to the romantic Isle of Skye then sail on to the beautiful Outer Hebridean Islands. Visit John o'Groats and the far north coast or climb the Cairngorms, one of Britain's last unspoilt areas. The choice is all yours. Available for either 8 or 15 days, the Wayfarer gives unlimited travel by rail throughout all of Scotland, and sailings on most of Caledonian MacBrayne's West Coast ferries, plus 1/3 off the P & O Scrabster to Orkney crossing and all participating bus services. Also included are 7/14 vouchers for use at any Scottish Youth Hostel.
>
> **Explore Scotland:** Our Explorer holiday gives you the freedom of Scotland. Where you go is up to you, the choice is almost as spectacular as the views. Enjoy 7 days unlimited coach travel on the services of Scottish Citylink Coaches. Discover all of the Scottish mainland plus the Isle of Skye. We also include 6 overnight vouchers for use at any Scottish Youth Hostel, an Explorer Ticket giving you free entry to many historic monuments and castles throughout Scotland.

Figure 1 From top, Carbisdale, Ayr and Loch Lomond

In the heart of Loch Lomond Regional Park, we provide a conference venue in our magnificent hostel at Auchendennan House, north of Balloch, which is one of our properties listed as being of architectural and historical significance. It sits in landscaped grounds near the shore of Loch Lomond, with conference rooms seating up to 120 participants, and there is residential accommodation for a maximum of 220 delegates.

RESPONDING TO GOVERNMENT POLICY

Like any other organisation, we have in recent years had to adapt our language and operational style to fall in line with current trends. For example, sustainable use of resources is now a high profile concept that appears at the top of political agendas, both nationally and internationally. The new concept says that sustainable development is when we use the resources inherited by ourselves in a manner which ensures that the needs of the present are met without compromising the ability of future generations to meet theirs. This is exactly what we have practised and preached since our foundation by 'recycling' old buildings for hostels and by encouraging our members to behave responsibly towards the countryside and those who live and work there.

A specific response to this new way of thinking was a decision, taken at the 1992 Conference of our International Federation, to adopt a Charter of Environmental Principles which national associations would implement within the policies of their own governments. Germany was the first to take action, and the Scottish Association has recently commissioned work to produce its own charter. The work is being done by the new Heritage Unit at the Robert Gordon University, and they have been asked to research and write a document that will deal with a broad range of prominent policy issues being tackled by Government at the present time. To establish a clear role for the Association, we have started by consulting all relevant public and quasi-public agencies and some key voluntary bodies, and this paper includes some of the ideas that have been put to us for consideration.

In our dealings with government, many of our old partnerships have had to undergo realignments due to organisational change, together with adjustment to attendant changes in language and blurring of conventional distinctions between landscape and wildlife, between protection and enjoyment, between conservation and enterprise, and between production and service activities in the economy. These trends are exemplified by the merger of the Countryside Commission and the Nature Conservancy Council into Scottish Natural Heritage which now has a combined concern across the subjects of landscape, wildlife, enjoyment and sustainability. The status as an Executive Agency for Historic Scotland has come at a time when their protection role has almost been overtaken by an active drive to attract people to their sites, including a 'friends' organisation, and finding new uses for some of their properties.

Reinforcing the many activities of local authorities, the recent creation of Local Enterprise Companies, including a remit for training, has been accompanied by stronger interest in and support for environmental conservation skills and green tourism enterprises. The Scottish Tourist Board and the local area boards have discovered that proper stewardship is important for their marketing of the environmental and cultural heritage, the fundamental attractions drawing visitors to Scotland. Add to this the recent review of priorities in support for the arts, which has led the Scottish Arts Council to indicate that there might be less for avant-garde minorities, more room for the applied arts, and closer attention to the role of the arts in attracting visitors.

There are two recent government policy initiatives that are of specific relevance to us. The first came in 1990 as a white paper, *This Common Inheritance: Britain's Environmental Strategy.* In addition to its commitment towards cleaning up the environment and reducing the causes of global warming (sustainability), the government gave high priority to preserving and enhancing Britain's natural and cultural heritage (historic buildings, sites and landscapes). Two of the stated heritage aims of specific interest to the hostelling movement, to which Ministers have pledged a commitment, were: first, promoting enjoyment and understanding of our heritage; second, encouraging private sector efforts, and making financial assistance available, to help meet the extra costs of maintaining and restoring heritage property.

In regard to enjoyment and understanding, we feel able to echo Alex Beith by saying that this is the area where we still make our main contribution and it remains our top priority. We were in the vanguard of heritage interpretation with our early guidebooks, and we will be going to government with proposals for how the Association can enhance its role in promoting enjoyment and understanding of our heritage. We can do this from a position of strength, as we already have a proven track record based on existing initiatives, and we will be studying the Smyth Report, *Learning for Life,* to determine how the Association can best help to implement its recommendations.

In regard to maintaining and restoring historic properties, the Association can refer to success in forging partnerships and seeking financial assistance from government and others. We are now looking for collaboration with bodies like Historic Scotland, the Architectural Heritage Society and the Garden History Society for expert help on aspects of restoring hostel properties to enhance their heritage value. We have already identified the subject as an issue to be looked at in partnership with government agencies (e.g. gardens, interior design, furniture and fittings), and we will be developing a new agenda on this front.

The main thrust of our study is naturally in relation to Scottish trends and strategic policies, and the second government document that is fundamental to our review was published by the Scottish Office in 1992. Entitled, *Rural Framework,* it set out a new agenda under the following themes:

1. Local Community and Added Value;
2. Diversity;
3. Quality and Effective Service Delivery;
4. Networks and Communications;
5. Europe.

A very striking thing about the consultation responses we have received, is the universal goodwill enjoyed by the Association. Success breeds success, and we have a long list of organisations who would like to be associated with this success, both existing and potential partners, many of whom are in a position to offer support. The following is a selection of issues raised by others which give pointers to where future priorities might lie, and these are discussed under the themes set out in Rural Framework.

LOCAL COMMUNITY AND ADDED VALUE

Partnerships and community involvement have always been a priority for the Association, as exemplified by the recently opened hostel in Port Charlotte on Islay. The whole venture was undertaken in close collaboration with the Islay National History Trust, and their collection and visitor facility occupies the ground floor of the hostel which was formerly the bonded warehouse of the Loch Indaal Distillery. The new hostel in Stirling is another story of partnership and collaboration with national and local agencies, as is the current project for a hostel at New Lanark, and it is gratifying that several new propositions of a similar kind have been put to us during the review which are now under consideration. Yet another example of community involvement, ad hoc perhaps and borne out of adversity, was when the Torridon hostel was used for teaching the local children after the roof of the school blew off in a gale.

In regard to added value, the Association can refer to contributions with its existing programme of activity holidays in partnership with local operators which produces local added value. Another opportunity for contribution towards economic viability of communities is to provide visitors with information about where to obtain locally produced goods. Where food is served at a hostel, there is also the possible challenge of providing a menu of local dishes, made with locally farmed ingredients, which would further enhance diversity.

We are mindful that there is scope for collaboration with the arts and crafts community. The recent formation of an Association for the Applied Arts and publication of the Charter for the Arts, have led us to the conclusion that hostels near to art schools might provide suitable venues for exhibition of work by students. If this was a success, the arrangements might be extended to provide space for exhibitions by local artists at certain times of the year, which we would regard as a positive way of contributing value-added input to local economies as a by-product of our main activity of hostel operation.

DIVERSITY

Here we refer to two aspects: a diversified local economy (as above) and diversity in the heritage of the hostels themselves. Taking the economy first, there is an enormous economic benefit to local communities from 630,000 bednights annually, and the visitors spend their money on a wide range of local goods and services. Second, in terms of the heritage value of the hostels, it is clear from our studies that the architectural heritage of many hostels is in itself an asset not fully appreciated. The Association is held in high regard for having saved many fine old buildings from falling into neglect. They range from listed mansion houses to modest vernacular buildings which would have disappeared long ago were it not for the Association. Our role in this regard has been greatly helped by The Gatliff Hebridean Hostels Trust which has restored several croft houses in the Outer Hebrides, and these are now operated as 'adopted' hostels.

In regard to the architectural heritage of our hostels, many have pointed out that more hostels could be furnished and decorated in a manner that better reflects local culture and traditions, including arts and crafts. There is a clear willingness in several organisations to help us with this, and we see no reason why the Association should not move up alongside the National Trust for Scotland to offer a worthwhile heritage experience at its own properties. Indeed, there are strong arguments why the two organisations should market joint tour packages because of their complementary resources, and Historic Scotland may be a third party in such a concordant. These are some of the ideas for how it might be possible to increase public awareness of the contribution made by the Association to the diversity and conservation of Scotland's architectural heritage.

QUALITY OF DELIVERY

Hostel bednights have increased steadily for six consecutive years, a resounding endorsement of high quality and effective delivery of services. However, in the drive to maintain these high standards, it is important that we do not lose the diversity of character which is so typical of our local hostels. Indeed, this is our great strength in appealing to a diversity of market segments, from those seeking the heritage experience of our historic urban centres to those who are drawn to the wildness of our remote islands, coast and uplands.

We have referred to the role of our wardens earlier in the paper. They combine the skills of an operational manager and tourist officer, and both roles are equally important for delivering an effective service of good quality. The latter is a dual function: one being concerned with providing access to our heritage through information and knowledge (explanatory publications and interpretation), the other being concerned with how to gain access in a physical sense (trail guides and street maps). In these capacities, the wardens need to work closely with local authority archaeologists, tour guides, area

Figure 2 From top, Wanlockhead, Strathpeffer and Aberdeen

tourist boards, museums, galleries and parks. The Association is grateful for the collaborative spirit shown by other parties involved in the exchange of tourist literature, and we would be keen to look at possible joint ventures to produce new material like local guidebooks, heritage trail leaflets and maps.

NETWORK AND COMMUNICATIONS

Improved roads and a nation-wide network of hostel accommodation means that Scotland can use its remoteness to full advantage. In relation to the high priority assigned by government to promoting enjoyment and understanding of the nation's heritage, the Association is well placed to enhance its contribution. We took a close interest in the 1974 policies proposed in, *A Park System for Scotland,* and the Association responded on two fronts. First, hostels are now providing accommodation in or near several parks. The Loch Lomond/Trossachs area has four, Edinburgh and Melrose serve the Pentland Hills, our warden in Falkland works closely with the Countryside Rangers in the Lomond Hills of Fife. Second, we have been established for a long time in the nation's other valued areas proposed for national parks in the 1990 report, *Scotland's Mountain Areas.* There are seven hostels in or close to the Cairngorm area, two in Glencoe/Glen Nevis and three in Wester Ross. The Association also keeps under constant review the emerging network of walkways and cycleways in Scotland, and we have referred elsewhere to the priority we have given to providing hostels for the convenience of walkers on the West Highland Way and the Southern Upland Way.

In relation to this theme, environmental education is potentially an attractive market for the Association. There are many reasons for this. One is the sad fact that many education authorities have had to close down their own residential field study centres to make economies in their budgets. They are looking at alternative options and several authorities have indicated that they would he keen to explore collaborative ventures with the Association. We will also be looking at other segments of the market, to calibrate the demand side of our formula used for deciding how we can best contribute to the overall strategy of access.

EUROPE

Britain's commitment to Europe has found physical manifestation in the Channel Tunnel, Scottish Office ministers say Scotland must develop its role in Europe, and the government is pushing a Bill through Parliament to reaffirm our membership of a unified Europe. In the search for a positive role in all this, we believe that the Association should draw on the strengths of its roots. Alex Beith wrote that these roots go back to the Rucksack Club of the 1930s, when young people of industrialised Central Scotland sallied forth into the countryside on foot and by bicycle for fresh air and communion with the natural world. In our age of green policies, it is proposed that we should revive the very heritage that Association members created in the early days: a heritage that has given us a special place in people's hearts and which has nurtured us as a movement ever since.

From its earliest days, the Association has had a strong international outlook, and over the years has welcomed large numbers of young Europeans to Scotland. The natural beauty and the unspoiled character of our countryside has a powerful attraction for young people from the Continent, e.g. the Germans now outnumber the English in our hostels, and they come with a strong commitment to environmental protection. As an international organisation in the new Europe we see it as our duty to make provision for them, along with our own members, and to fulfil their green expectations by the adoption of our forthcoming heritage charter. To this end, we are active in the Federation of Youth Hostel Associations in the European Community, which is encouraging a closer working relationship between the hostel organisations in the twelve member states, and the work of this Federation is already being recognised by the EC Commission through support for initiatives in respect of the environment, youth information and training programmes.

In moving towards a United Europe, we would like to build on our earlier vision for access in Scotland, shared with the Countryside Commission for Scotland and the local authorities. During the last 20 years, we gave top priority to creating hostel accommodation where required along the long distance walkways implemented by them. In partnership with those responsible for developing these routes, we sought to adhere to an early principle, recorded by Tom Hall in 1933. In his book, *Tramping Holidays in Scotland*, he wrote:

> The hostels did not appear haphazardly. From the beginning the idea was to extend gradually from different centres so that each hostel would be within walking distance of another in that district. Later it was planned to link up the different districts.

Our vision for Scotland was then, and it is the same now, that there would be a walkway from John o'Groats to Inverness as advocated by walking enthusiasts in Highland Region, which would link into the Great Glen Way to Fort William, as proposed by the Commission, and from there we already have the West Highland Way to Glasgow. From the 'European City of Culture' goes the Clyde Walkway, which when completed, will link with the Southern Upland Way to Melrose, whence into England via the Roman road of Dere Street which links into the Pennine Way down the spine of England. This route would eventually pick up the Thames Walk into London, and from there the North Downs Way already exists to take the walker to Dover or Folkestone.

Our continental colleagues have a long established system of routes, and on the French side the walker would pick up the existing network of Grandes Randonnés which runs across the country to the Mediterranean at Marseilles. Since we are already working towards the grand idea of a monetary union for the whole of Europe, it does not seem too fanciful for national routes systems to be linked into a grand European strategy for access. It could have spurs across the Alps and down the Apennine spine of Italy. Another spur could be across the Pyrenees and through Spain to the Rock of Gibraltar. Other options would be eastwards through Germany to the Carpathian Mountains or northwards through Belgium, the Netherlands and Scandinavia to the North Cape. This vision of access is not confined to the heritage of single nations, but extends to the natural and cultural riches of a whole continent.

This long-term strategy might be called the European Way or the European Trail. It would initially run from the Toe of Italy to the edge of Europe at John o'Groats, and it should be designed for both walkers and cyclists. A grand vision that would tickle the imagination of many, and it could become a reality if adopted as the master plan for access to Europe by the next generation of youth hostellers.

The authors

Philip Lawson is Chairman of the Scottish Youth Hostels Association, and a Director of the Scottish Rights of Way Society and the Gatliff Hebridean Hostels Trust. He is currently President of the Federation of Youth Hostel Associations in the European Community.

Magnus Fladmark is Director of The Robert Gordon University Heritage Unit, and he was Assistant Director of the Countryside Commission for Scotland 1976-92.

References

Beith, A., *Youth Hostelling in Scotland: the first twenty-five years,* SYHA, 1959.

Borthwick, A., *Always a Little Further,* Faber, 1939.

Grassl, A., and Heath, G., *The Magic Triangle,* International Youth Hostel Federation, 1982.

Countryside Commission for Scotland, *A Park System for Scotland,* CCS, 1974.

Countryside Commission for Scotland, *A Policy for Regional Parks in Scotland,* CCS, 1981.

Countryside Commission for Scotland, *Scotland's Mountain Areas: Conservation and Management,* CCS, 1990.

Department of the Environment et al, *This Common Inheritance: Britain's Environmental Strategy,* Cm 1200, HMSO, 1990.

Hall, T.S., *Tramping Holidays in Scotland,* Country Life, 1933.

Highlands and Islands Enterprise, *Tourism: The Way Forward,* HIE, 1992.

Historic Scotland, Corporate Plan 1992-95, HS, 1992.

Historic Scotland, *Safeguarding the Nation's Built Heritage*, Annual Report 1991-92, HS, 1992.

Humble, B.H., *Wayfaring Around Scotland*, Herbert Jenkins, 1936.

Lawson, J.P., *Hostels for Hikers: A pictorial history of the Scottish Youth Hostels Association's first fifty years*, SYHA, 1981.

Scottish Arts Council, *The Charter for the Arts in Scotland*, HMSO, 1992.

Scottish Landowners' Federation, *Towards Access Without Acrimony*, SLF, 1993.

Scottish Natural Heritage, *Enjoying the Outdoors: A Consultation Paper on Access to the Countryside for Enjoyment and Understanding*, SNH, 1992.

Scottish Office, *Rural Framework*, S.O., 1992.

Scottish Office, *Learning for Life: A National Strategy for Environmental Education in Scotland* (The Smyth Report), S.O., 1993.

Scottish Rights of Way Society, *Rights of Way: A Guide to the Law in Scotland*, SRWS (new ed.), 1991.

Scottish Tourist Board, *Tourism and the Scottish Environment: A Sustainable Partnership*, STB, 1992.

Smith, R., *Outdoor Scotland*, SYHA, 1981.

SYHA and NTS, *Touring Map of Scotland, Youth Hostels and Places to Visit*, SYHA and NTS, 1985.

Figure 3 Adopted Gatliff Trust hostels in the Outer Hebrides. From top, Berneray, Rhenigidale and Howmore

14

EXPLAINING THE LOCAL HERITAGE
The Role of a Regional Archaeologist

Ian Shepherd

Since its inception in 1975, Grampian Regional Council has recognised the importance of explaining the past through features surviving in today's landscape. The Council has regarded interpretation as an important tool for visitor enjoyment, environmental conservation and countryside planning. This paper concentrates on some key initiatives to explain the local heritage of the region, and readers are referred to the works of others for further introduction to the subject, e.g. Munro (1985); Magnusson (1983); Ritchie and Adamson (1981, pp178-82); Simpson (1976); Feachem (1963); Shepherd and Ralston (1979); Ritchie and Breeze (1991); the *Exploring Scotland's Heritage Series* (ed. A.Ritchie); Fowler (1987); Binks et al (1988); and Parker Pearson (1993). The essential elements of the classic definition of interpretation, according to Aldridge (1975, p1-3) can be recognised in the work carried out in Grampian:

> an aim to increase enjoyment
> an element of discovery
> an addition to understanding
> answers when questions arise
> inspiration/aesthetic awareness
> significance of the site: why is it important?
> a conservation message

In recent years we have added a more explicit economic justification for such work which was not evident earlier, e.g. Raymond Lamb's pioneering work in Orkney in 1986-87. The Westness Walk on the island of Rousay links features of several dates in a meaningful landscape study, and the Eday Heritage Walk brings together archaeology, landscape and nature conservation as it crosses the centre of Eday (Orkney Islands Council, a and b). Both are excellent examples of modest interpretive improvements. In addition to answering questions as they arise and communicating the significance of the sites, they have also been successful in attracting visitors, and thereby generating income vital to the continuation of these remote communities. These initiatives taught an important lesson: draw on the indigenous strengths of an area; identify what it has of visitor interest; assess its suitability to withstand visitor pressure, and go for it. The proposed Highland Heritage Network (Highland Regional Council, 1993) is similar, although wider in its aims in drawing in all aspects of landscape. In particular, it is hoped that it will be possible to co-ordinate the various interpretive initiatives currently underway in Highland Region, to assist in the selection of themes and sites, and in the production of high quality graphics and text.

INTERPRETATION OF THE REGION'S ARCHAEOLOGY

Strategic interpretation began with *Regional Interpretive Planning in Grampian* (1977): an early attempt by Trevor Sprott and Iain Slinn at strategic interpretive planning, made possible with the assistance of Don Aldridge and Valerie Thom from the Countryside Commission. It was revised as the *Regional Interpretive Strategy Review 1987*, when two areas of the region were identified as needing particular attention: the north coast of Buchan and the Mearns. In preparing this strategic overview, which has served as a role model, the utility of two tiers of local government was everyday apparent in the Council's ability to look at a region as a whole in a way that individual districts could not justify.

Both documents, the 1987 one in particular, focused on the importance of interpreting the cultural heritage, and highlighted the then poor state of interpretation at publicly accessible monuments. For many people the standard Government-issue blue metal sign remained the beginning and end of wisdom on the archaeology of an area, as distinctive a house style as the carefully-routed Forestry Commission boards. Much has been achieved by Historic Scotland, but there remain too many versions of language along the lines of a 'sepulchral monument of the Bronze Age' (currently at Cullerlie) for any of the conservation ethic to shine through.

There had been attempts at specific improvements in the 1970s. For example, the four-colour guidebook, *Early Grampian* (Shepherd and Ralston, 1979) was produced by the Council in 1979, and several leaflets on individual sites stemmed from the 1987 *Interpretive Strategy Review*. These are currently being re-presented in the house style of the new Economic Development and Planning Department. They relate mostly to certain Historic Scotland guardianship sites with minimal interpretation, such as the stone circle at Loanhead of Daviot, or the Picardy Stone, now blessed with an off-the-peg 'Picts' board, not specific to the site.

At the end of the 1970s, some work was also done with the Forestry Commission on interpreting certain monuments in their care in Kincardine and Deeside, e.g. the Nine Stanes stone circle at Mulloch and the long barrow at Capo. Plain boards of varnished pine were silk-screened with a simple

Figure 1 Drawings of carvings from the Picardy Stone (above left), an early Pictish symbol stone dating from the sixth or seventh century AD, and Rhynie Man, the earliest known figure carving from Grampian

text. Although they are still in place, the author of this paper is not sure to what extent he managed to inform the visitor given that, for instance on the Mulloch example, he omitted any mention of the date of the stone circle's construction.

THE HERITAGE FUND

More direct involvement with on-site interpretation flowed from creation of the Regional Heritage Fund, which began life as a proposal in the *Rural Area Structure Plan* (Grampian Regional Council, 1985, p79), and was finally established in 1987. It now has an annual allocation of £20,000. The guidelines for the Fund give equal weight to the preservation and interpretation of the region's heritage. The Fund has been used in various ways. In 1988 it was used to enable the Council to acquire the famous Pictish carving of the Rhynie Man in order to protect and display it in a public place (the foyer of the Regional Headquarters) as a new form of institutional art. This action was also intended to promote a new role for similar pieces of early sculpture, and it is gratifying to see that the Knocknagael boar stone has now been placed in the offices of Highland Regional Council.

Other uses of the Heritage Fund have included support for part of the publication cost of Charles McKean's excellent, *Architectural Guide to Banff & Buchan* (1990), and assistance with the establishment of a revolving fund for our local building preservation trust, the North East Scotland Preservation Trust. Currently we are committing funds (together with Gordon District Council and others) to the restoration of the Garlogie Beam Engine, near Dunecht, which will ultimately become a Museum of Power under the North East Scotland Museum Service. We are also near to concluding the purchase of the Aiky Brae Recumbent Stone Circle which, with support from Banff and Buchan District Council and the Local Enterprise Company, will enable us to clear the trees which were planted far too close in the mid 1970s. We are also planning to create a carpark and footpath, linking the circle to the Buchan Line walkway and Aden Country Park. For the site of the Neolithic timber hall at Balbridie on Deeside (Ralston, 1983 and Fladmark, 1991) we have commissioned an interpretive board to place the now bare field in its ancient landscape context.

We have also supported two research excavations in order to further our knowledge of the region's past, in particular, attempting to date several currently undated features. We are co-funding, with the National Museums of Scotland, Alan Saville's work at the Den of Boddam near Peterhead, which is revolutionising our understanding of the extent and complexity of flint-mining in prehistoric Buchan (Saville and Bridgman, 1992). A long-term aim of this project is to provide adequate interpretation to link the objects inside our museums to the sites from whence they came. At Romancampgate, near Fochabers, an excavation by G J Barclay has elegantly demonstrated the date in the region of a previously enigmatic class of monument, the pit circle. The interests of the natural heritage are also represented by our assistance to the

Woodland Trust in the purchase of Den Wood, near Oldmeldrum, a fine remnant semi-natural wood.

Partnership is an essential element in the use of the Heritage Fund. This can be seen at Kinloss Abbey where we have supported Moray District Council and Historic Scotland at the beginning of a programme of consolidation which will lead ultimately to the proper presentation and interpretation of this important medieval monument. We have also contributed towards the costs of opening the Joiner's Workshop at Fordyce, a new venture by Banff and Buchan District Council and the North East Scotland Museum Service, to restoring the Wine Tower at Fraserburgh and to the consolidation of Coxton Tower in Moray. Also in Moray, we have given grant assistance for the purchase by the North East Scotland Preservation Trust of a salmon-fishing ice house at Findhorn, which will be leased to a local heritage association as an interpretive facility. The bias towards the north coast of the region that will be evident in this catalogue is deliberate and stems from the 1987 *Interpretive Strategy Review.*

OTHER PLAYERS

It must be stressed that Grampian Regional Council is not working alone in its policy to improve heritage interpretation. Three district councils, in particular, have recognised the importance of the cultural heritage in serving local and visitor needs. These are Banff & Buchan, Moray and Gordon Districts. Their interest in the cultural heritage stems, I believe, from a realisation that it helps to foster a sense of place, and also because it can be used as an agent of economic development, by building on the indigenous strengths of an area. Such motives clearly present the archaeological curator with some dangers, but they also help to widen the importance of archaeology in the public's mind from simply a constraint to development. We are thus able to realise the conservation ends of interpretation as outlined at the beginning of this paper.

It enables us to transform the stone dump in the corner of a field that masks an early feature, like many of our neglected recumbent stone circles, into something that is part of the community. I firmly believe that local interest is the best protection that sites of less than national importance (i.e. 95% of our heritage) can acquire. Here, the newly formed Friends of Grampian Stones, has the potential to develop into a form of active local interest or support group not previously seen.

In 1990 an Archaeological Working Party of Banff and Buchan District Council identified two principal types of archaeological site as having the correct combination of local character and strong visitor interest. First, kirkyards such as Pitsligo old Kirk which is surrounded by a wealth of richly carved 17th Century tombstones, and second, promontory forts like Castle Point at Troup (Cullykhan) were seen to be of particular significance and potential. Since then, the District Council's Projects Officer has been able to link certain schemes to the Local Enterprise Company's environment fund, an important consideration in raising adequate finance to see ventures like the Observatory at Pitfour or the harbour at Port Erroll off the ground.

Banff and Buchan District Council, in partnership with the Regional Council, Historic Scotland and the National Galleries of Scotland, and with the help of Grampian Enterprise, is also involved in two much more elaborate projects. At Banff, William Adam's masterpiece, Duff House is being transformed into a Country House Gallery as an outstation of the National Galleries of Scotland. This will be managed by the local authorities. At Kinnaird Head, Fraserburgh, it is still hoped to create Scotland's only museum of seamarking, using objects (ranging from vast lens assemblies to lighthouse keepers' bibles and badges) in the lea of the first light to be lit by the Commissioners for Northern Lights in 1787. The partners for this initiative are the Regional Council, Grampian Enterprise and the Scottish Tourist Board, with active support from the Northern Lighthouse Board and the National Museums of Scotland.

Moray District has successfully developed its own approach to countryside interpretation, concentrating on small but useful displays throughout the district, some museum-based, others site-based and on the Speyside Way. Kincardine and Deeside District Council is currently developing interpretation at the Mill at Benholm and Tullich Kirk on Deeside, and it has longer-term plans for Kindrochit Castle, Braemar. The Council was a partner in the development of the recently completed Braemar Heritage Centre.

THE GORDON ARCHAEOLOGY TRAIL

Gordon District Council has made the most progress towards interpretation of the archaeological heritage. This has stemmed, in part, from a working party on tourism that has been sitting over the last three years. It is made up of officers and chaired by the district's economic development officer. The members are drawn from the district and regional councils, the area tourist board, Grampian Enterprise Ltd and the local museum service. A two-phase approach has been developed with the intention of interpreting the local landscape and thereby seeking to prolong the stay of visitors in the district.

Phase one consists of a trail, the Circle of Stones, comprising 16 sites, many already accessible by the public and state-managed. There are seven stone circles, three hillforts and six Pictish stone locations, (a total of 13 stones) representing a good cross-section of the early archaeology of the North East. Sites like the recumbent stone circle at Midmar Kirk, the ceremonial enclosure and avenue at Broomend of Crichie, the striking early historic hillfort on the Mither Tap o'Bennachie, the Pictish symbol stones at Logie House (with its wheel Ogam), and Kintore Kirk were identified as being both robust enough and sufficiently accessible to become visitor attractions. Consultants were appointed to prepare the copy and to design boards for car parks and sites. The land acquisition, where necessary for car parking and access, was handled in-house by Gordon District Council's landscape architect and countryside planners, while obtaining the necessary permission for signage was a career in itself.

Several sites are in the guardianship of the Secretary of State for Scotland, some with recently augmented interpretation already. The concept of the trail allows for different features of the same site type to be interpreted at different locations. For example, at Loanhead of Daviot, the group effort which would have been required to create the recumbent stone is contrasted with the apparent individuality of the adjacent, and much more modest, enclosed cremation cemetery. However, at Easter Aquorthies, the spectacular petrology of the stones can be stressed, in particular, the great gleaming jasper monolith which forms part of the circle. At other guardianship sites, the standardised interpretation will be customised to augment, for example, the all-purpose Pictish symbol board at the Picardy Stone and at the Brandsbutt Stone and several other locations to the north and the south.

Three hillforts are included in the trail, two of them located on high ground. The thinking behind including such serious climbs as Tap o'Noth at Rhynie is that you will probably need a bed for the night once you've completed the ascent! It is, in any case at 563 metres in height, a spectacular site. The trail is now underway, the first phase car parking has been completed, and the boards went up in mid 1993. A related interpretive publication is planned. Some sites were omitted owing to the length of negotiations, but it is still hoped that the Mains of Balquhain's magnificent quartz outlier can be included.

Meanwhile, consideration of Phase two, an orientation centre and archaeology park, required the appointment of other consultants. Whether the study should be concept-led or market-led provoked much debate. In the end it was decided to go for the concept focus as the market would depend on the quality of the product. This was not a self-evident proposition to many tourist professionals. The consultants were appointed early in 1991, and a market analysis was also commissioned to produce a basic business plan. The usual iterative process of site visits and interim presentations ensued. The result was a document presenting the concept and market analysis of the Gordon Archaeological Centre (Event, 1991). The centre will, it is hoped, form the hub of the trail, in close proximity to the A96 Aberdeen to Inverness trunk road, the main artery through the region. The interpretation centre is intended to interpret the sites and give people a vivid appreciation of prehistoric culture, religion, warfare and agriculture. Exhibits will be a combination of three dimensional and interactive displays in the form of an entertaining 'time tunnel' (Event, 1991).

The centre itself is intended to be an innovatory construction. Hidden under a grass dome structure, it will appear from the surrounding countryside as a small hill. In a central state-of-the-art theatre visitors will watch the ancient monuments come to life. They will view the moon rise over a stone circle reconstruction, and see the dramatic storming of a hill fort. The theatre will recreate the battle of Mons Graupius which may, if we believe Professor St Joseph, have taken place very near to the site proposed for the centre (1976). It is hoped that a new understanding of the sophistication of our ancestors and the impression they made on the landscape will result. A tour of the centre will culminate in the chance to enjoy the use of modern information technology for an interactive assignment, the Gordon Challenge. It will be tailored to suit the interest and mobility of each group or individual. The challenge will take people on a journey around a selection of archaeological sites, taking in some of Gordon's finest scenery. Sites can then be seen in their real settings, and they will provide the clues to solving the challenge. Conservation will be addressed in the challenge to reflect site sensitivity.

It is intended that the building would be surrounded by a series of full-size reconstructions of monuments which have not survived from prehistory, such as timber halls and round houses. A strong educational element would be offered through the opportunity to conduct experimental archaeology. In this some echoes of interpretation in France or Belgium may be discerned, but neither the Archeodrome at Dijon, nor Blicqies in south-east Belgium, are precisely similar. The Archaeological Park at Beynac in the Dordogne (Chevillot, 1992) is certainly an inspiration while the Archeon in Holland is altogether on a larger scale.

INTERPRETATION AND EDUCATION

Last but not least important is the educational use that can be made of archaeological resources as represented not only by the sites themselves but also by the information held on them. Since 1976, the Regional Council has been developing a Sites and Monuments Record which is now the most complete source of information on archaeological sites in the region. More than 8,000 sites are recorded, along with supporting information in the form of photographs, plans, reports and correspondence. In common with most of the other eight Site and Monument Records recently compiled by regional or island authorities in Scotland, ours is now computerised.

In 1992 we commissioned Elizabeth Curtis to conduct a study of our Sites and Monuments Record, arising from an action point in our Environmental Charter (Grampian Regional Council, 1991). We see the way forward, in the 5 to 14 age range, as a series of teachers' resource packages integrating archaeology in the curriculum. Maths, drama, English, and environmental studies can all benefit from using archaeology, and, in particular, from taking children to sites. The sites have been assessed for their potential to benefit children, and matters such as access, documentation, plans, and a series of suggested questions and projects prepared for the catchment area of one of our academies (Aboyne and Upper Deeside). Curtis has now produced a second pack, for Central and East Gordon, and we hope over the next few years to cover the whole region (Curtis, 1993).

I would like to conclude with the thought that archaeology has a much wider scope in local authorities, of whatever tier or boundary, than purely as a planning constraint. It can and must be embedded in the fabric of all council activities; to do this the Regional Archaeologist has 'a mission to explain' the past of his or her area to its inhabitants, and to its visitors. The best place to start is in the classroom to catch the children, and one of our major initiatives in this area is to have produced a *Directory of Environmental Study Sites* (1993) as part of the Grampian Environmental Education Development Programme.

The author

Ian A G Shepherd has been Regional Archaeologist for Grampian Regional Council since 1975 and he currently chairs the Association of Regional and Island Archaeologists. Editor of the *Proceedings of the Society of Antiquaries of Scotland 1982-91*, his research interests are the early Bronze Age, the Picts and the role of public archaeology. His published works include *Powerful Pots: beakers in north-east prehistory, Exploring Scotland's Heritage: Grampian* and the forthcoming, *An Architectural Guide to Gordon District*.

References

Aldridge, D., *Principles of countryside interpretation and interpretive planning*, HMSO, 1975.

Barclay, G. J., forthcoming *Excavation of pit circles at Bellie, Fochabers, Moray*, in Proc Soc Antiq Scot, 122, forthcoming.

Binks, G., Dyke J. and Dagnall P., *Visitors Welcome*, HMSO, 1988.

Chevillot, C., *Beynee's Archaeological park*, 1992.

Curtis, E ., *Archaeology and Education: integration and co-operation*, Lecture to   Institute of Field Archaeologists Conference, 1993.

Event, *Feasibility Study for an Archaeological Visitor Centre in Gordon*, Event Communications, 1991.

Feachem, R., *A guide to prehistoric Scotland*, Batsford, 1963.

Fladmark, J. et al, *Tomorrow's Architectural Heritage*, Mainstream, 1991.

Fowler, P. J., *The past in a foreign country*, in Proc Soc Antiq Scot, 117, 1987, pp.7-16.

Grampian Regional Council and Countryside Commission for Scotland, *Interpretive Planning in Grampian*, CRC and CCS, 1977.

Grampian Regional Council, *A Regional Interpretive Strategy Review*, GRC, 1987.

Grampian Regional Council, *Rural Area Structure Plan*, GRC, 1985.

Grampian Regional Council, *Environmental Charter*, GRC, 1991.

Grampian Regional Council, *Directory of Environmental Study Sites*, GRC, 1993.

Highland Regional Council, *An Interpretive Strategy for the Highland Region* (First draft), HRC, 1993.

McKean, C., *Banff and Buchan: an illustrated architectural guide*, RIAS, 1990.

Magnusson, M. (ed), *Echoes in Stone. 100 years of ancient monuments in Scotland*, HMSO, 1983.

Munro, R .W., *Monumental guidebook 'in State care'*, in Proc Soc Antiq Scot, 115, 1985, pp.3-14.

Orkney Islands Council, *Westness Walk, Rousay*, OIC, undated (a)..

Orkney Islands Council, *Eday Heritage Walk*, OIC, undated (b).

Parker Pearson, M., *Visitors Welcome*, in Hunter, J. and Ralston, I. (eds.), *Archaeological Resource Management in the UK*, Sutton, IFA, pp.225-31.

Ralston, I.B.M., *A timber hall at Balbridie Farm*, in Aberdeen Univ Rev, 168, 1982, pp.238-49.

Ritchie, A. and Breeze, D. J., *Invaders of Scotland*, 1991.

Ritchie, J.N.G. and Adamson, H., *Knappers, Dunbartonshire: a reassessment*, Proc Soc Antiq Scot, 111, 1981, pp.172-204.

Saville, A. and Bridgman,D., *Exploratory Work at Den of Boddam, a flint extraction site on the Buchan Gravels near Peterhead, north-east Scotland*, Quaternary Newsletter, 66, Feb 1992, pp.4-13.

Shepherd, I.A.G., *Archaeology in environmental conservation in Grampian*, in Selman, P., *Archaeology and Planning*, Stirling Univ., 1988, pp.27-35.

Shepherd, I.A.G. and Ralston, I.B.M., *Early Grampian*, Grampian Regional Council, 1979.

Simpson, W.D., *Dunnottar Castle: historical and descriptive*, Milne and Wyllies, 1976.

St Joseph, J.K., *The camp at Durno and Mons Graupius*, Britannia, 9, 1978, pp.271-88.

15

THE HERITAGE OF ABERDEEN

James Wyness

Our heritage is the sum of our collective past, and its influence upon us. It is the lifeblood of our community and its people, the product of their achievements, and the wellspring of future visions. An important duty of the ancient office of Lord Provost is to act as the symbolic guardian of the city's heritage and to foster pride and joy among the citizenry of belonging to that heritage.

In this paper I endeavour to draw out the main strands which have gone into weaving the rich tapestry of our local history. I dwell on those aspects which have shaped our destiny and have made Aberdeen what it is today, and I conclude by describing present facilities and programmes for providing access to our heritage.

GEOGRAPHY AND EARLY HISTORY

Aberdeen was built on seven small hummocks separated by wet, peaty hollows created at the end of the last Ice Age. Two of the larger hollows were permanently flooded: the Lochs of Aberdeen and Old Aberdeen. The feature which most encouraged a community to develop here was the great tidal basin of the river Dee. This provided a wide expanse of tidal mud flats with broad mussel and reedbeds which were separated from the grey North Sea by the sandy, finger-like promontory of Futty.

Great quantities of shells and other marine deposits attributed to pre-historic folk of 5000 BC have been found on the tidal sandbanks in the estuary and there is also considerable evidence of early man in the form of burial mounds and standing stones in and around the city. 3000 years later, immigrants from Holland and the Rhineland arrived in primitive crafts, using the sheltered estuary as a base for their early fishing expeditions. Over succeeding centuries settlements became established and were known to the Roman Legions who initially reached the area under Julius Agricola around AD 84. Ptolemy's map of Scotland of AD 145 shows Devana, a settlement on the bank of the Deva Fluvius, near what has become Aberdeen. The Roman camp at Normandykes, near Peterculter on the outskirts of Aberdeen, brought in most of their supplies by sea, using the sheltered Dee estuary. More visitations of an unfriendly nature occurred later in the 12th Century when the Viking King Eystein attacked Apardion, the Norse name for Aberdeen, as recorded by the bard:

> I heard the overthrow of people
> The clash of broken arms was loud
> The King destroyed the peace
> Of the dwellers in Apardion

Some years later, the ships of the Viking, Swein Asleifsson, entered the harbour to celebrate with Scotland's King in festivities lasting over a month, on a site where the present harbour office now stands.

The town's early status in Scotland's history was established during the reign of King David I when 'Aberdine' was made a Burgh in 1136. This was later confirmed by King William the Lion in 1180 who granted a charter guaranteeing the Burgh's trading rights. Despite its favoured status, early Aberdeen must have been little more than a cluster of wattle huts, in the vicinity of what is now the Castlegate. At this time the Don estuary was closer to the Dee. Between the rivers were open sand dunes, on the leeward side of which were scrubland, heather and pockets of soil which would have been among the first to be tilled.

In the river valleys, particularly the Don, oak would have been the commonest tree in a mixed deciduous forest of ash, hazel, and wych elm, with a sufficiently rich wildlife, to attract royal hunting parties. This woodland gradually became forest pasture, used by the town's domestic animals. As the forest dwindled, the burgh closed in on what was left of the Royal Forest of Stocket. In 1494, a legal dispute over the ownership of the forest was decided in favour of the burgh, and between 1494 and 1606 the last remnants of the forest disappeared forever.

The earliest representation of the Arms of Aberdeen was on the seal appended to an obligation given by Aberdeen to Henry VI for the ransom of James I during his captivity in England in 1423-24. It shows a three-spired building, probably a church, which developed into a tower within a double tressure decorated with sixteen fleu-de-lys. The supporters in the form of lions, changed to leopards by the Lord Lyon in 1674, hold a scroll bearing the inscription 'Bon-Accord'. The double tressure and supporters denote royal patronage that was given by Robert the Bruce for help received from Aberdonians who used 'Bon-Accord' as their password in 1308 when they razed the Castle, then held by the English.

OUR HARBOUR AND TRADE

The sheltered estuary of the Dee was the major factor in the development of the town in the 13th Century with the earliest regular sea-borne trade to Flanders. In the 15th Century, trade decreased when the Hanseatic towns

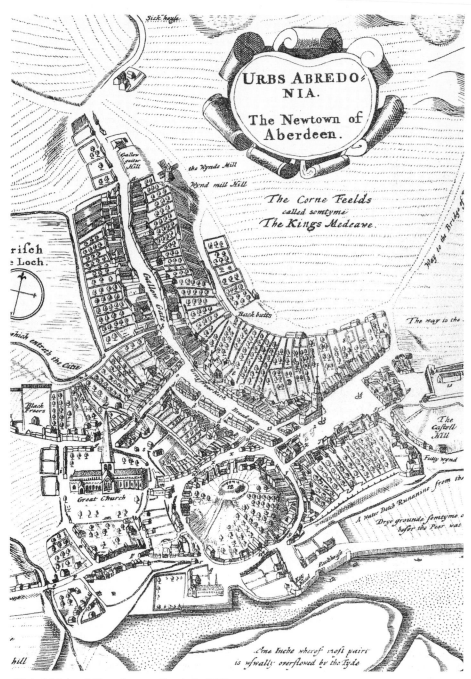

Inside the map:

Sick hoyle

URBS ABREDO-
NIA.

The Newtown of
Aberdeen.

the Wynde Mill

Wynd mill Hill

The Corne Feelds
called somtyme
The Kings Medeawe.

Gallow gaite Hill

Way to the Bridge of

rifch
e Loch.

The way to the

Back butts

which entreth the Cive

Black Freers

Broad gate

The Casstell Hill

Futty wynd

Great Church

A water Doth Runn into from the

Drye grounde somtyme
befor the Peor was

Backbutts

hill

One Inche wherof most pairt
is ufwally overflowed by the Tyde

Plate 1 Map of Aberdeen as it was in 1661

187

prohibited the importation of Scottish wool, but it then resumed and flourished with greater privileges being granted to Scottish merchants in Flanders. Wool, cloth, hides, furs, and salmon were exported, and wheat, provisions, wines, and a variety of luxury consumer goods were imported. Burgh records of this time show Aberdeen merchants willing and able to provide funds for the upkeep of city churches. Lack of good harbour facilities was not yet an obstacle as trade continued to develop, with traffic to ports in Scandinavia, Russia, Germany, Holland, Belgium, France, Spain, Portugal and the Mediterranean.

At this time Aberdeen harbour was the point of emigration for many who sought to avoid poverty, famine, and political or religious strife at home. It is said that Holland was over-run by Scots at this time, and many more emigrated to Poland which was then an attractive enterprise area. Notably, Robert Gordon of Straloch, benefited from trade with the Baltic area when, with wealth accumulated in Dantzig, he founded Robert Gordon's Hospital in 1731. More evidence of the munificence of the wealthy citizenry of Aberdeen is provided by an early example of the City's long links with shipbuilding and the Navy, when three ships of war were supplied in 1475 for the King and manned by 24 Aberdeen seamen.

In 1596, King James VI granted a charter to Aberdeen to collect a levy on ships entering the harbour to facilitate repairs to the harbour and the construction of a bulwark. This was erected along the Torry shore in 1607 but had little effect on the depth of the harbour entrance and was ultimately removed 200 years later. In 1610, David Anderson of Finzeaugh, known as 'Davie-do-a'thing', removed a large boulder which obstructed the harbour and in 1623 the quayhead was extended eastward by reclaiming the shorelands between the Denburn Estuary and Fittie.

New trades were established with Mediterranean ports and the New World. Indeed, it was an Aberdeen shipowner, John Burnet, who pioneered Scottish trade to the New World, a trade which gained in importance as many Aberdonians emigrated to the New World and the West Indies. Tobacco and sugar were being imported in large quantities, and Aberdonians were exporting wool, salmon, salted herring and wines from France. Towards the end of the century, exotic imports included hardwood and spices, and new street names like Jasmine Street, Lemon Street, etc. reflected the growth of this trade.

The 18th Century also saw the start of whaling, adding yet more pressure on the need for further development of the harbour. The turning point occurred in 1769 when the City invited the great 18th Century engineer, John Smeaton, to investigate the harbour entrance and suggest remedial measures to create greater depth at the bar. It was on Smeaton's recommendation that a pier was constructed at the north side of the harbour entrance on the Sandness, thereby providing entry and shelter for more and larger ships.

Early maps of the landscape between the Don and the Dee show an area denuded of trees, with a town on the Medieval pattern, centred around the church and market place. The amount of housing indicates a population which had probably trebled since the burgh register began in 1398. Today the

Royal Dee remains one of the great rivers of Europe and among the fairest water courses to grace a city, while the steep and wooded banks of the Don form a green and leafy enclave through the heart of the old industrial city.

RISE OF THE INDUSTRIAL CITY

The real growth of the city took place at the end of the 18th Century when Aberdeen rapidly became an industrial centre with a number of factories. The most important was Haddens, manufacturing stockings and woollen goods, Leys & Masson and Crudens, linen manufacturers, and Gordon and Barron, who produced cotton yarns and printed cloth. At its peak in 1840, the textile industry employed 12,000 people in some of the largest industrial units in Britain.

With the onset of depression in the early 1840s, industry began to experience difficulties and the result was a series of failures which saw only Richard's and Crombie survive. Three thousand workers lost their jobs and, in the industrial suburb of Woodside, the income of the inhabitants fell from £50,000 a year to £8,000. This dramatic collapse was due to the lack of cheap coal to power the new technology of that time.

A similar problem occurred in another long established industry, shipbuilding. At the beginning of the 19th Century, Aberdeen was a major shipbuilding centre, building more ships than any other British port. From around 1820 the introduction of steam-powered ships was a severe threat, since Aberdeen did not have easy access to the necessary coal and iron. Aberdeen's response was to build vessels for long-distance trades, where steam was not yet an advantage. The result was the golden age of the clippers when, between 1850 and 1870, superb ships like the Thermopylae and Yangtse won Aberdeen shipbuilders an unrivalled reputation. Advances in marine technology and the opening of the Suez Canal in 1869 ended this brief, but glorious, chapter.

Hall, Russell & Company began to build iron ships from 1867 onward but it was the emergence of a large fishing industry towards the end of the 19th Century which eventually provided the main source of demand for Aberdeen shipbuilders. Between 1886 and 1914, 496 steamtrawlers, 133 steam drifters and 23 steam liners were built. Two-thirds were for local owners, but such was Aberdeen's reputation that the remainder went to other ports of Scotland, major English fishing centres and abroad to Europe and South America.

The paper-making industry has a long history also, its origins going back to the 17th Century when the use of rags was the main raw material. Later, esparto grass and wood-pulp were imported through the harbour. Aberdeen, with its university, schools, printing firms, newspapers, law courts and offices, provided a ready market for the paper industry's products, although eventually firms grew to such an extent that most of the output was exported.

The most spectacular change to hit the city is of recent date. Since the 1960s, the development of North Sea oil and gas has had a major impact on our economy and the environment. Conservationists and planners, aware of the potential for damage to our heritage, have co-operated to minimise the adverse impact of new developments on the city's impressive granite heart. Industrial and residential estates have been built on the outskirts of the city, and we have endeavoured to preserve our superb environmental inheritance. Whatever yardsticks are employed, the growth of the North Sea oil and gas industry has been impressive and several factors have contributed to Aberdeen's emergence as the focus for the industry: proximity to the fields, harbour facilities, air services and road connections. Despite its association with major multi-national corporations, the exploration and production end of the oil industry is characterised by a fragmented commercial structure in which many activities are sub-contracted. This business environment promotes geographical concentration and guarantees Aberdeen's position for as long as the industry continues to operate in the North Sea.

AGRICULTURE AND FISHING

The industries which took advantage of the natural resources of the area were the enduring contributors to the economic development of 19th Century Aberdeen. As the main centre for trade in a mainly agricultural region, Aberdeen developed cattle markets and slaughter houses. This led, in turn, to subsidiary industries such as fertiliser plants, agricultural implement makers, hide and tallow works, fat refineries and perhaps, most spectacularly of all, the comb industry. In 1830 John Stewart moved from Edinburgh to Aberdeen to be nearer supplies of horn. By 1854 his factory produced nine million combs a year, employing 700 people. By the beginning of this century annual output had risen to an incredible 25 million. Today the region is still recognised world-wide as a producer of high-quality beef, cattle, pigs, poultry, barley and oats. Rather more romantically, our world-famous rose growers sell their products to all corners of the world.

The sea re-asserted its importance in 1882 when a group of local businessmen purchased the steam tug Toiler for use as a trawler and after six months fishing declared a dividend of 100%. Within a decade Aberdeen became the largest white-fish port in Scotland, with 38 home trawlers plus landings by many others. The reasons for this success were successive improvements to the port, particularly the completion of the Albert Basin in 1870, as well as good shipyards and repair facilities, a large local market, railway connections to the rest of Britain and good fishing grounds nearby. Because of good transport links, fish landed in Aberdeen was able to reach London in better condition than fish from the same grounds landed in Hull or Grimsby. Towards the end of the 19th Century, Aberdeen trawlers began to venture into the waters of the Northern Isles, Faroes and the Atlantic. Today, fish processing remains important with daily auction sales at the recently modernised fish market.

Perhaps the most well-known of Aberdeen's industries was granite. The industry began as a by-product of agricultural improvement, using boulders cleared from reclaimed land to produce paving stones. Although the earliest granite quarry (1604) supplied window sills and lintels, most pre-19th Century granite was chipped from the coastal cliffs at Nigg and Torry. As demand grew, an inland quarry was established on the rich seam of granite at Rubislaw. The hardness of granite, which had delayed the opening of quarries and its use as a building material, made it difficult to dress and polish the stone but in the 1830s Alexander Macdonald invented machinery to overcome the problems, bringing a tremendous surge of growth in the industry, with large numbers of granite polishing firms.

The modern City of Aberdeen may be said to have begun with the 19th Century and the building of Union Street as a costly and considerable engineering feat that required the construction of the Union Bridge, George Street and King Street. Marischal Street and others were thoroughfares of older date, like the Gallowgate, Shiprow and Guestrow. Although the forming of Union Street was of immediate benefit to the town for building purposes, its advantage as a main entrance from the south was not realised until the turnpike road was carried through Ruthrieston and Holburn to Union Place. King Street only became a main entrance from the north with the construction of the new Bridge of Don in 1830. Many other new streets were laid out from that time onwards, and a new town west of the Denburn began to spring up. The incorporated trades had a significant effect on the development of Union Street and the granite city.

Aberdeen exhibits a great diversity of building styles, but it was not until the commercial expansion in the 1800s that there was much scope for the architectural profession in Aberdeen. Nevertheless, architects of some stature were working in the city prior to the above date. Among these were James Gibbs who was responsible for the 18th Century fabric of the West Kirk, and there was John Smith who designed the colonnaded facade on the Union Street frontage of the St Nicholas churchyard. A little later in the century James Matthews was responsible for some fine buildings, including the Grammar School, Christ's College at Holburn Junction and the West Church of St Andrew.

However, it is to Archibald Simpson that the title 'Architect in granite' must go. It was he who shaped the modern day face of the city. Simpson used granite 'as the Egyptians did to bring out wide smooth masses contrasted with delicately cut mouldings'. Consequently, we are still able to enjoy the appearance of many attractive streets such as Albert Street, Bon Accord Crescent, and, of course, Union Street. The last of these was a costly and considerable engineering feat requiring the building of the Union Bridge, now one of the finest streets in Europe and due to celebrate its bi-centenary in 1994.

The kirk has been an important institution in shaping the destiny of our nation, as well as that of our city. St Ninian brought Christianity to Aberdeen in the 5th Century to lay the foundation on which our faith and religious institutions have flourished ever since. Although the See of Martlach was removed from 'Aberdon' in 1130, the rebuilding of what is now St Machar's Cathedral began about 1370. The other great building is St Nicholas, the first stone kirk which has stood as a symbol of Christianity in the heart of the city for almost a millennium. According to W.A. Brogden, it was founded before 1157 and known as the 'Mither Kirk'. It was the largest mediaeval Burgh Kirk in Scotland of which survive the 12th Century north transept, known as Collison's aisle, and St Mary's chapel. The groined vaulted crypt under the East Church was beautifully built in 1483 by Aberdeen's master mason, Sir Andrew Wrycht.

The religious history of the city is fascinating and did not produce the bigotry and excesses which so plagued the Central Belt and the West Coast. The City can boast of its tolerance and compassion and regard for property, artefacts and life. On the whole, the population accepted changes and turmoil created by outside forces like powerful families and national politics, e.g. Mary Stewart, the Earls of Huntly, the Marquis of Montrose etc. Indeed, it is claimed that the Reformation in Aberdeen was over in a week. Afterwards, artefacts in the churches were untouched, and even the Catholic Bishop kept his job and his flock, as well as Episcopalians who remained as numerous after as before. Threats to St Nicholas by 'dingers doon' were handled locally, and the congregation removed and sold valuables under threat by roup, using the finance to develop the harbour, repair the Brig of Balgownie, and even to buy arms for defence. Dissolution of the monasteries produced the finance to build Marischal College, and threats to King's College saw students organising the required defence. The emphasis in Aberdeen seems always to have been on pragmatism and compassion with an absence of excess in spiritual zeal. The main flock today remain Presbyterian, but there are large active Episcopalian and Catholic congregations as well as Congregationalists, Quakers, Pentacostalists etc. A mosque is in use and we have a small Jewish community.

Aberdeen has a long and distinguished reputation in the field of education. Today, standards in state and private schools are high. American, French and Dutch schools provide continuity of education for foreign visitors while special schools help deaf and physically or mentally handicapped children. There are a wide range of higher education establishments including two universities, the 500 year old ancient University of Aberdeen and the spanking-new Robert Gordon University. It is worth noting that between 1593 and 1860, Aberdeen, with Marischal College and King's College, was the only city in the UK with two universities, at a time when the whole of England and Wales made do with only two universities.

Founded by Bishop William Elphinstone in 1495, King's College, Aberdeen University, was to provide doctors, lawyers and clerics for the North-East of

Scotland. Indeed, it has the oldest English-speaking Medical School in the world, founded in 1497 over a hundred years before they discovered that blood circulated around the body. The University developed along European lines, drawing all that was best from the Renaissance. Marischal College was founded in 1593 as a consequence of the Scottish Reformation and the two existed uneasily side-by-side until a fairly acrimonious fusion in 1860. Today, a much enlarged and diversified University faces up to the challenges of the next 500 years as it approaches its Quincentenary. Today Aberdeen is renowned as a progressive centre for health care, mainly because of the university and some of the most advanced facilities and equipment have been funded, not from the public purse, but by the generosity of the local people, e.g. the Maternity Hospital, the Ophthalmology Department, the new Body Scanner. Sir Dugald Baird was a leading Obstetrician at a time when the 'pill' was first introduced to the world, and he coined the phrase 'the fifth freedom - freedom from fecundity'.

Our new university has a no less interesting heritage. Its foundation goes back to a bequest made in 1731 by a merchant, Robert Gordon, and the university started life in 1750 as a school for poor boys which developed into Robert Gordon's College in 1881, which soon thereafter absorbed the Aberdeen Mechanics' Institute. An other endowment from the local engineer John Gray added Gray's School of Science and Art in 1884, training responsibilities were transferred from The Aberdeen Pharmaceutical Society in 1898, and it became a central institution in 1903 under the name of Robert Gordon's Technical College. The term Institute of Technology was adopted in 1965, and since then several other disciplines have been incorporated. The present roll of 4500 students and 375 academic staff are organised into four faculties of Design, Health and Food, Management, and Science and Technology. It has a reputation for excellence using state-of-the-art technology for many subjects, particularly applied subjects and it was one of Scotland's largest polytechnic. In June 1992, it was granted University status as the Robert Gordon University, and during the same year it established a Heritage Unit under the direction of Magnus Fladmark.

With a wealth of specialised Research Institutes: the Rowett Research Institute, the Torry Research Station, the Macaulay Land Use Research Station, the Marine Laboratory, the Institute of Terrestrial Ecology, the Science and Technology Centre and the Offshore Technology Park with the world's only International Drilling and Down-hole Technology Centre, as well as the combined strengths of the two Universities' research resources, Aberdeen is well-placed to undertake the multi-disciplinary approach to research required by industry at a time when environmental issues are at the top of the political agenda. In 1993, the universities and these research organisations joined forces to establish the Aberdeen Research Consortium to take advantage of their combined strengths for marketing the research capabilities of the region and to act as a research base for the European Environmental Institute.

Among our illustrious institutions, we are very proud of the Gordon Highlanders. Formed in 1794 by the 4th Duke of Gordon with recruits from the extensive Gordon estates of Badenoch, Lochaber and Strathspey, and the counties of Aberdeen, Banff and Elgin. Legend tells of the recruits 'taking the shilling' with a kiss from the lips of Jean, the beautiful Duchess of Gordon. The Gordons first saw active service in Holland in 1799 and in its long history the regiment has won no less than 19 Victoria Crosses. We are ever hopeful that the history of the Gordon Highlanders will continue. It would be an immeasurable loss to the North East of Scotland to lose such an important part of our heritage, one in which so many take much justifiable pride, and whatever happens in the drive to merge Scottish regiments we shall continue to cherish the collection in their regimental museum in Viewfield Road.

OUR CULTURAL TRADITION

Central to our heritage are our language and our literature. The experience of John Galt's traveller when he alighted from the Edinburgh 'coach at the canny twa and twaetoun of Aberdeenawa' and had some doubts if the inhabitants spoke any Christian language is not unique, nor could it only have happened in 1793. The most casual visitor to the City is bound to be impressed by the vigour of the local speech called the Doric. The name comes from the ancient Greek and has long been used to describe northern tongues or accents, and it has as long a lineage as any other Anglo-Saxon tongue, coming to Grampian with the Normans in the 12th Century and gradually displacing Gaelic. By the 20th Century, the word had come to be applied mainly to the tongue of Grampian, with 'Lallans' or 'braid Scots' being accepted descriptions of the language elsewhere in Scotland. The main body of written Doric is poetry with its earliest known example being Barbour's *Brus*, poetry of the highest order. But most Doric poetry is to be found in the oral tradition. Grampian's many ballads, composed from the 14th to the 18th Centuries, were first collected by Greig and Duncan, and today work is continuing on an eight volume edition of the Greig Duncan Folk Song Collection.

By the late 19th Century, the agrarian life of Grampian was changing fast, and in the wake of the 1872 Education Act, literacy spread and with it, standard English. In reaction to this, poets like Charles Murray formed the vanguard of a vernacular movement, writing and publishing in Doric even from as far away as South Africa. His collection, *Hamewith*, is still in print. The new life of the 19th Century also produced a new form, the bothy ballad, and it is heartening to hear these passed on at such events as the Buchan Heritage Festival. Perhaps the greatest local writer drawing on the Doric tradition was Lewis Grassic Gibbon, born James Leslie Mitchell, before the pseudonym and *Sunset Song* brought him huge acclaim. Two more novels *Cloud Howe* and *Grey Granite* make up *A Scots Quair*, all fine works by any standards. Today the Doric remains much more than merely a form of speech: it is the embodiment of a whole way of life, intimately interwoven with the social and economic fabric of the region, and a cultural heritage of which to be proud.

Plate 2 Field Marshall Sir Donald Stewart (1824-1900) came from Forres and attended King's College Aberdeen, where he distinguished himself in Greek and Latin. He started as an ensign in the 9th Bengal Infantry and, after an illustrious military career, he rose to be Commander-in-Chief of the Indian Army 1881-85. On his return to Britain , he was invested with the insignia of the Grand Cross of the Star of India and served on the Council of the Secretary of State for India. He was the fourth officer of the Indian Army to reach the rank of Field Marshall.

Grampian can also boast a formidable number of renowned artists including George Jamesone who dominated Scottish portraiture in his day and whom Walpole called 'the Van Dyck of Scotland', James McBey, for whom North Africa was the inspiration and Joan Eardley, who, from her house on the coast at Catterline, painted haunting seascapes and landscapes.

In the field of traditional music, Grampian has long been unsurpassed, and her fiddle music was and remains seminal, now at the heart of the Scottish folk music revival. Grampian's greatest fiddler and composer, and a man of international renown, was James Scott Skinner. Today, these many facets of the artistic heritage are nurtured by organisations such as the North East Scotland Heritage Trust which aims to highlight the cultural heritage of the area, including the Doric language, so as to raise awareness and interest in schools and the wider community.

Other Aberdonians (using the term broadly to include the City's hinterland) have continued the rich seam of famous and inspirational characters who serve to bring focus to our rich and varied heritage. They include General Sir Patrick Gordon, a close associate of Peter the Great of Russia; Field Marshal Sir Donald Stewart, who was educated at Marischal College and became head of the Indian Army; Alexander Cruden, the compiler of the Bible Concordance; Mary Slessor, the missionary who devoted her life to the Calabar Mission in Africa; Thomas Blake Glover, who brought the railway to Japan; the photographer, George Washington Wilson; and Mary Garden, prima donna at the Paris Opera. Personalities of more recent vintage include Ian Wood, the industrialist; swimmers Ian Black, David Wilkie and Neil Cochran; Michael Clark, the dancer and choreographer; Andrew Cruickshank, the actor; the late Bill Gibb, the fashion designer; Evelyn Glennie, the percussion player; Denis Law, the footballer; Annie Lennox, the popsinger; and Robbie Shepherd, the broadcaster. No roll-call of our great heroes would be complete without mention of the Dons, the city's famous football club, founded in 1881 and winner of many honours, including the European Cup Winners Cup in the last decade.

ACCESS TO OUR HERITAGE

We have produced a trail leaflet of commemorative plaques in and around Aberdeen which indicate the place of birth or residence of many former citizens of significance: Harry Gordon, Willie Miller, Fraser Clyne, Provost Skene, Provost Ross, John Abercrombie, Isobel, Lady Aberdeen, William Ewart Gladstone, Dr Mary Esslemont, Lord Boothy, Donald Dewar, Alick Buchanan-Smith, Chris Anderson, Sir Alexander Anderson, John Smeaton, James Gibb, Archibald Simpson, John Smith, Sir David Gill, Alexander Macdonald, Prof John Clark Maxwell, and George Washington Wilson.

For public access and enjoyment of outdoor amenities, large areas of Aberdeen are laid out in public parks and gardens. Principal among these is Duthie Park, gifted to the City by Miss Duthie, with 125,000 rose bushes and Winter Gardens with a variety of familiar and exotic plants, notably 600 species of cacti. Others include Hazlehead with its three golf courses and famous maze; Westburn Park; Victoria Park with its gardens for the disabled and the blind; Seaton Park, first ever recipient of the 'Playground of the Year' award in 1976; Union Terrace Gardens, with its Victorian sunken gardens in the heart of the city that provides a natural amphitheatre for outdoor concerts; Johnstone Gardens with its stream, waterfalls, ponds and small rustic bridges; Doonies Farm, run by the City and open to the public with a wide range of livestock; and Lochinch Farm, which is being developed as a farming heritage centre.

The City provides a range of high quality venues for the performing arts, including His Majesty's Theatre opened in 1906, with a capacity for 2,550 and designed by the theatre architect, Frank Matcham. In 1975, the Theatre was bought by the City, and it was totally refurbished in 1980. Many top productions visit the city, and the box office has frequently been hard-pressed to cope with the demand of eager Aberdeen audiences. In Union Street there is the Music Hall, at the heart of concert life since 1822. It was refurbished in the mid 1980s and combines classical design and superb acoustics with comfortable modern facilities. The best of small scale touring theatre is presented at Aberdeen Arts Centre, along with productions by local drama groups. Our newest live arts venue, The Lemon Tree, opened in 1992 and features a Studio Theatre, three small workshops, and a Cafe Theatre.

The City has an Art Gallery of national standing and three very fine museums. They are James Dun's House and Provost Skene's House and then there is the Maritime Museum which interprets the shipbuilding, fishing and oil industries through its displays and excellent viewpoint from which it is possible to view ships in port. In this museum there is also an unique collection of oil related equipment, large scale models and audio-visual presentations. The University of Aberdeen's Anthropological Museum at Marischal College has an extensive collection outlining the history of the area from pre-historic times, and Peacock Artspace welcomes artists of all abilities to use the workshop facilities and visitors to its regularly changing exhibitions.

The Library Service offers the people of Aberdeen one of the most progressive library systems in the country through a network of 19 Branch Libraries and a large Central Library. In addition to lending out books, the libraries are used as venues for initiatives like the Reminiscence Project which has been established to record memories and the history of our heritage. Satrosphere is a much-admired attraction, that offers children an insight into the nature of the world around them. Constantly changing exhibits display the effects of the laws of physics and chemistry, as well as the geology of our environment. They invite participation and interaction by visitors, making sciences more exciting and attractive to both children and adults alike. It is designed to inspire young people to take an interest in the scientific world and help all visitors to appreciate and enjoy the world around them.

We also seek to give life to our heritage through an events programme, e.g. in 1991 saw the arrival in the City of the Cutty Sark Tall Ships Race and five days of exciting events culminating in the spectacular 'Parade of Sail'. The following year saw another unique occasion, when the City conferred its highest honour, the Freedom of the City, on H.M.S. Scylla. The vessel is a Leander Class frigate and the occasion marked 50 years of close association between the City and the Royal Navy.

We retain our strong foreign links, which have done so much in the past to enrich the heritage of Aberdeen, through our highly successful twinning programme, which in 1991 won the Royal Mail Twin Town Award for 'the Most Successful Twinned Town in the UK to Improve World Harmony'. The City has links with Regensburg, the Bavarian city on the banks of the Danube which has welcomed countless visitors from Aberdeen over the years; Clermont-Ferrand with which many social and cultural exchanges have taken place; Bulawayo, where the emphasis is on provision of aid via the Aberdeen Bulawayo Trust; Gomel, a link which has significantly emphasised the humanitarian aspect of twinning; and Stavanger with which the ancient links to our Viking cousins were revived and officially sealed in 1990.

Our environmental flagship initiative to secure a high quality of life into the next century is the Aberdeen City Centre Project which works to revitalise the historical core of the city around Union Street. Other projects include the Keep Aberdeen Tidy Campaign, which actively encourages people living in the city to help protect their environment; Links to the Future is developing a range of new facilities at the city's Beach area; and the Access to Leisure scheme entitles disabled and disadvantaged citizens free or discounted access to a wide variety of leisure and sports facilities.

In conclusion, this is the story of how the strands of our heritage overlap and interweave to make a pattern that is unique to our Aberdonian heritage tartan. Over the years, the enduring threads are of a community of people both canny and thrawn, whose path forward has been smoothed at various times by men and women of vision and enterprise. It is only by recognising quality and working to maintain it, that we can hope to uphold a heritage worthy of sharing with visitors to our granite city in the future.

The author

Dr James Wyness has been Lord Provost and Lord Lieutenant of the City of Aberdeen since May 1992. During his distinguished career as a local politician, having served as a city councillor since 1980, he has held numerous chairmanships of committees and boards, including being Convenor of the Policy Committee and Leader of the Council. His varied professional career has been in shipbuilding, the merchant navy and the teaching of history. His greatest personal interest is to encourage awareness and pride in the heritage of Aberdeen, and he was awarded an honorary doctorate by the Robert Gordon University in 1992.

References

Brogden, W.A., *Aberdeen: An Illustrated Architectural Guide*, R.I.A.S./Scottish Academic, 2nd ed., 1988.

Chapman, W.D. & Riley, C.F., *Granite City: A Plan for Aberdeen*, Batsford, 1982.

Fraser, G.M., *Aberdeen Street Names, their History, Meaning, and Personal Associations*, first published 1911, with a new foreword and supplement by M.Henderson, James G.Bisset, 1986.

Gibbon, L.G., *Sunset Song*,

Gibbon, L.G., *Gloud Howe*,

Gibbon, L.G., *Grey Granite*,

Graham, C., *Archibald Simpson -Architect of Aberdeen 1790-1847* (Bicentenary Edition), Aberdeen Civic Society, 1990.

Harris, P., *Aberdeen at War - A Pictorial Account 1939-45*, The Press & Journal in assoc. with Archive Pub.Ltd., 1987.

Harris, P., *Aberdeen Since 1900*, The Press & Journal & Evening Express in assoc. with Archive Pub.Ltd., 1988.

Keith, A., *A Thousand Years of Aberdeen*, AUP, 1972.

Keith, A., *Eminent Aberdonians*, Aberdeen Chamber of Commerce, 1984.

Leckie, R., *Grampian: A Country in Miniature*, Canongate, 1991.

MacKenzie, H., *The Third Statistical Account of Scotland - The City of Aberdeen*, Oliver & Boyd, 1953.

Murray, C., *Hamewith*,

Omand, D. (ed), *The Grampian Book*, The Northern Times Ltd., 1987.

Robbie, W., *Aberdeen - Its Traditions and History*, D.Wylie & Son, 1893.

Smith, J.S. (ed), *Old Aberdeen - Bishops, Burghess and Buildings*, AUP, 1991.

Stones, J. (ed), *A Tale of Two Burghs. The Archaeology of Old and New Aberdeen*, Aberdeen Art Gallery & Museums, 1987.

Turner, J.R., *Scotland's North Sea Gateway - Aberdeen Harbour 1136-1986*, AUP, 1986.

Wilkie, M. & Garden., E., *This Braif Toun*, Aberdeen Art Gallery & Museums, 1975.

Wyness, F., *City by the Grey North Sea*, Impulse, 1965.

Wyness, F., *Royal Valley - The Story of the Aberdeenshire Dee*, A.P.Reid, Aberdeen, 1968.

INTERPRETATION AND PRESENTATION

Studies in Telling the Story

Making the ordinary
seem extraordinary,
through interpretation

16

THE NORTH EAST OF SCOTLAND AGRICULTURAL HERITAGE CENTRE
Interpretation at Aden

Andrew Hill

Wedged between the Laigh o' Moray and the Howe o' the Mearns, the North East contains a quarter of Scotland's arable land, and consequently farming is an essential part of our rural life past and present. The story of this farming heritage is presented by the North East of Scotland Agricultural Heritage Centre, situated 30 miles north of Aberdeen, between the villages of Old Deer and Mintlaw, amongst the beautiful woodlands of Aden Country Park. Since its foundation by Banff and Buchan District Council in 1985, the Heritage Centre, which achieved provisional museum registration status at the outset of the Museums and Galleries Commission scheme, has aimed:

> to acquire, conserve, research, communicate and exhibit material and oral evidence of agricultural and rural life in North East Scotland, from the eighteenth century to the present day, for the purposes of study and enjoyment by the public.

Housed within the unique semi-circular Home Farm of the former Aden Estate, the Heritage Centre has become a focus for the preservation and display of this region's distinctive farming past. In the course of this overview I shall chart the phases of development, guiding principles and interpretive plan associated with the establishment of the Heritage Centre, but first an introduction to Aden's history.

THE RUSSELLS OF ADEN

The name Aden (pronounced Aa-den) is first recorded in the illuminated Celtic church manuscript, the Book of Deer, where it appears as a boundary marker for a gift of land to St Drostan's monastery at Old Deer. After the Wars of Independence, King Robert the Bruce rewarded his faithful supporter Sir Robert Keith, later the first Earl Marischal, with lands which became the barony of Aden. For the next three hundred years, Aden remained in the ownership of the Keith family but Aden's present appearance dates from the ownership of the Russell family.

Alexander Russell, a Banffshire laird, purchased the estate in 1758. Filled with contemporary ideas of farming 'Improvement' he reorganised his tenant farms, planted woods for shelter and built a modest house overlooking the South Ugie Water. Succeeding generations of Russells completed the transformation by building the unique steading, c1800, and enlarging the mansion in 1832 to plans by the Aberdeen architect, John Smith. The estate's wealth rested on farming and the Home Farm is a showpiece. The semi-circular steading came to include a sawmill, dairy, byres, stables, threshing mill and rooms for the farm servants. With not only farm and house staff but also gardener and lodge keepers, the estate was important to local employment and village shopkeepers. By late Victorian times the estate covered 31 square miles, making it one of the largest in Buchan.

Nevertheless, by the 1920s the house and beautiful gardens were in their last flowering. Spiralling maintenance costs when combined with falling farm income became burdensome, and finally in 1937 Sidney Russell sold Aden, much of Old Deer and the estate's remaining 52 farms. A succession of new owners used the estate mainly for shooting and instead of the care lavished by the Russells and their staff, the buildings were neglected and the grounds became overgrown.

ACQUISITION BY THE DISTRICT COUNCIL

In 1974 Aberdeen County Council decided to purchase the Aden Estate as part of its plans to provide housing at Mintlaw, but this was conditional on the policy woodlands being retained for the community's benefit. Local government reorganisation the following year meant it was the new Banff and Buchan District Council that took the decision in 1976 to develop the central part of the estate as a country park. Shortly after this, the District Council approved plans to restore the Home Farm with advice from Magnus Fladmark who supported an initial feasibility study funded by the Countryside Commission for Scotland et al. The intention was to provide a heritage centre for telling the estate's history, and the Council's decision was the start of putting into action a recommendation of the influential report, *Regional Interpretive Planning in Grampian* that had been jointly produced by the Countryside Commission for Scotland and Grampian Regional Council (1977).

Considerable financial assistance from the Countryside Commission and the Historic Buildings Council enabled the ambitious restoration programme to succeed, despite the project's total cost of £326,000. Furthermore, the quality of the restoration was commended by the Scottish Development Agency and the Royal Incorporation of Architects in Scotland (The

Regeneration of Scotland Design Award 1985) and by the Association for the Preservation of Rural Scotland in 1987. An imaginative exhibition was mounted based on the personal accounts of actual Aden Estate staff of the 1920s, and with the Country Park's official opening in 1980 by Viscount Whitelaw of Penrith, a nephew of the last Russell laird, the first phase of the Heritage Centre's development was completed.

THE ADAMSTON COLLECTION

The Grampian interpretive plan, referred to above, had also discussed the region's then sole agricultural museum at Adamston near Huntly. This substantial and significant collection of North East farming and rural craft material had been amassed by Hew McCall-Smith, but in September 1983 it was offered for sale. Encouraged by the National Museum of Antiquities of Scotland and the Countryside Commission, the District Council purchased the Adamston Collection with a view to augmenting the existing estate theme.

In order to assess and develop the newly acquired collection, a professional Curator was appointed in July 1984, initially for two years with grant-aid from the Countryside Commission for Scotland. The assessment included not only the documentation of the Adamston Collection, but of equal importance was the definition of the scope of an agricultural museum at Aden and establishing the parameters of the museum's collecting policy. The combination of restored nineteenth century estate farm buildings, regional farming collection, agricultural land and the proximity of the estate village of Old Deer made Aden the ideal location for a regional country life museum of national importance. This approach was wholly in keeping with an earlier joint policy document (Aldridge, 1972) on the creation of country life museums issued by the Scottish Country Life Museums Trust, the National Museum of Antiquities and the Countryside Commission, which identified the North East as one of twelve ethnological or cultural regions in Scotland with the potential to develop such a facility. The Scottish Museums Council and the North East of Scotland Museums Service supported this view and consequently this regional outlook was enshrined in the Heritage Centre's name, aims and collecting policy and these recommendations were approved by the District Council in January 1985.

After initial documentation and establishing the Heritage Centre's operational brief, the next priority was the conservation of the collection and this was made possible in 1985 by the leasing of a redundant factory unit encompassing 450 square metres of floor space for conversion as a conservation workshop and store. With assistance from the Scottish Museums Council, a specialist *Conservation Survey* (Hill, 1984) was undertaken. This study provided the plan for equipping the workshop with storage racking, environmental control and monitoring equipment, together with instructions for safe work procedures for first aid conservation. Subsequently, an Agricultural Engineer and two assistants were recruited to help with the collection's removal from Huntly and then the ongoing conservation and restoration programme could begin.

THEMES OF THE PLAN

As conservation progressed, consideration was given to an interpretive plan, since it was important to look at the former Adamston collection in relation to the existing theme of estate life, and also to consider future possibilities. Don Aldridge's excellent guide (Aldridge, 1975) to the subject of interpretive planning (updated 1993) proved invaluable to the drafting in 1985 of a five year Interpretive Plan (Hill, 1986), which included five interpretive themes:-

Aden Estate Story - existing exhibition and period Horseman's House (1983) augmented by a costumed interpretive guide(1985).
Weel Vrocht Grun (well worked ground) future synoptic exhibition to explain, using the Adamston collection and new donations, agricultural change in North East Scotland over two hundred years: requirements new exhibition hall, conservation of implements for display, design and production of exhibition, new marketing leaflet and poster.
Working Farm - future open-air section illustrating life on a small North East farm between 1930 and 1959, and including a reconstructed house and steading with twenty to thirty acres of land.
Estate & Village - future walking trail of the estate's buildings combined with a tour of Old Deer village highlighting the ties between farm and village.
Rural Heritage - future car trail of sites and interpretive facilities on particular agricultural or rural themes (e.g. Water power, Planned Village movement) throughout the North East.

This plan became the blueprint for the Heritage Centre's future programme of interpretation and presentation.

WEEL VROCHT GRUN

Following the permanent appointment of the museum's first Curator in 1986, work commenced on the second interpretive theme, Weel Vrocht Grun. This theme involved the construction of a purpose-built exhibition hall (300 square metres at a cost of £90,000) with grant-aid from the Countryside Commission for Scotland and the exhibition design and production (£50,000) with the assistance of the Scottish Museums Council. The exhibition was divided into four sections:

The Face of the North East - introduction to the region's farming;

The Changed Landscape - land clearance, drainage and enclosure associated with initial agricultural 'Improvement';
The Pattern of the Past - North East farming activity displayed according to the traditional six year crop rotation;
The Shape of the Present - innovative video cartoon illustrating the evolution of farming over the past forty years.

A companion booklet, *North East Farming Life* (Fenton, 1987), providing greater detail than could be included in the exhibition, was written by Dr Alexander Fenton who also opened the exhibition on 1st May 1987 as scheduled. The new exhibition attracted the interest of both local folk and visitors, and, together with the associated programme of promotion, had a very significant impact on visitor numbers. Visits almost doubled in 1987 to 51,236 peaking in 1989 with more than 61,000. The Heritage Centre's expanded catchment area could be gauged from the more dispersed origin of visitor survey respondents, and a better awareness of the Centre's educational value led to a corresponding increase in the number of guided school parties. Still wider recognition was conferred by the presentation of the second prize in the 1988 Scottish Museum of the Year awards and a Certificate of Distinction in the British Tourist Authority's Come to Britain Awards. This very positive reaction to the completion of the second phase of development, generated the momentum to investigate the feasibility of the third interpretive theme, the Working Farm.

THE WORKING FARM CONCEPT

Whilst existing exhibitions illustrated the daily routine of this estate's Home Farm and the changing face of North East farming, what was plainly missing was an opportunity for the visitor to experience traditional farming at first hand. Furthermore, the Interpretive Plan and subsequent Feasibility Study (Aldrige & White 1989) identified a number of advantages for the interpretation and management of the Working Farm, which would accrue to a reconstruction at Aden:

1. On-site comparison between a laird's home farm and a small tenant/owner occupier's farm; thereby interpreting the composition of the North East farming landscape.
2. Direct connection between the synoptic exhibition Weel Vrocht Grun that explains the context of the open-air operations of the working farm in terms of farming and technological changes over time.
3. Introductory video to the working farm shown in the Heritage Centre's video theatre.
4. Existing agricultural land of realistic acreage, twenty to thirty acres, screened by plantations ensuring the reconstruction

would neither impinge upon, nor be intruded upon, by the original estate buildings.

5. Existing on-site provision of necessary visitor facilities and security.

6. Finally, but importantly from a cost/benefit viewpoint, was diversifying the scope and increasing the attraction of Aden as the District's main tourist destination.

With the above considerations in mind it was decided to look for a representative North East small farm in keeping with the maximum acreage available within the park. Dr Ian Carter has shown in his book, *Farm Life in Northeast Scotland 1840-1914* (Carter, 1979) that the greatest proportion of holdings for central Buchan, some 50.1%, were between five and forty nine acres. Coincidentally therefore the small farm was more truly representative of early 20th Century North East farming than the Aden Home Farm. Indeed, Buchan estates were composed of numerous small tenant farms. In this case it was decided to find a farm with approximately thirty acres to match the acreage at Aden.

The selection of a suitable farm was narrowed down through use of Dr Bruce Walker's very helpful pilot study, *Farm Buildings in the Grampian Region* (Walker, 1979). This study sought: 'to identify the vernacular building styles most characteristic of farming in Grampian Region, or of more limited geographical areas within the region, as a first step towards ensuring the conservation of an adequate number of such buildings'. The pace of farm amalgamation noted, has in fact accelerated in recent years, to the extent that many a small farm is reduced to a few acres of paddock and a modernised farmhouse. Although the most common large farm steading layout was found to be a truncated 'H' plan, it was also appreciated that the type of terrain and soil quality tended to determine the proportion of large to small farms; and therefore differences in steading size and layout. In the Buchan area, where more than half the holdings were less than 50 acres, steading size reflected this fact and many smaller farms exhibit simpler 'L' or 'U' shaped layouts even though the accompanying farm house was often of the standard one and half storey dormer type.

Given the interpretive benefits of a farm reconstructed at Aden and the foregoing curatorial research into its selection, a specification of the farm sought comprised the following checklist of requirements:

Distance from Aden	: Less than 15 miles
Acreage	: 25-50 acres, preferably circa 30 acres
Construction date	: 1860-1920
Building plan	: Standard Buchan farmhouse with steading 'L' shaped with railway carriage, or 'U' shaped
Condition	: unaltered or little changed from 1930 to 1959; oral and/or

		documentary evidence if possible to record and date alteration
Completeness	:	Fixtures/fittings dating from the 1930s and including machinery and implements if possible
Contents	:	Past house/steading objects available for purchase or donation
Tenure	:	Probably owner occupier, but may have been tenant farm owned/built by an estate in the 19th Century
Oral & doc evidence	:	Same family's ownership throughout the era to be interpreted; estate records extant for the 19th Century

HARESHOWE OF IRONSIDE

The above specification was already in mind when the donation of an ox collar in 1986 called attention to the 30 acre farm of Hareshowe of Ironside, then owned by Margaret Barron, which was situated near New Deer some nine miles from Aden. A tour of the farm confirmed it fitted Dr Bruce Walker's description of the standard Buchan farm, even to the inclusion of a railway carriage on the fourth side of the farm close. Lastly, and very importantly for the successful documentation of the project, was the fact of the Barron family's long association with the farm since 1935, which of course coincided with the era chosen for interpretation. After discussion with the District's Leisure and Recreation Department, it became clear Miss Barron would herself be pleased to be associated with such an ambitious project if it proved viable.

It was to investigate the concept of a working farm, that the District Council approached the Scottish Development Agency in February 1988 for assistance towards a feasibility study. The consultants, Pieda and Ian White Associates, gathered information during the following summer and reported to a District Council working party in the Spring of 1989. The findings indicated that there was no perfect solution and a compromise over the question of authenticity would have to be accepted. Although moving a small farm from its original context inevitably prevented a totally authentic reconstruction, it was also the case that the Buchan landscape had itself altered so dramatically since the 1950s that new industrial field crops and modern sheds would impinge visually upon any in-situ reconstruction of an earlier farming era. The consultants tested Hareshowe of Ironside against the working farm specification, and concluded that it matched the blueprint.

Alhough this conclusion was very encouraging, it was the visit in June 1989 of the late Dr Malcolm S. Forbes that led to the start of the project's fund raising. His timely donation of £10,000 was welcomed by the District Council which that autumn endorsed approaches for grant-aid to the Countryside Commission, the Scottish Tourist Board and the Scottish

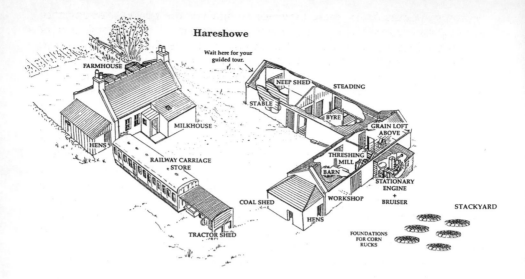

Hareshowe

FARMHOUSE

Wait here for your guided tour.

NEEP SHED

STEADING

STABLE

BYRE

MILKHOUSE

GRAIN LOFT ABOVE

HENS

THRESHING MILL

RAILWAY CARRIAGE STORE

BARN

STATIONARY ENGINE + BRUISER

COAL SHED

WORKSHOP

STACKYARD

HENS

TRACTOR SHED

FOUNDATIONS FOR CORN RUCKS

Figure 1 Schematic of Hareshowe, as reconstructed at the North East of Scotland Agricultural Heritage Centre, Aden country Park

Plate 1 The Aden Home Farm

Museums Council. All these agencies recognised the project's importance and together agreed to finance a large proportion of the total cost of £340,000. This in turn led to the appointment of Douglas T. Forrest, Architects of Cullen, already well-known for architectural restoration of historic properties in the North East, as project architects. Study trips were made to two pioneering open-air museums to discuss the philosophy of building construction and I am pleased to acknowledge the most helpful assistance given by John Gall at Beamish and Dr Alan Gailey at Cultra. After discussing the different emphases given to authenticity and interpretation at these renowned museums, it was decided that authentic reconstruction at Hareshowe should be taken as far as possible on those elements that could be seen by the public. With thirty years from which to choose to set the interpretation of the site, it was agreed to take the year 1955 as the base date, since it was the arrival of electricity that had last altered the farm. The changes that had occurred over the previous twenty years would be reviewed and interpreted by costumed interpretive guides.

The summer of 1990 saw the farm contents inventoried, and detailed plans of the buildings drawn, with their keystones numbered to enable exact reconstruction. This finally left the way clear for the appointed builders, A.D.Walker Ltd of Banff, to move on site at the end of September. The next seven months saw the dismantling, photographic recording (of exterior and interior structures), rebuilding and landscaping of the new site at Aden. This new site had formerly consisted of a 20 acre field with another 10 acre field alongside that offered expansion to a full 30 acres if required. Existing plantations screened the field and therefore the imported farm buildings do not impinge upon the architectural integrity of the original Aden buildings.

After the builders had completed reconstruction on schedule in April 1991, the museum's curatorial staff with the kind assistance of Miss Margaret Barron, reassembled the contents of each room in the house and put back in place all the fittings , implements and artefacts associated with the steading. Detailed job descriptions were written for the four costumed interpretive guides and staff with previous local farming experience were selected. The house and steading guides were then given individual training by Miss Barron herself. The whole process of dismantling and reconstruction was made into a ten minute video film entitled, 'It's mair like hame noo!', which is shown as an introduction to the site at the Heritage Centre, and has since won the Audio-Visual Presentation Prize at the 1992 Scottish Museum of the Year Awards. Finally, on 3rd May 1991 Jack Webster, Buchan journalist and television broadcaster, invited Miss Barron officially to open the new farm. Subsequent public reaction has been very favourable; most find it hard to believe it was not always there! In the course of the first season more than 14,000 visitors were welcomed and the farm was awarded a British Tourist Authority Come to Britain Certificate of Merit in 1992 and a Commendation from the Society for the Interpretation of Britain's Heritage in 1993.

It should be clear that the Hareshowe project could only confidently proceed because detailed primary historical research had been carried out by Carter, Fenton and Walker. A great debt is owed to the Scottish

Development Agency, the late Dr Malcolm Forbes and the central government funding agencies which worked together very effectively. As to the actual reconstruction, this task would have been impossible without the good humoured assistance of Miss Barron. Over the past season, the Assistant Curator has developed an interesting programme of demonstration events based at Hareshowe, including an appearance by the Scottish Horse Ploughing Champion team.

FUTURE PROSPECTS

So what of the future of the North East Scotland Heritage Centre and its interpretive plan? This museum has been exceptionally fortunate in the timing of its developments since the open window of economic opportunity seems to have now closed, but all the interpretive objectives have been either successfully achieved or are in process of attainment. The idea of a Rural Heritage car trail has been developed by the District's Tourist Board and the Heritage Centre now maintains its first outstation, the renovated Sandhaven Meal Mill, as a working exhibit. The last remaining interpretive theme, the Estate and Village walking trail, is still viable due to its low cost and it is hoped to include this theme as part of the updating and redesigning of the Aden Estate Story scheduled for completion in March 1995. Furthermore, with the end of the documentation backlog in sight, the heritage centre can look forward to full museum registration next year. It is through the efforts of many individuals and agencies that Aden has evolved, but special tribute must be paid to Prof. Alexander Fenton, Gilbert Carling and Don Aldridge.

Through the establishment of the Heritage Centre and by following a detailed plan of interpretation, the District Council has not only developed a significant addition to its tourist attractions, but more than that, it has preserved a representative picture of local twentieth century rural life, the importance of which will continue to increase with the passing of the years. I am confident that Aden will long continue to contribute to the understanding and quality of life of North East Scotland.

The author

Andrew F. Hill is Curator of the North East of Scotland Agricultural Heritage Centre and Country Park Manager in the Leisure & Recreation Department of Banff & Buchan District Council.

References

Aldridge, D., 'Museums and Historic Interpretation with reference to an Ideal National Pattern and the Scandinavian and American Analogies', *Country Life and Museums: an Ideal National Pattern*, Scottish Country Life Museums Trust & Countryside Commission for Scotland, 1972.

Aldridge, D., 'Principles of Countryside Interpretation and Interpretive Planning', *Guide to Countryside Interpretation Part One*, HMSO 1975.

Aldridge, D. *Site Interpretation: A Practical Guide*, Scottish Tourist Board, 1993.

Aldridge, D. and White, I. *Development and Management study for a working farm at Aden Country Park, Mintlaw*, 1989.

Carter, I. *Farm Life in Northeast Scotland 1840-1914*, Table 1.4, p.30, John Donald,1979.

Fenton, A. *North East Farming Life*, Banff and Buchan District Council ,1987.

Hill, A. F. *N.E. Scotland Agricultural Heritage Centre Interpretive Plan*, Banff and Buchan District Council, 1986.

Hill, L. J.K. *Conservation Survey and Report for the Aden Agricultural Heritage Centre*, Scottish Museums Council, 1984.

Regional Planning in Grampian, Countryside Commission for Scotland and Grampian Regional Council, 1977.

Walker, B. *Farm Buildings in the Grampian Region* 1979, Countryside Commission for Scotland, preface also Fenton, A. and Walker, B. *Rural Architecture of Scotland*, 1981, 183-210, John Donald.

17

THE NEW LANARK STORY

James Arnold

New Lanark is an historic cotton spinning village roughly equidistant from Glasgow and Edinburgh. It was founded by a partnership of David Dale, a Glasgow merchant, and Richard Arkwright, the English inventor. Together they harnessed the power of the Falls of Clyde as the river poured its way out of the Southern Uplands towards Glasgow. Fame on an international scale was achieved by David Dale's son-in-law, Robert Owen. He moved to live in the village in 1800 and it became the centre for a series of utopian experiments which attracted world attention. Cotton production survived from the 1780s till the late 1960s. Closure brought crisis. A housing association and a conservation trust were formed to pick up the remnants.

As well as being one of the foremost industrial heritage sites of the world, it is also special in terms of interpretation. The village is located close to the Falls of Clyde, one of the tourist sights of Scotland as early as the 18th Century. To the natural splendour of Corra Linn, the largest of the falls, was added the human construction of a utopian industrial colony. Robert Owen welcomed travellers from all over the world to see his wonderful achievements in constructing a better society. As well as welcoming visitors and encouraging them to sign the mill's Visitors' Book, he was also an active interpreter. His idea that, 'Of all truths it is the greatest, that man's character is formed for him and not by him', became a dominant theme in his philosophical propositions. He was prepared to make very substantial financial commitments to support this view. He built for this purpose in 1816 his New Institution for the Formation of Character, and in 1817 his School for Children. It is symbolic that these buildings, like the rest of New Lanark, remain virtually unchanged to this day.

Even when Owen left New Lanark after 1825, he did not cease his interpretive activity. He travelled extensively in Europe and America, promoting his ideas on social organisation. Among these ideas, New Lanark was always the prime example. Therefore, interpretation has been especially significant to New Lanark. The tradition which saw 400,000 visitors come to the village in 1992, was first nurtured during the Owenite period, and it is these special elements of heritage interpretation that this paper seeks to explore and explain. To do this it first examines the position in the 1970s, when key decisions were being made, and then it outlines the actual results achieved, with special attention to interpretation. Finally, it proposes a vision for the future - towards the interpretive millennium.

PRECARIOUS BEGINNINGS

In 1974 New Lanark Conservation Trust was established. It was a shell trust, rather like a shell economy. It was supported, on a short-term, temporary basis, by a combination of local and central government organisations. None of these wanted to take responsibility for the ruined, derelict, closed, decaying, rotting, depopulated, isolated, and insoluble problem that was New Lanark.

Unless specific project results could be identified and delivered, the Trust's core funding would collapse into a widening credibility gap, and the heritage represented by New Lanark would disappear by demolition. This was a real possibility in the 1970s. It has happened throughout the UK to other examples of industrial heritage. For the village to survive, the Trust had to deliver restoration and development projects on a scale as large as any in Scotland, but with no resources. The answer came, mainly as an accidental benefit, from central government unemployment relief schemes, and the Trust was able to capture a small part of the new monies made available through the Manpower Services Commission. For about a decade, large teams of workmen were harnessed to the cause of the 'revivification' of the village. By these means, not because of any specific grand design of governmental planning, was New Lanark saved.

Probably the most important principle was the use of unemployed labour as a resource to establish the foundations for future self-sufficiency. To do this, it was necessary to focus efforts on specific buildings and programmes that could generate economic returns. Failure to concentrate effort in these areas would only result in project collapse when the temporary resource was exhausted. It meant, for example, not having a large team of publicly financed guides who could give virtually every visitor individual attention. Market expectations would be distorted, and there was no prospect that such a level of support could be sustained.

The above background and challenges are significant because I believe these underlying features have constrained and directed our activities. The main influences on interpretive decisions have been the deep crisis of cultural confidence through which we have all been living, coupled with an absolute requirement for short-term, self-financing success. This displays only two of the mechanisms by which any interpretation is irrevocably linked to the circumstances of its time. Our interpretive proposals are rooted in our joint understanding of the times through which we are living, as well as the immediate pressure of production and delivery. From my observation it seems that most interpreters inhabit a similar, sometimes less demanding, environment. It would probably be more comfortable if we were able to escape the short-term pressures of economic necessity. However, if this luxury were possible for some of the luckier ones among us, we should remember that we would then be likely only to escape into the self-embrace of our own analytical subjectivity.

ESTABLISHING A TRACK RECORD

Progress since 1974 has led to current success. This is probably most evident in awards for conservation and tourism: a Europe Nostra Medal, the British Tourist Authority 'Come to Britain' Trophy, a Scottish 'Tourism Oscar', and so on.

Part of the reason for this success is that the village provides a particular and well-located example of industrial heritage which can be successfully exposed for the purposes of commercial tourism. This is not always possible, and for other sites is sometimes extremely difficult. However, New Lanark is a large and visually stunning site, able to attract and accept large numbers of visitors to its historic fabric with no real threat of damage to its virtually indestructible physical construction. In Scottish terms it would be able to accept the largest numbers of visitors imaginable, and there would be no prospect of significant damage caused by the endless shuffling of eroding feet, or even the caress of loving hands on soft stone. We have a large, but physically tough, site which is capable of absorbing as many visitors as we are ever likely to receive.

This, and the physical size of the site, has meant that we have been required to confront the issues raised by large scale tourism. Success and results were required fairly quickly. The growth rate since the acquisition of the industrial area in 1984 has been phenomenal - from zero paying visitors in 1988 to 150,000 in 1992. If a site as physically large as New Lanark is going to rely on tourists to provide economic support, then this has to be on a large scale, as reflected in the 400,000 total who visit the village each year.

Major elements in the paying attraction are: the physical grandeur of the landscape setting and site; the Falls of Clyde Nature Reserve; the historic character of the restored buildings; a dark-ride 'The Annie McLeod Experience' where a ten year old girl tells you of her life in Robert Owen's village; the working historic textile machinery; the imaginative use of audio-visual presentations; the catering and retail areas offering attractive leisure eating and shopping. The main, but not exclusive, focus of the attraction is certainly 'Annie McLeod' which is a powerful creative evocation of the feeling of New Lanark in the 1820s.

New Lanark has become, in Scottish terms, a major tourist attraction, where visitors pay for entry, which is revenue self-sufficient, rural, and which would be capable of self-sustaining growth. There is some public authority revenue core-funding, but this now represents less than 15% of total turnover, and is primarily directed towards development work. Public sector capital investment in the main visitor facility was approximately £1m, excluding the cost of labour provided through training or unemployment relief schemes. This combination of public sector capital investment from various sources has established a successful business activity based on tourism. Achieving this result has been a process of planning, design, hard work, and good fortune.

INNOCENCE v INTERPRETATION

Theoretically it is a valid option to do no interpretation, to have no interpretive provision, to allow the site or subject to speak for itself to all humanity. At various times I have found this an extremely alluring option, or at least to take the Ozymandias approach, in the words of P.B. Shelley:

> My name is Ozymandias, King of Kings:
> Look on my works, ye Mighty, and despair!
> Nothing beside remains. Round the decay
> Of that colossal wreck, boundless and bare
> The lone and level sands stretch far away.

This minimalist approach is potentially exceptionally comfortable. It permits the continued existence of an internalised, self-justifying procedure, which limits knowledge and understanding to a culturally privileged elite. If that elite group has shared assumptions it is not necessary to expose this esoteric understanding to general critical review and public consumption.

We manage to sustain a position of protected innocence for around 50% of our visitors. They are able to enjoy a free visit to one of the world's great sites with no requirement to engage in any interpretive procedure, other than to gaze at the ruins of the statue of Ozymandias as represented by the remnants of six-storey cotton mills. If these visitors gain anything from their visit, it is as a result of the interaction between their immediate visit and whatever they had in their heads before they arrived. As far as our surveys can determine, these innocent souls betray no particular dissatisfaction at having escaped our interpretive attentions. They profess to have enjoyed their visitation to an awe-inspiring historic village and depart with their original state of blissful innocence intact.

In its own way this is a humbling experience for the would-be interpreter. It raises key issues of why we should seek to interpret the site beyond this initial level, and of how difficult it is actively to engage the interest of most individual visitors.

THE FALLS OF CLYDE

At this point an intriguing prospect opens before us, and before our visitors. Corra Linn is the major feature of the nature reserve adjacent to the village.

The reserve covers nearly 80 acres and is owned and run by the Scottish Wildlife Trust. In interpretive terms, as well as the physical allure, it is a veritable Garden of Eden. There visitors promenade in sweetness and innocence - probably about 100,000 of them in any single year. Little distracts their attention from the diversion of enjoyment. Here there is only nature and the innocents. The human hand is confined to: hydro-electricity generation; control and management of the landscape for forestry and farming; the beaten path of the well-trodden route to pleasure; and a few vital safety signs. At least in interpretive matters, innocence is more fully sustained. Virtually all interpretation is confined to the wildlife visitor centre within the village of New Lanark itself. The voice of the interpreter is heard in this particular Garden of Eden only when a provided guide reveals the 'fruit of knowledge' to the visiting innocent.

This situation is more by accident than design, and it provides an interesting contrast to New Lanark itself. The focus of the Scottish Wildlife Trust is not to create a commercially-operated site where it is critically important to attract and explain the significance of the site to visitors for reasons of future economic development and survival. Rather, their interest is to preserve and manage, perhaps rather similarly to a museum curator and museum collections, for reasons which are internally justified and which do not require wider approval and support. I hasten to add that these observations are not intended to be critical. It is completely justifiable to take such a view of a resource, and, particularly if you are an independent owner, to treat the resource as you wish.

THE INTERPRETIVE SIGNIFICANCE OF NEW LANARK

Clearly, New Lanark has experienced a commercial requirement to interpret. Visitors are prepared to pay for access and understanding. When we charged for access alone, we charged less than one-fifth of the current £2.60 entrance fee. When we introduced interesting media systems to explain particular stories to people, we were able to increase the numbers to 150,000 at more than quintuple the original charges. To achieve these results was critical for the future of the village and the particular buildings involved: the Institute for the Formation of Character, the Engine House, and Mill Number Three. Revenue brought by visitors sustains the fabric of the buildings and provides 50 jobs. Further, it creates an enormous success at the heart of the Trust, and the heart of the village. Powerful and interesting interpretation has been crucial to the development of this position.

This economic imperative is reinforced by my view of New Lanark as a place of more than ordinary significance. In itself the physical presence of the village, and the mechanics of factory production, are strong enough stories. Particularly when, as in the case of the village, the package is so visually powerful, historically complete, and virtually undiluted by later development. However, the significance of the village goes far beyond this banal immediacy. In the works and presence of Robert Owen, and in the principles he sought to apply, we have one of the roots of the way we understand our society today. His physical contribution to New Lanark was primarily the community buildings: the Institute, the School, the Co-operative Village Store, and the Nursery. These represented the philosophy of a 19th Century reformer struggling to come to terms with the social changes wrought by the Industrial Revolution.

In interpretive terms it is helpful, but not vital, that Owen's views have remained so relevant, and are still the fundamentals of social debate. Poverty is only one example. Owen thought that society should be managed in a way that eliminated the concept of poverty. It was unacceptable that fellow human beings should be allowed to sink to the level of physical degradation that could be seen plainly in many parts of early 19th Century Britain, let alone the world. Underlying many of his views is a deep understanding and sympathy for the human condition, and a compelling desire to create a better future for us all.

A clear illustration can be understood by visiting other mill complexes, or other industrial sites. The story of production, its developments and recessions, are much the same in principle. The human beings involved could have been as benevolent as David Dale, the original founder of New Lanark, or as Titus Salt, the founder of Saltaire. Exposure to Owenism does mean that in visiting these other places you become aware that there is an element missing, and it is this element that gives New Lanark its key significance. It is Owen's visionary world view, and its relationship to New Lanark, which is the special significance of this place. This represents the real significance of New Lanark and the real challenge of interpretation. The challenges are surprisingly difficult to resolve. It appears to be much easier, to interpret a battle, a war-hero, the home of a noble family, or the humble memorabilia of provincial villages.

Research possibilities based on New Lanark and Robert Owen are prodigious. The bibliography of Owenite publications prepared by the National Library of Wales is a book in itself. To help overcome such a daunting prospect, I normally refer newcomers to J. Butt (1971) and Donnachie and Hewitt (1993). The sheer volume, as well as the depth and richness, of the material available has the potential to overwhelm the interpreter, and there is also the prospect of the piercing attention of the best academic brains in the country. Heritage interpretation is obviously no place for the faint-hearted. Planning and execution of sustained brilliance is required even to approach success. The interpretive disaster of an indifferent television programme, or a poor novel, can dissipate. Programmes are soon forgotten and books go out of print. However, heritage interpretation tends to adopt the status of hardware, and to last an uncomfortably long time.

Easy escape from these issues does not appear possible. We have become compulsive communicators. If we have found a place of significance, we as human beings are compelled to proclaim the news to the world. Our claims are racked-up by the competitive media system. How much of this is true can be gauged by considering the clandestine option. How could we keep such a secret? Perhaps, only if such revelation endangered the site. However, in an age of democracy such concealment is not likely to be acceptable. The people must know all, and it is in their right to decide acceptable limits. The 'fruit of knowledge' is available for free consumption via the market place.

Democracy and interpretation is an interesting issue, particularly in a democracy which provides most of the funds for the sites and the collections involved. To consider this, just look at the sites represented by the papers in this volume. Most are dependent for their present condition on substantial public funds, and also on the democratic manipulation of existing financial structures for their particular benefit. It is possible to continue to interpret for minorities, but in the end this privilege is dependent on the approval of the representatives of the people's majority. In these circumstances it is difficult to be anything but actively popularist in interpretation.

This implies a multi-layered approach to interpretation. If we are to seek to interpret to all our visitors, it would appear unwise to accept that any single approach will engage their interest. At New Lanark we have tried to structure a systematic presentation to our visitors which we hope will assist and encourage their progressive engagement with our interpretive arrangements.

PRIMARY INTERPRETATION

A decade of interpretive planning has resulted in a provision of various themes operating at different levels. Even for our most innocent visitor it is difficult to escape the First Interpreter. Even heaven-bent innocents would find it difficult to sustain their lack of knowledge when confronted by our initial signposting. Virtually all our visitors come to the car park. They disembark from their vehicles unassailed by anything other than a modest invocation to park in the correct place. Once free from their chariots, however, they become fair game for the arresting powers of one or two of our external signs.

Generally we use external interpretive panels, or signs, hardly at all. We are currently reviewing this position, but as a policy we have chosen to minimise the intrusion on the historic site which would be caused by modern signage. In particular we do not tell our visitors what a particular building is by fixing a descriptive plaque to it. Our signs tend to be of four types:

1. A first general orientation sign which gives people an initial understanding of what it is they are looking at, when it was built, and how important it is;
2. A group of signs on buildings help with identification of specific buildings, but at this stage not them all;
3. A group of signs giving minimal directions;
4. Temporary directional signs help to direct flow and focus attention. They intrude on the site but have no sense of permanence.

THE HERITAGE TRAIL

On top of this primary level of interpretation, we sell a Heritage Trail booklet to take the visitor around the village. About 10,000 are sold each year, for about £1 each. These provide a simple basic description of what the visitor sees, when, how, why and what it all means. The material is selected to take 30-45 minutes, and to keep visitors out of the residential areas of the village. The sequence of the walk has been carefully planned, and is as shown on the accompanying illustrative pages.

The trail booklet is deigned to guide you on a walk round the village, by following the numbers and the route map on the cover. The guide firstly covers village housing (1-6), starting at the Mill Gates where most of this can be seen from the village square, and visitors are encouraged to avoid straying into private property. The booklet covers the following: (a) Counting House; (b) Village Store; (c) Nursery Buildings; (d) New Buildings, (e) Village Housing, Long Row, Double Row, Rosedale Street; (f) Dale's and Owen's House; (g) the Institute for the Formation of Character; (h) Engine House, (i) Mill Lade; (j) the Mills; (k) Robert Owen's School for Children; (l) Foundry and Mechanics' Workshop; (m) Retort House; and (n) Falls of Clyde Nature Reserve.

The route is open-ended, in that it takes the visitor to the contemplation of the idyllic prospect represented by the Falls of Clyde nature reserve and its untold possibilities. Armed with this book visitors will gain a basic understanding of the village. They might even glean some knowledge of conservation and development, but this is not essential.

In the context of some of our later decisions it should be noted that the Heritage Trail is the basic interpretive tool which has been in use in New Lanark for over 15 years. It was preferred to external notices and signs, or listening posts, or audio-visual programmes, because it was self-financing, not visually intrusive in the historic fabric of the village, and could be operated flexibly by individuals or groups. It was also a souvenir which could be taken home to remind you of your visit and encourage you to return.

PUBLICATIONS

A range of other publications extends this initial descriptive theme into an array of printed information available on many aspects of the village. To the list of publications listed under references can be added those which are planned: a power trail, a booklet on village housing, and potentially many more. From the list of references it can be seen that there is a substantial tiered range of printed material which explains virtually every theme writers have been able to imagine, and which we have found useful to present to our public. The main themes are explored and re-explored at various levels suitable for a wide range of interest and attainment.

New Lanark
Heritage Trail

New Lanark Conservation Trust
Lanark ML11 9DG Telephone 0555 61345

New Lanark
Conservation

From the list of references it can also be seen that for some aspects, alternative media have been developed. Where it is suitable audio and video materials are available. These assist by providing a genuine range of options for the visitor. People buy the music to play in their car cassette systems as they leave the village. Ideally the interpretive script could be played before you arrive, but for other than organised coach tours this level of preliminary preparation is not likely to be attainable. New Lanark is fortunate in having developed a wide range of interpretative material in printed and related forms. This creates a solid interpretive base, which not only provides a simple introduction, but can inform even the most ardent academic.

THE NEW LANARK VISITOR CENTRE

Until 1988, New Lanark survived with no specific building identified as a separate visitor centre. However, in a real way this was simply a delay caused by restoration works, since from the Owenite period there had been the concept that the experience of visitors was enhanced by allowing access to major buildings. In the period in which this could not be achieved, we were the subject of criticism. It was something that visitors obviously missed.

A decision was taken that visitors ought to be encouraged to maintain that tradition established by Owen, and enter a visitor facility through the main porch of the Institute for the Formation of Character. It was just possible that this could have some beneficial impact on the personality. It was also the case that the building is at the centre of the village, as it was at the centre of Owen's philosophy. Therefore, by opening this community building for the purposes of our world visitor, we were continuing the original intention, and in physical terms re-asserting the importance of explaining the historic experience represented by New Lanark.

In terms of interpretive planning there are severe physical problems relating to access to historic buildings, especially access for the disabled and disadvantaged. To some extent these have been overcome by the construction of a ramped access system which allows individuals to follow a route through the ground floor of the Institute, into the adjacent Engine House, into the upper floor of the Institute (the Gallery Room). Visitors then cross a glazed bridge, which is a replica of an original corrugated-iron clad rope race, but which now transfers visitors into Level 5 of Mill Number Three. From here visitors enter and leave each floor of the mill via a continuation of the ramp, which is formed into a 'rectangular spiral' at the eastern end of the mill. In this way a route has been created through an historic complex, allowing visitor access to the upper floors of the cotton mills. Research, and our own experience, strongly indicated that the normal mill stairs were a most severe disincentive to visitors, and that without this access system the majority would never experience the spaces in the upper floors of the mill buildings.

The interpretive procedure which the visitor follows starts in the entrance area of the Institute. In each of the areas there are evident sub-themes, but I

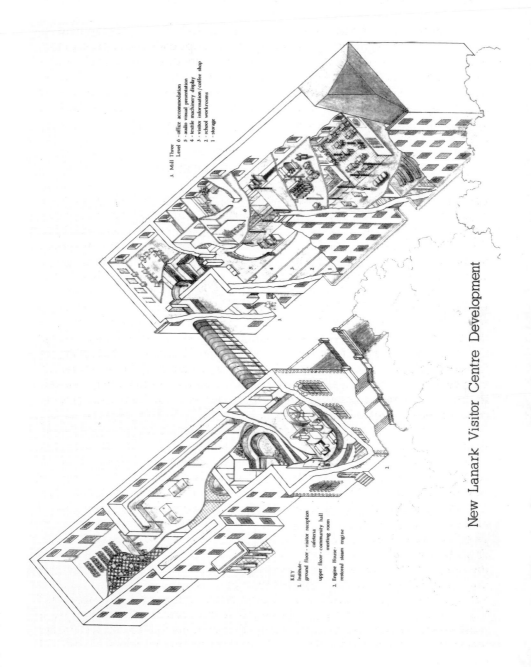

KEY:
1. Institute:
   ground floor - visitor reception
                  cafeteria
   upper floor - community hall
                 meeting room
2. Engine House:
   restored steam engine

3. Mill Three
   Level 6 - office accommodation
         5 - audio visual presentation
         4 - textile machinery display
         3 - visitor information / coffee shop
         2 - school workrooms
         1 - storage

New Lanark Visitor Centre Development

have sought to concentrate on the main thrust of the storyline. Before visitors have to pay for entry they can find out about the building they are in, and a basic introduction to New Lanark. The 'introduction' comprises: why and when the village was founded; what are the most significant aspects of its development; the general layout of the site; the modern, living community; and what else there is to see if they pay to enter the remainder of the complex. Fortunately, in 1992 we received 150,000 guests who were sufficiently encouraged by their initial experience to pay the entry charge.

Our introductory material is characteristic of much of our interpretation in the visitor centre. There is comparatively little text - we have become experts at minimalist captions. We have read the research, and it agrees with our experience, that the concentration span of visitors when reading captions is very, very short. We have been anxious to avoid the presentation of material to visitors which we know they will not consume. Therefore, we try to find alternative media to make our points. If captions are unavoidable, they are brief. You should be able to read our captions as you stroll past them. You will have perceived from our list of publications available for sale that there is ease of access to more detailed layers of information. The displays, particularly display boards and captions, accept that they can only tempt the appetite for what is a potential feast of data.

Having paid for entry, the visitor is introduced to the idea that 'power' is the basis on which New Lanark was founded. This is done by bringing inside the building a water exhibit. This contravenes the principle that the interpretation should occur where the site best illustrates the point being made, but the physical impossibility of achieving any rational sequence of explanation with this particular issue meant that we felt our approach to be justifiable. This is particularly the case when we are able to sustain the theme by entry into the Engine House and by the introduction of the idea of steam power and other forms of energy. How each of these is tackled is potentially the subject of a separate paper. At this stage it is sufficient to say that they provide the foundation for later understanding. It is interesting to note that the water power exhibit is entirely synthetic, and was constructed to serve a specific interpretive purpose. The mill steam engine is a genuine, twin-tandem, compound, 250hp example, by Petrie of Rochdale. It was saved from the Scottish Borders textile mill by the Trust more than 15 years ago. It replaces the original engine which was also a Petrie. It is an interesting speculation as to which, the synthetic exhibit or original artefact, is the more effective interpretive device.

Visitors then enter the Gallery Room of the Institute. The function and purpose of this room is outlined by a single display board, which explains the use of this grand and elegant room. Visitors can delay here to experience a 10 minute video. This is a video-disc system which, on demand, will reinforce the introductory story which visitors have already seen, explain more about the specific room in which they are, and tell them what to expect next. The purpose is to offer an alternative medium which is more acceptable to some of our visitors, and to re-assert the power/manufacturing/social organisation sequence.

Crossing the glazed bridge into Mill Number Three we hope will be an exciting architectural experience. Certainly it provides the opportunity of looking outward. New Lanark is a complicated site, and we are conscious of how frequently we need to allow visitors the opportunity of re-orientate themselves. To facilitate this, there are simple transparent viewpoint panels. These allow you to align the specific buildings with identification panel.

The bridge also provides a covered queuing area for visitors as they wait to enter Level 5 of Mill Number Three - 'The Annie McLeod Exprerience'. On approximately 20 peak days per year there is a queue of 1½ to 2 hours. On another 20 to 30 days there would be a queue of 20-30 minutes. It would be possible to arrange that this queue should be held outside the entrance to the buildings. However, the Scottish weather encouraged us to be friendly to our visiting queue, and to locate it inside, with a good vantage point, where visitors could be occupied by the view of other site activity. Initial survey investigations into the psychology of queuing have produced the surprising evidence that most visitors are happiest when they have queued longest. These early conclusions have not yet persuaded us fully of the advantages of arranging artificial queue procedures.

Peak demand is caused by the interest in The Annie McLeod Experience. This is a 10-minute controlled interpretive experience. Visitors sit in two-seater modules, suspended from a monorail. The modules are individually powered, and each has a separate compact disc sound system. Your individual commentary is by a 10 year old child, a mill-girl, who is part fiction and part fact, and is called Annie McLeod. She tells you of her life in New Lanark around about 1820. She speaks to you as a 'ghost' from the past, recounting a little of her life and experience. You travel in the dark, through a series of interconnected scenes, threaded together by Annie's commentary. Five languages in addition to English are available. The Annie McLeod Experience has been a most exciting interpretive adventure for New Lanark Conservation Trust. Our exit surveys indicate that it is the element of their visit that people remember most vividly.

This 'dark ride' has 22 modules and can deal with 264 people per hour. Over a six-hour day, for 360 days per annum, it could handle 570,240 visitors. Obviously it would be possible to extend the working day beyond six hours, but except on the very peak days this has not proved necessary. It can be operated by a single person, but on busy days two people are required. The total floor area of this exhibit is 6,000 sq.ft. From the 'dark ride' of Level 5 of Mill Number Three visitors spiral down the ramp system to Level 4 where they find working machinery and a series of displays:

1. Picking up the Threads, which tells of the story of textile manufacturing;
2. A Childhood of Love and Learning, which tells of the games and learning in which children engaged;
3. The Search for Universal Harmony, which is an audio-visual presentation of the ideas of Robert Owen.

It is important that there is a change of pace for visitors. In the Annie McLeod Experience, their timetable is controlled, as are the input and stimuli. On Level 4 the pace is self-regulated by the interest and engagement of the visitor. A major element of the engagement is an 84 ft. long, 392 spindle, spinning mule, driven by overhead line shafting. It is a noisy, sophisticated, mechanical spinning device, of the general type for which Mill 3 was originally constructed. It is operated by a mule-spinner. When it is switched on it demands your attention, and is virtually impossible to ignore. It was selected as the classic machine of the industrial revolution, which would engage visitors' attention and focus their interest. It is not usually operated for longer than 10 minutes at a time, in order that the noise does not drive away visitors. A silent, continuously running, video explains the process of spinning. When the machine stops the interpreter/operator explains the individual details of the mule.

The spinning machine is part of the 'Picking up the Threads' interpretive display which introduces visitors to some of the basic concepts: the increase in the use of cotton in the late 18th Century; a plantation system based on the exploitation of workers; the various processes of manufacture; the continuing success of cotton as a product; and other textile fibres. All these are touched on lightly. The main purpose is to introduce the visitor to the concepts, and allow a little further thought. Specialist publications on textiles and textile machinery are available at our retail outlet, but are rarely purchased.

'A Childhood of Love and Learning' picks up the child-related theme of The Annie McLeod Experience, and links through this to the experience of 'piecers' - the children who worked under the spinning mules. In the stories of the street games, and the copies of Robert Owen's 'Rolls of Time', there are the messages of what life was like before state education and television.

Finally, on this floor, 'The Quest for Universal Harmony' is an eight-minute audio-visual interpretation of Owen's philosophy as applied to our current lives. Using a Welsh-accented actor, some of the themes of Owen's life are given a pointed relevance to our current view of society. Examples of the related themes are, housing, education, trade unionism, social deprivation, internationalism, and the environment. While a historic chronology is sustained, each theme is brought forward into the life of the viewer. It is difficult to see how this could be done in any way other than by using audio-visual techniques. The use of display boards, or printed material, would be comparatively cumbersome. In a real sense, The Quest for Universal Harmony is the core of the interpretation of the extra dimension which is represented by New Lanark. It is a mechanism to illustrate the concept that the creation of economic wealth by the industrial revolution was not an end in itself.

We have tried to retain an open and spacious feeling on Level 4 of the mill, because it is the nearest we have to an original mill flat. The exhibition hangings are on heavy off-white calico, and while this creates a pleasant feeling in the area it restricts the capacity for captions. However, this is a welcome curtailment.

The average visitor spends 20-25 minutes on Level 4. Virtually all should see the spinning mule in operation. The most popular other single exhibit is 'The Rise and Fall of the Unscrupulous Master'. Children are able to climb over a cotton bale and the backs of slaves, and slide down under the glare of a mob of hostile workers, into the safe hands of Robert Owen. Glee and enthusiasm for this exhibit are most evident in those far too young to appreciate the significance of their actions.

Having completed their visit to Level 4 in their own time, visitors make their way through part of the ramp system to Level 3. Here the inevitable shop and catering facility awaits them. You can reach these areas without passing through the full system and without payment. From my previous explanations you will see that we regard items for sales as a significant part of our interpretation activity. Perhaps one of the most interesting items for sale, which illustrates this general principle, is a make-your-own Silent Monitor Kit. This was a small painted block of wood which Owen used as an instrument of social control. For a few pence you can extend the principle of economic and moral management to the late 20th Century.

Even in our cafeteria you are not safe from our interpretive attentions. Here we explain the most recent developments and plans for the village. It seems appropriate that as you consume your specialist ice cream, possibly a Corra Linn Cascade, or a Robert Owen's Ruin, you can peruse panels which give you the key dates of current progressed programmed development. Success is also interpreted within the ramp system itself. New Lanark has won virtually every major award, and we feel it is important that the visitor should know the opinions of those who have judged us in the past. This is one of the few areas where we have used a standardised display board and caption system.

If there is any single conclusion to be drawn from this wide range of interpretive provision, it is that the proposals made to visitors are essentially light and easily digested, and are available in a wide range of interesting forms. Our visitors come to us to have an enjoyable day out, and if we can educate them a little, as well as confirming their enjoyment, we feel we have been enormously successful in our limited interpretive objectives.

THE ANNIE MCLEOD EXPERIENCE

Since The Annie McLeod Experience is one of only two ride systems operating in Scotland, and is the only 'dark-ride', it is worth explaining its background. As a system, the provision uses simple, well-tried technology, which does not require much specialist attention. Down-time for emergency repair has been 10 hours in three years. Just under 0.5m people have visited it in this time. The internal scenes, of which there are 14, tend to use audio-visual or electronic techniques, and not formal built sets.

Very substantial flexibility is achieved by limiting the construction of internal sets. This is perhaps best illustrated by a November/December change which was introduced in 1991. The entire ride was converted in 24 hours to 'The Spirit of Christmas'. This provides a seasonal attraction which has made December our second busiest month and ensures that we are able to stay open all year. The interpretation of the Christmas theme is based on the change that has happened from Annie McLeod's day, to the modern festivity of tinsel and glitter. A commentary by Magnus Magnusson takes you through the story of change, and how it has altered our lives. The 1992/3 conversion time from 'Annie' to 'Spirit' was eight hours, and it was achieved overnight.

Therefore, the system is clearly no more than a sophisticated interpretive device, and at New Lanark it has been applied for a specific interpretive purpose. The decision to proceed with a proposal based on a dark-ride was taken in 1985-7. It was based on the village bicentennial celebrations in 1985, when Welfare State International were sponsored to conduct street theatre. They developed a theatrically enhanced guided tour, which involved some sensational events. The Battle of Trafalgar was re-fought on the Mill Lade. It was concluded with a plug being pulled which despatched 200 yellow ducks down the Clyde. However, one of their most successful sections was when the seance was held in one of the empty flats of the mill. Owen consulted spiritualists at the end of his life, so there was a strong historical connection. The result was a short, but very powerful and effective evocation of life in the early of the period village. We decided that The Welfare State had found an interesting solution to the problem of how to deal with the interpretive theme relating to village life in this early period. This was an issue which had been preoccupying us for some time, and we felt that their solution, of recreating the ghostly spirits of past residents, would allow us to develop an exciting and interesting response to this particular challenge.

We investigated every alternative to discover the best technique for the application of our draft proposal. We sought professional assistance, and eventually selected Renaissance Design Ltd. With them we decided that it should be a child who would be the medium to tell you the story. This was appropriate because of the Owenite tradition, but it also meant that a child would engage the attention of adults and be able to speak with a simple innocence not otherwise possible.

When we came to the conclusion that a dark ride system was the only mechanism which would allow us to control the telling of the story in a particular manner, we rejected this solution as being over-complex. We actively sought alternatives, but in the end the dark-ride solution offered very clear advantages over the management and control of visitors as they passed through the experience. With our own reservations in mind we built in maximum flexibility to allow for future change. We tried to keep the system as simple as possible commensurate with achieving the objectives.

For all its apparent technical complexity, the story which the system does tell you is both limited and controlled. You have a brief insight into the life of a little girl and her family in about 1820. Our ghost, good though she is, can give you no more that a glimpse back into her time. For most of our visitors that is quite enough.

It is interesting that part of the success of The Annie McLeod Experience rests on the act of travelling in a small module through a space, which in this case is fairly dark. This event has a special, extra, appeal for visitors, which is inexplicable in a mechanical sense. Their conveyance to the site by some form of road transport was far more sophisticated, but clearly they enjoy their more simple mode of transport. Over a year we probably receive around 20-25 people who feel uncomfortable on the ride, mostly because of claustrophobic or other nervous conditions. For most of the others the arrangement seems to provide a method by which their transportation involves them in active participation, however misguided is this judgement. We are still speculating on the basis for this consumer satisfaction.

My explanation of the development of The Annie McLeod Experience is to illustrate that it derives from a series of decisions based on interpretative planning, and a particular decision which related to issues of how best to interpret a particular theme about the early period of the village. It is not an expensive toy applied retrospectively as a solution looking for a problem. This particular medium, or collection of media, interprets best, for our purposes, this particular part of the story that we wish to tell. It is worth cautioning against the danger that an expensive ride system could be acquired as a solution to the wrong problem. Unless the facility is well planned and provides satisfactory interpretation, it could easily be ineffective. In these circumstances the operator would be left with an expensive, unsuccessful and large, white elephant. There have been a number of examples of such developments over the years.

GROUP VISITS

Probably the best interpreter remains the enthusiastic and skilled guide. They can be inspirational in their interpretation of a site or event. Our arrangement at New Lanark is that they add to the standard provisions available within the Visitor Centre. Around 30,000 visitors come in groups who have arranged booked guided tours. We have developed a fairly sophisticated booking system to try to ensure that we can match the most suitable guide to a particular group, in an effort to maximised interpretive success.

Most groups are educational, and they vary from university students to primary schools. All groups have to pay for their visit, and we treat them as individual clients. We pay attention to their physical needs with lavatories and packed lunch rooms, and we offer various levels of specialist tours to accommodate their particular requirements. In this way we try to adjust the interpretive opportunities of the village to meet the educational requirements of our visitors.

Essentially we do not see educational groups as being significantly different in principle from our other visitors. They all have special client needs, and it is our function to identify those needs and do our best to meet their justifiable requirements. All our visitors should undergo a learning experience when they visit us. Even our most casual visitor will, we hope, take away a little more understanding and a little more knowledge.

We do our best to accommodate disabled and disadvantaged groups. Our village and Visitor Centre are fairly wheelchair friendly. The village is in a steep valley and this is difficult to alter, but the Annie McLeod Experience has a wheelchair module, and wheelchairs can reach virtually all the site with no special arrangements. We are able to assist with deaf and blind groups, though we have had to draw the line at guide dogs visiting Annie McLeod. They have to wait while their owners experience the trip on their own. This success has been one of our great delights. We no longer have a gaggle of prams and wheelchairs which we are unable to accept. Now they flow through our system as part of our normal visitor arrangements.

INTO THE NEXT CENTURY

As a brief conclusion to this paper it is probably worth looking at some of our interpretive plans for New Lanark as we approach the year 2000. It is hoped to develop a series of additional interpretive sites around the core facility of the visitor centre:

1. The Village Store, the story of shopping and co-operativism; this had just opened at the time of writing;
2. Annie McLeod's House, typical of workers' housing conditions 1785-1999;
3. Robert Owen's House, the story of Owen and his family 1800-1850;
4. The School for Children, the story of education 1817-1999;
5. Specialist elements: a power trail following the development of power; an original house for specialist access; environmental impact of the village, etc.

When we have been able to complete all these, it will be time for a major review. The art of interpretation does not stand still. We are involved in a process of continuing improvement, but as we approach the millennium celebration we should step back a little from our project, and ask ourselves what special contribution it can make to our understanding of the 21st Century. In this respect we are like all interpreters, constantly re-assessing and re-analysing the basis and success of our activities. Certainly, the view which we present will be as seen through the prismatic distortion of the 21st Century. Interpretation is a creative activity, similar to the writing and production of theatrical plays, and for most theatres attracting audiences is of vital significance.

The author

James E. Arnold, MBE, is Director of the New Lanark Conservation Trust.

References

Donnachie & Hewitt, *Historic New Lanark*, Edinburgh University Press, 1993.
McLaren, D., *David Dale of New Lanark*,
Owen, R., *A New View of Society and Other Writings*, Penguin.
Butt, J.(ed), *Robert Owen Prince of Cotton Spinners*.

Available at New Lanark:
New Lanark Heritage Trail
Information Notes for Teachers
The Story of New Lanark
Detailed bibliography
Annie's Story (audio cassette tape)
Utopian Thought and Communal Experience - proceedings of international conference
    held in New Lanark 1988.
Robert Owen and Food - NLCT booklet
The New Lanark Village Store & Development of the Co-operative Movement - NLCT
    booklet
Thinking of Heritage - The Case of New Lanark, Lorna Davidson and Dennis Hardy,
    Middlesex University publications, resource pack incl. video and audio cassette.
The Story of New Lanark - short introductory video with commentary by Magnus
    Magnusson.
The New Lanark Spinning Mule - educational video, with subtitles
New Lanark Village Store - the Development of a Co-operative - New Lanark Conservation
Trust booklet.

18

CHATELHERAULT
The Restoration and Interpretation of a Folly

James Brockie

The story of Chatelherault, as a heritage area and country park, began in 1976, with the death of the 14th Duke of Hamilton. The ancient hunting lands, known as the High Parks, were offered up in lieu of death duties. Five hundred acres were acquired for the nation with support from the old National Land Fund and the Countryside Commission for Scotland, and a partnership was formed by the Commission, the Historic Buildings Division of the Scottish Office and Hamilton District Council.

Our initial investigations revealed what was once described as an 'embarrassment of goodies'. In our search through the mists of time for man's influence in the area, we discovered Bronze Age Man had lived here. His burial cists were discovered during sand excavations in the mid 1930s. Later hunter gatherers lived in the Gorge Area. Their defensive earth works can still be seen today. A recent archaeological dig uncovered a Roman coin on the site, perhaps indicating trade with their Roman neighbours on the other side of the Clyde.

The site is on the edge of Cadzow Forest, one of only two ancient woodlands in Scotland, said to have been planted by David I, 900 years ago. It is a royal hunting ground, where the Strathclyde kings would have hunted the boar, the deer and the wild white cattle. A few can still be seen today in the park. As the site became established as a seat of power, Cadzow Castle was built and the Hamiltons lived there until the 1500s. Today the ruined site has a mixture of structures including a 12th Century vaulted tower, 14th Century artillery fortification and 18th Century romantic additions.

Later the family took over the Monk's Orchard Tower in the Low Parks, and this was developed over the years into what became the finest building in Scotland, Hamilton Palace. Alas, it was demolished in the 1920s, and all that remains of that particular part of our heritage are two broken lines of trees that once formed the three and a half mile Grand Avenue. This feature, running north to south across the whole estate was designed by Alexander Edward for Anne, 3rd Duchess of Hamilton in 1708. Her grandson, the 5th Duke of Hamilton continued the improvements to the estate by constructing an ornate Dog Kennel at the southern end of the Avenue. This kennel, known as Chatelherault, was designed for the Duke by our great architect William Adam in 1732, and served many purposes: dog kennel, hunting lodge, summer retreat and garden ornament.

By the time of our acquisition, however, it had suffered the ravages of time and vandalism and the buildings were without roofs, floors and windows. Sand quarrying had started in the 1930s, in 1945 the avenue could still be seen, but three years later the quarrying had come to the rear of the lodge and by 1970 the avenue had gone and the workings were now right up to the front of the building, creating a desolate and threatened island in a landscape exhausted of sand.

RESTORATION OF THE LODGE

In what could only be described as an act of extreme bravery, Hamilton District Council and the Historic Building division decided to restore this ruin. Having no original drawings, we could only refer to engravings and Victorian photographs. A typical view of ordered Victorian neatness had turned into a nightmare of trees and scrub. For the next 10 years, painstaking restoration took place.

We were fortunate in finding the original quarry close to the building, and the slow process of stabilisation could begin. Temporary roofs allowed the shell to dry out, and stonework was examined. What could not last for 100 years was removed and new stones were cut to replace them. It was at this point our first craftsmen returned to the scene: the stonemasons. A lot of preparation could be carried out by modern machinery, but the demand was such that it took a team of 14 masons a full year to complete the external stonework. There are 29 hand carved urns on the roof alone.

After two and a half years the buildings were finally wind and weatherproof and we then looked to the interior of the Lodge. A 40 feet tall tree was removed from the Banqueting Hall. Thomas Clayton's beautiful plasterwork had been partially saved but the remaining sections had decayed beyond repair. A fire had occurred in the Banqueting Hall in 1945, destroying the room, including the ceiling. A photograph, the only one existing to show the complete ceiling, came from Country Life magazine and was used to compile new plans. These were then drawn to life size, modelled in clay, sent to Yorkshire and moulded into sections.

Our second group of craftsmen then arrived on the scene: the plasterers. Often having to refer to photographs, their work took a further two and a half years to complete. 15½ tons of fibrous plaster were required for the Banqueting Hall alone, and at long last the buildings were once again returned to their original grandeur. The painters were next to arrive. Using fragments of old plaster they were able to determine the original colours of the 1730s and, wherever possible, these colours were used on site.

At this stage there was a large space left where Wooton's painting of the 5th Duke and his racehorse, Victorious, once hung. The original, now housed in the Mellon Collection in Virginia, was photographed and reproduced on

Plate 1 The William Adam facade as it is today

Plate 2 Aerial view showing the courtyard of the Kennels (left) and the pattern of the restored parterre garden

canvas. The hanging of this painting in the restored hall returned the building to much as it was in Georgian times.

THE GARDENS

Out in the gardens, again we had no original drawings or plans. We could refer to paintings and old photographs through various periods, but the gardens were now completely overgrown. Our first job was to remove the Victorian elements: the monkey puzzles, the holly trees and the rose bushes. Archaeologists were brought in and slowly worked through the different forms the garden had taken until they arrived at a final soil profile. Once the archaeologists had completed their work, the area was grassed over and the profile was tested in sand, and it worked perfectly, so in 1976, the parterre was planted. A unique story of garden restoration in Scotland.

The terraced gardens were referred to in old records as being Dutch borders, but in Scottish terms this simply meant foreign in origin. The Victorian influence and later decay had left little of the original style. It was decided to return the borders to their original use, using only plants which pre-dated 1740. Plants were rarely grown for decoration at that time, but rather for their medicinal, culinary or dyeing properties. One flower was grown, however, heartsease or pansy as we know it today. This was sugared and placed on the beef as a digestive. The gardens are now a fascinating place to wander and discover the stories behind the plants.

THE KENNELS

To the rear of the terraced gardens, the actual Dog Kennels were situated. This was the working heart of the building and contained the Kennels, Gun Room, Slaughterhouse and Game Larders, none of which survived in their original form. So all was removed and a new structure erected to house our Interpretive Centre. During the restoration an Interpretive Planning Group was set up with members of Chatelherault staff and the Countryside Commission for Scotland. Our job was to create a linking theme which would arouse an interest in this 'embarrassment of goodies'. The amount of heritage and its diversity at first overwhelmed us: how could we link a Georgian Hunting Lodge with an Iron Age Fort, Coal mining, Ancient Oaks, White Cattle, Cadzow Castle, the Gorge and the River?

We were fortunate, during the restoration, to have an archival research team, founded by the Manpower Services Commission, overseen by Dundee University, which for six years examined the period around Chatelherault's construction. With access to the Duke of Hamilton's archives, we were able to build up a picture of the characters who lived and worked at Chatelherault and it was decided to use these characters to help tell the story of the Park. The Stonemason, the Forester, the Gardener and the Huntsman each now tell of his experience when the building was first in use and leads the visitor on to discover other times as well.

INTERPRETATION

The visitor coming to our interpretive centre is met by William Adam, discussing plans with the Duke and Duchess for the Hunting Lodge. Behind them is a 'trump loi' showing the romantic plans the Duke and Duchess have for the area. As visitors wander around the exhibition, they will be confronted with the smell of horse manure, a pack of hounds (one actually wags its tail) and the Huntsman barking out orders. On, through the forest, to the quarry where the Stonemason and the Forester are discussing the hunt the Duke is planning.

The smell of new mown hay and honeysuckle leads the visitor into the garden set where Hossack, the Gardener, is spying on two apprentices as they discuss the buxom maids and the work they have to do. A large back-drop shows the landscape of the Clyde Valley as it was in 1740 and a bust of William Adam comes to life to explain his plans. The visitor is then drawn back to the mural as a modern voice explains today's landscape. The visitor then discovers the source of the Hamilton's wealth as he enters the damp acrid coal mine and listens to George Peat, one of the miners, describing work at the coal face. Past the coal-mine the visitor comes to an area of dereliction, our 'nearly gone' section, that shows what had to be done to restore the area. On again to the 'land today' to re-meet the various characters and perhaps decide to go on the Gardeners Walk, the Stonemasons Road, the Foresters Path or the Huntsmans Ride. There is an audio-visual programme for the visitor who wants more details, but as visitors leave they will be introduced to the park rangers and their work, and perhaps be shown how they can discover more for themselves.

THE COUNTRY PARK

We have 500 acres of woodland with over 10 miles of footpaths. The Park is designed for passive recreation, somewhere to enjoy the peace and quiet of the countryside. Perhaps a Brownie pack on a ramble will cross this structure and want to know more about it? It is the Dukes Bridge, built in 1863 by William the 11th Duke of Hamilton. It is a 'B' listed structure about 80 feet above the river. The Duke died that same year and the people of Hamilton erected a monument in his honour. There are lots of these structures to discover around the park. Its natural history offers a lot of opportunities for the study of nature, and to expand this we have created small ponds and built bird hides. Imagine looking from these hides on to our new ponds on a Spring morning: children love water, it's a marvellous introduction to the countryside. With a pond net they can find frogs, toads, newts and leeches, thereby opening up a new world of discovery.

Our new marshes are now breeding grounds for dragonflies and damselflies in their metallic greens, golds, blues and reds and in the Autumn these same marshes encourage birds flying south from their breeding grounds to stop here and rest awhile. The meadows beyond the ponds have been developed to bring back the flowers that perhaps your grandparents once remembered, growing in our fields, and these, in turn, are now encouraging the insects, the bees and the butterflies to breed here. On 30 September 1987, the Park was opened by the Duke of Gloucester. We are still a fairly young Country Park and our planning since 1978 has brought us up to this point, but we can't sit on our laurels. We want to see lots of people enjoying the countryside.

We hope to see lots of happy, smiling faces. Our aim is for every individual to get something from the park - something to treasure, from experiencing the buildings, the wildlife, the White Cattle, the coal-mining, the pomp and circumstance of the Dukes. Whether our plan of interpretation has achieved this is for our visitors to judge, and they keep coming at a rate of about 300,000 annually.

The author

James Brockie is Manager of Chatelherault Country Park. He received an MBE in 1988 for his outstanding contribution to the restoration programme there and his energetic leadership to establish the Park as one of Scotland's premier visitor attractions.

References

Adam, W., *Vitruvius Scoticus.*

Campbell, A.B., *The Lanarkshire Miners - A social History of their Trade Unions 1775-1874.* John Donald.

Kaufman, E., *Architecture in the Age of Reason, Baroque and Post Baroque in England, Italy and France.*

Gifford, J., *William Adam 1689-1748*, Mainstream.

Miller, A.G., *Bronze Age Graves at Ferniegair, Hamilton*, Transactions of Glasgow Archaeological Society, Vol.11, 1947.

Pringle, D., *Cadzow Castle and The Castle of Hamilton, An Archaeological and Historical Conundrum.* Historic Buildings and Monuments.

Tait, A., *The Landscape Garden in Scotland, 1735-1835.* Edinburgh University Press.

Walker, M., Report by MSc Research Team, Chatelherault on Cadzow Castle.

Wallace, Dr M.N. & Talbot, E.J., *Report on Trench Survey of Cadzow Earthwork*, 1983.

Welfare, H.G., *A Bronze Age Cemetery at Ferniegair*, Proceedings of The Society of Antiquities of Scotland, 1974/5.

Wilson, G & Mortimer G., *The Medieval Environs of Hamilton - The Clyde and Avon Valley from Bothwell to Craignethan, 500 years ago.*

19

KELBURN COUNTRY CENTRE
Presenting a Family Heritage

The Earl of Glasgow

Inheriting too large a family home and a medium-sized estate in the West of Scotland is a mixed blessing. It is a particularly mixed blessing if it has been in your family for 800 years and you do not have sufficient independent means to support it. If there was a Rembrandt or a Louis XV Commode or something worth more than half a million hidden in the cellar, it would be easier, but the 6th Earl of Glasgow went bankrupt in 1888 to the tune of nearly a million pounds and the family have been struggling ever since.

I think it was the late Nicholas Ridley who said that people in large houses should stop whinging. If they haven't enough money to keep their houses they should sell them to people who have. To me, selling up never seemed an option. Kelburn is part of Scotland's heritage, it has been put in my care and I hope to pass it on to our son. To achieve this I have to make it pay for itself by maximising its natural assets and trying to minimise the effects of its natural disadvantages. As a principle, this seems pretty obvious, but, in practice, it can be quite difficult to do.

Kelburn is a three and a half thousand acre estate on the coast between Largs and Fairlie in North Ayrshire. A very significant part of the area's cultural landscape, it consists of two farms, 300 acres of commercial woodlands, 200 acres of amenity woods, a dozen cottages and the castle itself with its gardens and policies. My family, originally called de Boyville, were Norman and gained title to this bit of Scotland in 1145. Later the name was changed to Boyle. The original Norman keep was built in about 1200, and we make the claim that Kelburn is the oldest castle in Scotland to have been continuously inhabited by the same family. We also assert that the Battle of Largs in 1263 was fought on the shore at the bottom of our garden. By 1580, the Boyles who had been relatively insignificant up until that time, became richer and grander and the then Laird, John Boyle, enlarged his home considerably and converted it into a fashionable Z-plan castle.

In 1700, David Boyle, who was to become the first Earl of Glasgow, built a unique William-and-Mary mansion which was joined at an angle on to the old castle. (Castles had become unfashionable in the days of Enlightenment and the larger residence was now referred to as Kelburn House.) In 1890, a Victorian Wing was added and this remains the most recent addition. The result of continuous occupation and its several additions has resulted in Kelburn being a very lived-in but somewhat eccentric 'Grade A' building, with rooms on many different levels, bedrooms that used to be dining rooms, sitting rooms that used to be kitchens and passages that used to be solid stone walls. There is even a bathroom that may once have been a chapel, contained in the thickness of one of the walls. It has the very personal atmosphere of a house that is continuously being changed and converted to suit the needs of successive Countesses of Glasgow.

The gardens at Kelburn are a wealth of rhododendrons and exotic shrubs that thrive by the Gulf Stream. They are not exceptional by West Coast standards but have great character and historical interest. There are many unusual trees such as the two 1000 year old yews, the largest and oldest Monterey Pine in Scotland and the extraordinary Weeping Larch. But probably Kelburn's greatest assets are its Glen and its setting.

The Castle itself is built on the edge of a large burn (unsurprisingly called the Kel Burn), which rises a thousand feet up on the moors and drops to sea level, within the space of about half a mile, by means of many waterfalls and deep gorges. Winding up on both sides of the burn are paths that have been continuously maintained for the last 250 years or more. The glen is rich in wild flowers and ferns, trees and shrubs, some specifically planted but most self-seeded. It is both romantic and spectacular and has been praised by many visitors during the last three centuries. In 1773 the 3rd Countess commissioned Robert Adam to build a monument in one of the glen's most romantic spots to commemorate her husband's death.

Kelburn's other unique asset is its setting. The Castle stands one hundred feet above sea level overlooking the islands of the Firth of Clyde. It seems as if the place had been specially chosen to give a view through the gap between the nearer islands of Big and Little Cumbrae on to the further and larger islands of Bute and Arran with its hills rising to nearly 3000 feet.

My wife Isabel and I had always wanted to open Kelburn to the public, not only because it seemed the only practical method of generating revenue to help keep up the policies, but also because it was a new and exciting challenge. In 1977, when we opened Kelburn Country Centre, my father and stepmother were still living in the castle and there was no question of that being made available to the public. However, the 1700 home-farm building, mostly unused and in great need of renovation anyway, were only four hundred yards across the glen from the castle, and eminently suitable as a central point for the park.

The home farm buildings had not been fully in use since before World War I. In my great grandfather's day, though, they had housed a thriving community. They consisted of a stable, a byre, a piggery, a hen house, a joiner's shop, a laundry, a washhouse, six estate cottages and flats on the upper storeys to house the dairymaids and laundrymaids. Besides two dairymaids and three laundrymaids, the outdoor staff consisted of eight foresters, six gardeners, two gamekeeprs, an estate joiner, a carter and a

Plate 1 The present Earl and Countess of Glasgow

shepherd. With approximately twelve indoor staff, the 7th Earl was employing 35 people on the estate and he was not wealthy by the standards of most Scottish landed gentry.

With enthusiastic support and a generous grant from the Countryside Commission for Scotland, the old stables were converted into a tearoom, the old joiner's shop became the information office, the byre became an exhibition and display room and the laundry became the craft shop. A new toilet block and car park had to be built from scratch. Much money was spent on upgrading the paths in the glen and the bridges and walk-overs had to be built and replaced. Sign posts were erected, litter-bins and seats were constructed, a guide book was written by my father and me and the first brochure was printed, consisting mostly of my best photographs of Kelburn.

In adapting the old building of the home farm courtyard we took great care not to destroy their architectural integrity. External details were respected and the interiors were designed and simply decorated to be in keeping with the overall character. The 7th Earl added an architectural curiosity in 1898 when he erected a small building clad in corrugated iron to house his collection of artefacts and curiosities from the South Pacific after he had served his time as Governor of New Zealand. It sits by an ornamental pond, still serving its original purpose and standing as an interesting testament to 'hi-tech' architecture of a century ago.

I would like to say that we knew what we were doing, but that would only be half true. We knew what we wanted to show the public and how we were going to present it. But we had no business plan or budget. We decided to charge 40p for adults, 20p for children and hope for the best. That might have been a reasonable enough approach for the first year when everything was new and experimental, but, in retrospect, it was a great mistake to have taken the same cavalier attitude towards pricing and budgeting for the following years too. We had much more energy and enthusiasm than business sense.

In the nest six years we increased our visitor numbers from 9,000 in 1977 to 60,000 in 1982. During the same time through, we spent a lot of money introducing new attractions and improving the facilities. We started pony trekking and introduced a ranger service, we increased the size of the shop with a grant from the Scottish Tourist Board and built an extra toiled block with assistance from the Countryside Commission. I designed a Children's Stockade and the Royal Marines built us an adventure course. We converted an estate cottage into an ice-cream shop and put up a rangers' shed. We laid down much more paving in the farm courtyard and spent a fortune turning an abandoned swamp into an ornamental duck pond. We constructed new paths and bridges in the glen and a special path down to the waterfall pool, set in a spectacular sandstone grotto just below the caste.

On the surface, Kelburn Country Centre was a huge success. It was increasing its visitor numbers every year, it attracted a lot of publicity and in 1979 it won a special Glasgow Herald Award for the Best Tearoom of the Year. The tearoom, like the rest of the Centre, was regarded as very good value. And so it was, because it was making a yearly loss and the overdraft was steadily rising. In 1982, we were still charging only 80p for an adult and

40p for a child as entrance fee. Because we were in recession, I was nervous of setting a price that might put people off. I rationalised my losses to the bank manager and my accountant with the argument that I was making major capital improvements to the building and amenities and that, if I didn't have the Country Centre, I would have to pay more than its loss to maintain the existing gardens and policies anyway.

In 1984, we had an excellent summer and a record number of 76,400 visitors , the most we had ever had. The entrance fee was £1 for adults and 60p for children and even with the high visitor numbers we never quite made a profit. But it was not till we had been through 1985 and 1986 that I finally starting taking the finances seriously. 1985 was the worst summer we have ever had. It rained every day throughout the whole of July and August. By the beginning of august, all holidaymakers in the west of Scotland had decided to cut their losses and go home. Watching television at home was cheaper than watching it in a boarding house in Largs. In the following year, there was a teachers' strike and so we didn't have the school parties that are essential to our business in late May and June. In those two years we made a combined trading loss of over £120,000, and with my existing debt to the bank, we had to sell our London house to bring our borrowing back under control.

Experience had shown several difficulties facing anyone wanting to make a country park pay in the west of Scotland. The most obvious one is the unreliability of the weather. It is difficult to exaggerate the effect of the climate on visitor numbers. For instance, in 1988, Easter Monday was a brilliantly sunny day and we had 1,194 visitors. But on Easter Monday in 1991 it poured with rain all day and eleven people came. About 70% of our visitors come from the Glasgow conurbation and on good days they will flock to the coast, and many come specifically to Kelburn. But on wet days, they will stay at home.

So is there any way of counteracting the effects of bad weather? One way is to persuade groups, who get a generous reduction on their entrance fee, to book in advance for a specific day and offer them wet weather cover in case they are unlucky. In 1987, with a grant from the Countryside Commission, we erected a special building which we call 'The Pavilion'. Its simple architectural form makes it fit comfortably into the surrounding landscape, and its flexible interior was designed specifically to provide shelter for groups and also to house exhibitions and hold special events. In this way, approximately 28,000 people a year come to Kelburn in booked groups, which is about twice as many as we could attract before we had our custom-built weather cover.

Another suggested solution to protect us from the uncertainty of weather is to introduce a major undercover attraction at Kelburn, which would attract visitors regardless of the climate. In principle, this seems a good idea, but there are two problems. A major indoor attraction capable of providing room for over 300 people at one time would be very costly, and, even with a grant, a daunting prospect to somebody with a large overdraft. But even if we had such a facility, would it be enough to entice the families of Glasgow and

Paisley to drive for 50 minutes in pouring rain, when they could much more easily find their recreation at the local leisure centre or swimming pool round the corner? Maybe it would depend on the quality of the attraction. But everything that is unique and inimitable at Kelburn, and most of the attractions we are likely to develop in the future, are natural and historical and out-of-doors. Anything we create indoors is liable to seem artificial unless it is an appropriate Exhibition or Interpretation of some aspect ofKelburn. In 1990 we converted the old hen house, a long narrow building, into a room to display a cartoon exhibition telling the story of the Boyle Family history. Don Aldridge, who is one of Britain's foremost consultants in interpretation as well as an idiosyncratic artist in his own right, has created a picture gallery of colourful and irreverent cartoons that both educate and entertain. But an exhibit like this is not enough to attract visitors on wet days. The opening of the castle itself might be a sufficient attraction when it rains, but I return to that issue later.

Although weather is our biggest imponderable, there are other handicaps to be overcome. For instance, our location. If you were a leisure entrepreneur wishing to establish a theme park in Scotland, you wouldn't choose to have it on the Ayrshire Coast. You would place it somewhere in a triangle that has Glasgow and Loch Lomond to the west, Edinburgh to the east and Perth to the north. Within that triangle you would have the largest concentration of Scotland's population and be close to one or more of the traditional tourist routes. At Kelburn, we do have the benefit of being in an area that has long been a traditional playground for Glaswegians but we are far from any tourist route. And that is largely because no serious attempt has ever been made to market the Firth of Clyde as a tourist destination. Against this argument though, it is worth noting that Culzean Country Park and castle, which is even further off the beaten track, claims over 300,000 visitors a year. This is more than four times as many as Kelburn, although, of course, there are other reasons for Culzean's superior drawing power.

Then there is the question of competition. Since Kelburn opened in 1977, several new country parks and leisure attractions have opened and are competing with us for the day-tripper market. Kelburn is always in danger of falling between too stools. At one extreme, there are an increasing number of local authority owned country parks, where people can enjoy the beauties of the countryside free of charge. At the other extreme, there are the multi-million pound theme parks, more expensive than Kelburn but offering more streamlined forms of entertainment, and usually protected from the weather. There is also the question of publicity and promotion. It is very difficult to gauge how much money and time should be spent on this, particular when a spell of bad weather can virtually drown the effects of the most carefully managed publicity campaign.

If one wanted proof of the effects of publicity and competition, there is no better example than the damage we suffered from the Glasgow Garden Festival in 1988. About £40m was spent on the Glasgow Garden Festival and eight million of that on publicity. The Festival was primarily targeted at the day-tripper and particularly those living within 50 miles of Glasgow. Because

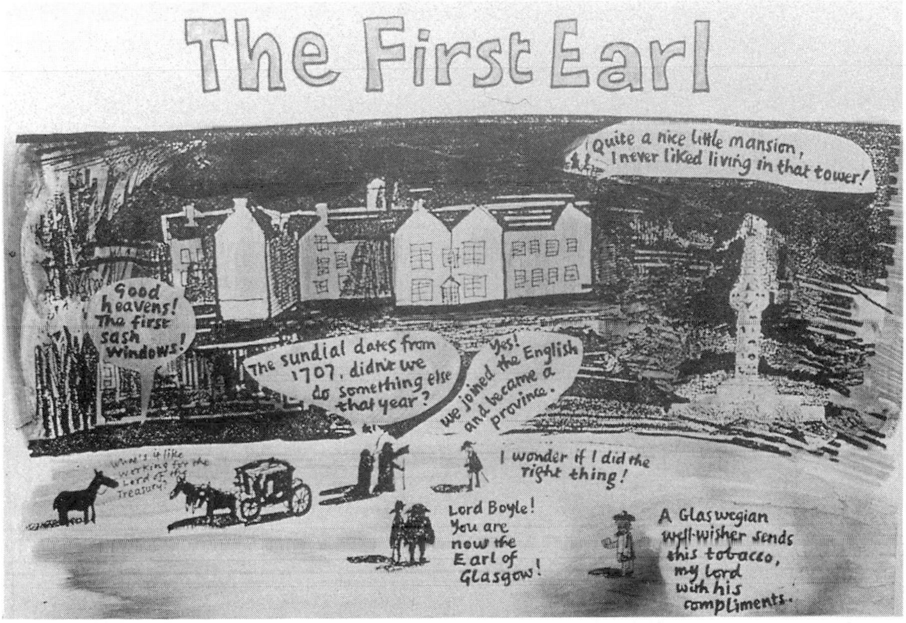

Plate 2 One of Don Aldridge cartoons telling the story of the Boyle Family history

Plate 3 Kelburn as it looked in the 19th Century

it was a one-off event for 1988 only, many groups and nearly all the school parties who would normally have come to Kelburn made the Festival the destination for their yearly trip. Every day in July and August the attractions of the Garden Festival were advertised on television, and there was no way we could compete with that. The result was that, instead of our average number of 75,000 visitors in a year, we were down to 53,000.

Even when you can clearly identify the problems of a country park, the solutions are not easy to find. Certain things, though, are essential if you want to survive as a business. You must have something to offer the visitor that is unique and cannot easily be copied by shrewd entrepreneurs with a better site than you. For instance, you cannot afford to be seen as just another country park or just another Scottish castle and you must constantly publicise what you have that is different. You must also budget very carefully and always charge the amount necessary to give yourself a reasonable chance of showing a profit. Of course, higher charges will put some people off, but those who have decided they want to see or experience what you have to offer will not be deterred by the cost.

In 1984 my father died and in 1985 Isabel and I moved into Kelburn Castle. Although country parks have been known to earn money, large castles or stately homes, particularly if they are Grade A buildings, are invariably financial liabilities. In the early days, it was our plan to persuade Americans to come to Kelburn as paying guests. With a golf course on our doorstep, many opportunities for sailing and trips to the Islands, as well as the facilities the Castle and Park, we thought we were on to a good way of earning some money. We spent several thousand pounds doing up some of the bedrooms and putting in extra baths and showers. We made a business trip to the US, seeking out the most promising travel agents and visiting wealthy contacts. However, although we succeeded in getting a few American guests to stay, they tended to come too infrequently, in couples and stay for no more than two nights at a time. Providing first class accommodation and meals as well as bright and intelligent conversation for one couple every fortnight or so, turned out to be a lot of work for relatively little reward. What we needed were groups of Americans staying for at least three nights. So far, we have only occasionally succeeded in realising this, but, more successfully, we have started catering for large groups of Americans and Europeans who come for dinner. Forty or fifty people for cocktails and a four course dinner is profitable and often enjoyable. By now, Isabel and her staff have turned the management of these dinners into a fine art.

We were reluctant to open the castle to the public, except as an obligation to Historic Scotland who make it an understandable condition of the grant. For one reason it is our home and we and our children live in the whole building during the summer, and, for another, it could not easily be opened to the public at the same time as entertaining guests who are paying large sums for Kelburn's exclusivity. But this year, for the first time, we have decided to abandon paying guests and open the castle to the public in July and August. It will be inconvenient but it may bring more people into the country park and it is one attraction that is not dependent on the weather.

Various advisors and consultants have suggested that Kelburn would attract many more visitors if the castle was permanently open. I'm sure they are right but that too presents new problems. Besides the damage of continual wear and tear and the cost of providing adequate security, there is the paradox that Kelburn's biggest selling point is its claim to have been continuously lived in by the same family for 800 years. The more the public have access to the rooms we normally use, the less genuinely lived-in the castle becomes.

The most valuable thing we have to offer is the continuity of our history. We and our family are still part of that history. The Castle is not a museum or a converted hotel or a National Trust property. It is still a family home and that refers to the gardens and policies too. But living in the 1990s, the price we must pay to keep it as such is to open our doors to the public, forgo some of our privacy, and try to run a successful business. Nobody in their right mind would take on such a business if they had a choice. But I do not have a choice. At least, I have certainly been conditioned into believing that I do not. It is a lot of work and a big financial worry. But is also a challenge and a mission, and there is something very satisfying in that.

The author

The present and 10th Earl of Glasgow (Patrick Robin Archibald Boyle) is the owner of Kelburn Estate. He went to university in Paris and, before returning to Kelburn, to establish the country centre, he was an independent television producer. The principal guidebooks *Kelburn Country Centre* and *The Trees of Kelburn*, were written by himself.

References

Boyle, D., 9th Earl of Glasgow, *Tales from the Scottish Lairds –Kelburn Castle*, Jarrold Colour Publications, Norwich, pp.131-140.

Gow, I., *Scottish Renaissance Interiors –Glasgow's Seat*, Moubray House Press, pp.49-59.

Hill, O., *Scottish Castles of the 16th and 17th Centuries*, Country Life, pp.15, 150.

Leighton, J.M., *Beauties of Clyde*, Joseph Swan, Glasgow, p.227.

MacGibbon, D and Ross, T., *Castellated and Domestic Architecture of Scotland*, David Douglas, Edinburgh, vol.4, pp.24-31 (Kelburn), vol.5, p.553 (Kelburn).

Mackenzie, A.,,, *At kelburn with the Boyles*, in Scottish world, Spring 1993, pp.44-45.

Pont, T., *Cunninghame*, John Tweed, Glasgow, pp.224-228.

Kelburn Country Centre: Guide Book & Maps.
The Trees at Kelburn: an Illustrated Guide.

20

BAXTERS AND ITS VISITOR CENTRE

Gordon Baxter and Finlay Weir

The aim of the company, through its visitor centre, has been to combine interpretation of the Baxter family heritage with that of the local area. The story of the centre also provides an insight into how to satisfy the curiosity of the visiting public for the workings of a food factory with a worldwide reputation for its fine products. The style and methodology of interpretation in the centre has worked successfully, as it is now one of the biggest tourist attractions in the North East of Scotland, receiving 180,000 visitors annually.

INSPIRATION OF THE IDEA

The visitor centre, as we know it today, had its beginnings in 1985. Its origins, however, go much further back to my father, William Baxter, who was born in 1877. He was a great chap: self-educated, hard-working, and a total quality practitioner fifty long years ago. With his new wife, Ethel, he struck out on his own in 1914 to establish a small preserve-making business. The pair of them, with few resources, literally slaved to lay its foundations, but Willie Baxter had a sense of vision, and a fine memory to recall the old days. I loved my bedside chats with him in the 1960s towards the end of his career. He lived for 96½ years and, when he passed on, was the proudest man in Scotland.

I had come across an old photograph of my father, with his father and his brother George, outside the old grocery shop in the village, with their staff of three plus the cellarman who looked after the whisky stocks. I wanted to know more about it, and asked him to tell me about the old grocery shop, how it started in 1868, his own early days as message boy, salesman, traveller to London to sell his wares, and to France to buy fine provisions, wines and epicurean foods for the great aristocrats of that time who used to join Royalty at Gordon Castle, Fochabers, to shoot pheasants and fish for salmon in the great River Spey. The village grocer, my father, had to keep good groceries ! At the time of our bedside talks in the 1960s the shop on Spey Street, Fochabers was a broken-down, decaying ruin; an occasional storehouse, it smelt of paraffin and was home to generations of mice and lonely cats. As my father's stories of fifty years before unfolded, the Baxter history began to take on a new meaning to me.

Some years earlier I had made the first of many visits to the USA to try to sell my wares - my wife's canned soups and my mother's jams and jellies. The USA was to become a second home for me and the source of many ideas which later I tried to apply in my own business. One cold winter's afternoon, I made a presentation to Scottie Wilson, then the Chief Buyer at the Jewel Tea Company in Chicago. Scottie could see that I was an earnest, independent, fellow Scot who believed passionately in the quality of the goods I had to sell. He began to tell me about a new concept previously, to the best of my knowledge, unheard of in Scotland. It was called 'marketing'. It meant, in effect, to find out what your customer needs, or could be persuaded to require, and then make it. Not the other way round!

For me that meant that I had to try to tailor my products to the US consumers. There was no question of getting them to buy Royal Game Soup if it contained a high proportion of well-matured and marinated Highland venison and pheasant, or to purchase Seville Orange Marmalade if they were accustomed to more bland flavours - 'light beige' flavour as one of our great chefs used to say of American taste buds.

In effect, I had to turn our business upside down if we wished to succeed. I am glad we did, for the Baxter business today is a thousand times bigger than it was when I started in 1946.

My travels to America with my wife, Ena, took us to Washington DC, the headquarters of government and, by a gentle process of osmosis, at weekends to the great centres of history, Mount Vernon, the home of George Washington, Montechello, home of Thomas Jefferson, and finally to Williamsburg, Virginia. Here Laurence Rockefeller and his associates produced a reconstruction of the small town, a key centre of ferment and political discussion in Colonial America in pre-1769 times. Williamsburg made a tremendous impact on Ena and me. That, coupled with our new ideas about marketing Baxters, was the catalyst which led ultimately to the development of our visitor centre in Fochabers.

The marketing business, it seems to me, is a fairly straightforward commonsense discipline, but if one can add to it flavour, imagination, vision and warmth it becomes much more exciting and worthwhile.

So the idea was born of taking my grandfather's rather broken-down old shop from Spey Street in our native village of Fochabers and transferring it one mile west, across dear old Spey bridge, to a lovely site at the factory at the side of the river. We took it down stone by stone in 1966 with the windows, the lamp posts, outside lights and the iron railings against which message bikes had been placed and horses hitched. Eventually, it was lovingly restored and opened by my father, William Baxter, on 28 November 1968 when he was in his 91st year.

I am proud to say that the Baxter shop has been the centrepiece of many colourful and successful British trade promotions in overseas markets, such as Gimbels, New York 1967, Nieman-Marcus, Dallas, Texas in 1968, Macy's of New York in 1969, Nodriska Kompaniet, Stockholm in 1970 and Takishamaya in Tokyo, Japan in 1973 among others. In recent years we have added a replica of my grandfather's whisky cellar and another retail establishment, Mrs. Baxter's Victorian Kitchen, which offers a wide range of high quality cookery and gift items. There is also an extremely popular fast food restaurant situated on a glorious site overlooking our noble salmon river to the hills beyond. It is said to be the most popular tourist centre in North East Scotland, and the eighth most successful industrial tourist centre in the United Kingdom. Not a bad endorsement, considering its humble beginnings.

My family were not too keen on my idea to move the shop from Fochabers. 'Are you sure you are not wasting good money on this idea, Gordon?' my father once said. 'You know, you'll need every penny you can get to buy machines for those new soups your wife is making, they're good and will do well, but you must have proper equipment to make them.' Most of our staff, too, were doubtful, the old ones would smile wryly, shake their heads and say little. The younger managers envied the apparent misappropriation of funds which they thought could have been well used in their own departments. Actually, the establishment of the original George Baxter shop, including the old wooden counters, fittings and lighting, cost us just under two thousand pounds. But my wife Ena and I had faith in our little project and were determined to see it through.

MAKING IT WORK

The majority of visitors will have planned their visit based on high expectations gleaned from our publicity leaflet or, hopefully, by word of mouth from other well satisfied customers who have previously enjoyed the experience. It is extremely important, therefore, that the first impact on approaching the environs of the factory and visitor centre is a good one and to this end great care has been taken to ensure that the environment is in keeping with this expectation, i.e. tidy and well maintained grounds, clearly signposted and with easy access to the car park.

A fully tarmacked road and car park for over one hundred vehicles is provided, together with eight coach stances. The car park is beautifully sited with unbeatable views of the River Spey. A prime consideration in laying out this facility was access for disabled persons, and coaches and cars are encouraged to stop adjacent to the reception area for the convenience and comfort of the less mobile visitors.

Well appointed toilets are a most important feature of the facilities and are designed to accommodate coach loads of visitors. This is a vital facility and indeed, at one time, Baxters was the only site which could suitably accommodate coach parties in this part of the North East. The ease of access for these large vehicles is also very much appreciated by coach drivers and contributes greatly to the number of visiting coaches.

Many of the visitors choose to make this a holiday occasion and picnic tables and facilities are provided for this purpose. A short walk leads the visitor to the reception area where they receive a friendly welcome and are given an outline of the facilities available. In this area they are formed into groups, each receiving a coloured badge to ensure that access to the audio-visual show is on a 'first come, first served' basis. In the reception area there are interesting photographs, aerial views of the factory, etc., and postcards of the local area may be purchased. Also available is an extensive selection of leaflets advertising other tourist centres and places of interest within Moray District and further afield to whet the appetite, not only for a Baxters visit, but also to assist the visitor to fully enjoy the experience of Moray.

THE BAXTER EXPERIENCE

An audio-visual presentation takes place every fifteen minutes in a specially constructed cinema holding about 50 people. To avoid congestion, the visitors enter by one door and leave by another, into a secondary area. The film covers the Baxter story over its four generations, highlights the company's activities both at home and abroad, and also introduces the visitor to the attractions of the full 'Baxter Experience' which they can enjoy later in the day.

For those who wish, a factory tour is arranged, and at this point smaller groups of no more than fifteen people are introduced to a specially trained guide who then escorts the guests around the factory. As Baxters is a food manufacturing company the visitors view the factory from a specially constructed viewing gallery equipped with an audio system and furnished with wall displays. This separates the public from the hazards of the factory operations and also assists the guides who do not have to speak above the noise of the machinery.

The final section of the tour, which lasts some 20 minutes or so, is via an open gallery in the labelling department where the visitors are no longer insulated from the factory experience and feel the hustle and bustle associated with a high volume manufacturing operation. With the formal part of the tour over, guests are invited to visit the Old Shop, where they are welcomed by an old-fashioned grocer, complete with white apron, who will guide them round. This is a highly atmospheric display, just as it was some 100 years ago.

Adjacent to the Old Shop and its fascinating contents, is an exhibition of pictorial presentations, dealing in a little more detail with the history and

Plate 1 Preparing the gingerbread in the Victorian Kitchen

Plate 2 A welcome smile from the grocer in the Old Shop

heritage of the business. Of special note is the desk and ledgers of George Baxter and original invoices, which can be freely examined and are just as they were when in use. It is worth mentioning that, despite the tens of thousands of visitors who have passed through this area, not one case of vandalism or damage to these items has occurred.

Following a look at the memorabilia and history of the business, there is an opportunity to view the entire range of Baxter products together with tasteful, predominantly Scottish, quality goods which are on display in the George Baxter Cellar. This building reproduces the original shop in Fochabers and its atmosphere is appropriately reflected in the decor. This retail operation provides a useful opportunity for us to illustrate the diversity of our products, as well as for the visitor to indulge in a small gift or souvenir for those at home.

The most recent addition to the visitor centre is the Victorian Kitchen. This is a retail outlet offering more sophisticated wares and taking its theme from the old kitchen at Brodie Castle with flagstones, open ovens and a cat sitting comfortably at the fireside. The ladies serving in the kitchen are appropriately attired in mob caps with Victorian aprons. A tiny kitchen produces Eyemouth Tarts and Fochabers Gingerbread. The Gingerbread in the oven creates a mouth-watering aroma to tempt the appetite.

Attached to the Victorian kitchen is a splendid restaurant which seats 120. In addition to the normal fare expected, a special experience in mouth-watering pancakes, made to order and served with world class preserves, honey and whipped cream, is very popular with visitors. The restaurant is sited to take advantage of superlative views over the River Spey. In fair weather, an attractive patio area in front of the restaurant allows visitors to relax out of doors, enjoy a beer or a glass of wine in the sun, and admire the view. To add further enjoyment to the day, a fold of Highland Cattle graze contentedly in fields adjacent to the visitor centre. These animals are extensively photographed and add something a little special to the experience of a day at Baxters.

For the more adventurous, however, a Nature Trail along the Spey and up the adjacent Break's Hill provides those who wish to stretch their legs a little, with an unsurpassed view of the river as it winds some five miles to the sea. It should be emphasised that the whole experience of the time at Baxters is entirely free, our only reward being a satisfied customer, a warm feeling for Baxters and its world famous brand name, and an opportunity to demonstrate to the world the beauty and heritage of this wonderful countryside and business with which we are so closely involved.

REACHING OUR CUSTOMERS

At an early stage, it was found that leaflets provided the most effective method of creating awareness of the attraction. These contain a brief history of the company, descriptions of the facilities, and some attractive photographs and are distributed to all tourist information centres, hotels and attractions from the Borders to the North of Scotland, some 3,500 outlets in all. A simple computerised data base facilitates correspondence with all outlets over the course of the year. The leaflet is printed in five languages and is targeted mainly at car, train and air travellers.

A high proportion of visits are made up of those travelling by coach. Arrangements are made with the companies directly, or at the Scottish Trade and Travel Exhibition held every April. The visitor centre is a very popular destination for coach parties as the 130 seat restaurant has ample capacity. This is quite rare within the area. Coaches often arrive without prior booking, as sometimes the destination is left to the driver's and courier's discretion.

ADVERTISING AND PUBLIC RELATIONS

Conventional advertising in weekly or monthly publications has been less effective than using annual publications or brochures. However, at key times of the year, local advertising works well for those travelling within the area, or indeed, local residents. Success breeds success. Other than the leaflet, public relations has been found to be the most effective means of communication. It is a means whereby the wider story can be disseminated.

There is a story to tell and many approaches to take, e.g. family owned and run, 125 years in business, the 'quality' approach, a million visitors welcomed, an interesting history, a beautiful site and, above all, the centre itself - a powerful public relations tool. Every public relations opportunity is exploited, using a specialist company.

The completion of the Prize Draw card after the factory tour provides us with the names and addresses of visitors, who qualify for a regular draw of a super Baxter hamper, and provide a facility for direct contact with our consumers at a later date. Of particular note is that all the company's advertising and public relations for the purpose of consumer and trade are cross-referenced to the visitor centre and the Company's heritage.

COLLABORATING WITH OTHERS

The common strengths of family ownership, quality of product and location within the Moray area led to an association between Baxters, Glenfarcles Distillery and Johnstones of Elgin which is marketed as 'Quality around Speyside'. We have produced a theme trail leaflet together. These combined strengths add greater public relations opportunities and offer to the visitor the opportunity to visit all three attractions in one day. Of importance also is the buying power of the three businesses which creates economies in leaflet distribution and printing.

THE BENEFITS

In the early days, the visitor to Baxters was exposed to the complete range of products manufactured at Fochabers in the hope that he would influence his local grocer to stock new varieties. Things have changed in recent years, and, sadly, the customer has less influence on the trade. Today's main objective is to provide our customer with an opportunity to spend some happy hours in a beautiful setting with much of interest around, and to create a warm feeling about Baxters, its brand name and its high quality products.

There is little doubt that linking the family story, the place and the marvellous heritage of Speyside does deliver a memorable impact which is proving of great benefit to our own business, the wider community and the local economy.

The authors

Gordon Baxter and Finlay Weir are respectively Chairman and Operations Director of Baxters of Speyside. They gratefully acknowledge the assistance of the Director of G & E Baxter Ltd, Michael Baxter, in writing this paper.

References

Banks, C., in *The Grocer*, March 1993, p.70.
Barber, L., in *Sunday Express Magazine*, 1987.
Daunt, M., *Scottish Quest*, 1993, p.43-46.
Financial Times, 6 Aug. 1992.
Moir, J., in *Guardian*, 16 Dec. 1992.
National Grocer Magazine, 1992.
Nuttall, R., in *Mail on Sunday*, 29 Jan 1989.
Ramm, M., in *Mrs Beeton Magazine*, Aug.1992.

21

THE BRITISH GOLF MUSEUM

Peter Lewis

Depicting history in a single subject museum is a very different proposition from writing a book or giving a lecture. Museums are three dimensional experiences. They need to be highly visual and at the same time act as a catalyst for learning. The scholarship needs to be present in the interpretation of the displays but it must work at a fairly basic level. A fundamental consideration of any museum should always be the amount of detailed information presented to the public in any display. I believe that the function of the public displays in a museum should be to stimulate interest in a subject or subjects. A visitor can then learn more by subsequent visits, buying a book in the shop, contacting the curatorial staff for more detailed information on a specific inquiry or any combination of all three. At the end of the day, a visit to a museum should be an enjoyable experience and not a hard slog.

Sports museums are about games that people play. This has many different connotations. It means that they are about social history, economic history and the history of technology. Their collections contain decorative art, applied art, fine art, books, archival material and possibly even archaeological material. In many ways, they are no different from many multi-discipline museums except that the entire range of the collection focuses on a single application of these disciplines. All sports involve movement and thus the use of interactive technology becomes a very important aspect in the interpretation of the subject. Moving image of a game in progress is worth more than volumes of text.

THE BRITISH GOLF MUSEUM

Opened in 1990, the British Golf Museum at St Andrews tells the story of golf in Britain and British influence abroad from the middle ages to the present day. This has meant looking beyond Scotland itself and trying to set the

Plate 1 Interactive technology in use at the British Golf Museum

development of the game in its full context in the UK. This is achieved through a combination of objects, illustrations, text and interactive touch screen displays. There are three factors that dictate the interpretation of one's subject: the scope and nature of the collection itself, the amount of space available in which to display it and the funds available to build the displays. The scope and nature of the collection should effectively dictate how best to use the building and the budget. In simple terms, one can only build a display when one has something to show.

The museum is set out chronologically and each gallery has a well defined theme, each display case within the gallery tells a story related to that theme, and each object on display contributes to that story. This paper is structured to take the reader through the chronological journey of a visitor to St Andrews.

INTERACTIVE TECHNOLOGY

The use of interactive technology is a very important part of the museum's interpretative techniques. Over the last few years, there has been a tremendous increase in the use of interactive displays in museums which provide a means of involving visitors in the interpretation of a museum. There is no difference between preparing the design for an interactive display and for a three dimensional object; what is important to remember is that the display must have a purpose and then fulfil it.

The British Golf Museum was the first museum in Europe to use the CD-I (Compact Disc-Interactive) system developed by Philips Electronics. It also uses Philips Laservision players controlled by personal computers. The museum is set out chronologically and divided into 15 permanent galleries and one temporary exhibition gallery. There are eight Laservision workstations and six CD-I displays integrated into eight of the galleries, containing 149 audio-visual programmes. Multiple touch-screens are used in two galleries giving a total of 12 workstations in the museum. In addition there is one CD-I workstation in the temporary exhibition gallery which allows us to show a variety of different CD-I discs while another CD-I display uses a simple button to activate the single programme on the disc. In the last two years, another three interactive workstations have been added to the museum.

In the design of these interactive displays, we adhered to six basic concepts:

> **Integration.** The workstations were both thematically and physically integrated into the museum, and it was decided that each touch screen would only contain programmes that dealt with the specific gallery in which it was located. In all, the 13 touch screens were divided between eight galleries.

Format. There were with a few exceptions two basic formats used. The main format was an introductory audio-visual programme, a selection of biographies of famous players, a selection of accounts of dramatic golf matches, relevant statistical information for the theme of the display and one or more audio-visual programmes dealing with a topic unique to the theme of the display. The non-statistical audio-visuals used a combination of still and moving images with a voice over narration to tell their story. The remaining two were both quizzes, which used a different format consisting of text only multiple choice questions.

Good viewing. From a content point of view each audio-visual had to be not only historically accurate but also provide good viewing. Thus, whenever possible audio-visuals incorporated anecdotes or interesting story lines.

Simple to use. From a visitor's point of view, each touch-screen had to be extremely user friendly to visitors of widely diverging ages, all of whom would be literally just passing by. This is achieved by having very simple menus with clear instructions. It is possible to stop any audio-visual once it has started and return to the menu screen.

Length of audio-visuals. Most museum visitors have a remarkably short concentration span and the time spent watching audio-visuals is deceptive so we endeavoured to keep all of ours between 60 and 70 seconds long.

Visitor satisfaction. A touch screen can only be used by one visitor at a time and the actual screens are quite small. In order to reconcile this very one-on-one individual experience with the need to have a large throughput of visitors, especially in the summer season, we use large slave monitors suspended above the touch screens. These allow groups of visitors to view a programme activated by someone else. Also by spreading workstations throughout the museum, visitors can move from one to another in the hope that they will eventually be able to use one themselves.

THEMES AND OBJECTS

A specific problem with sports museums, especially with golf, is that visitors often have a preconceived erroneous idea of what the museum will be like. They think that it will be simply a larger version of a club trophy room. In our case they often think that it will consist of endless cases of clubs, balls and trophies with little or no interpretation and therefore quite dull. We worked very hard to avoid this. The basic philosophy was to constantly vary what the visitor was looking at in terms of themes and objects.

A conscious decision was made from the start that the museum would cover the whole chronological span of the game. Thus the modern period is given as much weight as the 18th and 19th century developments. I feel very strongly that a museum must collect for tomorrow as well as for today. The latest club and ball designs are of as much interest to us as 18th and 19th century ones; the late 20th century champions are as important as the late 19th century ones. If we do not stay up to date, we cannot properly represent the modern game.

THE ORIGINS OF GOLF

The first theme encountered by a visitor to the museum is that of the Origins of Golf. In recent decades, there has been a great deal of debate about the origins of golf, most of which misses the basic point. Ball and stick games constantly evolve throughout history; they do not happen overnight. It is rather futile to try and find a date or a precise origin for any one game. Golf was one of many ball and stick games played during the middle ages. What seems to have distinguished Scottish golf from other British or Continental games was that the object was to put the ball into a hole in the ground by hitting it with a stick.

These games all undoubtedly influenced one another, but there can be little doubt that golf as it is played today took root on the east coast of Scotland in the middle ages, some time before 1457 and from there it eventually spread to the rest of the British Isles and then the world. This is covered by a display of objects and a CD-I programme which illustrates the different games.

The visitor then moves on to Golf and the Stuart Monarchs 1457-1649. The earliest surviving written reference to golf dates from 1457, which does not mean there were no mentions of the game prior to that date, but simply that it is the earliest to survive the ravages of time. It is also worth noting that the word golf is indeed spelled 'Golf' and not 'Gowf', a corruption in the 18th century printed text. Golf was almost exclusively, with very few exceptions, a Scottish sport and a letter of 1691 refers to St Andrews as 'the metropolis of golfing'.

1700 - 1840

Golf in the 18th Century deals with the structure of golf in this period. The formation of the early golfing societies and the social side of these societies is depicted in a tableau with a commentary of two gentlemen making bets prior to their match and the players standing alongside a silver club. Betting was an integral part of virtually all 18th century sporting activities. The mid-18th century was also a great time for codifying rules of games and golf was no exception. The earliest surviving rules of the game, those formatted by The Gentlemen Golfers of Leith in 1744 are reproduced. Also featured in this gallery is the earliest provenanced set of golf clubs in the country dating from about 1700 and known as the Troon Collection. These eight clubs were found concealed in a cupboard at 160 High Street, Hull in 1898 and were wrapped in a newspaper dated 1741.

Next comes the gallery Golf c1800-1840 which features an impressive range of clubs made by Hugh Philp and Tom Morris and feather balls made by Allan Robertson and the Gourlays. The feather ball is rather misunderstood. It actually flew quite well. When the gutty ball came into being, it did not travel any further than the feathery. The problem with the feathery was that in wet weather it tended to go soft, losing its shape and it easily split into pieces if it was mis-hit, especially with iron clubs. This is why iron clubs were rarely used up to the middle of the century. They were clubs of last resort only to be used to get out of extremely rough ground or ruts. Thus players used an array of wooden spoons where modern golfers would use irons. The feathery was also difficult to make and very expensive.

We also tell the story of the relationship between Robertson, Morris and Col J.O. Fairlie. Morris worked for Robertson as a ball maker. When the gutty first appeared around 1849, Robertson, jealous of his livelihood, made Morris swear never to play with the new ball. However, one day Morris ran out of balls when playing a match on the Old Course and his opponent gave him a gutty with which to play. Robertson had stern words with Morris when he came off the course. Shortly thereafter, Morris left Robertson's employ and Fairlie, the leading amateur of his day and Morris' patron, secured for Tom the appointment of Custodian of the Links at the new club in Prestwick in 1851, where he stayed for 14 years. This effectively illustrates the social structure of the time as well as changes in equipment.

CLUBS AND BALLS

We then proceed to the gallery on club and ball development c1850 to c1890. The gutty ball was a solid piece of gutta percha, which was the juice of the palaquinium genus of trees in the far east. It was much harder than the feathery and necessitated changes in club design. The faces and necks of wooded clubs needed to be strengthened and then eventually the shape changed from the long nose to the shorter type still in use today. Iron clubs came into greater use as they no longer damaged the ball and it was easier to hit lofted shots with them rather than using wooden spoons. Iron club making became much more skilful. This is illustrated by the clubs on display.

One of the mistakes that appears in many books is that with the advent of the gutty ball, golf became much more popular. This is simply not true. The rapid growth of golf in Britain in the late 19th Century was the result of a number of factors that go beyond the introduction of the new ball. Although the cost of the gutty ball brought the game within the reach of many more people, golf only spread slowly after its introduction. The table below shows

Plate 2 Players at Leith Links Tournament May 17, 1867

Plate 3 Advertisement for the Haskell Ball (Golf Illustrated, April 15, 1904)

the growth in the number of clubs in Scotland and England between 1850 and 1913:

	1850	1870	1880	1888	1893	1902	1913
Scotland	22	50	84	164	301	606	1,022
England	2	9	21	31	356	751	1,469

SOCIAL CHANGE AFTER 1850

Something else besides the gutty ball and then the rubber cored ball in 1902 caused this explosion.

The popularity of golf was part of a massive social change that took place in Britain in the second half of the 19th century. It was this social change, which in turn was fuelled by the advent of the railway and then other forms of transport, which was the catalyst for the popularity of golf.

The railway broke down many social and physical barriers as all classes of people were able to travel countrywide. In the 1880s, the safety bicycle had been introduced, providing a cheap form of transport for both men and women and by the turn of the century, the motor car was beginning to become a factor in the growth of transport. In turn, roads and public transport systems in the major cities developed, especially around London.

Concurrent with these developments, the social impact of the industrial revolution had reached a peak by the 1870s with a decline in countryside population and a massive increase in city populations and the emergence of a large middle class. This in turn led to a new attitude towards sports. Organised games had become virtually compulsory in the rapidly growing number of public schools, where it was felt that sports were an important part of the moulding of a British gentleman.

Organised sports as we know them today emerged out of all this change. The Football Association was formed in 1863 and the Scottish Football Association was formed a decade later in 1873; the English Football League came into being in 1888 and the Scottish one two years later in 1890. The Rugby Football Union was formed in 1871 and the Scottish one in 1874. The Northern Rugby Football Union, later to be known as the Rugby League broke away from the RFU in 1895. In 1874, Major Wingfield patented a game called Sphairistike which rapidly became known as Lawn Tennis. The game underwent major rules changes in 1877 and the first Wimbledon Championship was held that same year. 1877 also saw the first international cricket match between England and Australia. That game was seeing a transition from sporadic county matches and itinerant travelling eleven teams to a county championship by the 1890s, with the M.C.C. taking responsibility for determining the championship in 1895.

In Scotland, golf had a long tradition of public courses. This was not the case in England, where the game grew largely within the confines of private clubs. Therefore golf in Scotland was played by a much broader social spectrum of people than in England. These complex issues, by necessity, are simplified and reduced to five text panels but the underpinning knowledge exists and has been published by the museum.

THE OPEN CHAMPIONSHIP

Next comes a gallery about the origins of the Open Championship and Professional Golfers c1860-c1890. In one of history's little ironies, the first Open was not an open competition - it was for professionals only. Amateurs were allowed to play the next year in 1861. Before 1863, when the first prize money of £10 was offered, the winner received a medal but no money.

The development of the Open Championship is one of the major themes of the museum. We illustrate this early period of the Open with replicas of the Belt and Claret Jug Trophy and we have an impressive array of artefacts used by, won by or made by Open Champions of this period. The audio-visuals in the interactive display very much relate to the objects on display.

AMATEUR GOLF

Next comes the story of Amateur golf c1880-c1914. One of the highlights of this gallery is the stunning collection of 124 medals won by John Laidlay. We also have displays about other famous amateurs and club life in the period. There is a touch screen dealing with Amateur Golf 1885-1914, which offers the choice of an overview, biographies of 10 famous players, accounts of 10 dramatic matches, a feature on club life and a feature on Mens' Fashions.

Up to this point in the museum, there has been an emphasis on golf in Scotland, because that is where most of the events depicted took place. However, as the game swept England, so the emphasis changes. No distinction is made between Scottish and other British events. Subjects are covered on the grounds of what is in the collection and the relative importance of the topic rather than its regional basis. From a content point of view the nature of the objects on display also changes. Up until 1860, virtually all the displays contain clubs, balls or ball making equipment. As the game grows in popularity so the surviving artefacts become much more diverse and we are able to start building medals, trophies, clothing and decorative art objects into our displays. The visual aspect of the displays starts to take on a very different look.

The gallery of Early Ladies Golf features a look at the range of competitions that the ladies played in contrast to the previous galleries where the emphasis was on individual winners.

The twin themes of equipment development and fruits of victory come together in Golf c1890-c1914. There is a display of unusual clubs, most of which were illegal by 1910 which is then contrasted by a display of conventional clubs. The impact of the rubber cored ball is dealt with in detail. The display on professional golf in the period includes a wide selection of medals, trophies and miscellaneous memorabilia that belonged to the leading professionals. The strides in technology in this period are best represented by the fact that the touch screen in this gallery contains the earliest moving image in the museum, dating from 1908.

The next gallery, The Administration of Golf, incorporates three interactive displays because the subject matter is not very visual. The first deals with the history and functions of the Royal & Ancient Club at St Andrews, the second is about all the other ruling bodies in golf and the third is a very popular quiz about the rules of golf. Opposite that is the Auchterlonie Workshop tableau, which shows the father and son, Willie and Laurie Auchterlonie at work making hand crafted clubs.

POST WORLD WAR I

The resumption of golf after World War I marks another watershed in the nature of the material put on display. Up to 1914, British golfers dominated the world scene. Then after the war, American golfers come to the fore. They began coming to Britain on a regular basis and winning the Open and the Amateur. This period also saw the start of regular international team matches. American golfers such as Bobby Jones and Walter Hagen started to make a big impact on British golf during this period and are therefore represented in the museum along with the leading British professionals and amateurs of the period. The museum takes on a truly international aspect that did not exist in earlier time periods or galleries. This is all done in the context of overseas golfers' impact in Britain or the travels of British players abroad. This applies to both the three dimensional displays and the touch screens.

The two major equipment changes in this era are dealt with in detail, namely the advent of rules governing the size and weight of balls and the introduction of steel shafted clubs.

The impact of American and European golfers on British golf continues to be well represented in the Golf Since 1946 Gallery. This gallery looks at the significant changes in equipment and features many objects relating to Open and Amateur Champions as well as to other significant British tournaments. There are also three touch screens, two dealing with post war golf and the third is a general quiz covering the full history of the game. This is the most popular gallery in the museum because almost all our visitors can relate to the people, events and equipment depicted in it.

TEMPORARY EXHIBITIONS AND THEATRES

The Temporary Exhibition Gallery is used to stage short exhibitions of national and international importance. These are chosen so that they compliment or expand upon the permanent exhibits. Also in this gallery is another touch screen, featuring a variety of different CD-I programs, of which the most popular is an animated sudden death play off on the old Course featuring historic players and equipment. Finally, the Audio Visual Theatre seats 48 and shows a selection of historic golfing films.

And so ends the tour of the museum, which starts very much as a Scottish story, becomes a British one, and then ultimately an international one. In short it reflects the changes in society from the middle ages to the present day.

MUSEUMS OF SPORT

Sports museums are rare in the UK and even rarer in Scotland. In terms of major museums, there is the Wimbledon Lawn Tennis Museum, the Lords Cricket Museum, the National Horseracing Museum at Newmarket and the British Golf Museum in St Andrews. Each of these are located at the emotional centre of their respective sports. In Scotland, in addition to golf in St Andrews, there will be an expanded Scottish Rugby Union Museum at Murrayfield and plans are afoot for a Scottish Football Museum in Glasgow, which is being tried out initially on a temporary basis in a small space.

The concept of sports museums is not nearly as ingrained within society in Britain, or Scotland, as it is in the United States. There, each of the major sports is represented by at least one museum attracting six figure visitor numbers. In Britain, sports museums are hard to sell to the general public. The assumption that everybody who plays a specific sport will be interested in the history of that sport is not correct. Therefore sports museums in this country need to be modest in size but not in ambition.

I believe that the British Golf Museum has shown the way ahead with its use of interactive technology which is seamlessly integrated with three dimensional displays. In America, the National Baseball Hall of Fame and Museum in Cooperstown, New York, the National Museum of Racing and Hall of Fame in Saratoga Springs, New York, the Kentucky Derby Museum in Louisville, Kentucky, the Pro Football Hall of Fame in Canton, Ohio, and the Basketball Hall of Fame in Springfield, Massachusetts, all use interactive technology in a similar manner to the British Golf Museum but not as effectively. However all but the Pro Football Hall of Fame, use a different application of new technologies - namely stunning multimedia state-of-the-art film or tape/slide shown in a large single location.

To be successful in attracting visitors, any sports museum in this country will need to have outstanding visual displays combined with intelligent use of interactive technology and/or complex multimedia theatre presentations. To be successful in historical/research terms, any single sports museum should also be constantly evaluating its own sport's history in the context of social history along with the broad spectrum of the overall history of British sports in general. Apart from a general museum of Scottish sports, the obvious candidates for special provision in Scotland are curling, shinty, mountaineering and skiing.

The author

Peter Lewis is Director of The British Golf Museum at St Andrews. One of his major publications is *British Professional Golf in the Age of the Triumvirate 1894-1914* (Grant Books, 1993).

References

Bearman, D. (ed), *Hypermedia & Interactivity in Museums - Proceedings of an International Conference*, Pittsburgh, October 1991.

Brailsford, D., *British Sport - A Social History*, Cambridge 1992.

Cornish, G.S. & Whitten, R.E., *The Golf Course*, London 1981.

Cousins, G., *Golf in Britain*, London 1975.

Cousins, G., *Lords of the Links*, London 1977.

Darwin, B., *British Golf*, London 1946.

Davies, M. (ed), *The Museums Journal*, Vol.90 No.8, August 1990.

Davies, M. (ed), *The Museums Journal*, Vol.93 No.2, February 1993.

Geddes, O., *A Swing Through Time*, HMSO 1992.

Henderson, I. & Stirk D., *Golf in the Making*, Crawley 1979.

Hobbs, M., *British Open Champions*, London 1991.

Hoffos, S., *Multimedia and the Interactive Display in Museums, Exhibitions and Libraries*, London 1992.

Leach, H., *Great Golfers in the Making*, London 1907.

Lewis, P.N., *Great British Golf* (CD-I disc), Philips 1992.

Lewis, P.N., *British Golf Museum Guide*, St Andrews 1991.

Ryde, P., *Royal & Ancient Championship Records 1860-1980*, St Andrews 1981.

Vamplew, W., *Play Up & Play the Game*, Cambridge 1988.

Viney, L., *The Royal & Ancient Book of Golf Records*, London 1991.

22

AT THEIR COUNTRY'S CALL
The Heritage of Soldiering in Scotland

Stephen Wood

Scotland's soldiers, or, more particularly, her Highland soldiers, represent internationally an advertising symbol of iconographic proportions. The kilted and feather-bonneted Highland soldier now joins the Breton *pêcheur*, the Bavarian *bauer*, the Spanish *torero* and the Venetian *gondoliere* as a human symbol of his country. It is ironic, I feel, that all these icons represent not so much their nations but, rather, microcosmic cultural groups within those nations, nations that have now not only engulfed but also sanitised, polished and rediscovered those cultures for the benefits of national tourism. One need not be either cynical or dismissive of this; it is but part of the business of caricature and caricature has a long and colourful history.

Equally long and colourful is the military history of Scotland, both as a nation in its own right and within the broader compass of the military history of Britain. Scotland is a country in which the importance of tourism to the national economy has never been so great, especially when compared to the more long-standing generators of revenue now in decline. Under circumstances of military retrenchment and retreat from global commitments, it is inevitable that Scotland's soldiers will diminish in quantity. It is unlikely that their fading away will proportionately reduce either military museums or military collections in the public domain and, indeed, the converse may actually be the case, rather as a decline in the shipbuilding and fishing industries has paralleled the growth of maritime museums and collections. The national caricatures that I referred to above are themselves a product of the nostalgia industry and, given their entrenched position and the fact that few first-time visitors to Scotland visit without preconceived notions of kilt-and-bagpipes combination, it seems unlikely that a perceived diminution of demand for the national stereotype will occur. In other words, we have to accept that we are stuck with military history, like it or not.

If we accept that we are stuck with it, its material culture and its residual attitudes (for and against), how are we to interpret it? The title of this paper is deliberately both provocative and laced with double-meaning. I intend to examine not only what might be done but also, more particularly, what

Plate 1 The regimental museum as old clothes shop: that of the Gordon Highlanders in Aberdeen, 1983 (author's photograph).

Plate 2 Interpretative and multi-media: the Gordons' regimental museum in 1993 (author's photograph)

might be done better than it is at present. Thus, the people who are at the call of their country are not just those whose stories are being interpreted (or not) but also those charged with the interpretation.

I have worked in Scotland for 10 years, having known the country well beforehand. In the last decade, purely coincidentally I am sure, great advances have been made in the level of interpretation of military history to be found here. This is not unique to Scotland, fortunately, but it has meant that Scotland's interpretation of its martial past has caught up with developments elsewhere in the UK. This is not the time or place to be complacent or smug however – associated though those two attributes inevitably are with Englishmen; much more remains to be done as scholarship advances, as fashions change and as the generations and the years depart. As a prelude to examining what might be done, I would like to examine the changes that have taken place in the last decade.

The most stereotypical of military displays are those established in regimental museums, of which Scotland has eight (nine if you count, as I think you should, the museum of the King's Own Scottish Borderers in Berwick-upon-Tweed). The passions and loyalties generated by the clannish nature of the Army's regimental system in Scotland have been constantly in the news in recent years, as the Keep Our Scottish Battalions campaign has mustered support from most levels of society for its resistance to the amalgamations of regiments.

Although regimental museums have been, in many ways, the Cinderellas of the professional museum world, I have not encountered many in which the curators and trustees have had any of the doubts or uncertainties of that world concerning their role or their target audience: targets and roles are, after all, their business, and overt doubt is not a quality of leadership. Successive Ministry of Defence surveys, reports and recommendations have consistently identified the principal roles of the regimental museums as: (i) an aid to recruitment, and (ii) Keeping the Army in the Public Eye. It is for the perpetration of these roles that the MoD continues to fund them, since it isn't in the heritage business, other than coincidentally.

In the dear departed 1950s, regimental museums' displays tended to be notable for their clutter, lack of interpretation and what a generation of anthropologists still then in nappies would later describe as 'cultural ethnocentricity'. In this, the regimental museums were largely indistinguishable from most other museums. But the years advanced, the 1960s and 1970s wrought great changes in interpretation in museums, piles of dusty old tat were unearthed in cellars, rediscovered as 'ethnographic material culture' and treated with curatorial reverence. The regimental museums slumbered on, largely unchanged and increasingly distanced from their peers in the post-National Service decades. In Scotland they tended to resemble family shrines (which, in part, of course, they were and are) or old clothes shops. As any semblance of military history was swept, with a shudder, from local authority museums, so it became ossified in regimental museums: it was the worst of all possible worlds.

Reduced defence budgets since the 1970s have inevitably meant less money for regimental museums. Increased availability of grant-aid, tested against the ability to demonstrate not only value for money but also curatorial standards and customer service has meant that, increasingly, Scotland's regimental museums have been drawn into the professional museum sphere. Added to a gradual change in attitude has been the fortuitous geographical link between five of these museums and substantial developments in the world of site interpretation; thus, newly-displayed and interpreted regimental museums now exist in the Historic Scotland properties of Edinburgh and Stirling Castles and Fort George and in the English Heritage property of Berwick-upon-Tweed's Barracks.

I refer to the business of co-operational site interpretation of military history below, but, before that, it is worth pointing out that the importance of the museum interpretation of military history, even in its inevitably parochial regimental sense, has been recognised by the Scottish Tourist Board and the Museums and Galleries Improvements Fund, which is underwritten by the Wolfson Foundation, both of which made generous grant-aid available to the new museum of The Royal Scots in Edinburgh Castle. These grants recognise the intrinsic importance of the museum interpretation of military history, and with this recognition it can be said that Scotland's regimental museums have come of age. Further evidence of this maturity of outlook has been a recent agreement between the Cameronians' Museum in Hamilton and its neighbouring local authority museum. This recognises not only their physical proximity but also the fact that the regiment's history is inexorably intertwined with that of the area, a fact recognised by all - too - few local authority museums.

All the changes in regimental museums notwithstanding, most still retain their shrine-like qualities and I believe that, despite the purist reservations of some modern curators, visitor surveys would show that this aspect does not jar with the museums' audiences. Indeed, it might be said that those regimental museums which have retained the shrine concept have, in so doing, retained both the baby and the bath water. This, for instance, is what makes the new museum of the Argyll and Sutherland Highlanders in Stirling Castle a successful modern regimental museum in the traditional mould; by contrast, that of The Royal Scots in Edinburgh Castle demonstrates modernity but in a more clinical and information-intensive way. Each has its appeal but I suspect that the Argylls' has the edge in visitor satisfaction.

Both these museums have large captive audiences by virtue of their situations within Historic Scotland properties and both probably gain more than they lose by their relationships with their landlord. However, Historic Scotland itself interprets military history as part of its site interpretation: in the barrack rooms and Grand Magazine at Fort George, in more barrack rooms in Stirling Castle and in the military prison in Edinburgh Castle.

The minutiae of the soldier's life is not an easy concept to interpret and in the thirty years since the ending of National Service it has become an experience increasingly remote from the majority of the population. In the same period, the dreadful trauma of Northern Ireland's misery and the

Plate 3 Historic Scotland's tableau interpretation: an officer's quarters in Fort George (c.1815), 1990 (by courtesy of Historic Scotland)

growth of world-wide terrorist activity has led to an unsurprising repugnance on the part of a post-Imperial generation for the overt trappings of soldiering. Thus, the interpretation of military history by civilians on military sites – as opposed to that in the regimental museums - has tended to concentrate on what little of the soldier's life can be easily and comprehensibly interpreted: hence the fascination for barrack room vignettes.

Considerations of cost and, I suspect, a slight quasi-academic nervousness, have prevented Historic Scotland from going the whole hog and constructing a military Jorvik-type interpretation or going headlong into 'living history' in the North American style. As a result, while the tableaux are admirable, carefully researched and generally visitor-friendly in their interpretation, they are, perhaps, more limited in their impact and achievement as regards visitor-experience than they might have been had Historic Scotland not applied the same rigidly high standards to them which it habitually (and quite rightly) applies to its interpretation and conservation of the buildings in its care. It may be that a more co-operative approach, a concept to which I shall return in my conclusions, would have yielded a more exciting and less traditional result.

Although neither institution may care for the comparison, the activities of the National Trust for Scotland may be bracketed, for the purpose of this paper, with those of Historic Scotland as regards the interpretation of military history. The National Trust has busied itself in military interpretation within the past decade and has achieved considerable success (although echoes of Samuel Johnson's comments about woman's preaching may uncharitably have occurred to those whose view of the Trust's predilections has been formed by caricature). While I take very considerable issue indeed with aspects of the Trust's interpretation of the battle of Culloden, I am happy to recognise and to acknowledge that what is there now (or, in the case of the trees and the road, what is not) is a vast improvement on the battlefield as it was before the Trust's improvements to it. It is probable that a more objective approach to the battle, to the wider history of Jacobitism and to the *dramatis personae* of the '45 Rebellion, would not have appealed to the battlefield's audience and, indeed, might have led to a repeat performance of the battle itself: scholars - real, imagined or putative - and fans of the Duke of Cumberland just have to grin and bear it.

In my view, one of the greatest strengths of the National Trust is its ability to assess correctly its visitors' expectations and to produce interpretations which satisfy them, even if, in the process, those expectations are neither heightened nor especially challenged. Thus, while Culloden may irritate pedants like me, it is clearly widely popular and successful, factors which, after all, are measurable indicators of the Trust's performance. Similarly, while the display of weaponry-as-wallpaper at Culzean may make the odd (I mean 'odd' in more than one sense) weapons specialist wince, it has a respectable pedigree, enhances the impressiveness of the Castle interior and has considerable popular appeal. Much the same applies at Fyvie Castle, where the use of weaponry as interior decoration accompanies one of the finest military paintings which Scotland possesses, Batoni's 'Colonel William Gordon of Fyvie', and other military portraits to interpret the inevitable association of the house and its history with gentlemen who were also soldiers.

This interpretation is taken to its greatest extent by the Trust at Leith Hall, where a great quantity of family uniforms, weapons and other relics have been, I think, successfully used to bring what would otherwise be just another minor 'stately home' alive, through the interpretation of the careers of several of its occupants. While few Trust properties have been as fortunate as Leith Hall in retaining such quantities of their occupiers' belongings, it is also true that few have not had owners or occupiers with military connections. The nature of British society from the mid-17th to the mid-20th centuries meant that few people remained untouched or unaffected by the armed forces, to varying extents, and to ignore this factor is to censor historical interpretation. I very much hope that the experience of co-operation between the National Trust for Scotland and the National Museums of Scotland over Leith Hall and, to a much lesser extent, over the new Visitor Centre at Killiecrankie will lead to similar future exercises in co-operative interpretation, which can only benefit Scotland's visitors.

An area in which the interpretation of soldiering tends to be notable by its absence is in the local authority museums of Scotland. This absence, and it is now decreasing, is largely a hangover from the attitudes of the 1960s and was brought about either from ignorance – military history and its artefacts are specialised subjects after all – or hostility. Notable successes in putting military history into its social history context have taken place in recent years in several local museums in Scotland and younger and more enlightened generations of curators, leaving aside the political complexions of their governing bodies, seem less willing automatically to consign their military collections to the kind of *oubliette* once occupied by their ethnography collections. Several local museums have important collections of military materials; those in Glasgow, Stirling and Perth provide examples which spring most readily to mind. In North-East Fife in 1992, the District Museums Service actually staged two temporary exhibitions with military themes: one, in Newburgh, based upon a private collection - very successfully put into its local context; the other, in St Andrews, showing the socio-military interaction that the last war made inevitable for local people. Glasgow's arms, armour and military history galleries are of international renown and reflect the status of Glasgow's collections; in Perth military items have been incorporated into a permanent exhibition on the region's history; in Inverness a display on road-building in the Highlands places a military operation in its social, economic and political context. The message throughout is simple: military history is not something to be afraid of or prejudiced against, it is an inevitable part of any nation's history and, in Scotland, is very close to the surface of that history. Be enthralled by it, if you must; be repelled by it, if you wish, but don't ignore it. Scotland's local authority museums are waking up to this message.

Plate 4 A family's service, lives and careers in context: the National Trust for Scotland's displays at Leith Hall, 1991 (by courtesy of the National Trust for Scotland).

Plate 5 The civilian element in military history interpretation: the Home Front exhibition in St Andrews Museum 1992 (by courtesy of NE Fife Museums Service).

The encouragement of links between the regimental museums and local authority museums should have as its eventual goal a balanced interpretation of the history of Scotland's regions. This should be presented to visitors in a way which makes the essential point that soldiers and civilians in this country have never been that far apart, even when they have been violently in opposition to each other. Each of Scotland's institutions which makes the effort to interpret military history, no matter how or whatever the view it takes of its subject, can benefit by actively seeking to co-operate with other institutions at work in the field. This co-operative concept it not one unique to military history; indeed, it permeates the day-to-day life of all of us at work in the heritage, museums and galleries sector of the arts in Scotland. However, it is apparent that more might be done to institute regular co-operation between institutions in order to ensure that visitors' experience of every facet of military history is enhanced.

In the Scottish United Services Museum, Scotland's national museum of the armed services, we take this need for co-operation and balanced interpretation seriously, as do our peer departments of the National Museums of Scotland, and we make it our business to respond as positively as our limited resources allow to requests for co-operation. We are slowly altering our displays at Edinburgh Castle from ones erected by curators for other curators to ones that we anticipate will satisfy the expectations of our visitors, who represent a cross-section of Scotland's annual tourist traffic. This involves, in part, the removal of a traditional military museum's rather incestuous clutter and replacing it with comprehensible displays deliberately aimed at visitors who have, on average, less than an hour to spend on our premises and who generally have either (or both) a limited and/or romantic notion of Scotland's history.

While I like to think we have made great advances in this area of interpretation, I realise that we still have a long way to go and that our very best efforts have to be set against the expectations of increasingly sophisticated visitors; like all museums, we have to be aware of the danger of our displays being obsolete by the time they are completed. A reduction in the sheer overwhelming quantity of items which we display will result in much more material being available for use elsewhere and although some has been targeted for use in the Museum of Scotland, I would very much like to see us making items available as loans to sites where they would be appropriate, welcome and adequately protected.

The very fact that a Convention such as this can be arranged under the modern interpretation of the word heritage, and by so doing represent so many diverse – yet associated – parts of its resultant industry, indicates that there must be unlimited potential for co-operative ventures, not only in terms of museums or other displays but also in terms of interpretation, marketing and information exchange. That it was thought worthwhile to include the military history factor in this Convention, I regard as a major step forward. Although I fully appreciated that its importance and relevance may still be a matter of some doubt for many, I hope that the attitudes represented in the pages of this paper will have provided not only food for thought but also the

Plate 6 Incestuous and unreconstructed clutter: displays at the Scottish United Services Museum, largely unchanged in style since the 1930s, 1993 (by courtesy of the Trustees of the national Museums of Scotland)

basis for the future co-operation among those of us employed in the heritage industry which I regard as essential to its successful pursuit.

The author

Stephen Wood is Keeper of the Scottish United Services Museum in Edinburgh Castle. Publications include *The Scottish Soldier* (Archive Publications 1987), *In the Finest Tradition* (Mainstream 1988), *The Auld Alliance* (Mainstream 1989).

References

Aldridge, D., *Site Interpretation: A Practical Guide*, Scottish Tourist Board, 1993.

Articles in *Soldiering On*, Museums Association Journal, November 1991.

Preece, G., *The Museum of the Manchesters: a social and regimental history*, Museums Association Journal, September 1987.

Thorburn, W.A., *Military History as a Museum Subject*, Museums Association Journal, December 1962.

The Museums of the Armed Services: a report by a working party, Museums and Galleries Commission, HMSO 1990.

Wood, S., *Too serious a business to be left to military men: a personal view of the military museum's role today*, from Museum, c.1985, pp.20-26.

Wood, S., *Stands Scotland where it did?: developments in Scotland's national military museum*, Journal of the Society for Army Historical Research, Summer 1987, pp.63-66.

Wood, S., *Military museums and the Army: the view from Scotland*, British Army Review, 86, August 1987, pp.57-64.

Wood, S., *Military museums: the national perspective*, Museums Journal, 87(2), September 1987, pp.65-66.

Wood, S., *Obfuscation, irritation or obliteration?: the interpretation of military collections in British museums of the 1980s*, Social History Curators' Group Journal, 15, 1988, pp.4-6.

THE ARTS AND CRAFTS
Calling upon the Muses

Art has boundaries
of neither time nor place,
yet, it is unique
to where and when it was begotten

23

OUR HERITAGE
Not Just an Armchair at the Fireside of History

Duncan Macmillan

In 1817, as he returned to Scotland after some years absence, the artist David Wilkie wrote of his native land:

> Scotland is most remarkable as a volume of history. It is the land of tradition and of poetry. Every district has some scene in it of real or fictitious events, treasured with a sort of religious care in the minds of the inhabitants and giving dignity to places that in every other respect would to the man of he world be considered barren and unprofitable.

It is a familiar, a too familiar, vision of our country that countless tourists and visitors subscribe to unquestioningly as they gaze too often with unacknowledged bafflement at landscapes that must sometimes still seem barren and unprofitable. Indeed, Wilkie was writing before the agricultural revolution, then already in progress, had finally irrevocably changed the face of the country. If we understood our own heritage better and the motives that gave rise to the very concept of 'heritage', perhaps we could do more to dispel this bafflement, but, also, we might be able to draw more effectively ourselves on the resources that this idea holds and which inspired our forbears.

Yet Wilkie was one of the greatest imaginative artists Scotland has produced and, when he wrote this, he was reacting to the achievement of the man who did more than any other to shape the modern image of Scotland, Walter Scott. It was Scott above all who inhabited the Scottish landscape with history and poetry in the popular imagination in the way that Wilkie describes. Scott himself drew on a European inspiration, but it is nevertheless true that he in turn did much to open the imaginative dimension of history for all of Europe by showing that it was not some kind of Titanic march of great events, but the sum of countless, individual human experiences. The Scottish perspective on heritage is therefore a special one.

Within Scotland, Scott himself was responding to the inspiration of an earlier generation for whom the landscape had proved a rich and various source of inspiration. Indeed, in some ways Scott's own conservatism has disguised the radical inspiration that led men to search in the past and in the natural world for ideals and for tools with which to set right some of the wrongs of the present.

RADICAL CONVERGENCE IN THE ENLIGHTENMENT

Landscape is central to the idea of heritage and in one way or another, any discussion always returns to the idea of 'the cultured landscape'. But why do we value the landscape so highly and what has landscape to do with culture? It is a comparatively modern view. In painting, for instance, the idea of a 'national landscape' was born with the Dutch in the 17th Century. It was taken up by the Scots in a rather different way in the following century and has played a central part in all aspects of Scottish life since then. As early as 1724, the poet Allan Ramsay wrote of 'that natural strength of Thought and Simplicity of Style that our Forefathers practised' and then he went on:

> When these good old Bards wrote, we had not yet made Use of imported Trimmings upon our Cloaths, nor of Foreign Embroidery in our Writings. Their Poetry is the Product of their own Country, not pilfered and spoiled in the Transportation from abroad: Their Images are native, and their Landskips domestick: copied from the Fields and Meadows we every Day behold.

In a way that already suggests very clearly something of the modern idea of heritage, Ramsay identifies virtues of simplicity and strength located in the past and reflecting the landscape. The national heritage was therefore seen as a witness of a heroic past, simpler, stronger and more honest than the present and so it came to stand not just for a familiar environment, but for a whole set of values. As he presents this idea, however, Ramsay also combines the imagery of painting and poetry and in the period of the Scottish Enlightenment, not just these two, but music, history and science as well all found inspiration in the landscape. Often as they did so, what we see as separate branches of knowledge, overlapped and informed each other. In a way, the Enlightenment was like the Renaissance in this. Its peculiar intellectual and imaginative strength reflected the way that the different branches of thought were convergent. Their representatives could speak to each other on common ground. This is indeed a heritage without boundaries, and in the Enlightenment, if the central discipline was philosophy, an important part of the common ground was landscape. It is really from there, though it is much debased, that our modern attitude to landscape derives.

The music of the people as it was preserved in custom and oral tradition was seen by men like Ramsay as the truest kind of poetry and song. It was described as the product of the landscape just like the flora and fauna. For instance, in the introduction to his first collection of *Scots Songs* (1769), David Herd, who was one of the pioneers of the collection of folk song, commented on the special distinction of the Scottish musical tradition and reflected on 'the romantic face of the country and the pastoral life of the great part of its inhabitants; circumstances no doubt highly favourable to poetry and song.' Folk song and folk music were seen as 'natural' therefore and when Herd's contemporary David Allan painted the *Highland Dance*, set outside Blair Castle, he imitated the simplicity and unselfconsciousness of the dancers in the way that he painted. When Raeburn painted *Neil Gow*, the greatest Scots fiddler (and a musician strictly in the oral tradition), he imitated these same values, but in addition he matched the strength and vigour of Gow's music in the simplicity and directness of his own painting.

Music and dance are social models too. In the 18th Century they were seen as representing the natural harmony of a society at peace with itself. Indeed, in one theory, music predated language in the evolution of society, thus the very origin of society was harmony. It was the continuation of this in contemporary agricultural life that David Allan sought to represent in his painting of *The Penny Wedding*. It was a model of a society co-operating without the divisiveness of private property.

The dance and its music, located in the life of such country people living in the landscape, were held to be as natural as the hills or the waterfalls that Charles Stueart painted for Blair Castle also in the 1760s. The Hermitage on the Falls of Bran at Dunkeld associates Steuart's painting of the same falls with the legendary Gaelic bard Ossian. The sound of the waterfall as it is caught and focused in the echoing chamber of the summer house over the water is identified with his music, the music of nature.

In 1771, Alexander Runciman, close friend of Herd and Steuart drew a remarkable picture of Ossian. He shows him as the primeval musician, his harp in his hand. The wind is blowing through the trees behind him and through the strings of his harp. It is almost as though, like the music of the waterfall at the Hermitage, it is the music of the wind itself that we would hear were we able to listen to his song. Thus Ossian is presented as a poet whose art was completely at one with the natural world. He is not just in the landscape. He is part of it and this was how Runciman painted him the following year in Ossian's Hall at Penicuik House, tragically destroyed by fire in 1899.

In his drawing of Ossian, Runciman has deliberately set out to emulate what he saw as the primitive qualities of his poetry: spontaneity, energy and lack of finish. Hugh Blair, Ossian's champion wrote of this primitivism:

> Irregular and unpolished we may expect the productions of uncultivated ages to be; but abounding, at the same time, with that enthusiasm, that vehemence and fire, which are the soul of poetry. For many circumstances of those times which we call barbarous, are favourable to the poetical spirit. That state in which human nature shoots wild and free, though unfit for other improvements, certainly encourages the high exertion of fancy and passion.

Runciman's drawing defies the idea that art is governed by rules which establish norms of correctness and it stands at the beginning of the history of modern art as the artist turns away from these rules to seek to emulate the spontaneity of primitive expression. Blair's friend, Adam Fergusson, expressed it very clearly when he wrote:

> The artless song of the savage, the heroic legend of the bard, have sometimes a magnificent beauty, which no change of language can improve, and no refinements of the critic reform.

Runciman was searching for an image that would reflect the idea that in our primitive origins, we were actually in tune with the natural world in this way. He was trying to catch an idea of value through re-identification with nature and was seeking it, not in the recent past, but in the most remote past in which one could hope to recognise the still uncorrupted state of human nature in its childhood. (This perspective of human history as covering only a limited and relatively short span of time, as we shall see, could not survive the implications of the new geology set out by James Hutton only a few years later.)

NATURE AND TRUE VALUES

In the drawing too, the two principal, interdependent concerns of heritage are focused, the past and the natural world. In fact, the idea of heritage and the idea of modern art have ultimately very similar origins, but these things were harnessed then to very different purposes from those with which we now normally identify them. We could ourselves perhaps still find this motive to true recreation in our love of wilderness and our sense of the need to preserve it, if we were to understand its origins more clearly. As it appears here for the first time, it is not just to defend nature against the ravages of man's 'civilisation', nor is it to preserve the past as a refuge in the face of the manifest insecurity of the future. It is to seek to rediscover and preserve a sense of the natural origins of man and so a hope of remaining in touch with the possibility of what is natural in ourselves, or even to recreate it by learning from the past in the process of true recreation.

David Allan and Runciman were both in Rome for a time around 1770 where they were part of an influential Scottish group, a central part of the artistic community that made Rome at the time very much what Paris was 150 years later. The leading artist in this group was a Scot, Gavin Hamilton, and it is really with Hamilton that we can first identify these ideas. Ideas that are still very relevant about the importance of the past as containing moral examples and the kind of values that might be rediscovered by a return to first principles. It was above all in the imagination that such moral resources were sought.

As it was presented by Enlightenment thinkers like Hutcheson, Hume, Adam Fergusson, or Adam Smith, the imagination was the faculty of moral sense, of feeling and of sympathy, indeed of all the social virtues. The artistic cult of the imagination which is still so prevalent had its origins here.

Plate 1 'Princes Street with the Royal Institution Building under Construction' by Alexander Nasmyth, 1825 (National Gallery of Scotland)

Hamilton's paintings of Homeric subjects do not look 'primitive' to our eyes, yet they were seen in that light by contemporaries, as an attempt to match the passionate grandeur of human behaviour when the imagination was still free and in touch with the nature in us, before it became the servant of convention. So potent were these ideas that almost two hundred years later we find them summarised in one of the principal texts of modern art, Andre Breton's first *Manifesto of Surrealism* (1924):

> Cette imagination qui n'admettait pas des bornes, on ne lui permet plus de s'éxercer que selon les lois d'une utilité arbitraire, elle est incapable d'assumer longtemps ce rôle inférieur et, aux environs de la vingtième année, préfère, en général, abandonner l'homme à son destin sans lumière.

Hamilton not only inspired the young Scots in his circle. The French painter David who became the principal painter of the French Revolution was initially also one of his followers and this is a reminder both of how these ideas were working on a European stage, and of how they were in origin socially and politically radical. They were not confined in their significance to some autonomous province of 'art'.

IN HARMONY WITH NATURE

In Scotland, Alexander Nasmyth and Robert Burns, close friends, were among those who championed the ideals of the French Revolution. Nasmyth was also a pupil of Runciman. Wilkie called him the father of Scottish landscape and Nasmyth's landscapes are really the first to focus that image of Scotland with which we have since become so familiar. Typical of Nasmyth's painting is a view of what we would call a historic building, set in a wide landscape. It is characteristic of Scotland that where there is cultivation, it is also almost always possible to see wilderness and Nasmyth focuses this very beautifully as a metaphor of man in nature. He creates an image of balance between the human and cultivated and the wild and natural. His pictures have a sense of calm and continuity. These are pictures that might be easily enrolled in that kind of enterprise which seeks to impose modern conservative ideas on to the past so that it looks smug and cosy, but Nasmyth really was a radical and his vision of the balance of man and nature was close to the ideals that inspired the French Revolution. The idea of man in harmony with nature was an objective to be achieved by social and political change. It was not yet a fact. Nasmyth share the idealism implicit in Runciman's drawing.

In his later career, Nasmyth advised extensively on the layout of landscapes surrounding Scottish homes. One of the most interesting related paintings is his view of Inveraray from the sea which includes the new town of Inveraray and the castle whose grounds Nasmyth planned. Nasmyth's two principal paintings of Edinburgh, *Edinburgh from Prince's Street* and *Edinburgh from the Calton Hill*, present just that idea, the creation of a new natural environment for man, the city, and within it the dignity of labour, seen in Prince's Street during the day with the citizens going about their business; and the place of leisure in true recreation as the same citizens enjoy a well earned rest during a midsummer evening in the light of the sunset on Calton Hill. The model of social reform is present too in the image of Calton Jail, although, in the middle distance, the tomb of the philosopher Hume presides over it all.

Nasmyth's contemporary, John Clerk of Eldin, had a very similar approach to landscape. It was as a branch of historical investigation, close indeed to archaeology and in the origins of the modern study of history laid in the 18th Century by men like Hume, making sense of the landscape in this way was an important aid to investigation. (For the flip side remember Jonathan Oldbuck's enthusiasm for unexplained mounds in Walter Scott's novel, *The Antiquary*.) John Clerk was brother-in-law to Robert Adam and his view of the historic landscape of Scotland closely parallels the inspiration of Adam's castle style, as at Culzean or at Seton for example. These should not be seen as merely nostalgic and fanciful therefore, but as an attempt to capture qualities of strength, simplicity and imaginative force in an architecture of the present. This is why Gothic became the favourite architecture to express both the ideals of religion and of democracy.

ART AND SCIENCE

Nasmyth was a talented engineer. He seems to have done the drawings for Patrick Miller's first successful steamship. He devised the shaft-propeller which has influenced all subsequent ship design and the bow and string bridge which was one of the principal forms of 19th Century iron construction. He shared his enthusiasm for ship design with Raeburn and it is recorded that Raeburn once fell into Stockbridge Pond, trying out one of his own ship models. He was wearing a heavy coat and had to be fished out by his servant.

It was this kind of link between art and science that led to John Clerk's collaboration as a landscape artist with James Hutton whose *Theory of the Earth* (1785) not only founded the science of geology, but also changed our world view beyond recovery. Long before Darwin, it was Hutton's perception of the nature of geological time and, within that vast framework, the instability and impermanence of the earth's surface that cracked irrevocably the foundations of our old certainties based on the bible story of creation and the primitive, anthropocentric vision of the universe enshrined in Christianity. His theory recognised that the earth was the product of unceasing, and still continuing, processes of change over immense periods of time and he set out his conclusions in *The Abstract* thus:

> 1st That it had required an indefinite space of time to have produced the land which now appears. 2dly, That an equal space had been employed upon the construction of that former land from whence the materials came;

lastly, That there is at present laying at the bottom of the ocean the foundation of future land, which is to appear after an indefinite space of time.

It was a profound step in the march of human knowledge that nevertheless had its origins in a familiar landscape. Hutton began by reflecting on the structure of Arthur's Seat and based his principal conclusions on two sites in Scotland: Glen Tilt and the Isle of Arran. James Nasmyth, Alexander's son who became a distinguished Victorian engineer, remembered as a boy walking on Arthur's Seat with his father in the company of such eminent men of science as David Brewster and hearing these things discussed.

DIVERGENT VALUES AND DISLOCATION

Hutton, following close on the troubling impact of Hume's scepticism, introduced a further insecurity to western thought by changing our perception of the scale of creation in such a way that it was impossible any longer to believed that man could be the centre of a universe that was so vast in time. In 1858 William Dyce painted a picture that explicitly focused the anxiety that such ideas brought to any thinking Christian, and again he did so in the landscape. Dyce, a native of Aberdeen, was a Christian with an active interest in science. (He was also a relation by marriage to James Clerk Maxwell whose portrait he painted as a boy.) His painting of *Pegwell Bay: a Recollection of October 5, 1858* takes the second part of its title from the presence of a comet in the sky which was at its most brilliant on that day. The movement of the tides over the rocks in the foreground sets the theme of time, but it is time beyond human comprehension; the time of geology in the rocks and especially in cliffs behind and of astronomy in the path of the comet in the sky, swinging through the solar system like a pendulum whose single sweep is greater than the span of human life. In the immediate foreground, members of Dyce's own family set the paltry scale of humanity against these immensities. It was just such anxieties that brought Dyce's contemporary, and also a Christian and also a student of landscape, the geologist Hugh Miller to commit suicide shortly before Dyce painted this picture.

Such intellectual and spiritual anxieties were compounded in the mid-19th Century by the spectacle of radical social change, also in response to new and original thinking based in the landscape. Nasmyth's landscapes were essentially a vision of Scotland before the agricultural revolution changed the face of the countryside. Burns and Robert Fergusson both present a Rousseauesque vision of the old order in rural Scotland as enshrining a democratic ideal. David Allan illustrates it in his *Penny Wedding*, his illustrations to Allan Ramsay's *The Gentle Shepherd*, or to the songs that Burns was editing for the music publisher George Thomson, but it was also the ideas of the enlightenment that shattered this ideal.

Ideas of agricultural economics and the improvement of methods of cultivation led to enclosure, dispossession and the creation of the urban proletariat on which the industrial revolution was founded, exploiting such new technology of the Enlightenment as the steam engine of James Watt. It meant literally a change in the culture of landscape. The modern Highlands, cleared in the name of improvement, are the grimmest testimony to this change, the result of a dissociation of sensibility which made it possible to separate economic welfare from human welfare. They are commemorated in one of the greatest Scottish paintings, *The Sailing of the Emigrant Ship*, by William McTaggart, painted almost exactly one hundred years ago, which records with tragic economy the uprooting and destruction of an ancient people.

The human cost of this change was vividly presented very early on in two of the most important Scottish pictures of the early 19th Century, *The Penny Wedding* and *Distraining for Rent*, in which Wilkie comments directly on the dislocation of a once harmonious order based on human relationships and its replacement by alienation, the condition of modern urban man.

The first picture shows the old order, before the agricultural revolution where the music of the dance symbolises the harmony in society. The second picture shows the unjust distraint of the goods of a tenant farmer. The implicit motive for his being driven from his farm is the landlord's economic advantage. His neighbours rally round him in the name of humanity, but are powerless as the bailiff and his men poind his goods in the name of the law. The inhumanity of the action is doubly stressed by the way that they are in the act of taking the very symbols of domestic care, love and warmth, the baby's cradle and the bedclothes from the bed.

Here Wilkie is using the past as a vehicle for criticism of the present and as a model for the reassertion of human values, just as Runciman had done, but now in a context of real anxiety. It was a crisis of conscience. Wilkie saw clearly as did his contemporary and friend, Thomas Chalmers, that economic change was being pursued at an unacceptable human cost. Indeed Wilkie's opposition of past and present was taken up by Thomas Carlyle who became one of the leading social critics of the 19th Century.

The idea of the seamless garment of society may have been largely imaginary, but now it was well and truly torn. However, it would be unfair to suppose, as we often do, that our ancestors merely turned their backs on these anxieties. 1993 is the 150th anniversary of the 'Disruption' in the Scottish Kirk when, led by Chalmers, the evangelical party left the established church to create the Free Kirk. This too was a reaffirmation of the radical implications of the past, of the past not seen as a kind of refuge from the present, but turning to the tradition of John Knox and the ideal of a society that was both democratic and spiritual as a way of tackling the present problems of the 19th Century. The gravity of the issues that faced the people who led the Disruption is measured by the gap between Nasmyth's vision of Utopia and the promise of progress and the reality of it as it is described in James Thomson's grim, poetic account of a great modern city, *The City of Dreadful Night* (1874), exactly 50 years later.

THE PAST IS NOT PASSIVE

Carlyle left a deep mark on the 19th Century, but his ideas for a Scottish National Portrait Gallery bore specific fruit and for the time being this is with us still (It is threatened by the proposed Gallery of Scottish Art). It is of course an important repository of our heritage. The idea of it demonstrates how Carlyle saw heritage in terms of individuals and above all therefore in terms of actions. The past is not passive.

Carlyle and above all Ruskin who became very much his disciple were part of the inspiration of those who founded the first modern heritage societies, moves which were a reaction to the conditions of the present certainly, as Wilkie's paintings had been, but which lost none of the radical intention that had informed so much of this kind of activity hitherto. Heritage was an instrument of social criticism. For William Morris, for instance, generally credited with being one of the prime movers in one of the first effective heritage societies, the importance of the past was closely associated with radical ideas. As it had done for the artists of the 18th Century, it provided a model on which the reform of the present could be based. Ideas of social reconstruction through the dignity of labour found a model in the place of the artist in society in the Middle Ages, for instance. In consequence, art was given a central place in the social ideals of Morris and his friends who formed the Arts and Crafts movement. The movement represented an attempt, following the failure of the spiritual revival of the mid-century to do so, to find in social reconstruction led by the ideals of art a genuine alternative to economic and material wealth as the highest social goods.

THE VISION OF GEDDES

In Scotland, it was Patrick Geddes above all who focused these ideas. For his vision of the reconstruction of society, however, he also turned again to landscape and to history for inspiration. He is best remembered as the father of modern town planning, but he was much more. Town planning as he saw it was the spatial form of social thought. Essentially, as a biologist, he saw society as an organism. Through this organic view of things, he became a pioneer of ecology and his vision of town planning was in itself ecological. It involved seeing society as part of the wider ecology of the environment that sustained it, as an organism among organisms that were mutually sustaining. To understand it, the whole environment needed to be described and this was the basis of Gedde's invention of the regional report. These regional reports were inspired by a botanical model created by Charles Flahault in his description of the interdependence of species and their common dependence on the environment that in part they together created, but as he applied these ideas to society, Geddes saw that history and so heritage were an integral part of the organism. These were the memory of a society and so contained the root of its identity. A society without heritage was like an amnesiac. It could not know who it was.

Geddes' was a reforming vision. For him, heritage was not an armchair drawn up at the fireside of history, a comfortable refuge from the real and present world. He understood that we need the past, that we cannot live by it, but that it is vital both to our sense of who we are and as a model and stimulus for change. In his vision for the reconstruction of human society, he also took from Morris and from Ruskin and the older moral reformers the idea of art as enshrining the highest aspirations for society, especially public art. This was a belief that he held in common with Morris's associate, Walter Crane. Public art said Crane was the 'highest form of popular art'. On another occasion he wrote: 'Monumental art demands the sympathy of a people bound together by common feelings . . . sensible both of the joy and the tragedy of life, delighting in phantasy and in invention, and, above all, in the beauty of form and colour.'

In the tradition of Scott, Geddes saw that this kind of sympathy depended on a sense of history too and that it was vital that 'heritage' played an active part in the reconstruction of self-respect and a sense of value in the present and for the future rooted in it. To this end, Geddes promoted all kinds of schemes. These included an immense commitment to the regeneration of Edinburgh's Old Town so that it should balance the New Town and not be displaced by it. The decay of the Old Town symbolised a dangerous neglect of the past. The old and the new should complement each other. The Outlook Tower that he built was a symbol of this. In the prismatic mirror of its camera obscura, the two towns were joined in a single image, just as they had been by Nasmyth.

Geddes also promoted these ideas through the building of Ramsay Gardens in the Scottish vernacular style, incidentally using colour very imaginatively in a way that is typical of the Arts and Crafts movement, and incorporating Allan Ramsay's mid-18th Century house in he middle of the composition with a completely harmonious effect.

The new complex was to be a colony for Town and Gown. This was typical of Geddes. It was a specifically convergent exercise intended to bring people together from different walks of life and with different habits of thought. It was also a base for the first summer schools which had the same consciously convergent, generalist syllabus. Nearby too he created the first student residences. Within Ramsay Gardens, Geddes commissioned mural decoration on the theme of Scottish history from John Duncan. Elsewhere he promoted mural decoration by Phoebe Traquhair, the first really successful, professional woman artist in 19th Century Britain, William Hole and others as a way of reintroducing art into life and, with it, a sense of values which should include a sense of history.

Geddes believed that cities set in the landscape of their regions were the natural form of human organisation, as the beehive is to the bee, but he saw the modern city with great clarity. He saw that it was in a state of constant change as a reflection of its vitality, but he saw that much of the contemporary urban environment was acutely unhealthy and dislocated, reflecting alienation and the careless pursuit of profit. He described this fully in a major exhibition on the theme of Edinburgh in 1910, but his vision is now more readily accessible to us in Muihead Bone's contemporary drawings of modern Glasgow.

Geddes' vision of human ecology as a microcosm of the ecological macrocosm was prophetic in its urgency. From an early date, he saw the risk of extending the alienation of the 19th Century into the whole field of human endeavour and separating the human sciences from the technological. It was this, the substitution of divergence for convergence that was surely the message of Stevenson's famous story which Geddes often quoted, Dr Jekyll and Mr Hyde. Mr Hyde was the product of Dr Jekyll's apparently innocent, scientific inquiry given a life of its own as it diverged from the controlling humanity of its creator to become a monster. Geddes was a biologist, in his own phrase a 'professor of life'. In a chilling neologism, he expressed what he saw as the fatal risk in this divergence by matching his own profession with its logical opposite, the necrologist, the 'professor of death': Mr Hyde as the scientist working outside the controlling values of humanity. In this tradition, as Wilkie had demonstrated at the beginning of the century, the past heritage was seen as an essential repository of these human values and so vital to the maintenance of balance.

OUR FRAGILE FUTURE

Tragically Geddes' prophetic vision was borne out in the events of World War I where technology ran amok, unchecked by any human or natural restraint. Again it was Muirhead Bone who appeared as the fittest interpreter of this awfulness, not by trying to find an emotional key shrill enough to match its horror, an impossible task, but by an almost laconic account of the absolute denaturing of landscape and the human presence in it. Are these too 'cultured landscapes'? It seem regrettable, but they must be so.

It may seem ironic, but it is surely fitting that within the spirit of Geddes' social ideal of art, one of the greatest achievements was the Scottish National War Memorial built to commemorate the terrible human loss of this dreadful war. It was the product of an unparalleled team effort with a group of artists working under the leadership of Robert Lorimer. Walter Crane had written:

> It seems to me if we wish to realise the ideal of a great and harmonious art, which shall be capable of expressing the best that is in us . . . We shall have to learn the great lesson of unity through fraternal co-operation and sympathy, the particular work of each, however individual and free in artistic expression, falling naturally into its due place in a harmonious scheme. Let us cultivate technical skill and knowledge to the utmost, but let us not neglect our imagination, sense of beauty and sympathy, or else we shall have nothing to express.

Crane's ideal is once again the ideal of convergence, this time through co-operation. The War Memorial is a symbol of a community acting together to express in its tragic loss the values that, it was hoped, properly articulated could prevent anything so awful ever happening again.

A few years after the National War Memorial, William Johnstone's painting *A Point in Time*, was conceived as a kind of personal war memorial. The picture 'grew out of my horror of the disease of war, of the anticipation of future tragedy.' It is an extraordinary landscape, inhabited by memories of time and place like the novels of Lewis Grassic Gibbon or Neil Gunn. The picture is one of the great products of the Scottish Renaissance, a movement led by Hugh MacDiarmid, but which took its title and part at least of its inspiration from Geddes and that still hinged on the idea that heritage can be a force for change, drawing on continuity for strength as a way of focusing value and identity in the present and for the future, and searching for the unspoiled in the dream or perhaps in the memory of innocence. Johnstone and his younger associates, especially Alan Davie, were particularly interested in children, in child art and in the Jungian idea of a kind of internal heritage that is a link to prehistory within us.

The Scottish Renaissance approach to the idea of heritage is, however, perhaps most clearly apparent amongst our contemporaries in the work of Will Maclean, who has sought to focus both the loss and the great continuities of Gaelic culture in his art. Once again it is located in landscape in the way that Runciman's or David Allan's was. The landscape shapes and is shaped by the human presence, although in the Highlands it is too often tragically the human absence.

Much of Maclean's work draws its inspiration from images of fishing, the human activity in which we are still closest to our hunter-gatherer ancestors. Neil Gunn wrote of them:

> They were hunters, hunting the northern seas as their remote ancestors had hunted the forests and the grasslands.

Following the lead of the great Gaelic poet Sorley MacLean, Will Maclean also makes a connection in his works between the inhumanity of the Clearances and the even greater destructive power of a very different kind of hunter, the sinister presence in the waters of the north west of nuclear submarines from the Firth of Clyde. *Inner Sound* for instance is a construction with the broken boarded window of a deserted croft house and the black conning tower of a submarine visible through it. It echoes two lines by Sorley MacLean from his poem *Hallaig*:

> Tha bùird is tàirnean air anuinneig
> troimh'm faca mi an Aird an Iar.
> (The window is nailed and boarded
> through which I saw the West.)

It is the ultimate vision of the desolation anticipated by Wilkie in *Distraining for Rent* and of the destruction foreseen by Geddes.

In spite of such pessimism, convergence is the theme of much of the recent work of an older contemporary, Eduardo Paolozzi. In the exhibition, *Nullius in Verba* at the Talbot Rice Gallery five years ago, following Geddes and inspired too by other thinkers of the Arts and Crafts movement like Morris and Crane, he specifically tackled the tragic divergence of art and science with works like his great *Newton*, or in his *Self-Portrait as Hephaestos*.

It is, however, with another great contemporary that I shall close. Ian Hamilton Finlay's garden at Little Sparta in Lanarkshire is in the long tradition of Scottish gardens which are such an important part of our heritage. It is heritage in the simplest sense, but it is also part of this much more complex tradition that I have been trying to trace, in which the values enshrined in heritage are moral, not simply material, and a resource for change in the struggle to create and to maintain a better world.

With Finlay's garden we return to the artist-poet in the landscape like Runciman's Ossian, for Finlay is a poet as well as an artist, and the garden itself is a poetic composition: an articulated landscape or truly a cultured landscape. However, a garden 1000 feet up on a Scottish hillside is a very different kind of statement to that offered by the optimism of Runciman's image of Ossian as a child of nature. The pastoral tradition, its poetry and its ideal are a constant inspiration for Finlay. The pastoral which recalls the austerity of 'that natural strength of Thought and Simplicity of Style' that Allan Ramsay identified. But for Finlay this austerity suggests that darker pastoral imagery of Poussin's *Et In Arcadia Ego*. It speaks to us about the need for order in the face of the power and incipient disorder of nature, and of the violence and destructiveness of human nature as it has been manifested in the 20th Century, a frequent theme in the imagery of the garden. It is a metaphor for the world as we have made it, for our heritage and its precariousness, and how we must learn from it, or risk losing it all. As you reach the top of the garden at the edge of the open moor there is a single stone inscribed with a single world – FRAGILE.

The author

Dr Duncan Macmillan is Curator of the Talbot Rice Gallery, and Reader in Fine Art at Edinburgh University. He is Chairman of the Scottish Society of Art History and he wrote the much acclaimed major work, *Scottish Art 1460-1990*, published in 1990.

References

Blair, H. *A Critical Dissertation on the Poems of Ossian*, 1764.
Crane, W. *The Claims of Decorative Art* (London 1890) p134.
Crane, W. *Bases of Design*, p36
Fergusson, A. *An Essay on Civil Society* (1767, Edinburgh 1966) p173.
Gunn, N. *Highland River*(1937, London 1960), p.215.

Hutton, J. *The 1785 Abstract of James Hutton's Theory of the Earth* (Edinburgh 1987) pp27-8.

Johnstone, W. *Points in Time* (London 1980) p116.

Breton, A., *First Surrealist Manifesto*, 1924, Hal,(Paris 1962), p16.

Ramsay, A. Preface to *The Evergreen*, 1724.

Wilkie, D. MS Letter to Perry Nursey, 5 Nov. 1817, Trinity College, Cambridge.

Plate 2 Alexander Runciman's 'Ossian Playing his Harp', 1771 (National Gallery of Scotland)

24

THE TIMELESS HERITAGE OF MUSIC

John Purser

When people wish to evoke the past or enliven the present, whether it be for the opening of a restored building, an 18th Century fashion parade, an exhibition on St Margaret, a programme for a visitor centre, or a television ramble through a remnant of the great Caledonian Forest, they nearly always end up with the thing they should have begun with – music. At the last minute a telephone call confirms that they cannot either commence or conclude their presentation without a piece of music. What, they ask me, would be suitable to play? My dentist lives off the grinding of my teeth that ensues when I have to try and respond to their fait accompli. Here is an imagined, but absolutely typical example:

SELF: 'Do you have any mention of bishop's bells in this programme evoking the world of Iona?'

VOICE AT END OF TELEPHONE: 'No, should we?'

SELF: 'Well, not only can you see bells made for those early missionaries from as old as the 8th and 9th Centuries, you can hear them, ring them, and they make a very special sound and there are lots of wonderful stories attached to them . . oh . . I see . . it is too late now. What about mention of early Christian chant and poetry?'

VOICE: 'We had to concentrate on the architecture and landscape. We have this very beautiful sequence approaching the abbey at sunset . . we thought a sort of soft Runrig number or something to set the scene . . .'

SELF (choking): 'Did you know that virtually everything that took place in those buildings was sung? That they were built partly for their acoustical properties and that there exist very lovely mediaeval chants in honour of St Columba, some referring to stories you may well have included in your script?'

VOICE (unmoved): 'Oh we've got a mediaeval chant in already – my sister has a CD of Gregorian chant sung by the monks in France – it sounds splendid, very atmospheric you know.'

Now what I should say is 'You are careless ignorant swine. The chants you have used are not appropriate to the place, the era, the time of year, or the proper service for the time of day; you have given credence to the idea that our music was non-existent, you have filled the purse of a foreign record producer, in the process misusing his product and abusing your own, and you have advertised to the many visitors and viewers who know more than you do, that you are either lazy, stupid or disgracefully badly informed; above all, you have missed the chance of creating something of poetic beauty or arresting energy which would have been wholly relevant and magically illuminating – please shrivel up and die.' Instead it is I who must shrivel.

This, sadly, is by no means a worst case scenario, the St Mungo exhibition being a classic example, so distressingly bad that I insist on naming it. The causes are ignorance, bad planning, and lack of source material. They go hand in hand.

That Scotland should be a particular offender is a particular tragedy. Not only because we ought to present ourselves to the world, and be able to see and hear ourselves, for what we were and are, just like any other nation; but also because Scotland is incredibly rich in terms of its musical heritage. It is that heritage which I wish broadly to outline, though as far as the musical historical map of Scotland is concerned I only have space to present you with a cheap tourist guide showing the coast and a few pretty castles and things, dotted about on the mainland.

As regards the broad outline, Scottish music, both traditional and classical, has many distinguishing traits. We have given the world its first triangular frame harp; we have exported our powerful bagpipes and their repertoire to every corner of the globe; we have been the originators of at least two dance forms - the reel and the strathspey; we have developed a melodic style often easily recognised, and that finds echoes in the ways we harmonise melody. We have retained styles of embellishment in instrumental and vocal music which seem to connect us with he Middle East through links which have now been broken for hundreds of years. Our classical composers from the 16th century to the present day have made use of these characteristic traits and have themselves been major contributors to Scotland's leading role in the study and preservation of traditional music and folklore in general.

In terms of detail, however, to map Scotland's music would require that almost the entire country be on a scale of an inch to the mile. That is how closely the music integrates with the geography. For instance, scarcely a battlefield is unrecorded in song, indeed songs and music often provide us with information about the site, the outcome, and people's perception of that outcome, sometimes from both sides of the story. The Battle of Harlaw is an example. Inverlochy is recorded in song by the man who planned its conduct. The Flowers of the Forest keeps alive the memory of a battlefield of almost 500 years ago, Flodden in 1513, with its heart-rending tune at least as old as the early 17th Century and quite possibly as old as the battle itself.

There are songs and tunes for our remotest rocks – Sula Sgeir, St Kilda – or for many more journeys across water than that of *Over the Sea to Skye*. On the mainland, every second farm in Aberdeenshire seems to get a mention in some bothy ballad or other. An early 20th Century song takes us in from Eaglesham to Glasgow on the morning milk cart, enacting a real-life courtship that took place on the journey. There is music for cathedrals and churches in every corner of the land, much of it ancient; for Glasgow, Stirling, Edinburgh, Aberdeen, Kirkwall, St Andrews, Arbroath, Incholm, Iona. The castles have their music. From Kilravock and Kelly castles comes the brilliant Mannheim style of the Earl of Kelly's symphonies and chamber music. In Crathes an entire ceiling is given over to paintings of early 17th Century musicians. At Dunvegan the silver chanter of legend is still honoured in bagpipe recitals. From Coll comes the clarsach lament for the execution of Charles I. One could go on for weeks in this way.

As for he human history, well, the music often is the history. Not just the facts, but the feelings about the facts. Music is the living history, unfrozen, awaking in a fine musician the same emotions it evoked centuries before, so that the tears will course down the cheeks of a tinker as she sings of the brutal beating of Mill of Tiftie's Annie in the late 17th Century, conscious of the link between her own humanity and that of the girl who died at the hands of her own family for her love of a young trumpeter. The ruined mill exists. The gravestone exists. On the turrets of Fyvie there is a little stone trumpeter. The song itself illuminates social status and prejudice in the period, for Annie was considered by her miller father to be too superior to Lord Fyvie's trumpeter to be allowed to marry him. The song's existence and survival also indicate that from the outset there was strong feeling against such prejudice – feeling still felt about an event of no historical consequence to the world at large, and yet of the deepest consequence to us all. The tinker who sings it accompanies herself on the harmonium. That tells us something too about what sorts of skills are valued and acquired in different sections of society.

My task is impossible, so I shall sketch merely, giving some examples of how our music relates to other more carefully studied aspects of our heritage. I shall take a few random headings as my guide. Archaeology, Natural History, Labour, Language, Economics, International Relations, Architecture and Landscape Gardening. I could chose many more examples for each that I have done, and many other headings: the Church, Education, Agriculture, Fishing, Industry. Music has touched them all, frequently commenting and illuminating. I could even choose music for its own sake! We are truly embarrassed with riches.

ARCHAEOLOGY

I can tell you of six different sites where there are ringing rocks with ancient associations, one still with votive offerings of copper coins on its top, waiting for the petulant drummer to strike sound from the stone, sometimes as clear as a bell. When it comes to bells we have a number of the oldest and most interesting in Europe, some as near their probable original sites as can be conceived.

We can go back further than the bells, and hear the sound of the 8th Century BC, a more living presence than any story board, telling us also of the nature of the cult which spawned such magnificent bronze horns and rattles, based on the horns and testicles of the totemic bull, indicating that their users had probably mastered the art of circular breathing, never mind casting techniques we are bard put to it to reproduce today.

We can re-create the sounds of a battle with the Romans, comparing the iron Age Celtic horns, used by the mercenary cavalrymen, with the carnyx, the magnificent beaten bronze Celtic trumpet, carried aloft by the proto-Picts in stunning array. The materials these instrument are made of tell their own stories. They define the metallurgy, the trading connections, the tools, the astonishing skills. The forms evoked are testimony to their powers of observation and refined abstraction, even telling us something of their religion.

Above all we can hear these instruments speak as they spoke two or three thousand years ago, in their own true accents. They are the nearest thing to lie that we can evoke, for they breathe and activate the air, and the variety of sounds they produce tells us much about their likely function.

NATURAL HISTORY

Birds, animals, plants, elements, they are all there in Scottish music. The carnyx is a superb stylised rendition of a wild board in aggressive mood. His tongue and jaw move, his mouth makes sounds.

The pre-Christian lament, the pi-li-li-liu, enshrines the evocative calls of the sea-shore redshank in its very notes and syllables, as a symbol of the passage from life to death, between land and ocean. Its mournful cry has even been translated on to the bagpipes, providing us with an archetypal music of lament.

Many bird calls have been superbly imitated in Gaelic, and other are evoked in song so well that specific types or behaviour patterns of birds can be identified: Buick swans in Barra, or black guillemots attracting their young off the cliffs and on to the wing. Even the threatened rasp of the corncrake is evoked with affection in a 19th Century love song, for he is heard at that time of the evening when lovers are at last free from work to enjoy each other's company. On the humorous side, the hen is brilliantly imitated marching over the midden in a fiddle piece.

Whole mountains are adored. A vast piobaireachd song from the 18th Century has been written entirely in praise of Ben Doran and its flora and fauna, the wonderful rhythmic changes in the music bringing to life the prancing steps of the young hinds on its slopes, the text cruelly reminding us of how our mountains have been subsequently denuded by sheep.

The glens are described from as long ago as Deirdre's mediaeval lament on leaving Scotland; or claimed vauntingly in a bagpipe piece called *The Glen is Mine*, or tenderly evoked in a piano piece by Hamish MacCunn, whose Overture *Land of the Mountain and the Flood* bespeaks its own nature.

The rivers and seas are everywhere, one of our finest pieces of fiddle music is rightly called *The Spey in Spate*, for that is what it was intended to sound like, and its succeeds; but the *Sweet Afton* will flow forever gently in song.

As for flowers, 96 different ones are assigned to 96 different sonatas by Oswald, composed in the mid-18th Century.

LABOUR

Scotland is especially rich in work songs. Through these we can reconstruct the rhythms and tempo of work. Rowing, waulking cloth, churning butter, grinding oats, milking the cow, dandling the baby, spinning wool, herding cattle, reaping corn - there is even a Gaelic song whose melody seems to follow the unruly sheep dog described by the words. Songs of the sea abound. Our whaling past, the herring fishing, the song of a St Kilda cliff-climber, a tune to attract seals, a song sung by a selchie – half-human, half-seal. There are street-trading songs, including seven street cries from the 17th Century arranged so they can be sung simultaneously. There are mill songs, coal-mining songs, protest songs, or the gently humming buzz of the 'trump' – the jew's harp – which protests at nothing, but was a nice cheap instrument you could tuck in your pocket and play in an idle moment if you have breath.

LANGUAGE

Music remembers many things forgotten by the spoken sentences and the books we make out of them. Music remembers Latin, Celtic Latin, orthodox Latin, bad Latin, 18th Century Latin. Music remembers Norn – the last scraps of true Norn were collected from the mouths of singers in a rowing song and a ballad of King Orfeo in Shetland. Gaelic steps into the day wrapped in the cloak of its song. In the choruses of its work songs, syllables are sung which have no phonic equivalent in modern Gaelic, reminders of ancient sounds that would otherwise have passed from the lips of men and women. It remembers the ancient poetry which, in many cases, could not be recalled without melody or intonation so wedded are the two. It keeps alive Scots in song and bothy ballad, otherwise a stranger to the lips and ears of many Scottish people. It admits English.

In doing these vital services to the history of our literature, music also guides us towards an understanding of rhythmic emphasis, intonation, rhyme and assonance, and, in the conservative styles of traditional performers, retains the accents and vocabulary of otherwise forgotten times. It is the essential, though frequently missing, partner to much of our poetry which was written to be sung, not merely spoken. Above all, the music gives vent to the feelings evoked by the text.

ECONOMICS

The instruments of music are fascinating indicators of the economic climate in which they were generated. The deposition in a bog pool of a vast number of incredibly skilfully made bronze iron age horns, tells us that bronze and the artistry that went with it was plentiful. The refinement of the workmanship on the beaten bronze carnyx tells us of a society wealthy enough to support the highest levels of time-consuming craftsmanship. The fact that from early mediaeval times the clarsach was played with the fingernails tells us of the support of a class of people who never undertook any manual labour whatever. They, and the pipers and bards were granted lands held over hundreds of years. The value placed upon music by early societies is reflected in the considerable attention given to it on the Pictish carvings, themselves evidence of highly skilled craftsmen who were capable of planning complex work, as well as executing it in a manner far more durable than our own crumbling concrete.

When we come to music written on manuscripts we re given an idea of the amount of time a composer or copyist was able to afford to give to his work. The forces required for the execution of that work, and their expertise, all tell us much. Simple monks on Iona? Yes, but if, as is widely accepted, the Book of Kells was produced there, then the quality of vellum alone, never mind what was put on it, is of a standard never surpassed. Vellum was skilfully prepared from calf skins. It was expensive, but they could afford it. The blue colour they used beautifully but sparingly, could only by made from lapis lazuli imported from Afghanistan. They therefore had wide trading links. Music for that community or its successors survives in a 13th Century manuscript, and, as with many music manuscripts, it has much relevance to the world of the find arts, as well as containing early Celtic Latin poetry set to music in complex intertwining structures which mirror the incredibly complex deigns in the book illuminations. Such structures could only have been evolved or understood by people with a great deal of time free from physical necessities to cultivate their minds.

The virtuosic chants in the 13th Century St Andrew Music Book could only have been performed by an expert soloist. Somehow he must have been trained and maintained. So too the man who wrote the music down, and the choristers who provided the mainstay of the services. The ruins of that great cathedral give us only a faint clue of its true glories, but listen to the music that we know for a fact was sung in it in its heyday in the 13th-14th Centuries and you are instantly transported into a world of deep religious conviction, artistic beauty and breathtaking display which makes clear that at one time those ruins housed some of the finest music-making in Europe, as indeed they had to since they were the focus of a major pilgrimage which must have been of considerable economic significance to the area. It was a high-class tourist trap as well as one of the most important Western European pleas of worship dedicated to the world's firs Christian, St Andrew.

Likewise, the works of Robert Carver in the 16th Century could only be sung by choirs kept in constant training to the highest standards known In Europe. Some of the music carries with it architectural implications to which I will return. This sort of evidence should be carefully considered before judging the economic state of society on the basis of a failed onion crop, or a debt written off, a battle lost, or an austere taste in architecture as at Dunblane.

At a simple level of overt intentions on the part of leading economists, we have Sir John Clerk, architect and chief financier of the Act of Union of 1707. As a young man he wrote a cantata on the Carien scheme, Scotland's disastrous venture into colonialism. The originai motives and feelings of one of the most significant legal and financial players of the day are enshrined in that cantata, but no economist studies it and few are the historians who have availed themselves of the fascinating facts that its text was written in Latin by a Dutchman, citizen of a young country also fighting for its international trading rights. Ramsay's song on the South Sea Bubble speculators is kept alive by the folk singers, not by the book. At the raw edge of the economy, food and the gathering of it are recorded more truthfully and poignantly in the songs of the tatty howkers than in the statistics of the economists. In song the reality and the meaning of the reality come together.

INTERNATIONAL RELATIONS

Listen to William Kinloch's late 16th Century description of the Battle of Pavie. It is a virtuoso solo piece for virginals, composed some 60 years after the famous battle in which a Spanish and Papal alliance defeated the French, capturing their King Francis I and thereby ensuring that his reforming zeal did not take hold in France. Why should a Scot evoke this event so long afterwards? Because it was the last legendary mediaeval style engagement of men of honour? Or because Kinloch was a spy for Mary Queen of Scots during her captivity? If the latter, then the piece of evidence of a Roman Catholic faction in the Scottish court willing to listen to such a piece with its triumphant Spanish dance at the conclusion, even though the Scots had, as usual, been fighting on the side of the French.

Go to Bannockburn and, if you are lucky, you will hear Scots Wha Hae, the name given by Burns to the ancient tune of Hey Tutti Tatti. If there are Frenchmen reading this, they may know that it was to the sound of that tune that Joan of Arc entered Orleans when the gates of the city were opened to her by its bishop who came from the borders of Scotland, bishop Kirkpatrick.

Perhaps they will even have hears it played by French military bands who include it in their music books. It is striking evidence, surviving to the present day, of the indebtedness of the French to the Scots mercenaries and Scottish foreign policy, for the survival of their nation at its must crucial period.

Read the petition of the Scottish composer, Tobias Hume, in conjunction with his music for viola-da-gamba, including his battle pieces, and you are escorted into the extraordinary political anomalies of the lifestyle of a soldier of fortune in the service of the highest bidders in Sweden, Russia, Poland, and so on, who comes to London hoping to milk the Scottish court which had established itself there at the union of the crowns. Or listen to Calum Ruadh singing his song about the tragedy of Arnhem and you will spare yourself the trouble of whole chapters of commentary.

In our own times, the Freedom-Come-All-Ye of Hamish Henderson still acts as an important political force in forming opinion and sustaining loyalty to a cause. Part of is strength is derived from the fact that it was designed to be sung to a bagpipe tune which saw long military service throughout the world. Scottish musicians are, many of them, globe-trotters, living off the fascination of other nations with the beauty of our music, especially in Germany, Sweden, Norway, Canada, the USA, New Zealand, Iceland, but also in other less obvious places such as China and Oman.

ARCHITECTURE AND LANDSCAPE GARDENING

From mediaeval music galley to modern concert hall, there is evidence for the determining factor of music in architectural design in some of our most important buildings. Every church is a place of singing. Before the reformation scarcely anything took place in churches without singing. The echoey acoustics are no accident of scale, but deliberate policy, with great potential when handled by singers who understand the acoustical space. Rosslyn chapel choir is carved all over, but the most significant carvings are those of musicians, as is the case in Linlithgow royal chapel. Stirling Parish Church was probably partly supervised in its building by a composer, Robert Carver, whose music absolutely required space, vertical and horizontal, for the vast sound of his ten part mas or his nineteen part motet to blossom. Likewise, the mid-18th Century St Cecilia's Hall, always intended for music, was probably overseen by the Earl of Kelly.

Proportion in music and architecture are often compared and, in the case of Sir John Clerk, the two skills come together in one man, fascinated by principles of structure which are as clear in his music as they are in his masterpiece, Mavisbank House, and the symbolism of his tunnel and grotto through a steep hill into an Arcadian valley, is described by him in terms of a musical progression.

But readers can provide examples for themselves. I have scarcely begun and am past my allotted space in this volume. Suffice it to say that our nation's history, landscape and inhabitants (in whatever form of plant or creature), have found individual expression over the centuries in our distinctive handling of the art of music, which speaks internationally; but the appreciation of which is processed in the deepest parts of each individual human brain.

The author

Dr John Purser is a graduate of Glasgow University and the Royal Scottish Academy of Music and Drama. A polymath of Renaissance stature, his distinguished career has embraced work as a composer, musician, poet, dramatist, broadcaster, writer and university lecturer. He is best known for his energetic campaigning for Scottish culture, which has included a major BBC Radio Scotland programme on the history of Scottish music, and he wrote *Scotland's Music* (Mainstream, 1991).

References

Alburger, M.A., *Scottish Fiddlers and their Music*, Gollancz, London 1983.

Baltie, D., *Musical Scotland*, J. and R. Parlane, Paisley, 1894.

Collinson, F. *The Traditional and National Music of Scotland*, Routledge Kegan Paul, London, 1966 and 1970.

Dalyell, Sir J. G., *Musical Memoirs of Scotland*, Edinburgh, 1849.

Dauney, W., *Ancient Scottish Melodies*, The Edinburgh Printing and Publishing Company, Edinburgh 1838.

Diem, N., *Beitrage zur Geschichte der Schottischen Musik im XVII Jahrhundert*, Kommissions-Verlag von Hug & Co., Zurich and Leipzig, 1919.

Elliot, K., *Early Scottish Keyboard Music*, Stainer & Bell, 1958 and 1967.

Elliot, K., *Fourteen Psalm Settings*, Oxford University Press, 1960.

Elliot K., and Rimmer, Frederick, *A History of Scottish Music*, BBC, London 1973.

Elliot, K., and Shire, H.M., *Music of Scotland* (Volume XV of *Musica Britannica*), Stainer and Bell, London 1957, 1964 and 1975.

Emmerson, G. S., *Rantin' Pipe and Tremblin' String*, Dent, London, 1971.

Farmer, H.G., *A History of Music in Scotland*, Hinrichsen, London, 1947.

Farmer, H.G., *Music Making in the Olden Days*, Hinrichsen, London, 1950.

Fiske, R., *English Theatre Music in the Eighteenth Century*, OUP, Oxford 1986.

Fiske, R., *Scotland in Music*, Cambridge University Press, 1983.

Glen, J., *Early Scottish Melodies*, J & R Glen, Edinburgh, 1900.

Harris, D. F., *Saint Cecelia's Hall in the Niddry Wind*, Oliphant Anderson and Ferrier, Edinburgh, 1899.

Johnson, D., *Music and Society in Lowland Scotland in the Eighteenth Century*, Oxford University Press, London, 1972.

Munro, A., *The Folk Music Revival in Scotland*, Kahn & Averill, London, 1984,

Oliver, C., *It is a Curious Story. The Tale of Scottish Opera 1962 to 1987*, Mainstream Publishing.

Patrick, M., *Four Centuries of Scottish Psalmody*, Oxford University Press, London 1949.

Purser, J., *Is the Red Light On?* BBC Scotland 1987.

Shire, H.M., *Song, Dance and Poetry of the Court of Scotland Under King James VI*, Cambridge University Press, 1969.

Wilson, C., *Scottish Opera: The First Ten Years*, Collins.

The Companion to Gaelic Scotland, Derrick Thomson (ed.) Blackwell Reference, Oxford 1983.

25

THE SCOTTISH TRADITION OF STORY TELLING

Donald Archie MacDonald

To attempt a description of Scottish storytelling anything like adequately in the space allowed is a daunting task. The situation is not a simple one, either historically or currently. There is, in fact, no such thing as a single, monolithic tradition of Scottish oral narrative. What we do have is a web of many strands and of manifold complexity. One important factor is that there are three languages involved: Gaelic, Scots and English. True, there is a fair amount in common regarding social function and style. However, the differences are, I believe, sufficient to require that at least the Gaelic heritage and the Scots heritage be viewed through rather different lenses. They should, in effect, be approached as distinct and yet mutually complementary areas of Scottish tradition.

First of all, I would like to deal briefly with some aspects of scholarship and terminology: terms such as Tale, Folktale, Legend, Saga, Fable, Myth and so on. All of these, and others, are often used loosely, interchangeably and confusingly. However, there is now a certain measure of agreement among scholars working in the area of oral narrative as to how such terms should be used. As a starting point, there is *The International Popular Tale* or *The International Folktale*. Over the better part of the past two hundred years, it has become increasingly recognised that there exists a considerable body of stories which have been recorded in numerous versions, in many parts of the world, but especially in Europe and Asia. While the details of these tales may often vary, the basic plots remain remarkably stable, having apparently easily crossed geographical and linguistic boundaries in the course of their migrations. Many theories have been advanced and argued over as to the explanations for this phenomenon. These I cannot enter into here, but I should at least mention the following Classification.

THE AARNE-THOMPSON CLASSIFICATION

This classification was the product of work by the Finnish scholar Antti Aarne, first published in 1910 under the title *Verzeichnis der Märchentypen*. A revised and translated version was published in 1928 by the American scholar Stith Thompson as *The Types of the Folktale*. Thompson published a further revised and enlarged edition in 1961, reprinted in 1964. The result is what is usually called the Aarne-Thompson Classification, abbreviated as AT. Upwards of a thousand tales are listed and numbered, and their hypothetical archetypes summarised. Some of these summary plots are simple, others much more complex. The international distribution of all versions known to Thompson is also listed and the main bibliographical references given. The vast majority of the tales are shown to have some sort of international distribution, many of them having a very wide one.

Despite criticism, the Aarne-Thompson system has come to be regarded as a most useful means of tale classification and has served as a model for organising many national collections. Its numbering system is used in archival and research work in many institutions, including the School of Scottish Studies at Edinburgh University and the Department of Irish Folklore (formerly the Irish Folklore Commission) at University College, Dublin. The five main headings of the classification are as follows:

I   Animal Tales
II   Ordinary Folk Tales
III Jokes and Anecdotes
IV   Formula Tales
V   Unclassified Tales

Headings I to IV are further subdivided. For instance, II Ordinary Folk Tales, which is the section into which most of the great international tale-types fall, is subdivided as follows:

A   Tales of Magic (or Wonder Tales as many prefer to call them or, indeed Fairy Tales. This last is really a very inappropriate term, as fairies as such do not usually feature in such stores at all). This sub-heading includes Supernatural Adversaries; Supernatural or Enchanted Husbands, Wives or Other Relatives; Superantural Tasks; Supernatural Helpers; Magic Objects; Supernatural Power or Knowledge; Other Tales of the Supernatural.

B   Religious Tales

C   Novellas or Romantic Tales

D   Tales of the Stupid Ogre

Well known examples of Animal Tales are AT 1, *The Fox the Wolf and the Fish*, and AT 6 where the animal captor is persuaded to talk and release his victim, usually told of the cock and the fox. Both of these occur in Scottish tradition. Animal Tales are usually fairly simple in plot, sometimes incorporating no more than one basic narrative motif. Many of them have a very wide international distribution.

I have already mentioned Class II, 'Ordinary Folk Tales', as the one into which most of the great complex international tales fall. Good examples are AT 300 *The Dragon Slayer*, AT 303 *The Twins or Blood Brothers*, AT 313/314 *The Magic Flight* and AT 510 *Cinderella*, all of which often have complex plots and all of which are listed in sub-division A of Class II, that is to say as Tales of Magic/Wonder Tales. *The Dragon Slayer* and *The Twins* are sometimes found compounded in one complex story and, indeed, this compounding of the two is also to be found in Scottish tradition. Incidentally, the earliest identified version of *The Twins* is claimed to occur in an Egyptian papyrus of 1250 B.C. and the earliest version of *The Magic Flight* in a Chinese text of the 9th Century A.D., to cite only two examples of early occurrence of tales which have been recorded from oral tradition in Scotland in our own time.

Again in Class II, I should mention briefly sub-division C, Novellas or Romantic Tales. Although, in terms of structure, Novellas are not unlike the Tales of Magic or Wonder Tales of sub-division A, such as *The Twins* and *Cinderella*, and although there can be a good deal of overlapping between the two kinds, there are still considerable differences between the Tales of Magic and the Novella.

As Stith Thompson has pointed out, the Tale of Magic 'moves in an unreal world without definite locality or definite characters and is filled with the marvellous. In this never-never world humble heroes kill adversaries, succeed to kingdoms and marry princesses.' On the other hand in the Novella 'the action occurs in a real world with definite time and place. They are such as apparently call for the hearer's belief in a way that the Tale of Magic does not.' He points to the Adventures of Sinbad the Sailor as a good example of the Novella (Thompson 1946).

Another good example of the Novella, and one which has been recorded in a number of Scottish versions, both Scots and Gaelic, is AT 922, listed under the heading *The Shepherd substituting for the Priest answers the King's Questions*. This is, of course, the widely known story of *The King and the Abbot*, better known in English versions in ballad form, but ranging internationally as a story from Ireland to India, in a considerable number of variants. There is nothing particularly magical or marvellous or heroic in this story. It is naturalistic and quite down-to-earth. It is, in fact, a typical Novella.

Numerous examples of well-known stories could also be cited from Class III, Jokes and Anecdotes. This, by the way, can be a rather misleading designation. Some of the so-called 'anecdotes' can be quite substantial stories and, some of the 'jokes' I would hardly call jokes as such. Some of these, too, can be well-developed stories. The *Whittington's Cat* type of story, AT 1651, is often cited as a good example of its class. The hero takes a cat to a land where cats are unknown and sells it for a fortune. This story again has a wide distribution, including examples from Scotland. It also illustrates quite well the point I have just made: it does not seem to me to fit very easily under a heading of either Joke or Anecdote.

A good example of Class IV, Formula Tales, is AT 2030 *The Old Woman and her Pig*: the pig won't jump over the style and the old woman cannot get home, again a widely distributed tale with a number of Scottish versions.

One could easily go on multiplying examples, but I think what has been said above may be sufficient to confirm that there exists a considerable body of tales, of diverse kinds, which, on examination, are found to be widely distributed around the world, having apparently crossed many geographical and linguistic boundaries. This is the type of situation we have in mind when we speak of the International (Popular) Tale or the International Folktale.

The Aarne-Thompson Classification is an indispensable guide for anyone proposing to take a serious interest in the subject. The other standard tool is Stith Thompson's six volume *Motif Index of Folk Literature* (Thompson 1955-58). Motifs, which I have mentioned already, are the basic factors or ideas of narrative: such as the assistance supplied to the hero or heroine by grateful animals or other supernatural helpers; the wicked stepmother; the fight with a dragon, and so on. Some of the simpler tales, for instance the Cock and the Fox story, really contain only one single motif. In complex tales such as *The Twins* or *The Dragon Slayer* there are a large number of such basic narrative ideas woven into the plot. The Thompson Index, often abbreviated as ST, gives a complete listing of all the motifs which the author has been able to identify. He has grouped them in accordance with certain principles and allotted a number to each individual motif.

The best introduction in short compass that I know to the International Tale and associated scholarship is to be found in the first two chapters of Kenneth Jackson's admirable book *The International Popular Tale and Early Welsh Tradition* (Jackson 1961) now unfortuately out of print. These two chapters are: 'I - The International Popular Tale: Characteristics' and 'II - The International Popular Tale: Origin, Diffusion and Recitation'. I can recommend them with enthusiasm to anyone who does not already know them.

THE BROTHERS GRIMM

The world's best known published collection of International type tales is of course the famous *Kinder und Hausmärchen* (Children's and Household Tales) of the German brothers Jacob and Wilhelm Grimm, first published in 1812. It has been widely translated and has appeared in many editions: in English as the well known *Grimm's Fairy Tales*. Märchen is a diminutive of the word mär, meaning a short story. The Grimms themselves extended the term märchen to include Popular Tales, or Folktales, of all kinds and numbers of other scholars have also used the word with this extended meaning. Others have suggested that märchen should more usefully be restricted to the Tales of Magic, or Wonder Tales, or Fairy Tales, which I have mentioned already - that is Division A of Class II in the Aarne-Thompson Classification. It is in this sense that the term märchen is probably most commonly used now.

Mention of the Grimm collections, incidentally, prompts the reflection that equally good and frequently better versions of these same international tales have been recorded from Scottish storytellers, both Gaelic and Scots, for the better part of two centuries. Yet generations of Scottish children, and indeed

314

adults, have become thoroughly familiar with Grimm's Fairy Tales without ever becoming aware of the riches on their own doorstep.

The other German term associated with storytelling that one most often meets is Sage, plural Sagen. The most commonly accepted English equivalent is Legend or Local Legend. Already in the early 19th Century the Grimms were concerned with the similarities and differences between Märchen and Sagen, or Magical Tales and Legends and this is a subject which has interested scholars ever since. In 1844 Jacob Grimm observed:

> The Märchen is with good reason distinguished from the Sage, though by turns they play into one another. Looser, less fettered than Sagen the Märchen lacks that local habitation which hampers the Sage but makes it the more homelike. The Märchen flies, the Sage walks, knocks at your door ... As the Märchen stands related to the Sage, so does the Sage to history and so, we may add, does history to real life.

This may be rather fancifully expressed, but the point is valid. What distinguishes the Sage/Legend from the (Wonder) Tale is that the legend is associated with the local area, with local landscapes, with real historical characters, and was frequently believed to be true.

OTHER CLASSIFICATIONS

Various classifications for legends have been proposed from time to time. Among them are:

1. Etiological and Eschatological Legends. These include explanatory stories about the creation of the world and the origin of things, striking natural phenomena and the nature of plants and animals. Place name legends could also come under this heading or under 2.

2. Historical Legends. These may concern local hero-figures, clan warfare, oppressive landlords, stories attached to placenames and prehistoric ruins.

3. Legends of Supernatural Beings and Forces or Mythical Legends. These are concerned with supernatural beings and people with supernatural knowledge and powers, ghosts, black and white magic, protection and destruction of property, and so on.

4. Religious Legends or Myths of Gods and Heroes. These include stories about saints, martyrs, miracles and the like, often deriving from medieval written sources.

Scottish tradition - and especially Gaelic tradition - is very rich in Historical and Supernatural Legends, with Clan Legends being a particularly remarkable phenomenon, really without parallel in modern Europe.

Some Legend types have been identified as migratory, crossing geographical and linguistic boundaries in a manner very similar to the International Tales to which I was referring earlier. A special study of these was made by the Norwegian scholar Reidar Th. Christiansen who devised a classification extending the Aarne-Thompson numerical system from No.3000 upwards and using summary outlines based particularly on Norwegian versions.Christiansen's classification entitled *The Migratory Legends* was published in 1958. In very meagre outline the system is as follows, with ML representing Migratory Legends:

> ML 3000-3025 The Black Book of Magic. The Experts
> ML 3030-3080 Witches and Witchcraft
> ML 4000-4050 Legends of the Human Soul, of Ghosts and Revenants
> ML 4050-4090 Spirits of Rivers, Lakes and the Sea
> ML 5000-5050 Trolls and Giants
> ML 5050-6070 The Fairies
> ML 7000-7020ML Domestic Spirits, Nisse, Haugetusse, Tusse, Gobonden
> ML 7050-8025 Local Legends of Places, Events and Persons

Many of these Migratory Legend types have been found to be shared by the whole north western seaboard of Europe, including Scotland and Ireland.

I might perhaps add that, while the system used at the School of Scottish Studies for legend indexing does make some use of the Christiansen system, there is also in use a wide-ranging index for Scottish Witch and Scottish Fairy Legends, devised by the Archivist of the School, Dr Alan Bruford. The system uses the prefixes W and F. There is a tremendous wealth of supernatural Legend material in the archives of the School, particularly from the Gaelic areas and the Northern Isles.

SOME THOMPSON DEFINITIONS

I should like to mention four further items which have given rise to considerable confusion: Myth, Fable, Saga and Hero Tale. I have found Stith Thompson's preferred definitions useful in all four cases (Thompson 1951):

> **Myth**: He prefers to limit this term to stories of semi-divine heroes and of the origin of things, usually through the agency of these sacred beings. He adds that Myths are intimately connected with religious beliefs and practices.
> **Fable**: He suggests that, when an Animal Tale is told with an acknowleded moral purpose, it should be classed as a Fable, the

moral purpose being the essential quality which distinguishes the Fable from other Animal Tales.

Saga: He proposes that this term should be restricted to the literary tales of an Heroic Age, such as those of Scandinavia and Ireland, and not used loosely to mean 'a story.'

Hero Tale: He points out that this term has been used of both Märchen and Novellas. He would prefer to see it restricted to tales concerning a cluster or series of adventures involving the same hero, e.g. Hercules. He also acknowledges the use of the term for some of the great Gaelic heroic tales which are the common property of Ireland and Scotland.

JOHN FRANCIS CAMPBELL OF ISLAY

When we turn to look at the practice and social function of storytelling in Scottish society, it quickly becomes clear that much more is known about the situation in the Gaelic areas than in the Scots speaking areas. There are a number of reasons for this. A good deal of what we do know about such matters comes from the writings of collectors and, from the time of John Francis Campbell in the mid 19th century down to the present day, the Gaelic tradition has, generally speaking, been much more actively collected. This is partly because its presence was more obvious on the ground, and quite largely also due to the influence of Campbell and his helpers and followers - even down to the present day. Campbell's seminal four volume work *Popular Tales of the West Highlands* was published between 1860 and 1862 and re-issued in 1890, with two further volumes based on his manuscripts appearing in 1940 and 1960.

Campbell's work included the Gaelic texts exactly as taken down by his scribes and also very literal translation by himself. Almost equally importantly, Volume I contains an introduction of 128 pages which describes in detail his working methods, his views on what he was doing, and his estimation of the value of the storytelling tradition and its wider implications.

STORYTELLING IN GAELIC SOCIETY

For Gaelic Scotland we also have the advantage of a considerable body of Irish evidence. In both countries a system of 'Heroic Age' values remained very much in force well into fairly modern times. In a sense society remained in many ways 'Medieval' and the Renaissance had little real impact. The main reasons for this situation are to be sought in matters historical and political which are beyond the scope of the present paper.

However, while ties remained close many Scottish Gaels continued to look back to Ireland for the sources of their civilisation and this was nowhere more evident than among the literati of the Bardic Schools who continued, even in Scotland, to write in a classical form of Gaelic based on Early Modern

Irish. One of the most striking cases in point is provided by the MacMhuirich family of bards and scholars who, though of Irish origin, became established at the court of the Lords of the Isles and latterly were attached to the house of MacDonald of Clanranald in South Uist until the mid 18th century.

The collapse of the old social order - in the 17th Century in Ireland and the 18th century in Gaelic Scotland - meant that the remnants of this privileged educated elite of bards and tradition bearers became reduced to the ranks of the ordinary population.They brought with them, however, a considerable detritus of their learning and, indeed, some of their manuscript compendia of poetry, history and tales. There is evidence that stories were being read from some of these manuscripts in South Uist in the 19th century, as was also happening in Ireland.

There had, indeed, obviously been a constant process of give and take going on between the written tradition and the oral tradition for centuries, as there had in other medieval societies. There can be little doubt, however, that a number of Heroic Romances have survived to be recorded from oral tradition in the present century because of the influence of the old bardic scholars and their manuscripts. Such romances were being composed in the Gaelic world, mainly in Ireland, between the 14th and 19th Centuries. They fulfilled much the same function for the Gaelic aristocracy as other Medieval Romances did elsewhere in Europe: tales of voyages, adventure, combat against odds, wooings, magic. Examples are *Conall Gulbann* (a Romance concerning an Irish prince of that name); *Sgeulachd an Dìthreibhich* (The Tale of the Hermit); *An Ceatharnach Caol Riabhach* (The Lean Grizzled Champion) to mention three that have survived to be recorded from oral tradition for the archives of the School of Scottish Studies, founded in 1951. Sometimes the oral versions make better impact as stories than their manuscript exemplars. The standard work on these Romances is Alan Bruford's *Gaelic Folk Tales and Mediaeval Romances* (Bruford, 1969).

It was these Romances, along with the earlier Hero Tales of the Cuchulainn and Fenian Cycles, plus some of the great International Wonder Tales such as AT 300 *The Dragon Slayer*, AT 303 *The Twins*, AT 313/4 *The Magic Flight*, that furnished the most highly prized aspects of the Gaelic storyteller's repertoire, both in Scotland and Ireland. On these they concentrated their best skills and it is in them that one is most likely to find the 'curious impassioned and sentimental language' referred to by J. F. Campbell and the decorative 'runs' - the ornate archaistic passages with which significant scenes such as entry into battle or setting out on a sea-voyage were highlighted

Not all International Tales had anything like the same prestige. Good storytellers, almost always men, would not be expected to concern themselves with Animal Tales, for instance or, for that matter, with most Supernatural Legends of fairies and ghosts. Legends of inter clan feuding and cattle raiding would, however, be regarded as fit for a talented performer and for the usual adult audience – again mainly male. Less prestigious tales and legends would be relegated to the family circle, often perhaps told by women to children.

Even by Campbell of Islay's time in the mid 19th Century this big tradition of Gaelic storytelling was in sharp decline in most Gaelic speaking areas of the Mainland Highlands. In the Outer Hebrides however, and particularly in the Uists and Barra, the tradition was still in full vigour and still socially functional.People still gathered, particularly in the long winter evenings, to listen and to tell stories and good performers were eagerly sought after and had a considerable prestige in the community.

CEILIDHING

Stories could be told on any occasion which involved people meeting together, but the most important focus was certainly the 'taigh céilidh' - the céilidh house. This would be simply a popular family home in the community where people met together to tell and listen to stories, to sing songs, to exchange local news and gossip, even to play cards or to dance. There might be several such 'schools' in a community. Céilidhing basically simply means 'going visiting.' For much of the evening normal household tasks such as carding, spinning, or twisting heather rope would often continue, but when serious storytelling started close attention and strict silence were usually expected - apart from apt exclamations as the audience reacted to some incident in the story or appreciative or critical comment at the end of a performance.

Despite emigration, the Clearances, the collapse of the kelp industry, potato famines, the hostility of some fundamentalist clergymen, and the imposition of a totally English based system of education in the 1870s, storytelling still continued to hold its ground in some remote areas into the present century. Lack of educational and economic opportunities still continued to keep many of the more intelligent people at home and a basic subsistence economy saw to it that competitive social pressures in the modern sense scarcely existed. Such a setting did, however, provide a very suitable environment for a lively oral tradition. Well within living memory these Island communities still held numbers of men and women, often monoglot Gaelic speakers and lacking any kind of formal education, who might have achieved very successful careers had the opportunities existed.

Such people staying at home were the leavening influence on the rural life of the Highlands and Islands, as indeed elsewhere, and from their ranks were normally drawn the best of the bearers of oral tradition. Their social function was a natural consequence of the conditions of the society in which they lived. They supplied the needs that are now catered for by books, newspapers, films, radio and television. Under these circumstances artistry in telling a story, a good memory and an extensive repertoire were obviously highly prized qualifications and they were assiduously cultivated.

One constantly hears of astonishing feats of memory: it was not unusual for a practised storyteller, even in recent times, to be able to memorize long and complex tales at one hearing. The importance of telling a tale oneself, as soon as possible after hearing it, has sometimes been stressed. Visual imagery would also seem to have played a vital role and sheer verbal memory has clearly been a factor, for instance in some long tales told virtually word for word by the late Duncan MacDonald of South Uist (d. 1954) on a number of separate occasions.

The First World War is often mentioned as an important watershed. Constant news of deaths and woundings cast a gloom over whole communities. Though house-to-house visiting still went on, the old style of ceilidhing began to decline sharply. After the war many ex-servicemen sought employment and homes on the mainland. Accelerating processes of economic, social and educational change contributed to the decay of the old system.

As the demand for the services of storytellers declined so did their number and their prestige. Today there are very few left who can tell any of the major tales and those with even a reasonably large repertoire of any kind are very few indeed. Some are more or less 'passive' tradition bearers who, through an early interest and the excellence of their memories are able to recall some of what they heard in their youth – for the benefit of collectors, broadcasters or students.

Most of the Gaelic stories one hears nowadays are of the shorter, more anecdotal and legend types. Telling tends to be restricted to interested individuals who swap yarns, or to the family circle. There seems to be a certain amount of social function still in such circumstances and this is perhaps especially so among some Gaelic speaking traveller or tinker families, as it is among their Scots speaking counterparts.

SCOTS STORYTELLING

Some of what has been said above in relation to Gaelic can also be applied with considerable relevance to Scots storytelling. For instance, evening visiting among neighbours, very much akin to Gaelic céilidhing, continued into the present century in some Scots speaking crofting areas. This was particularly so in Shetland where a strong tradition of local and supernatural legend telling survived well enough to be recorded in recent years by local collectors and broadcasters as well as by members of staff of the School of Scottish Studies.

Bothy life on farms provided another active focus for storytelling, as well as for music-making, ballad and song. Even in such cases, however, it has been very much a legend and anecdote dominated tradition with little evidence of any kind of major Wonder Tale telling having continued into anything like recent times.

From a situation where Wonder Tale telling was probably widespread throughout the whole of Scotland as an evening entertainment in the 18th Century, collectors such as Robert Chambers and Peter Buchan, operating in the early part of the 19th Century, some half-century before Campbell of Islay

Plate 1 Collecting tales, Paisley 1870. L to R, Lachlan MacNeill, Storyteller; John Francis Campbell; Hector MacLean, Collector/Schoolmaster. See J.H. Delargy 'Three Men of Islay' in *Scottish Studies* vol.iv, 1960.

Plate 2 Collecting tales, Edinburgh 1990. Duncan Williamson being filmed by Fred Kent and Donald A. MacDonald (photo by Ian MacKenzie)

began his major work in the Gaelic area, believed that they were collecting the last vestiges of Wonder Tales from Scots tradition. The sum total of Scots Märchen in the collections of Chambers and Buchan amounts to thirty: sixteen in Chambers and fourteen in Buchan. In a letter of 1827 to Charles Kirkpatrick Sharpe, the ballad collector and antiquary, Buchan reports that '... ancient fabulous Scottish tales ... are now wearing obsolete, being discarded from the farmer's ingle cheek.'

TRAVELLERS' STORIES

Nobody would probably have been more surprised than Chambers and Buchan had they been told that a major stream of high storytelling, of Märchen, was surviving more or less undercover, to emerge in the second half of the 20th Century, largely through the activities of a School of Scottish Studies and allied collectors, among an overlooked and frequently despised social stratum of Scottish life, the Travelling People or Tinkers. To quote my colleague Dr Alan Bruford (1982) '... a trickle of Scots Wonder Tales first tapped in the fifties among the travelling people or tinkers is now becoming a torrent, and now for the first time since 1859 more interesting traditional tales are being collected in Scots than in Gaelic.'

These stories span the whole spectrum of International type tales outlined at the beginning of this paper with the addition of some typically Traveller Legends of Burkers or body snatchers. Other types of legend tradition do not seem to figure as strongly in the traveller repertoire - probably because such local legends are usually products of a more settled population and often linked to specific local areas and features. However, the range of Märchen type stories known to living traveller tellers such as Duncan Williamson, Willie MacPhee and Stanley Robertson is enormous and probably not yet fully recorded.

It is a great source of satisfaction that even now it is possible, in the live performances of such men, and in videotaped recordings of other men and women, both Scots and Gaelic, to experience an ancient and highly developed Scottish art-form at first or near-first-hand. To be involved in even one live storytelling session is to be forcefully reminded that this is a dramatic art – no less visual than aural. Even if not any longer in the céilidh house or round the camp-fire, here are all the tricks of gesture, of eye-contact, of emphasis, of body-language and style that are so individual and yet so obviously part of a tradition. And in some of the Scots Traveller tales here are still the decorative runs, similar in some ways to the Gaelic runs referred to above but almost certainly in this case deriving from a parallel Scots tradition.

What the future holds for Scottish storytelling is uncertain. There is certainly a current revival of interest and participation, both at audience and performance level. Good storytellers can draw considerable numbers and hold their audiences spellbound at folk festivals and other arranged venues. Numbers of schools are showing an active interest and many of the younger generation are now able to hear and to learn from first-rate living exponents of the art.

Storytelling was the cultural lifeblood of our traditional communities, and I would venture to suggest that, as an art form, it should be given higher priority by those concerned with heritage interpretation at visitor attractions such as historic houses, parks, museums and galleries. An injection of storytelling into existing programmes and special events built around Scotland's narrative tradition would add a valuable dimension to interpretation of the nation's heritage.

The author

Donald Archie MacDonald is a broadcaster, lecturer and writer, now the Deputy Director of the School of Scottish Studies at the University of Edinburgh, his alma mater. A native of North Uist, he has studied the Celtic and Scandinavian languages. He was Assistant Keeper at the National Library of Scotland with responsibility for the Gaelic Manuscript Archive, served on the Gaelic Books Council, and has lectured in Ireland and Canada. He is an authority on the works of JohnFrancis Campbell of Islay.

References

Aarne-Thompson (Aarne, Antti and Thompson, Stith) *The Types of the Folktale, a Classification and Bibliography*, F.F. Communications- 184. Helsinki, 1961.

Bruford, A.,*Gaelic Folk-Tales and Mediaeval Romances,* Dublin.1969.

Bruford, A.,'Scots Storytelling, Traditional', in *A Companion to Scottish Culture*, ed. David Daiches, London,1982.

Bruford, A.,*The Green Man of Knowledge and Other Scots Traditional Tales*, Aberdeen,1983.

Buchan, P.,*Ancient Scottish Tales*, ed. J.A. Fairley, Peterhead,1908..

Campbell, J. F.*Popular Tales of the West Highlands*, 4 vols, Edinburgh,1860-62.

Campbell, J.L.,*Stories from South Uist told by Angus MacLellan,* London,1961.

Chambers, R., *Popular Rhymes of Scotland*, New edition,. Edinburgh and London,1892.

Christiansen, R.Th.*The Migratory Legends*, F.F. Communications, 175, Helsinki,1958..

Delargy, J.H.,' The Gaelic Storyteller', Proceedings of the British Academy 31. London,1945.

Douglas, S. *The King o the Black Art and Other Folk Tales*, Aberdeen,1987.

Jackson, K.H.,*The International Popular Tale and Early Welsh Tradition*, Cardiff,1961.

MacDonald, D.A.,'Gaelic Storytelling, Traditional' in *A Companion to Scottish Culture*, ed. David Daiches. London,.1981.

MacNeil, J. N.,*Tales Until Dawn*, ed. and trans. John Shaw. Kingston and Montreal,1987.

Robertson, S., *Exodus to Alford*, Nairn,1988.

Thompson, S.,*Motif-Index of Folk Literature*, 2nd ed., 6 vols. Helsinki,1955-58.

Thompson, S.,*The Folktale*,. New York,1946.

Williamson, D.and L.,*Fireside Tales of the Traveller Children*,Edinburgh,1983.

Williamson, D.and L.,*A Thorn in the King's Foot*, Harmondsworth,1987.

Plate 3 Duncan Williamson painted by Caroline Miller (1993) against the landscape of Loch Fyneside in Argyll where he was born. A story teller of travelling stock going back to Viking times, he is one of today's great exponents of the art and, together with his wife Linda, has published several collections of stories

26

EVERYMAN'S FURNITURE IN LOWLAND SCOTLAND

David Jones

Recent years have seen a lively interest in the architecture of the smaller house in Scotland, fostered by societies such as the Scottish Vernacular Buildings Working Group, but little serious attempt has been made to investigate how these buildings were furnished. Common types have certainly been identified; the box bed, for example, is widely recorded and collected, and some regional chairmaking traditions are recognised. However, if we ask specific questions about say, the furniture of Lanarkshire miners' dwellings 1840-1900, or the type of chairs one might expect to find in an agricultural labourer's cottage in 19th Century Forfarshire, it becomes clear that research has hardly begun. The way forward is to undertake detailed studies in each region of the country. This brief survey will focus on just a few key types existing in the Lowlands from the 18th to the early 20th Centuries.

A range of sources can be consulted in an investigation of the frequently anonymous common furniture to be found in small urban and rural dwellings. For example, manuscript account books kept by city or country wrights can provide illuminating detail about the repertoire of furniture made in a particular area, or perhaps enough firmly provenanced items might survive to enable identification of specific regional features. However, in a society where inevitable modernisation and a market for antiques has caused the dispersal and destruction of much common furniture, such survivals are rare. A useful, if scattered, source with which to begin research into everyman's furniture is the photograph. Enough photographs exist for example, of 19th Century fishing families and their belongings in St. Andrews, to enable an accurate analysis of some of the basic furniture types which they used at work and home.

Prominent in these working scenes is the small boarded stool or 'creepie' which occurs so frequently in the small Lowland household. The creepie is very simply constructed of sawn boards nailed together to form a seat, legs and strengthening side aprons. Shapes are cut out of the vertical end boards to form the legs. The stool's main use in the St. Andrews photographs is as seating, conveniently close to the ground for reaching bait from creels or handling nets. The work takes place outside, emphasising the portability of these stools. It is clear that they were carried about according to need and used both in the home and at work. Before the advent of fixed pews in the 18th Century, small stools of different designs, but almost always with carrying holes in the seat, were taken to church to sit on. These could also be used outside on occasions such as Holy Fairs. However, the creepie was not just a seat, but also a stand, as is evident in the St. Andrews scenes. The woman in Plate 4 for instance, is using a large creepie as an angled stand to support a pile of line at arm level.

In his studies of Lowland cottage interiors of the 1820s, the Edinburgh artist Walter Geikie provided similar evidence for the creepie's use as a versatile stand inside the house. He illustrated multiple creepies sometimes stacked against a wall, but also in use to elevate water vessels, washing tubs, or pots by the hearth. It is apparent that creepies used as stands by day would be used as seats by night when everybody was gathered together in the house. The stool, which survives Scotland in great numbers, is clearly a piece of multi-purpose furniture but this versatility can apply also to the chair. This too, can function as a stand or table, particularly when used in conjunction with a stool. Plate 4 illustrates that what we categorise today as children's chairs were used by adults when it was necessary to work close to the ground. Like stools, chairs served many purposes and cannot be too narrowly defined.

As in Scandinavia, common chairs in Lowland Scotland were frequently made in native woods according to fashionable or once-fashionable designs. Usually following 18th Century patterns, but made by local wrights using local methods of construction, these were made in large numbers throughout the 18th and 19th Centuries. An example is Plate 1, a splat backed chair from North East Fife made in Scots Laburnum (Cytisus Alpinus). It is notable for its low proportions which make it suitable for a low roomed cottage, and for its wood type: this densely grained worm-resistant timber was commonly used in Fife and Forfarshire during the 18th and early 19th Centuries. The seat is inset or 'dyked in' so that the rails form a wall around the seat board. It is a vernacular chair in that it is made of native wood and has distinctly regional features of construction, but at the same time it has clear connections with a tradition of designed furniture.

In contrast, the rural and to some extent the urban populations of England were served by easily recognisable chair types which were products of craft traditions. For example, the ladderback chairs of Lancashire and Cheshire or the hoop backed Windsor chairs of the Thames Valley were locally distinct types simply made primarily from turned components. They had no connection with fashionable design or cabinet maker's methods. Such a clear distinction between 'everyman's' furniture and its 'genteel' counterparts did not exist in Lowland Scotland where craft traditions in furniture making were virtually unknown. Thus the mainstream vernacular furniture of the area was related to fashionable furniture at the top of the social scale. The dominant influence was the tradition of cabinet making.

Plate 1 Late 18th or early 19th Century laburnum splat-backed chair from Fife (private collection)

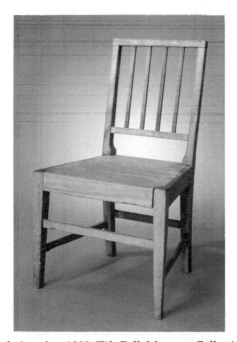

Plate 2 Brander back chair, ash, c 1800 (Fife Folk Museum Collection)

A clear illustration of this is the 'brander back' chair. This type is characterised by its square back which frames a row of plain banisters (usually three). The stay rail is raised slightly above the seat to form part of the back frame. It is frequently referred to in Scotland as a brander back because of its resemblance to a brander or gridiron. Most common in Perthshire and Eastern Scotland, this pattern was made by city cabinet makers and country wrights alike. For example, George Sandeman of Perth made a documented set for his daughter's Edinburgh townhouse in 1789; these were genteel chairs with carved detail including fishtail terminals on the banisters. A year earlier, John Tweedie, wright in Biggar, had made a very plain precentor's chair to the same pattern for St Mary's Kirk in that town. This however was quite definitely a common chair with no carved decoration. It was made from local ash and constructed with simple, square section banisters. A pictorial illustration of the brander back's place in the common household is given by Tom Faed's choice of the type in his print of a cottage interior for *The Cottar's Saturday Night* published in the early 1820s.

Moving on from the brander back which is was a late 18th Century pattern, to the early 19th Century, it can be seen that common regional chair types in the cabinet making tradition continued to flourish. With the advent of industrialisation, some were even adopted by furniture making companies for mass production. As population began to shift, regional boundaries expanded and it seems that at first, there was no strict line of demarcation between the ordinary furniture of the countryside and city. Perhaps the best example of closely related rural and urban tradition during this period is that of the 'Glasgow' and 'Edinburgh' chair types. Both were generalised regional patterns given these names by the large firms who began to produce them in volume. They were retailed as kitchen chairs.

The Glasgow chair had a top rail inserted between the stiles and a distinctive, centrally placed stay rail which could take a number of forms, the most common in the Glasgow area being a straight edged rail with the upper edge curving up to a central tab. These chairs inherited many of the constructional features of the eighteenth century Lowland tradition, such as the dyked seat, and are particularly recognisable by their front legs, which have a pronounced taper on all four sides. The Edinburgh chair had a yoke shaped top rail placed over the stiles and a plain stay rail. It did not always have a dyked seat and was frequently made with turned front and splayed back legs.

These chairs often appeared alongside each other in 19th Century trade catalogues and were made in large numbers for both urban and country markets (in the latter case by mail order) by firms such as Wylie and Lochhead and Christie and Miller of Falkirk. Until the 1930s they were also made according to local variations by country wrights across Central Scotland from Dumbartonshire to the Fife coast. In Anstruther for instance, Edinburgh pattern chairs were made from sycamore with broad yokes overhanging the stiles. In North Lanarkshire, Glasgow pattern chairs sometimes had a stay rail shaped like a wheelwright's spokeshave.

The demise of the Scottish common chair came with the introduction of the

Plate 3 Designs from Francis East & Co., Dundee, showing Edinburgh (top) and Glasgow (bottom) pattern chairs (Francis East collection, Dundee Art Galleries & Museums, Dundee)

Utility Furniture Scheme from 1943 under which factories were requisitioned and turned over to making a small repertoire of economical chairs chosen from existing English prototypes. The most popular pattern became the standard hoop backed Windsor, whose region of origin was the High Wycombe/Thames valley area of Southern England.

In terms of usefulness, it can be said that the stool scores over the chair, but in terms of basic necessity the bed comes first. The box bed was to be found in a wide range of households including farmhouses, inns, fishermens', miners' and weavers' cottages in Lowland Scotland but it is chiefly associated with the one or two roomed cottage of the married agricultural worker or hind. The married farmhand in the nineteenth century had to purchase his own furniture and freestanding box beds, the principal items, required a considerable financial outlay. James Robb, author *The Cottage, the Bothy and the Kitchen, being an Inquiry into the Conditions of Agricultural Labourers in Scotland*, 1861, recorded the generally-held opinion that ploughmen married too young, before they had saved sufficient to purchase furniture. He added: 'The consequence is that many of them remain for years in debt to country wrights who of course repay themselves for their long outlay by charging heavy prices for the articles.'

The box bed was a prestige item in the homes of those who could afford to buy one new, and indeed many box beds in Berwickshire, East Lothian, Fife and Forfarshire had a fitting pedigree. Their design, a simple keystoned arch and pilasters beneath a cornice, was derived from Paladio's *QuattroLibri dell'architecttura*, 1570. This once again underlined the strong link between Scotland's common furniture and professionally designed patterns. The records of Mary's Chapel, Edinburgh show that the box or 'closs' bed was one of four standard essay pieces executed by apprentice wrights and that architectural design sources were prescribed by masters. For example, on 14 July 1683 the wright Charles George's essay piece was:' ane Closs bed the lidds to be of raysd work out of the timber it self angled from poynt to poynt with ane dorick entablature, to be all done in wainscott.' These architectural patterns were common to the Eastern Lowlands; other distinctive regional box bed patterns remain to be identified.

To be seen as the owner of an expensive new bed was socially important, but to have too many beds in the living space was an obvious indication of an overcrowded house. A solution was to have some beds disguised as other pieces of furniture, such as clothes presses. Press beds were designed to be compact and portable pieces of furniture suitable for placing against a wall; they were deliberately constructed to resemble clothes chests and the bedstead part folded up to be concealed when not in use. Although few early examples survive, documentary sources, particularly household inventories, indicate that this type of bedstead was well known in 17th Century Scotland and that it enjoyed an enduring popularity in the small household until the 1930s. Twentieth century examples, (many now converted into wardrobes), can still be found on the second hand market in Scottish cities such as Glasgow.

Like the press bed, the bed settee performed a flexible function in the one or two roomed household. This appears, along with chair beds, in the first Glasgow *Cabinet Makers' Price Book* of 1809, but it enjoyed a heyday in the 1930s and 1940s. Several firms came to specialise in their manufacture, including Goorsh Bros of Glasgow, Alexanders of Rutherglen, MacGregors of Renfrew and The Dayanite Company of Edinburgh. Space saving was the clear priority in all these bed types and they were common to the urban room and kitchen and single end as well as the rural cottage.

A type which was apparently unique to the tenement was the 'hurly bed'. This was a shallow wooden box with slatted bottom raised on legs with castors. It could be stored in the space beneath an alcove or set in bed and wheeled out at night for children to sleep in. These are now scarce, but well recorded in photographs and oral recollections. The use of a large number of bed types in the small Lowland household was geared to the accommodation of children and extended families in a small space and, as with items such as stools and tables, involved much moving around and putting away of furniture at different times of the day. The closest modern analogy must be that of living in a caravan or boat, in which tables and beds have to be brought out for use, in which washing of people, clothes and preparation of food all takes place at the same sink or water source and where most of the furniture is designed or adapted for neat and ingenious storage. Surviving physical evidence, reports on living conditions and the published observations of architectural commentators indicate that the 19th Century agricultural labourer's cottage had fewer 'fittings' designed for storage that its urban counterpart the tenement flat. For example, larders, press cupboards and coal bunkers were not commonplace as they were in the homes of city dwellers in comparable regular employment.

Throughout the 19th Century the most widely used item of storage furniture remained the kist. This was certainly not static; most examples had carrying handles and before coming to the family home, may have been used by men as lodging boxes in bothies or by women in accommodation associated with migrant labour such as fish processing or domestic service. The standard design of Lowland kist was a rectangular box with a fitted till or 'shottle' and perhaps a small drawer at one end of the interior underneath a deep lid which again was usually of dyked construction. The lid was therefore not a flat board but had a frieze which contained a keyhole and lock. On more elaborate examples this frieze was sometimes scratch beaded. Geikie's sketches illustrate how kists could be used as bench seating at a table or placed in rows immediately in front of box bed openings.

Until the late 19th Century, wardrobes were conspicuously absent in the small Lowland home. In the rural cottage clothes could be stored in kists or inside box beds but in the urban household the principal item of storage furniture was the chest of drawers. One distinctive pattern came to dominate during the 19th century; this was the so-called 'Lum chest'. The type was sufficiently idiosyncratic and occurred with such frequency in Lowland Scotland that it was cited as a 'Scotch Chest' when the design appeared in English trade catalogues. Its characteristic feature was a deep, square drawer used for the purpose of stowing hats, such as women's mutches or the man's lum hat, which gave the popular name to these chests. In a small room such as a single end, a lum chest might seem enormous, but the design was adapted for maximum storage capacity in the minimum of floorspace. Dimensions always favoured height over depth so the chest did not project into a room and the top, frequently over five feet from the floor, could be used for display of china and other ornaments. William Bow of Glasgow's *Illustrated Catalogue* (1908) shows lum chests of different sizes and decoration ranging in price from £3 19s 6d to £6 10s; they were relatively expensive items in showy mahogany veneers but they could be bought on credit.

Except in cases of extreme poverty such as the inhabitants of common lodging houses or sub-let rooms, to whom the luxury of furniture was not a high priority, costly furniture was a general feature of the 'ordinary' household in which the occupants were not always on the move and where a steady income enabled the payment of credit terms. The two great features of small homes were the chest of drawers and the bed. In the rural cottage the bed took prominence and in the city tenement the chest of drawers was the chief investment. Proud householders strove to outdo each other in the quality and fashionability of these items.

For everyman in Lowland Scotland space-saving qualities and prestige value were desired from certain types of furniture. At first, rural traditions served the new industrial centres reflecting distinct regional preferences; these were frequently quite subtle differences that were found in constructional details and type of wood The common Lowland chair for instance, was generally based upon a designed pattern reflecting the historical education of the Scottish wright, and could be made from laburnum or pine, alder or ash, depending on its region of origin. It must not be seen as simply a debased version of a sophisticated source, because it was a vernacular standard and the equivalent of common furniture made in the craft tradition in other European countries. Urban fashion came to predominate and mahogany veneer became ubiquitous, but regional types remained a strong part of Lowland culture until at least the 1930s. Continued fieldwork will gradually complete our knowledge of this rich pattern of regional difference and perhaps one day contribute to a Lowland Folk Museum, for an area in which 'everyman' is united by the use of a common language and was once united by the use of common types of furniture.

The author

David Jones is a lecturer in furniture history at the University of St Andrews where he is developing a centre of excellence for this neglected subject. He organised the successful 1987 exhibition, *Looking at Scottish Furniture*, which was shown in Glasgow and St Andrews, and is Editor of the journal, *Regional Furniture*. He is currently working on a *Dictionary of Scottish furniture Makers 1660-1840*.

References

Jones, D., 'Box Beds in Eastern Scotland', in *Regional Furniture V*, pp.79-85, 1991.

Jones, D., 'The Press Bed in Scotland', Scottish Society of Art Historians, *Proceedings*, 1988.

Jones, D., 'Scotch Chests', in *Regional Furniture II*.

Jones, D., *Looking at Scottish Furniture: A Documented Anthology 1570-1900*, St. Andrews and Glasgow 1987.

Jones, D., 'Scottish Cabinet Makers' Price Books, 1805-1825, in *Regional Furniture III*, 1989.

Jones, D., 'The Laburnum Tradition in Scotland', in *Regional Furniture VI*, 1992.

Plate 4 A 'creepie' being used as a stand outside 21 North Street, St.Andrews, c1900 (St Andrews Preservation Trust Collection; photograph, W.Patrick)

27

BOWYERY AND FLETCHING
The Ancient Crafts of Archery

Hugh Soar

We can have no idea of how or where the principle of shooting with a bow was first discovered. What seems probable is that by the late Stone Age a simple bow had evolved. Man had discovered that by converting potential to kinetic energy, he could influence the order of things. Partly for the better: bow-hunting was effective, and economic of manpower. Partly for the worse, since these new found 'stand-off' capability would revolutionise warfare.

EARLY EVIDENCE

Whilst drawings of bow-men may date from the seventh millennium, bows themselves are conspicuously absent from early sites. That found at Rotten Bottom in the Tweedsmuir Hills of Dumfriesshire has been radio-carbon dated to 4040 – 3540 BC, and is thus amongst the earliest of the prehistoric weapons so far found in Great Britain, ante-dating the Ashcott Heath and Meare Heath bows of Somerset by a thousand years. These latter, broadly contemporary in age, are interesting in that they show totally dissimilar profiles and cross-sections (Figure 1), each of which are recognisable in today's bows.

Mesolithic rock pictures on Eastern Spain clearly show the bow and arrow in use for both hunting and combat. That from the Cueva de los Caballos, Castellon, vividly portrays a herd of deer being driven into a line of archers; only the trees or rocks are missing for this to be a medieval 'bow and stable' hunting stand. The apparent appearance of vanes (fletchings) at this early stage in the development of the weapon suggests an understanding of simple aero-dynamics: the stability imparted to a shaft when fletched. Certainly the principle of 'three-vane' fletching was known to the 'Alpine ice-man'; evolution perhaps by trial and error.

Creation of a stable shaft, able to travel in an arc and to connect with its target is fundamental to archery. The relation of arrow whippiness (spine) to bow draw-weight is important if a shaft is to fly true. The ability of an arrow to travel 'round' a bow-limb instead of along the apparent line of flight –

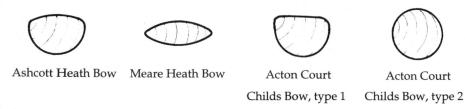

Ashcott Heath Bow   Meare Heath Bow   Acton Court   Acton Court

Childs Bow, type 1   Childs Bow, type 2

Figure 1 Typical cross-sections of bows. (Ashcott Heath Bow: acknowledgements to the Prehistoric Society. Acton Court Childs Bow: acknowledgements to the Bath Archaeological Trust)

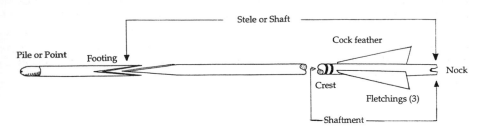

Figure 2 Named parts of the arrow

creating a phenomenon known as the 'archers paradox' – was seemingly familiar to prehistoric bowmen and fletchers. The making of an arrow is a thing no less worthy of respect than the bow itself. To paraphrase Ishi, the last of the Californian Yana Indians: 'Any stick, him do for bow – arrows kill deer! ' and again, 'Any young man, him make a bow – old man, many years experience, make arrows.' A simple philosophy, but exact.

For a bow to be of use, a suitable string and considerable draw-force are needed. Early man neither had, nor needed to have the one-hundred pound bows which his descendants handled with such consummate skill; but his bow-string had still to arrest the bow-limbs after they had discharged the arrow. The material of which it was made had perforce to be stout enough for the purpose. Primitive archers are known to have used rawhide, sinew, animal gut, and plant-fibre to string their bows, and it is likely that these were in use during prehistoric times. Ishi the Yana Indian made his strings from the finer tendons of a deer's shank which he chewed until soft, and then twisted tightly into a cord which served for a bow of about 45lbs in draw-weight, adequate enough for the despatch of small game.

A suitable elastic quality is necessary for the cast: the propulsive capability of a bow. The tensile and the compressive elements of the chosen wood must be compatible with what is required of the weapon, and this naturally limits the choice. Of only slightly less importance are the profile and cross-section employed by the bow-maker. Each plays its part in determining the quality of the bow: the former by producing 'arcs of force', the latter by balancing the 'neutral' and the 'medial' axes of the limb in such a way that compression fracture or 'crysalling' is avoided (*Archery: the Technical Side*, National Field Archery Association, 1947).

It is of interest that the flatter of the two sections (Figure 1) has been shown to be the more efficient in research by Paul E. Klopsteg in 1931. A replica of the Meare Heath bow was made, and was shot by a top archer at the 1963 Meeting of the Grand Western Archery Society, and it is recorded that at his third shot he hit the target 60 yards away. For all that, however, it was the high-cambered section which pre-dominated, and we meet this section regularly during historic times.

BOWS AND MATERIALS

There have been four recognisable types of long-bow across the centuries. Chief among these was the formidable battle-weapon, the great war-bow of our ancestors, and a prime reason for our claim to be a martial nation. Second but pre-dating it was the hunting bow, a weapon lighter in draw-weight, often camouflaged, but in almost daily use to cull for kitchen or for sport. Used by skilled foresters and hunters, well versed in their art, it despatched the broad-headed hunting shafts which killed so effectively either directly or by haemorrhage.

Third, the peasant's bow – a 'bough bow' fashioned from hedge-yew or other wood readily come by and made by those who hunted in the forests, often illegally. Used legitimately by, among others, the cattle drovers on their way from the Borders to Eastern England, it was a universal weapon, doubling as a yoke to carry water buckets, a goad to guide the beasts, and a ready means of defence and 'pot hunting'. Crude and unpretentious but powerful, it was truly the 'people's weapon'. Last is the recreational bow that is lighter in draw-weight than its cousins to match its lighter arrows, and shorter to permit greater cast. It has evolved across the years to be the weapon which is familiar to us today – the bow most accessible for study since creating it is still a living art.

Bow-making or bowyery requires skills enshrined in a long craft tradition. Apprenticeships were lengthy, often exceeding seven years before mastery was deemed to be complete. A variety of woods were in use during earlier times, and we know something of these through the writings of Roger Ascham, man of letters, author of *Toxophilus, the Schole, or Partitions of Shooting* published in 1544, and amongst the first of the books written and published in English. Ascham wrote with both passion and knowledge. He was adamant that yew was the superior wood, and was dismissive of the others:

> As for Brazell, Elme, Wyche and Ash, experience doth prove them to be meane for bowes (and so to conclude) Yew of all other things is that whereof perfect shooting would have a bow made.

Brazell wood has been identified as Caesalpina echinate, known popularly as Pernambuco Wood. Pink in colour, it was imported from South America for use in dyeing. A dense wood, it was used also for 'footing' or 'piecing' arrows, together with the native wood, holly. This process was designed to conserve and strengthen them (Figure 2).

The reference to Elme and Wyche is interesting. Giraldus Cambrensis, in his 12th Century description of the bow-wood used by the South Welsh, refers to 'ilmellis silvestribus', believed alternatively to be 'ulmus glabra huds', referred to by Statute as wych hazel in the context of bowyery. Wych-hazel, or wych-elm, (the names are synonymous) is common in the West and North of England, Wales and Scotland and is superior as a bow wood to ulmus procxera or Common Elm. Relevant as an aside is wych's Germanic root 'wik', meaning bend.

Bow-making materials were defined by Statute as were so many matters pertinent to archery:

> Bowers, for every bow of yew, are to make two of elm, Wych or other wood of mean price, and if they be found to do the contrary, to be committed to gaol for the space of eight days or more.

Yew has always been the preferred bow-wood because the combination of sap-wood and heart-wood provides tensile and compressive strength in correct proportions and the distinctive colour of each allows exactness as the stave is fashioned. Of the many species and sub-species of yew, two are used today. The war-bow was fashioned from Taxus baccata . The other, Taxus brevifolia, indigenous to the USA, is used for recreational weapons of distinction. The English specie of Taxus baccata made, and makes a tolerable bow, but wood from the Spanish Pyrenees and Northern Italy was prized above all other during the hey-day of the bowyer.

THE BOWYER AND THE FLETCHER

Although the majority of the country's bowyers almost certainly worked in comparative isolation, others were gathered in craft-guilds. Of these, the City of London Livery Companies of Bowyers and of Fletchers were arguably predominant. Formed in the 14th Century and fiercely independent of each other since their division in 1370, they survive today largely as charitable institutions, but still with interest and influence in archery matters. Provincial Guilds were also formed with close links to other trades, and they survived well into the 16th century. That at Chester incorporated with the Hoopers Company, whilst the Bristol (Bristowe) Guild severed contact with the Hoopers to establish its own Ordinances in 1479. Whether these were subsequently renewed is uncertain, but there is no doubt that individual bowyers and fletchers in Bristol were engaging apprentices into the 1550s, often from many miles away. Gormanstown in Ireland, and curiously enough Chester, appear on the Rolls, among many other places.

At least one apprentice stayed in his adopted city after his term was ended. Richard Vykeris, son of a Husbandman from Astely in Worcestershire, was put with John Powell, bowyer, in 1535 for a seven year apprenticeship. In 1543, Richard, now married to Isabella, took an apprentice himself as a practising Bristol bowyer. As one might expect, bowyers were outnumbered by fletchers, and it was not unusual for women to engage in the latter trade. When John Badnall, a Bristol fletcher died in the mid-1540s, his wife Lucy took over the business, engaging apprentices in her own right, as a 'widow fletcher' according to the Rolls. Arrow making and fletching is not demanding of strength, as is bowyery, and many aspects of the task are better suited to nimble fingers than the horny hands of men-folk. Unlike the Company of Longbowstringmakers of London, formed in 1415 by Prescription, the Stringers of Bristol were seemingly attached to no guild. These local string makers were Barbers by trade, although it is as Stringers that they took apprentices.

The stages in the formation of both bows and arrows are described in Randle Holme's *Academy of Armoury* (1688, facsimile 1905). Although written well after the war-bow had ceased in use, there can be little doubt that the practices had earlier application. The 'working' of the bow was, in sequence: the 'stave' or staff (so called when cleft from the log) was roughly hewn with a hatchet, and 'pointed' or tapered with a 'float' or rasp. It was then planed and straightened if crooked, 'horned' (to protect the upper and lower limb tips, and 'notched' to take a bow-string (initially a 'tillering-string'). It was next 'tillered' to bring the limbs around in true compass by rasping where needed, polished or 'stoned', and finally rubbed with boars-tooth and oil cloth to shine and seal the finish.

Making the arrow involved taking the rough wood, pointing it out, or rounding it with a knife. Then shaving or planing it round with a hollow plane, smoothing it with a fish-skin (dog-fish skin was very suitable), slitting it to take the horn sliver, and cross-slitting to form the nock or notch which fitted on the string. Tapering the foot to take the shoulder of the pile, and glueing this on completed the operation (see Figure 2 for technical terms).

Drawing the feathers for fletching required cutting, or stripping them from their quills; paring the backs to make them lie close to the stele, 'ribbing' them by cutting away the 'side-skirts', cutting to length and shape, and pressing them in a wet cloth to keep them flat. Next came 'glazing' or varnishing the shaftment with glue, 'feathering' -glueing on the three fletches, 'poising' the arrows to match for weight and length, and finally 'twirling' or turning them in the hand to check for straightness.

With minor exceptions these are the sequences followed by bowyers and fletchers today. Traditional bowyers of today might saw rather than split to produce a stave, all in the interest of economy when bow-wood is scarce. Lamination is practised now, again because of timber shortages, and 'backed' bows in which tensile strength is provided by a hickory strip are the rule rather than the exception. Fortunately, modern glues set rapidly, which the animal glues of old did not, and it is no longer necessary for joints to be set aside for a year to cure.

Today's arrow making 'from the plank' is little different to that of the 17th century. The square from which the shaft or 'stele' is formed is habitually sawn and planed initially on a 'shuting block'. Although fish-skin (particularly dog-fish skin) will certainly smooth, and purists still use it, most modern fletchers have succumbed to modern technology and finish the stele with sand or glass-paper. Fletching jigs are invariably used to affix the fletchings, although the earlier practice of dribbling hot animal glue on the skirt of the fletch, placing it on the shaftment and cooling it with breath would perhaps be an alternative if animal glue were more easily come by. Apprentice Rolls occasionally listed the tools which the apprentice acquired at the end of his time. Thus, in 1552, young Thomas Hinton took with him four shaves, one pair of shears, one plane and one paring knife to start him on his way as a fletcher.

Bowyery was, and still is an art form. To create a bow is to tame and train a piece of wood to one's will and to imbue it with purpose. Until shortage of raw materials forced change, bows were invariably formed from self-staves, laminated staves appearing only as the weapon declined in use for war. A bow is shaped to create a profile and the required cross-section. It is this latter which will influence cast, reliability, and function. The earliest association of section with purpose occurs within the French manuscript *L'art d'archerie*, a work pre-dating Ascham by some forty years. From this we learn of the two principal cross-sections in being at the turn of the 15th Century: 'square' and 'round'. The former was recommended for target and butt shooting, the latter for flight, or distance target work. Although full details of the Tudor war-bows recovered from the war-ship Mary-Rose have yet to be released, there are indications of the use of these cross-sections in abundance. Clearly, bows were not created by chance.

RECREATIONAL ARCHERY

Whilst recognising its importance we will, for the purpose of this paper, exclude hunting in the context of recreational archery. Archery as a pastime is surely as old as the bow itself. For even the seven year old lad of Tudor times, sporting with his bow and arrows as statute required was preparing for the day when he might defend his country. Andres Boorde, physician to Henry VIII commented that 'A pair of Butts is a decent thing about a mansyon place.' There is little doubt that 'garden butts' were as popular in the 16th century as in the 19th. Sadly, not all observed basic rules of safety, and the cold text of many a Coroner's Report told of deaths by misadventure of youngsters who strayed into the path of arrows.

Deserving of recognition, if not of fame, was one Henry Pert, a Tudor gentleman of Welbeck in Nottinghamshire, who in the cause of personal research contrived to shoot himself in the head. This experience proved terminal and the Coroner, curious no doubt as to Mr Pert's modus operandi, established that he was apparently accustomed to using too short an arrow.

Despite a paucity of examples for study, it is still possible to follow the development of the recreational weapon; to note the disappearance of one feature, and the appearance of another. Thus, two features present on 17th and 18th century bows are no longer found today. The 'belly wedge', designed to avoid damage to the bow if an arrow were overdrawn, was a feature of 17th century weapons, when it was described as a 'cork', or 'noche'. It is present on a bow made by Grant of Kilwinning dating from the mid-18th century, and on another by Muir of Edinburgh of early 19th century date, although it is absent from the later Scottish bows and had apparently been dropped from mainstream English bowyery practice much earlier.

A feature which is unlikely to re-appear is the 'side-nock' or stringing-groove. This arrangement permitted easier 'bracing' or stringing of the 'heavy' bow, and there is some evidence that side-nocking was a regular practice amongst 16th century bowyers. Certainly the 18th century bowyer Grant incorporated the feature within his weapons. Although it does not appear on later Scottish bows, it was, together with the belly wedge, seemingly confined to Scotland where heavier bows for distance shooting were in regular use.

Understandably, few recreational weapons have survived. However, two children's long-bows have been recovered from an archaeological excavation at Acton Court, Bristol. Examination of these shows an interesting difference in cross-section. One is low-cambered with a flat back, fore-runner of a shape that was common in the 18th and 19th centuries. The other was elliptical, a 'war-bow' in miniature, which was a shape less frequently encountered in later times. The pattern of recreational bowyery in England was strongly

Figure 3 Miss Queenie Newall (top left), National Lady Champion, 1911, 1912 and Olympic Champion, 1908. Top right, Mr Willy Dod, National Champion, 1909, 1911 and Olympic Champion, 1908. Middle, a bowyer tillering a bow. Bottom, a fletcher preparing an arrow shaft

influenced by Thomas Waring (died 1805) who, following the revival of interest in the pastime amongst the gentry, developed skills learned many years earlier from the Kersall family of bowyers in Manchester. Waring's selection of cross-section and profile may thus have reflected mainstream bowyery practice, differing little from the low-cambered sections seen in one of the Acton Court bows.

Another feature, surviving from the 18th into the mid-19th century, was the 'purging hole' formed when shaping the horn tips and designed to avoid hydraulic pressure when gluing the tips to the bow. Shapes of horn tips altered significantly from the 1850s onwards, when the finely formed 'flat-face' nocks were replaced by others with 'side-faces' bought in from the Continent of Europe.

Although British bowyers remained largely faithful to the traditional long-bow profile, the influence of continental design was occasionally felt, and bows with 'recurved' limbs appeared. Known today as 'Burgundian bows', these graceful weapons appear in 17th century paintings in both Scotland and England. Although one English bowyer at least fashioned them in the 19th Century, they were seldom seen in post-revival archery, and made no impact on the competitive scene.

Omitting hunting, which had a dual purpose anyway, there have been many forms of recreational archery, e.g. distance shooting with 'standard' battle-shafts, and 'flight' arrows; butt shooting, which includes target archery; clout shooting at known marks, and roving archery at un-marked distances; 'Popinjay' (in Scotland, Papingo); shooting 'under the line', and wand or prick shooting. In respect of shooting for distance, exemplified by 16th century 'standard arrow' contests and their successors, the 'pound arrow' meetings had undeniable military use. Valuable prizes were offered, and competition was probably keen.

Whilst quasi-battle practice was smiled on by authority, less favourably received was butt-shooting at shorter known distances. Men were expected to be strong shooters and to 'keep a length' and bow shot was some 12 score yards, while butt shooting took place at about half that distance. Nevertheless, the need for close-range accuracy was recognised by the military. An early form used in France, for which there is circumstantial evidence here, was 'shooting under the line'. The distance between two targets was bisected by a taut line suspended between two poles. Archers shot from one target to the other, keeping their shafts below the line. There were penalties for going over the line.

Roving, particularly between marks of unspecified distances, was encouraged as in modern field archery, not just because it developed intuitive accuracy, but because it had the archer walking in the open air. Archery was even regarded as the 'cure-all' of disease, and many were the poems, and lengthy the prose extolling its beneficial properties.

Popinjay, 'tir à la perche' in France, and Papingo in Scotland, was once widely practised in England. Originally involving a tethered bird on a high pole, this was eventually replace by a stylised 'roost' of birds and chicks. The ancient society of Kilwinning Archers' Papingo Meeting, first held in the 15th century still takes place, and archers annually 'ding doon the doo' to the acclaim of their peers. Perhaps originating from a need to aim at an acute angle towards an enemy perched on a castle wall, it is now seldom practised in England.

Target archery survives of course, and now formalised and shot to inflexible rules. In earlier days clubs shot to please themselves, and distances, target colours, and numbers of arrows even, varied sometimes at an official's whim. It was not until the 1840s that matters stabilised, and recognised 'Rounds' established. That for men was inaugurated at the National Archery Meeting of 1844, the first of the present series, whilst that for women followed a year or two later. Until the formation of an International Governing Body in 1931 these were the principal Competitive Rounds.

Although the long-bow continues to flourish in Britain under the benevolent eye of the British Long-Bow Society, traditional archery is very much a minority sport. Today's target archery is conducted with weapons that derive from quite a different stock based on modern technology. But a strong preoccupation with 'state of the art' equipment is encouraging many archers towards a renewed interest in the simpler bow, and it is hoped that the division between 'traditionalists' and those solely concerned with target accuracy will in future become less pronounced.

THE BOW AND ARROW IN POETRY

The muse is no stranger to the bow and arrow. Couplet and verses, both heroic and prosaic span the years. From Michael Drayton's *Agincourt*, we have the following lines on a battle theme:

> When from a meadow by,: Like a storm suddenly,
> The English Archery, struck the French horses.
> With Spanish yewgh so strong,: Arrows a clothyard long,
> That like to Serpents stung, piercing the weather.

Robert Shotterel, 17th century poet, and sometime Captain of the Society of Finsbury Archers stressed the beneficial properties of recreational archery:

> A Whole-some Pastime which all Sports exceeds,
> And he who shooting loves, no physic needs.
> A noble Archer his own Doctor is, and soars above the reach
> of rank disease.
> Agues and lazy fevers are for those who cherish the repute of
> Guns, not Bows!

Fittingly for a paper delivered north of the Border, the last word should come from Peter Muir, bow-maker in the 19th century to the Royal Company of Archers, the Queen's Bodyguard for Scotland:

It lengthens life, it strengthens limb,
It adds to beauty's glow.
Disease flies off on rapid wing,
From him that twangs the bow.

The author

Hugh Soar is Freeman of the Worshipful Company of Fletchers and Honorary Secretary of the British Long-Bow Society.

References

Ascham, R., *Toxophilus*, 1544, Reprint.
Bradbury, J., *The Medieval Archer*, Boydell & Brewer, 1992.
Duff, J., *Bows and Arrows*, 1927, Reprint.
Hansard, G.A., *TheBook of Archery*, 1841.
Hardy, R., *Long-Bow*, Patrick Stephens. J.H. Haynes, 2nd Edition, 1992.
Hodgkin, A.E., *The Archers Craft*, Faber & Faber, 1951/74.
Longman & Walrond, *Archery*,The Badminton Library Series, 1894.
Roberts, T., *The English Bowman*, Geo Shumway, Penn, 1801.

28

HERITAGE IS IN THE HEARTH

Elisabeth Luard

Ask any one of us what we understand to be our heritage, and no two of us will give the same reply. In this very diversity of opinion lies the truth. Our heritage is most broadly defined by landscape and the character of the people. It is most clearly visible in our artefacts: in architecture and paintings and music, in poetry and song and story telling. But it is the sights and sounds and smells of home, of our domestic hearth, which most truly reflect our heritage. It is when gathered round the dinner-table that we have the most vivid awareness of tribal identity.

By our culinary habit we know ourselves, and we value the traditions which make us different from our neighbours. We are what we eat, and we underline our separateness by referring to other 'tribes' by what we perceive as their preferred diet: consumers of frogs' legs or eaters of salted cabbage, to put it politely. We know exactly what we mean when we tap our noses and say 'it doesn't smell right'. We do indeed smell of what we eat. Food taboos, voluntary abstentions and religious dietary laws, serve to reinforce this olfactory distinction. Yet, knowing who we are, taking pride in the traditions of the community, can make us able to be generous, eager to share what we, and others, perceive as valuable.

The Scottish people, particularly in the outlying districts, are naturally hospitable. Perhaps this is because a rural, isolated population takes strength and confidence from an independent way of life. Frugality and self-sufficiency breed a sturdy, kindly people with a tradition of hospitality to strangers, but the independent life is hard. Yet, for those island-dwellers who live all year round with the difficulty and expense of ferry-crossings, which make daily necessities more costly, there is the compensation of a gentle pace of life, a community where people matter more than possessions, a soft climate, fish in the sea and berries on the hill, and the most glorious landscape on earth.

It is this, the crofting tradition, which most truly reflects the national domestic identity of Scotland. We see ourselves most clearly in a culinary habit dictated by season, availability of raw materials and fuel for the heat source; using ingredients which can be harvested, husbanded or hunted locally; limited by access to trade routes. As for the recipes, until recently there was no need to write them down. Indeed it remains a hard task, since the husbandry of the raw materials is as important as the culinary skills. Such knowledge is most easily passed from one generation to the next: father to son, mother to daughter.

A strong oral tradition, underpinned by the lessons learned by example, is the hardest to uproot. It cannot be rewritten, as can the history books or even the images on a television screen, to confirm the authority of a new power. The housewife may have new crops to accommodate, new ingredients to supplement the old, new gadgets, from the pestle and mortar to the food-processor, to cut down her labours. New recipes and imported delicacies make a welcome change. But nevertheless, underlying the new skills and foodstuffs, is the old tradition, in the case of the Celts, the lightest finger on the rolling pin, an in-born instinct for baking, a patient hand on the boiling pot.

THE CELTIC LEGACY

In the Celtic domestic tradition, a powerful influence on Scotland's culinary habits, can be found the last remnants of that shadowy civilisation which flourished during the millennium before Christ. The Celts were first and foremost homesteaders, independent farmers, a settled peasantry, tilling the soil and raising stock. For 500 years their civilisation flourished in the good lands of Germany and France. Squeezed between the Romans and the Germanic tribes, the Celts retreated to the outlying, less habitable areas of Europe, where they are to be found today.

Traditionally, the Celts are primary producers who take their goods to market. This gives access to new ideas and the intellectual hybrid vigour of the towns. To this day, there is an expressed preference for living close to a main thoroughfare. The wealth of the pre-Diaspora Celts derived from food production, supplemented by mercenary soldiering, mining and the exploitation of mineral resources: gold, tin, iron, silver, lead and salt. It can be argued that the most important of these was salt. Not only essential to the human diet, but used, pre-refrigeration, for the conservation of perishable foodstuffs: meat and fish, cheese, butter, even vegetables. Europe is criss-crossed with the old 'salt roads', and country people will still point them out. There is some suggestion that the Celts once controlled this trade in certain parts.

Traditional Celtic crops are the upland grains such as oats and barley, root vegetables, with kale or cabbage as the cultivated greens. The Celtic housewife has never set undue store by vegetables, and prefers meat when she can get it. So, harvests permitting, she fed surplus grain to the barnyard animals, and the Celts can claim to be the first (late pre-Roman Iron Age) in Britain to domesticate wild fowl: ducks (mallard) and geese (greylag, barnacle). It is thought they learned the trick from their cousins the Gauls, who also supplied them with chickens, descendants of the jungle fowl of North India and Borneo, courtesy of the Romans.

The Celts have a well-documented fondness for liquor. In the early days, trade routes up and down the Rhone were set up so that southern wine might be delivered to northern markets. At first wine was imported from Italy or Greece in amphorae, later the southern Gauls made their own, and the northerners learned to make mead, apple and pear wine, wheat and barley beer flavoured with herbs. Coopering, the making of barrels essential for the storing and maturing of liquor as well as salting food, was an acknowledged Celtic skill.

The cooking-fire is the heart of the Celtic home, unlike Mediterranean nations, where the population takes its leisure on the stoop or in the street; or those once nomadic populations such as Hungary's Magyars, who, whenever possible, take the cooking pail into the yard.

Heavy-duty iron utensils are characteristic of the Celts. Such containers can be heated swiftly, and will keep the heat for a long time, a necessity when fuel is scarce and keeping warm is a major preoccupation. Celtic hearth utensils are the bakestone (girdle, griddle, planc etc.) on which bread, pancakes, oatcakes etc. are cooked on top-heat; and the round-bellied cooking pot, variously filled with porridges made of oats or barley, and post-Columbus, cornmeal and potatoes. The cooking fire is traditionally used for roasting and toasting, and the pot used to boil meats and slow-simmer stews. The same pot, with its lid upturned and coals heaped on the top, served as a primitive baking oven.

THE CULINARY LANDSCAPE

This brings me to our native culinary landscape - a subject which I was privileged to explore at some length last year, when compiling a series on regional Scottish food for my newspaper, *The Scotsman*. Here in Aberdeen, is one of Scotland's deep-sea ports that have long formed the backbone of country's prosperity. Lerwick, Peterhead and Ullapool land the bulk of the fish caught in and around our waters. The great fishing port of Aberdeen, where much of the harbour space has been taken over by oil industry vessels, still handles a fair proportion of the daily catch, supplying the smokeries of the east coast. The bulk of the white-fish catch is haddock and cod.

Shoal-fish, such as herring and mackerel, are by their nature peripatetic, their migration dictated by some random piscine compass. The herring fleets had no option but to follow the shoals, and land the catch where it was most convenient. Within living memory, the fishwives followed the fleets around on land, ready to process the 'silver darlings', a role now taken on by the big factory ships.

The traditional method of conserving the catch was either simply wind-drying, salting and drying, or salting and smoking. The smoke was an addition made necessary when the British climate became wetter around two thousand years ago. All the famous Scottish smoked fish: salmon, kippers, haddie, and the Arbroath smokie belong to this tradition. You can make the general distinction that the use of a smoke-cure indicates a damp climate.

Further north, the Shetlands and Orkney take their culinary cue from Scandinavia (as do many of the islands), where brining (or salting and wind-drying) remains the traditional cure.

The Central Highlands, the Grampians and the mighty Cairngorms, lie at Scotland's heart. Here, in these sparsely populated regions, with high hills, heath-clad moorland, wooded valleys and the last of the ancient forests, is game in plenty. Grouse, partridge and capecaillie, red and roe deer, rabbit and hare are on the menu. Where there's grouse there are berries: the king of the game birds is a fussy eater. In high summer the moors and birch woods are carpeted with low berry-bearing shrubs: bilberries and cranberries and those small fruits which ripen rapidly in the long days of our short northern summer.

There is salmon in the rivers, fish in the burns and edible fungi in the autumn woods. And on the hillside there is wild thyme and juniper berries to be gathered to perfume a stalker's stew. Malt whisky is distilled throughout the area, and the fertile farmland of the Spey's alluvial plain supplies vegetables, soft fruit and dairy produce to Scotland's largest canning and preserving business at Fochabers.

The Highland region, its southern border formed by the Great Glen, covers half of Scotland's entire land-mass, but a mere one-twentieth of the population lives there. Of these a quarter cluster round Inverness. The short-horn herds of the Black Isle, the peninsula north of Inverness, produce some of the best beef in Scotland. Inland, lochs and rivers thread the high hills, with forest and peat-bog providing a wild larder of game, a landscape which accommodates a high proportion of Scotland's deer-farms. The ocean is never far away, and the weather dominates husbandry, whether by sea or land. For the past decade, salmon-farming has been the main growth industry, supplementing the trouble-beset herring fisheries as the major food industry.

Of the northerly islands, Skye is the largest and easiest of access from the mainland. The windy Outer Hebrides, of which Lewis, Harris and the Uists are principal, remain strongholds of the Celtic tradition, with Gaelic a living language. The eastern archipelago of Orkney and Shetland owes much of its rugged way of life to the Scandinavian influence, with upland grains and fish traditionally providing the bulk of the diet. Small-holding and fishing are the traditional occupations – landscape and season still dictate the daily dinner. Storable grains and tinned goods fill the larder. Salt fish, salt mutton and potatoes provide many a winter meal. And for the rest, baking is the great strength of the Celts, the use of top-heat and the girdle being the traditional, and most economical, way of preparing food where fuel is scarce and hard to gather.

The spectacular beauty of the West Coast, and the area's relative accessibility make this one of our most popular tourist destinations. The rock coastline provides sheltered sea-lochs, providing a fine haul of shellfish and crustaceans. With the ocean's resources proving finite, new marine industries include the cultivation of oysters and rope-grown mussels.

On the mainland, Loch Fyne traditionally has the finest herring for kippering. Of the western inner isles, Jura specialises in scallops; Islay has its distilleries and makes excellent butter; windy Tiree, nowadays a mecca for surfers, still crops kelp, has fine beef and grows bulbs for export in its sandy machair; Coll has the most delicately flavoured lamb; and my husband's home-island of Mull makes what I would count the finest cheese in the highlands. There are still crofting communities on all the islands, although the townships are no longer up to strength, and these days only the hardy few stick to the old agricultural methods of the small-holder.

Berries are big business in Tayside. Around Blairgowrie, where the soft-fruit industry had its beginnings in the 1920s, there is the highest concentration of raspberry farms in the world. Most of the crop goes to the preserve-makers of Dundee, with only a small proportion of the crop sold fresh. Dundee acquired its first marmalade factory in about 1800, using fruit landed from the merchant ships which used Dundee's port. From the same source came the imported spices, almonds and raisins which the bakers of Dundee use to make their famous cake. The fields of Fife are rich and fertile, producing much of Scotland's barley – raw material for the breweries and distilleries, with market gardens serving the cities of the east coast.

On the Carse of Gowrie, the monks of the Abbey of Coupar Angus taught the locals the art of gardening and the use of herbs – the archives of Perthshire record the sales of the product of fish ponds, beehives, orchards and dovecotes. Even today, gardeners will tell you that when the soil is newly dug, some of the old medicinal herbs miraculously appear. The potato crop was once exported throughout Port Allen to the Low Countries, a one-way trade which brought the boats back ballasted with Dutch soil, which the market gardeners immediately dug into their own vegetable yards to lighten the heavy clay.

The great city of Edinburgh has always depended on her fertile hinterland to supply her citizens with fresh food - her market garden is the coastal strip stretching up to North Berwick, where two thirds of Scotland's vegetables are grown. The rich agricultural land of Mid and East Lothian supplies cereals to the city, with barley for the breweries concentrated around Fountainbridge. Here the main food industry is the milling of grain, a spin-off from the days when wheat and corn were shipped out from the port.

The royal stamp of approval on horticulture was bestowed by David I, who endowed the abbey at Holyrood, and laid out the gardens and orchards below Castle Rock. The Royal Botanic Garden, once the Physic Garden supplying the university's renowned medical school, has long played a key role in persuading the Scots to change their eating habits. Post-Columbus, the garden championed the cause of the New World's vegetables, above all the mighty potato, now an integral part of Scotland's daily dinner. So, if vegetarianism is to be the diet of the future, Edinburgh can provide the philosophical will: the population of the 400 year old university ensures the city's vegetarian restaurants and wholefood stores are well-patronised.

Glasgow's culinary traditions remain rooted in the trade from which she earns her living. Imports, both of produce and people, have always added diversity to her table. Salt, sugar and spice were essential preservatives in pre-refrigeration days, supplied first by trade with the East, later by the West

Indies. The establishment of trade routes with the Americas brought the vegetables of the New World to Glasgow's market gardens: the agriculturists of the Clyde Valley made a name for themselves as tomato-growers and the farmers of Ayrshire were reputed to have been the first in Scotland to plant potatoes.

The native Ayrshire breed is the closest we have to the original wild cattle of these islands, providing dairy-products for Glasgow. Ayrshire bacon, a relative newcomer, is a spin-off from dairy-farming: pigs thrive on the whey and buttermilk from the butter and cheese-makers. In ship-victualling ports there are always offal and sausage dishes. Meat, beef and pork in particular, was salted and barrelled for the Atlantic crossing, so inevitably the cheaper more perishable parts of the animal were either paid as part of the barrellers' wages, or were bought by the urban poor. As might be expected, Glasgow has fine gourmet shopping, with groceries imported from all over the world. Her position as the gateway to the Highlands ensures access to the best of Scottish produce.

The flocks which graze the rolling hills of the Borders produce tender lamb and fine wool for the knitwear industry. The valleys provide pasture for dairy and beef herds. To the west is the wild and beautiful Galloway peninsula, gateway to Ireland, but still one of the least-known of Scotland's ancient provinces. The handsome Galloway Belties are hard to find these days, replaced with more profitable beasts. Several cheeses are made locally, including the traditional Galloway Cheddar as well as several fine newcomers.

There is fish in plenty throughout the region, both freshwater and salt. Salmon comes from the Tweed, a historic herring fleet bases itself at Eyemouth on the west coast, Kircudbright crops shellfish from Wigtown Bay, and the little harbours of Galloway still shelter a small inshore fleet. Farmed trout from the hatcheries of Dumfries supply the smokeries of Annan. Dumfries has market gardens, and the sandy soil and mild winter climate round Wigtown produces very early potatoes. Over on the east, the fertile Merse grows vegetables for the pot, barley for soups and for the brewers and distillers; and wheat for the fine baking at which local housewives traditionally excel.

ECO-CATERING

From the above analysis it is reasonable to conclude that Scottish raw materials and native culinary skills are second to none. Unfortunately our culinary reputation is based more on our ability to export our produce, than our skill in presenting it on a plate to our visitors. You can have some truly horrible culinary experiences in public places. That said, there is no doubt there has been general improvement at the top level of our public catering. Most of our celebrated chefs understand the virtues, and the selling power, of using locally grown produce in season. But if we are to do ourselves justice, we must find ways of translating these advances into less ambitious establishments. And we must do so naturally, from within, by using local traditions and local ingredients.

With this in mind, I would like to propose a new standard in public catering in Scotland, and to suggest that this is one area in which we might give a lead to other nations. Let us call it Eco-catering, a deliberately workmanlike term, but it serves to suggest its meaning. To qualify as an Eco-caterer, an establishment would offer dishes inspired by local tradition, using ingredients as far as possible grown, husbanded or cropped within a certain radius. There would be a conscious effort to recruit local labour, and to use local skills, particularly in the goods offered for sale as souvenirs. When costing such an enterprise (and I have no doubt that just as toy seals made in the Philippines are cheaper than hand-knits from a local knitter, beef burgers which originate from a cattle ranch in Argentina are more profitable than a collop from an Aberdeen Angus), it might be useful to consider the hidden price-tag. These include the negative impact on the environment of trucking in supplies from outside, cost of access (roads and bridges to carry heavy loads), the true cost in unemployment and loss of traditional skills, and that unmeasurable but vital ingredient – quality of life as expressed in pride in a community's identity.

It might be possible, perhaps through the Scottish Women's Rural Institute, to organise demonstrations in heritage centres of local domestic skills. Where skills have been lost, the preparation of fish, the distinctive uses of upland grains, wild-gathering, to bring in outsiders to impart their knowledge. This would have value as entertainment, as education (domestic habit as living history), and to give back a sense of pride in old skills. Other nations are already attempting similar schemes. On recent travels in France, I noticed that local 'Syndicates of Initiative' declared a day when those who wished to learn how to prune the olive trees were invited to observe and assist the pruners at work.

The benefits of active local involvement in tourist catering would be a visible and tangible (edible) vocabulary with which to welcome visitors, whether native or stranger. And the dialogue between visitors and visited would provide access to a real record of our traditions, many of which, for practical, political or social reasons, have disappeared underground. Such centres would provide an anvil for forging links between the tourist industry, and at a very basic 'household' level with local communities, particularly with women working and caring for families at home.

The role of The Robert Gordon University Heritage Unit and the School of Food and Consumer Studies in all this might be to offer guidelines and practical advice on the raw materials and culinary habit appropriate in any given area, to look for ways of co-operating with existing official bodies, to champion the cause of the small producers and suppliers seeking to conform with the new EEC regulations, to look for liaison and co-operation with local communities.

I would hope too that we might be able to provide a scheme for rewarding our children for active care of their heritage: they are already becoming the most aware of the difficulties besetting the planet. I envisage some kind of step-by-step qualification, much like that already in place for First Aid or the Duke of Edinburgh Award sceheme, leading youngsters in the direction of higher qualifications at a college or university when they grow up. Finally, the University could provide a clearing house for knowledge and a marketplace for traditional skills. This would be particularly valuable when those with the financial resources to set up an enterprise might not be best placed to know how to fit them into the social and geographical landscape.

An appreciation of our culinary traditions is not merely the frill on grandmother's apron, but essential to the proper understanding of who we are. Our heritage is the ancestral hearth-fire, fuelled by all those things which burn most brightly in our hearts. It shapes our perception of the future as well as our memories of the past. Women have always known that the wooden spoon is mightier than the sword. The hand that stirs the porridge rules the world.

The author

Elisabeth Luard is a distinguished wildlife artist and an internationally renowned writer and broadcaster on the ethnology of cooking. Her books include *European Peasant Cookery* (1986), *Princess and the Pheasant* (1987), *The Barricaded Larder* (1988), *Sainsbury's the Cooking of Spain* (1991), *European Festival Food (1990)* and *The Flavours of Andalucia* (1991). She writes for the *Scotsman* and *Country Living*, and won the 1992 Glenfiddich Award for the best cookery book of the year.

References

van Bath and B.S.Slicher, *The Agrarian History of Western Europe AD 500-1850*, London, 1963.
Beeton, I., *Household Management* (1912 Edition), Ward Lock, London.
Blum, J., *The Edn of the Old Order in Rural Europe*, Princeton, USA, 1978.
Blum, J.(ed), *Our Forgotten Past*, Thames & Hudson, London, 1982.
Boswell, J.,*Journal of a Tour to the Hebrides*, London 1785.
Dabitesse, M.L., *Revolution Silencieuse*, Paris, 1931.
Davidson, A., *North Atlantic Seafood*, Viking, London, 1979.
Franklin, S.H., *The European Peasantry*, London, 1969.
Grant, E. of Rothiemurchus, *Memoirs of a Highland Lady*, Edinburgh, 1830.
Henderson, T.F., *Old World Scotland*, Edinburgh, 1893.
Johnston, I.C., *The Cook and Housewife's Manual of Mrs Margaret Dods*, 1826.
Lovell, M.S., *Edible Molluscs of Great Britain and Ireland*, London ,1867.
Mabey, R., *Food for Free*, Collins, London, 1972.
McGee, H., *On Food and Cooking*, Scribner, USA, 1985.
McNeill, F.M., *The Scots Kitchen*, Blackie, Edinburgh, 1929.

Oyler, P., *The Generous Earth*, Harmondsworth, London, 1961.
Raymont, L., *The Peasants*, Knopf, USA, 1925.
Warrington, D., *The Economics of Peasant Farming*, London, 1964.
Wilson, C.A., *Food and Drink in Britain*, Constable, London, 1973.